Edited by Çiğdem Kâğıtçıbaşı
With the assistance of Diane Sunar

SEX ROLES, FAMILY, & COMMUNITY IN TURKEY

● Indiana University Turkish Studies 3 ●
General Editor For the Series:
İlhan Başgöz

Library of Congress Catalog Card Number: 82-084525
Printed in the United States of America

All orders should be addressed to:
General Editor, Turkish Studies
143 Goodbody Hall, Indiana University
Bloomington, Indiana 47405

CONTENTS

PREFACE

The idea of editing a book consisting of contributions from social scientists doing work in Turkey was suggested to me by Professor İlhan Başgöz, who also graciously offered to publish it in the Indiana University Turkish Studies Series. I greatly appreciate his encouragement and support. I have learned through the two years of work leading to this volume that it is a difficult, interesting and challenging task to edit a book of original essays. I have been assisted greatly in this work by my friend and colleague Dr. Diane Sunar, who, in addition to the stylistic editing of the English usage, also helped me with the substantive work. Special thanks are due to her.

Partial financial support was provided by Boğaziçi University Faculty of Administrative Sciences, Institute for Research and Application in Administrative Sciences and by Indiana University Turkish Studies Publication Series. I thank these institutions for their support. Katherine Çizakça and Birsen Çarmıklı typed the manuscript efficiently, not missing impossible deadlines, which I appreciate. Iris Şeğikyan and Yasemin Ogan helped with the preparation of the manuscript and the index. My husband, Oğuz Kâğıtçıbaşı, and my children, Elif and Emrah, provided me with love, understanding and encouragement, as usual, for which I feel grateful and lucky.

Without doubt, this book belongs to its contributors—the sixteen social scientists from whose work it benefited. I have learned a great deal about Turkish society from their essays, and I believe readers, also, will find them interesting and informative. Based on original research, observations and experiences, these essays provide us with insight into sex roles, family and community in Turkey. I appreciate greatly the valuable contributions made to this volume by my colleagues.

In spite of a growing awareness of the importance of Turkish studies for a better understanding of the Turkish society and the larger Middle-Eastern–Mediterranean culture area, social science literature on Turkey is limited in volume. It is to be hoped that this collection will be a contribution to that literature.

Çiğdem Kâğıtçıbaşı
Istanbul, March 1981

INTRODUCTION

Çiğdem Kâğıtçıbaşı

This volume attempts to study some of the complex interrelations among sex roles, family and the community in a rapidly changing society—Turkey. It is a first book of its kind, aiming to describe and understand Turkish society at the grassroots level, bringing together fifteen studies utilizing a micro-analytical approach. Within this approach, the changing family, its structure and dynamics are of focal interest. Intrafamily sex roles, women's status and related attitudes are inherent to this interest. The changing community forms the context in which the family relates to its social environment and adjusts to it. At times, however, maladjustment and crises rather than healthy adjustment may occur, resulting in individual and social problems. These different aspects of a changing society comprise the basis of this volume.

The Turkish society under study is a highly complex, heterogenous one with a diversity of ethnic, cultural, and religious conglomerations, differentiated along social class, rural-urban and development dimensions. Various lines of historical-cultural influence have molded this society, the main ones being: the nomadic-Turkish, Anatolian, Islamic-Middle Eastern and the Mediterranean.

Furthermore, this is a society undergoing rapid social change. Social change involves, on the one hand, modifications of social structure and, on the other hand, modifications in attitudes, beliefs and values. More specifically, shifts in the demographic composition of the rural and urban areas; increased differentiation and specialization of production, industrial growth and other related changes in economy and social structure precipitate modifications in family structure, functioning and dynamics. Corollary changes in individual attitudes, beliefs and aspirations as well as in social values and norms make the picture very complex, indeed.

It is obviously very difficult, if not impossible, to describe such complex phenomena in any comprehensive and exhaustive fashion, and this volume does not make such a claim. On the contrary, one must admit, from the start, its limited nature. Its limitations derive both from its self-imposed micro orientation and from the bounds of available research.

Social structure, dynamics and change have been approached in this volume mainly from a micro-analytical orientation, focusing on the individual, sex roles, family and community. The main goal has been to reach down to the basic units and institutions of a changing society and to grasp the mechanisms and the dynamics of change. This choice is both a strength and a limitation of the volume. It is a strength in the sense that it allows systematic disclosure and analysis of phenomena at a particular level of abstraction. It is, at the same time, a limitation in that it does not cover phenomena at a higher level of generality, namely macro or societal level. Thus, for example, issues relating to national economics and politics, religion and history are not included in the volume. This is due both to the main goal pursued, as explained above, and, as related to it, the impossibility of covering everything about a society in a single volume. Thus the choice of micro-level analysis of sex roles, family and the community.

What the present volume can cover is also limited, naturally, by the extent of available research. Social science research in Turkey in the past few decades has focused largely on social change and problems of development. Within this context, migration from rural areas to urban centers; marginal settlement in the periphery of the large cities (the so-called squatter areas or shanty towns known as *gecekondu* in Turkey); changing attitudes and values; family structure and dynamics; sex roles; education and labor force participation of women and socialization of children have been focal points of interest for the researcher. These typical issues, are, therefore, reflected in the chapters of this volume, together with other topics extending from these into further problem areas.

Social Sciences in Turkey

A discussion might be in order here about the state of the social sciences in Turkey and the role of the social scientist in the context of social change and development. Benedict, Tümertekin, and Mansur (1974, p. VII-X) briefly reviewed the development of social sciences in Turkey in the 1960s, comparing previously published bibliographic studies of Kolars (1962) and Beeley (1969). They noted the emergence of a cadre of indigenous social scientists and viewed this as a function of two developments: namely,the establishment of new social science departments in universities attracting young academicians with foreign training, and the recruitment of social scientists from universities to participate in national planning and development efforts. Kâğıtçıbaşı(1976, p. 285-320) also reviewed the development of social sciences in Turkey, focusing mainly on social psychology as an inter-disciplinary research area, and noticing the institutional and academic development of the field mainly in the 1960s and 70s.

From these reviews and others (Magnarella and Türkdoğan, 1976; LeCompte, 1980), as well as from bibliographic works (Tezcan, 1969; Tugaç, 1970; Ergil, 1971; Arı, 1977; Kâğıtçıbaşı, 1976, p. 323-42 and Bilgin, 1979), it can be seen that empirical social science research in Turkey is of recent origin. Studies have been conducted in both rural and urban field settings, involving large scale surveys or in-depth anthropological analyses; and problems of social change and development have been the main topics of interest. Especially in the beginning, theory construction lagged behind, as researchers mainly used theories developed in the West, and the impression of foreign scholarship was noticeable in the ensuing literature (Benedict, Tümertekin and Mansur, 1974, p. VIII).

In the past decade, however, together with an increase in the number of social science research projects, new orientations, conceptualizations and hypotheses about Turkish society have been generated, which owe less to Western theorizing. Thus Turkish social science has achieved some autonomy and maturity, although it is not altogether independent of Western influence, for social science is international.

Also, in terms of the numbers of social scientists and the volume of research, Turkish social science occupies a leading role in the Middle East.[1] Thus, today social science in Turkey has reached a stage where it can and should reach out into the international scene to make itself heard. A volume such as this one is a step in that direction.

As for the role of the social scientist in the context of social change and development in a country like Turkey, one can say that the more social science becomes established, the greater responsibility falls upon the social scientist to contribute to development. With the greater salience of social issues, more problem-oriented research comes to the fore. Given the pressing problems of development and the need to channel social scientific research into the study of these issues, the potential value of the social scientist emerges in understanding the process of development and in facilitating it. This can be fulfilled only through careful study, description and analysis of the society, its continuities and change. The studies reported in this volume are endeavors toward that end.

An overview of some of the findings of previous social science research in Turkey might provide the context within which the specific findings, interpretations and discussions presented in the chapters of this volume may be better understood.

The Traditional Sociocultural Context

Widespread social change is almost an everyday matter for people in Turkey. It is most noticeable in the waves of rural to urban migration and international migration occurring unceasingly since the early 1950s (see Abadan-Unat, and Şenyapılı in this volume). Concomitant with geographic mobility is what might be called "psychological mobility"—people changing. Technological innovation in agriculture and monetized agricultural economy, land fragmentation and shifts in income distribution, the growth of urban industry, cultural diffusion, education and the mass media have all been precipitators of this social change.

To understand this change, however, we have to grasp that which is changing, namely, the traditional agrarian society—the core of society at large and the main source of its cultural values. Thus, research has focused on rural society both in its own right and also as a standard or reference point in comparison to which modifications in values, outlooks and ways of life can be understood.

Family Structure:

The peasant village is often described as an isolated, small agricultural community characterized by a patrilocal and patriarchal family system and closely knit kinship and family relations (e.g. Kolars, 1962; Stirling, 1965). Though it was generally assumed that the typical rural family was patriarchally extended, national surveys (Timur, 1972; Kâğıtçıbaşı, 1981) and other studies have shown this not to be the case (see also Duben in this volume). Indeed, today it can be stated that the majority of families, even in rural areas, are nuclear and probably always have been.

The dynamic nature of the family as it undergoes modifications in the face of changing socio-economic conditions in Turkey is also apparent from research results. For example, a typical pattern of change through the life cycle of the rural family involves first the newly married couple living with the husband's parents as a valued pattern and due to economic necessities (patriarchally extended family), then moving out as the young man gains more income and autonomy (nuclear family) and then later on, the aged parent(s) moving in again for protection in old age ("transient extended" family) (Timur, 1972; Kandiyoti, 1974; Tanyol, 1960-61; Kıray, 1974). Indeed, economic necessities may force adjustments of the family which go against age-old cultural norms and conventions, such as establishing matrilocal households (Hinderink and Kıray, 1970; Kıray, 1974, p. 198).

However, even when conjugal families live in separate households, the functions of an extended family are served by them in that they are called upon to provide material support when needed, forming what might be called the "functionally extended family" (Kâğıtçıbaşı, 1977). Thus, close family ties extending into kinship relations serve an important function of security in times of crisis and conflict, often faced by the families undergoing change in both the rural and the marginal urban context (Kongar, 1972; Şenyapılı, 1978; Karpat, 1976; Stirling, 1965; Kolars, 1962; Kıray, 1974; see also Duben, Abadan-Unat, Şenyapılı and Okman Fişek in this volume). As noted by these researchers, the spatial proximity of the separate family and kin households, even in urban areas, symbolizes and may further strengthen the close mutual bonds of family and kin. Mutual support within the family is the rule. Thus, for example, older brothers are expected to help finance younger siblings' education and be available for assistance to their parents in old age (Kâğıtçıbaşı, 1979; see also Kâğıtçıbaşı in this volume).

Values Concerning the Family:

Values about the family appear to be more in line with the above-mentioned prevalent functions than with the actual family structures. Even though the majority of families are nuclear, the extended family is the ideal, especially in rural areas (Timur, 1972).

This ideal reflects conventions and expectations of living in old age with the adult son's family and being supported by him (Timur,

1972; Kâğıtçıbaşı, 1979, 1981). Underlying this ideal is, on the one hand, economic necessity, mainly lack of institutional support or other means of old age security, resulting in dependence on children and a consequntly high value put on children's loyalty to the parents and the family (see Kâğıtçıbaşı in this volume). On the other hand, idealization of the extended family is partly the continuation of a tradition or a sign of longing for the past, as well as a sort of status aspiration. Generally, rural patriarchally extended families have been the rich families which can afford to keep all the family members under the same roof, as they have large land holdings to live on. Consequently, in the eyes of the poor peasant, the extended family has been identified with wealth, thus symbolizing an ideal.

Marriage, Bride Price, Inheritance:
    Today civil marriage is generally practiced with or without an additional religious ceremony (e. g. Tanyol, 1960-61; Türkdoğan, 1965; Şahinkaya, 1970). However, the practice of religious marriage alone has not disappeared. Thus, in 1933, 1945, 1950 and 1956 laws were passed for the legitimation of children born out of civil wedlock (Abadan-Unat, 1979). Polygamy was prohibited in 1926, with the acceptance of the Swiss civil code. Nevertheless, it is still possible to see it in some regions, though it is rare and was not very common even before 1926 (Tanyol, 1960-61; Stirling, 1965; Erdentuğ, 1959; Şahinkaya, 1970; Magnarella, 1973, 1974). Endogamous marriage is found to be a common practice (e.g., Magnarella and Türkdoğan, 1973; Meeker, 1976) as a means of maintaining local cohesiveness and control over land. It may even have political implications (Aswad, 1974).
    Marriage in the rural context appears to assume more of a social than an individual or conjugal character, as a means of establishing economic and social ties. It is especially instrumental in strengthening existing kinship relations or extending them outside the village to similar ethnic groups or in forming neighborhood and territorial ties (e.g., Magnarella and Türkdoğan, 1973), and in increasing the number of relations and friends who are potential sources of aid (Magnarella, 1974, 1979).
    In view of the various functions served by arranged marriage in the peasant culture, it is possible to understand why abduction and elopement are not condoned. The responses to such action range

from tolerance (Türkdoğan, 1965; Meeker, 1976) to strong disapproval and even vengeance and strike between the families involved (Yasa, 1962; Stirling, 1965; Emiroğlu, 1972; Tezcan, 1972). It is also seen as a breach of the proper standards for formal marriage and the financial contract, namely, the bride price.

The attitudes and values concerning the bride price reflect both the traditional functions it serves and also its dysfunction. On the one hand it is valued as a symbol of chastity and for the economic gains it brings in exchange for the loss of labor (of the girl). On the other hand, it is considered dysfunctional, as the inability to pay it may result in abduction (Emiroğlu, 1972), and unfair and useless even in eastern Anatolia where it is widespread (Türkdoğan, 1976). An alleged function of bride price is providing support for the wife in case of divorce, yet divorce is quite rare in rural Turkey (see Levine in this volume), as it is not condoned and is resorted to only under extreme conditions. Another alleged function of bride price is providing security for the wife after the husband's death.

Even though under the civil code women have inheritance rights equal to men's, in some traditional areas women still get either nothing or half of what men get, and inheritance issues are resolved informally within the family or the village (e.g. Stirling, 1965; Erdentuğ, 1956; Türkdoğan, 1965; Magnarella, 1979, p. 24-25), as indeed are most disputes (Starr, 1978). This practice is, however, on the decline (Emiroğlu, 1972), and equal sharing is common in urban areas.

Kinship and Community:
The closely knit family extends into the kin, and often members of a whole village are related to each other through marriages and blood relations. Thus, kinship ties form the basis of social relations in the rural setting. Especially brothers and agnates are the closest of kin, who must stand together in disputes and who are called upon for help, support, defense and even revenge (Stirling, 1965; Tezcan, 1972).

With economic change, increased mobility and outmigration from the village, however, this pattern of lifelong daily contact, mutual services and solidarity is weakening (Jaquette and Erkut, 1975; Magnarella, 1979). Still, in times of need and crisis, family and kin are called upon for help (Kıray, 1974, p. 200; Karpat, 1976; Kongar, 1972; see also Şenyapılı and Duben in this volume). For example, if the husband has to leave the village for long periods to work in the city or abroad, he may leave his wife with his or her parents. When this is not possible, other kin take over this function (Emiroğlu, 1972; Abadan-Unat, 1976; see also Abadan-Unat in this volume). Similarly, kinship ties are functional in shared agricultural work, housebuilding, childcare, etc., and this function continues even in the urban *gecekondu* context.

If, due to mobility, the kin are dispersed and kinship ties weaken, the neighborhood may assume greater importance as a support system (Kandiyoti, 1977). This support would continue being important as long as basic needs remain unfulfilled by public services (Kongar, 1972, p. 138-39; Kâğıtçıbaşı, 1975; Karpat, 1976; see also Heper and Şenyapılı in this volume).

Thus, as family extends into kin, so kinship extends into neighborhood and community in terms of a network of bonds involving duties, responsibilities, common concerns, support and help. In the face-to-face interpersonal relations of the small community everybody is a "significant other," and nobody can be ignored; thus, other-directed behavior tendencies develop from childhood on. Helling (1966) observed, for example, that the adults with whom the village child interacts are more numerous and have more control over him than is the case for the child in the middle class urban family. In other words, in the village setting the child is not socialized in a family only, but also in a kinship-community system characterized by mutual obligations. Expectations from the child, accordingly, are not only individual and familial, but communal as well.

Group Loyalties and Respect for Authority:

The loyalty of the "traditional" man is not to himself but to his in-group; the self is in the service of the group (Spencer, 1960; Helling, 1966; Kâğıtçıbaşı, 1970; Dubetsky, 1976). Traditional values revolve around loyalty to the in-group (family-kin-community), symbolized by respect for its elders, which culminates in a general respect for authority. This is a social value which has been found to be strong even among young people in the urban setting (Kâğıtçıbaşı, 1970).

Loyalty to and respect for state authority can be interpreted as a generalization of respect for authority, resulting in nationalism and patriotism and involving a personal need to serve the country (Hyman, Payaslıoğlu and Frey, 1958; Frey, 1966; Kâğıtçıbaşı, 1970, 1973; Gökay and Topçu, 1971; Tezcan, 1974).

There is often a deep concern with being accepted by the all-important ingroup. The same group loyalty is observed even in the behavior of small town merchants and shop keepers (Benedict, 1974), who consider competitive behavior stemming from envy of another's business shameful. Such values appear to be remnants of the past where they were functional within the guilds. Yet, they linger on though they may be dysfunctional in modern competitive capitalist society.

Even in the small production and factory context, such community-oriented values may persist, although a factory is supposed to function on such universalistic principles as efficiency, rationality, skill and achievement. Dubetsky (1976) notes, for example, that in the small factory context, trustworthiness and loyalty are the desired qualities of a worker, and the personal relationship between the worker and the patron is emphasized. Accordingly, workers are selected from among kin or from the same community from which the patron comes. Bonds of trust, solidarity, respect, loyalty and obligation between the patron and the worker also reflect a shared value system, a traditional morality (Dubetsky, 1977). Thus, typically rural patron-client relations persist even in the urban non-agricultural production (see also Kıray in this volume).

Loyalty and respect within the family, kinship and the community extend most thoroughly to those in the established positions of power. In the family it is the father. In the rural community, age, land ownership, material wealth, and family descent are important sources of power, status and prestige (e.g. Eberhard, 1954; Stirling, 1953, 1965; Avcıoğlu, 1971; Benedict, 1974). However, with changes in agricultural technology, shifts in income distribution, emergence of new types of income generating activities and with mobility of people, the control of fathers over their sons and consequently respect for the elderly is weakening (Kandiyoti, 1974; Kıray, 1968, 1974). Thus, young men assume the decision-making roles and autonomy, as they can deal more effectively with changing conditions (see also Kıray in this volume).

Community Religion:
Karpat (1976) notes that to be a Muslim for the villager and the *gecekondu* dweller (urban migrant) means first of all to be a part of a community. Thus, religious affiliations often intermix with group loyalties (Dubetsky, 1977; Meeker, 1976). Accordingly, religion is more of a

communal than an individual affair; it feeds on community loyalties and, in turn, reinforces them.

Another important characteristic of community religion is its concreteness. To the peasant and the *gecekondu* dweller it means a set of rules and regulations about every-day behavior rather than an abstract system of ethnics. Concrete expression of these characteristics is the community (Karpat, 1976).

Mardin (1969) proposed that "folk religion" assumes a special significance during the process of fast social change and modernization. Through social change, the security-providing primary relationships weaken, often without being replaced by institutional support. At such time individuals search for security and identity in the folk culture and folk religion that they create, superstitions often being an inherent part of this folk religion. This, of course, is the much noted "support function" of religion, not so different from that of family, kinship and community.

As male and female religious activities are separate in both rural and urban context, religion sustains separation of the sexes, as much ethnographic evidence shows. Furthermore, there is often an intermixing of religious and sexual rules of conduct (e. g., Turhan, 1951; Köknel, 1970; Meeker, 1976; Dubetsky, 1977; Tezcan, 1972).

With social change and urbanization, religiosity is generally found to weaken and is replaced at least to some extent by secular values (e.g.Kâğıtçıbaşı, 1973; Emiroğlu, 1972; Kıray, 1968). Yet, this is far from being a smooth unidirectional change; reversals, reactions and revivals are possible. As Bingöllü-Toprak (1979) notes, for example, the Islamic framework, endorsing separation of the sexes, is persistent among both the elite and the masses, in spite of Atatürk's reforms. Furthermore, this framework is sometimes propagated for political purposes, as was done by the National Salvation Party in the 1970s.

We will not enter a discussion here of the role of Islam as a formal religion, as community religion is our main interest, and the former has been studied extensively. (For accounts of Islam and women in the Middle East and North Africa, see, for example, Mernissi, 1975, and Beck and Keddie, 1978).

Sex Roles:

The "second class status" of women in the Middle East is also seen in Turkey. A great deal of research in both rural and urban context has focused on women's roles in Turkey (e.g., Kâğıtçıbaşı,

1973, 1974, 1975, 1977, 1982; Kandiyoti, 1974, 1977; Abadan-Unat, 1976; Kıray, 1975, 1976; Fallers and Fallers, 1976; Meeker, 1976; Magnarella, 1974; Aswad, 1974, 1978; Mansur, 1978; see also Kandoyoti in this volume). Similar work on women in the larger Middle Eastern culural area is much more extensive, of course. (See, for example, the 142-item annotated bibliography of Gulick and Gulick, 1974; and the more extensive bibliography on the Middle East by Helmer and Toth, 1980.) Here only background information on Turkey will be provided.

A seminar was held on "Women in Turkish Society" in Istanbul in 1978, and a volume both in Turkish and English ensued from it (Abadan-Unat, 1979, 1982), to which seventeen women social scientists contributed. This is a topic of great interest, concern and extensive research, thus its heavy weight in this volume, also. Here only a general summary will be provided as background information for the chapters dealing with sex roles.

In the peasant village women's status is still largely evaluated in terms of age and childbearing. Abadan et al. (1976) have noted, for example, that in recent years the position of "the woman" has improved more than that of "the young woman," who is still subject to strict social control. Stirling (1965) earlier stated that village women accept their overall inferiority as part of the metaphysical order, but their immersion in a world of their own greatly mitigates this inferiority. Clearly defined sex roles, division of labor and separate social networks may both help the women endure the status difference and yet at the same time serve to reinforce and perpetuate this difference. Lack of sharing and overlap between traditional male and female sex-roles, coupled with supportive same-sex friendship/kinship networks further contribute to this separation extending even into towns (Kâğıtçıbaşı, 1977, 1982; Kandiyoti, 1977; Benedict, 1974; Magnarella, 1974; Karpat, 1976; see also Kandiyoti and Olson in this volume).

Quite basic to sex role segregation and the subordination of women is the concept of *namus* (honor), referring to the sexual modesty of a woman. The implication is that men control the sexuality of their women, and men have honor when their control is socially recognized and legitimized (Stirling, 1965; Magnarella, 1974: Meeker, 1976; Dubetsky, 1976).

Honor reflects the other-directed, small, face-to-face character of social relations within the community, the great significance of others' evaluations and the shame (*ayıp*) orientation. Men apply communal standards to insure their honor which is communally validated, so that without conventions there be no honor (Meeker, 1976). Accordingly, the reaction to an insult to honor should also be public: thus, the ensuing disputes, fights or even blood feud are communal, not private affairs. All reinforce the close ties among the individual, family, kin and community, so much so that sometimes the honor of a whole village or community is affected by the honor of a man (see Özgür and Sunar and Magnarella in this volume).

Within the family, therefore, young women are controlled, and their status is low. Especially the young bride is expected to serve all the adults within the patrilocal household. Once she bears a son, however, her status increases, and it reaches its peak when the son grows up and brings in a bride, the cycle thus repeating itself. Hence, every woman in the traditional rural society wants a son; if she does not bear one, her marriage may be endangered.

A woman with sons will never be in want or homeless, thus a son is a "permanent acquisition" (Stirling, 1965). This is in contrast to a daughter, who when she is of an age to be useful, leaves the household to get married. Thus, the widespread preference for sons (Başaran, 1971; Kâğıtçıbaşı, 1981; see also Kâğıtçıbaşı in this volume).

When a son is so highly valued, and brings so much to his mother, it is only natural that he is given much love, protection and indulgence by her. Thus, observers note that the mother's relationship to her son is intimate and affectionate, in contrast with that of the father, who is stern (see also Okman Fişek in this volume). In fact, the mother often protects the son from the father's disciplinary acts (Kıray, 1979, p. 363). The mother-son relationship is generally stronger and more important than the husband-wife relationship in the traditional family, where any public show of affection between spouses is disapproved (Stirling, 1965; Kandiyoti, 1977). In fact, it is considered bad taste for a man to talk about his wife in the company of others, and often the word "family" is used to mean "wife" (see also Olson in this volume). However, even though for the woman the mother-son relationship is of greatest value, for the man the relationship to his agnates—to his father and brother—is more important, this lack of symmetry reflecting the inferior status of women (Stirling, 1965).

Male decision making in the family is widespread; communication and role sharing between spouses is limited, indicating well differentiated and non-overlapping sex roles. Furthermore, this pattern extends even into urban areas (Timur, 1972; Kâğıtçıbaşı, 1981; see also Olson, Kandiyoti and Kâğıtçıbaşı in this volume).

Furthermore, in the urban context, intergenerational continuities in sex role self-concepts and sex role definitions are observed (Kâğıtçıbaşı, 1973, 1977; Kâğıtçıbaşı and Kansu, 1976-77).

Education and professionalization of women appear to be the key "psychological mobilizers" in this respect (Kâğıtçıbaşı, 1982), rather than mere participation in the labor force. Women's work, indeed, is hardly the "modernizer" it is assumed to be (Kâğıtçıbaşı, 1979a; see also Kuyaş in this volume).

Women's Work:

Women's work in the near-subsistence rural economy is unpaid and is often not considered "work," for it is, rather, a total life style. It is not differentiated as to locality or time (two or three different types of work may be done in the same place and at the same time, such as food production, housework and childcare); neither does it involve specialization or formal training. Thus, when asked if they work, women often answer, "No."

Underestimation of women's work also derives from social values which assign the provider role to men. In the idealized image of the affluent family, the woman does not have to work, an image which is especially prevalent in urban and small town culture (Kâğıtçıbaşı, 1982; Kandiyoti, 1977), and is spreading among gecekondu dwellers and villagers, who emulate towns people (Şenyapılı, 1978; Abadan-Unat, 1979). It is reflected in the Turkish expression which describes a non-working wife or daughter as, literally, "sitting at home" (evde oturur). This image is a remote ideal, indeed, especially in the near-subsistence economy of the peasant village where women have, rather, a "beast of burden" role (Kandiyoti, 1977, p. 59).

With the introduction of modern technology into agriculture and the participation of rural production in the national economy, the above-described situation of a near-subsistence rural economy has changed in many areas. Cash cropping and farm mechanization have rendered small family enterprises untenable, the result being the spread of larger agricultural production, integrated with nationwide market economy, and utilizing sophisticated technology and employing wage labor.

The main effect of this economic-structural change on rural women has been a general reduction in their work load. With farm mechanization and the monopoly of such farming by men, women's farming has decreased in quantity. Furthermore, with the introduction of a consumption economy in the form of ready-made clothing, fuel and food, and even bread into an increasing number of villages, women's domestic chores have also decreased. This change has been considered to have a positive effect on women's well-being, relieving them of some of their heavy burdens (Emiroğlu, 1972). It has also been interpreted as a negative influence both in Turkey and abroad, as undermining the importance of women's production, and increasing the productivity gap between men and women, thus decreasing the latter's status (Boserup, 1970; Kandiyoti, 1974; Tinker, 1976). It can also be claimed that decreased work load has alienated women from production and has stressed their reproductive role.

In certain areas, with the participation of men in factory work, an opposite outcome of economic-structural change has taken place, resulting in "feminization of agriculture," (as also observed in some socialist economies, e.g., Cernea, 1978). In this case women are again disadvantaged, as they are completely tied down in agricultural and domestic work and do not have access to the education and mobility which men enjoy (see also Özbay in this volume). Indeed, 88% of the economically-active female population in Turkey is involved in agriculture, compared with 4% in industry and 8% in services, the corresponding figures for males being 50%, 16%, and 30% (1975 census figures).

When we turn from rural to urban areas, women's labor force participation decreases in line with the above figures; thus, a strong negative relationship pertains between socio-economic development and women's labor work participation (r = -0.88; Kazgan, 1979, p. 158). A notable urban bipolar pattern also appears, with substantial numbers of non-skilled workers (about half of the total) and professional women (30%), with a relative lack of semi-skilled women in between—a situation very different from that found in industrial nations (Kazgan, 1979; see also Kandiyoti in this volume).

The substantial percentage of professional, highly educated, highly skilled women is notable in view of the low overall female education and skills in the country. This apparently ironic phenomenon has been explained in terms of class distinctions and conflicts as well as women's utilization of other women's services without threatening male sex roles (Öncü, 1979; see also Kandiyoti and Erkut in this volume).

Social Change and Migration:

Migration from rural to urban areas has been so pervasive in the past three decades that it has been, by itself, a major instigator of social change. Yener shows that during 1960-65, 880,000 people migrated from rural to urban areas, constituting 65% of the growth of 1,361,000 in urban populations during this time (reported in Tuncer, 1976, p. 107). A great deal of research has been conducted on migrants (*gecekondu* dwellers), especially in the metropolitan areas (see also Şenyapılı and Heper in this volume). Most of this work notes value changes accompanying or following migration and new life styles (Suzuki, 1960, 1964, 1966; Hart, 1969; Yasa, 1970; Levine, 1973a, 1973b; Kongar, 1972; Karpat, 1976; Gökçe, 1976; Şenyapılı, 1978). However, confusion rather than replacement of old values by new ones may ensue from migration, and this is often attributed to a time gap between the abandonment of the old values and the subsequent adoption of new ones to replace them.

Scarcity of stable, well-paying jobs, feelings of alienation and insecurity, e.g., occupying a marginal status in society, further aggravate problems of adjustment. It is in this context of insecurity that the material and emotional support of the community assumes key importance. As many families from the same village commonly move to the same *gecekondu* area at various times, village and kinship solidarity is extended into the city. Communal help can be functional in the solution of such diverse problems as building a house, finding a job, obtaining credit, obtaining access to some health services, etc. (see Şenyapılı and Heper in this volume).

However, these ties of support and solidarity functioning as a "buffer mechanism" (Kıray, 1964, 1968, 1974) may also hinder rapid adjustment and the development of an urban identity. If informal support systems and primary relationships are available to fall back on, new formal institutional mechanisms and secondary relationships may not be attempted, as they are much harder to establish (see Heper in this volume). This situation might also perpetuate reidentification with the rural village values at the expense of new urban values (Yasa, 1970). Levine (1973) has, for example, delineated three different adjustment styles of the gecekondu dweller, namely "urban modern" with an ideology of "embourgeoisment"; "urban identity" showing "emulation"; and "traditionalism" or a defensive identification with the village behind. Adjustment to urban living may also pass through phases. Karpat (1976), for example, has differentiated four phases in the progressive individual urbanization and identification with the city through time: symbolically significant change in dress; participation in the material aspects of the city; establishing relations with city people; and full identification with the city and alienation from the village.

Full urban identification, however, is dependent on integration into the urban economy through stable employment in industrial production or services, i.e., through a shift from informal, marginal types of self-employment into the formal, organized sector (Şenyapılı, 1979; Tekeli, 1977; Tekeli and Erder, 1978). This is a difficult, time-consuming process, as it depends on the national economy and resources. At the level of the individual and the community, this process inevitably involves changes in attitudes and values, i.e., psychological outlook and life styles, though as indicated before, not necessarily in the form of a smooth transition from a "traditional" to a "modern" outlook.

This overview has sought to present, on the one hand, a selective picture of social science research, its interest areas and main findings, relevant to the topics covered in this volume. On the other hand, it has aimed to provide a background for the chapters by drawing the main lines of the socio-cultural base against which they can be considered. Especially for the reader not familiar with Turkish studies and with Turkish society, such a general framework should be a helpful introduction to the chapters included in the volume. This overview, however, has not attempted an exhaustive, encyclopedic coverage of social science research in Turkey, nor a comprehensive picture of the Turkish society. Rather, it includes what I considered to be of relevance to the chapters of the volume and helpful in placing them into context. Together with the greater availability of research in certain topical areas, my own interests and limitations of knowledge have inevitably dictated the coverage of this overview.

Organization of the Volume and Chapter Summaries

The chapters in this volume are organized into four parts: family structure; sex roles; the changing community, urban and rural; and family and social problems. Their lengths differ, with the second part including the largest number of chapters. Again, the availability of research and access to the researchers, as well as the perceived current relevance of the topics, have played a role in this.

Most of the authors are Turkish social scientists currently involved in research in Turkey. Contributions from foreign social scientists are few in number. This is mainly due to the fact that not many foreign social scientists are presently involved in this kind of micro-analytic research on Turkey. The resulting distribution, indeed, reflects the present social science scene in Turkey, with a much greater amount of indigenous research and less dependence on foreign scholarship than was true in the 50s and 60s.

The fact that all but one of the Turkish contributors to the volume are women is unintended and striking. This, in itself, is a reflection of the relative prevalence of women in the professions, which Erkut discusses in her chapter and to which Kandiyoti also refers. Also, women social scientists, more than men, have focused their attention on sex roles and the family. This is a common phenomenon but is especially true in Turkey.

Given these general observations, let us turn now to summaries of the chapters comprising the four parts. Part I deals with family structure in Turkey and involves various considerations of this structure, based on observations and research findings. An analysis of family structure is basic to understanding family dynamics and sex roles; accordingly, this is the first part in the volume.

Olson questions the validity of the evolutionary "Western" model of conjugal role relationships, whose central dimension is dominance and which assumes a shift from the "traditional family structure" to the "modern family structure." The former is character- ized by extended household setting and male domination, whereas the latter is assumed to involve egalitarian, companionate conjugal relations and joint decision-making. Both on the basis of available evidence and on her own observations, Olson rejects the "Western" model for Turkey in favor of a "social network" approach building on Bott's (1957) and Smith's (1973) formulations. According to Olson, "duo-focality," implying different social networks and different domains of action for the spouses, is a dimension more fundamental than male dominance. In fact, she goes so far as to call male dominance a myth which is created and perpetuated by the existence of sexual segregation in Turkey and also in other Mediterranean societies. Though this last claim may be queried for Turkey on the basis of much research evidence (see also Kandiyoti, Kuyaş and Kâğıtçıbaşı in this volume for differing views), the concept of duofocality indeed provides insight into the Turkish family structure. Olson provides detailed anthropological case material from both rural and urban families aptly demonstrating her theoretical conceptualizations of the duofocal family structure and segregated conjugal role relationships.

Duben, in his chapter on the significance of family and kinship in Turkey, uses the word "significance" in two senses: first, to refer to the statistical prevalence of various family types over time;

secondly, to refer to certain cultural phenomena, such as the use of a kinship idiom to structure social relations among kin and non-kin alike. In contrast to much of the writing on family and social change in Turkey, Duben argues that the rapid changes of the last three decades, including migration to the cities, have had little impact on the family. Where changes have taken place, they have done so among long-time middle and upper income urban families, which have hardly been studied. He further claims that despite the overwhelming prevalence of nuclear family residence, extended family and wider kinship ties have not decreased in importance in the city, especially at the upper rather than the lower end of the socio-economic spectrum. Finally, he contends that one can understand a large range of social relationships in the city which fall somewhere between the most impersonal and the most intimate by seeing them as governed by what he calls a kinship idiom. He thus applies certain recent thinking in social anthropology in the fields of kinship and culture to areas of Turkish society where they have not been applied before.

Part II is about sex roles and contains six chapters, organized in three subsections: overview and women's education; sex roles and family dynamics; and sex roles and migration. The first subsection aims to present an overview of sex roles and women's education as the basis of women's sex-role status in Turkey. Both urban and rural contexts are taken into consideration.

Kandiyoti provides us with an overview of women's plight in Turkey, mainly in the context of urban change. Basing her discussions on numerous research results, she studies women belonging to different socio-economic strata and ecological settings. These are, in order, women in shanty towns; lower middle class and "traditional" middle-class women; and the educated middle and upper-middle class women. She notes a common feature in the adjustment of urban women across these socio-economic strata, namely, they do not in any way challenge the male role (this point is further discussed in Erkut's chapter which follows). To achieve this, lower class urban women may retreat into domesticity, or if they have to work, it is considered unimportant or temporary. In the case of lower-middle class women, subordination is reflected in very limited access to the outside world. Even in the case of professional women, husbands "continue to be sheltered from new role demands." Kandiyoti predicts difficult choices and adjustments for women in response to economic problems and makes the apparently paradoxical claim that as men become more economically dependent on women, "their patriarchal control will be tightened rather than relaxed." (Evidence supporting this view is also presented by Kuyaş in this part.) Ultimately, however, she contends that confrontation of the issue of division of labor within the household will be inevitable and will continue a real challenge for women.

Erkut addresses the apparently ironic fact that "despite the low levels of educational attainment for women in general, substantial numbers of Turkish women obtain professional degrees and practice in what are considered to be male-dominated occupations in the West." She explained that this has come about as women have been able to pursue professional careers without posing a threat to the male sex role and its privileged status (elaborating the point made by Kandiyoti in the previous chapter). Highly educated women have had access to the support and services of other women, from the extended family and kin or from among the less advantaged, so that their professional roles have not had to hinge upon their husbands' help in carrying out domestic chores. Men have thus enjoyed the enhanced family prestige and income provided by career women, without themselves losing any status or enduring more work, having the best of two worlds, so to speak. Erkut points out, in other words, that men are the real beneficiaries of "the rise of a few women made possible by the exploitation of many," as noted in the Third World by, for example, Safilios-Rothschild (1974) and Öncü (1979). Thus, positive attitudes toward professional education of elite women exist side by side with negative attitudes toward women's universal education deriving from traditional culture. This is, however, viewed to be a precarious situation likely to change by the decreasing buying power of elite families or increasing employment opportunities for domestic workers, with resulting implications for conjugal sex role sharing and conflict among the elite.

Özbay studies women's education, also, but from a different perspective, namely, within the context of property relations and as it relates to labor force participation in rural Turkey. She notes, first of all, that "both the labor force participation rates and educational attainment of men and women are getting further apart to the detriment of women" in Turkey, considering both rural and urban areas. Furthermore, women's labor force participation is decreasing, though it is still high; and women's literacy is increasing, though still low. Thus, the apparent paradoxical situation: women's increasing literacy rates coincide with their decreasing labor force participation in Turkey, a situation which holds in the rural but not in the urban areas.

Özbay delineates four different types of agricultural production and property structures: large agricultural enterprises; medium size agricultural enterprises; small agricultural enterprises; and landless wage labor. She studies women's labor force participation and education in four villages from different regions which exemplify these four types of agricultural production. It is found that the structures which necessitate heavy involvement of women in agricultural work create obstacles for their education, thus perpetuating their low status. Özbay predicts that the division of labor between the sexes in agricultural production will increasingly resemble the pattern of "feminized agricultural production," with implications for an even greater educational and status gap between the two sexes. Her findings and predictions oppose those claiming decreased involvement of women in agricultural production, discussed before (e.g., Boserup, 1970; Kandiyoti, 1974; and Tinker, 1976).

The second subsection of Part II focuses on sex roles and family dynamics, penetrating into the family and studying roles, values, preferences and power relations. Chapter 6 by Kâğıtçıbaşı presents the picture at a nation-wide level; Chapter 7 by Kuyaş concentrates on the urban scene.

Kâğıtçıbaşı reports the main findings of the Turkish "Value of Children Study," which she carried out with a nationally representative sample of married respondents, mostly women. In understanding fertility, values attributed to children, sex roles and family dynamics appear to be important intra-family factors which are affected by socio-economic development. Specifically, with development and especially with education, the perceived economic value of children decreases, but their perceived psychological value increases, at least in relative terms. As the economic value is cumulative with child numbers, whereas psychological value is not, the result is lowered fertility. Thus, the value of children forms an explanatory link, at the individual level, between level of development and fertility rates. The economic value of children goes hand in hand with son preference, as sons are more dependable sources of economic benefits, especially in old age. This is of key importance in the socio-cultural-economic context where partiarchal traditions are strong and institutional old age support is lacking. The dependent, inferior status of the uneducated woman is crucial in this context. It is apparent in widespread male decision making and low levels of communication and role sharing between spouses. It is an inherent part of a general pattern of interdependent relationships appearing first as dependency of the child on the parents and then as the reversal of this relationship. Socio-economic development and especially women's education and professionalization are the key precipitators of change in this pattern.

Kuyaş studies power relations in urban middle and lower class families and asks whether and how female labor affects them. She questions the validity of the "modernization theories," which depend on the "resource model," in explaining intra-familial power relations in developing countries like Turkey. Indeed, in accordance with previous findings from Greece and Yugoslavia, Kuyaş finds greater intra-familial male power in the lower classes where males have less resources (such as income and occupation) than in the middle classes. Investigating women's perceptions of relative male and female power within the family, and their normative preferences regarding power distribution in the family, the social class effect is found to be striking, whereas that of women's employment is negligible. Specifically, middle class women perceive mutuality or sharing between spouses and think this is how it should be (normative preference), whereas lower class women perceive almost total male control, but again feel this is how it should be. Kuyaş views the powerlessness of women (mainly lower class) and the patriarchal, familistic values they possess as "a function of the level and mode of their continuing responsibility in the family," together with the persistent ideology of the primacy of the family.

The third subsection of Part II covers sex roles in the context of migration from Turkey into Europe. A phenomenon of great prevalence and importance, migration has reshaped the country in the last three decades. In this section its effects at the level of the family are analyzed. In Part III its effect at the community level will be investigated.

Abadan-Unat studies migration of Turkish workers into European countries and focuses her attention mainly on its effects on women's roles. She presents the problem in its wider historical perspective and as shaped by national and international policies reflecting mainly the economic needs of the receiving countries. Thus, such key issues as whether the migrant worker can bring his wife and family with him into the receiving country; whether the man or the woman will be the migrant worker; in what type of a job, with what benefits, and for how long, are determined more by frequently changing policies rather than by the individuals involved. Adjustment problems of the family, accordingly, depend largely on the type of migration undergone. When the woman is the migrant, alienation and isolation are the main causes of stress, together with a too-heavy work load. When the woman is left behind, problems of family fragmentation go hand in hand with greater autonomy of the woman. Migration does not inevitably increase women's options, as sex roles and decision making within the family do not change easily. "Nevertheless, migration imbues participants with an increased awareness of change," the reaction to this change depending on environmental support, family background and individual characteristics.

Part III extends from the family into the community. Following the previous section, Chapters 9 and 10 by Şenyapılı and Heper focus on the squatter *gecekondu* community, which has come into existence as a result of rural to urban migration. Chapter 11 by Kıray studies the changes in a rural community. All three analyze the dynamics of social change which the community undergoes in response to changing demands from the economy and the larger social environment.

Şenyapılı studies both the *gecekondu* family and neighborhood through economic change in the last three decades. She claims that *gecekondu* families have now become permanent and essential factors in the urban economy. In return, however, they have received economic and social support sufficient only to enable them to maintain their present position. As they are still bound in the small-scale, even marginal, job range of the economy, they have limited income. Together with their low education levels and cultural differences, this situation is the cause of their segregation from the urban society proper. It is found, for example, that even though *gecekondu* families have consumption patterns similar to those of the middle class urbanites, they still can not make full use of urban services and spaces. Even though *gecekondu* dwellers are permanent features of the urban economy and urban life, since they are, in effect, owners of valuable plots in urban areas and are involved in small-scale economic work, they are not fully integrated into the urban culture. Furthermore, Şenyapılı does not foresee any basic change in this situation unless the employment structure changes.

Heper also focuses on a *gecekondu* community and studies the mechanisms through which services were procured, thus "shaping the course of change from below." He notes that the initial survival of the community was assured through the tenacity of the dwellers themselves, who had no other option but to hold on to their plots and squatter houses. After the initial formation of the community, public services such as a school, roads, sewer system, water and electricity were obtained not through organized interest group activity, nor through policy planning of public agencies, but rather through the efforts of a few individuals and through chance factors. Furthermore, these individual initiators of change dealt with the bureaucracy by utilizing their status (at times based only on old age and a white beard), personal acquaintances and connections, and by resorting to political pressure and taking advantage of every opportunity available. Thus, faced on the one hand with bureaucratic unresponsiveness and ineffectiveness, and on the other with their low capacity to organize in formal structures and to articulate their demands, the *gecekondu* dwellers have mobilized their culturally provided skills and their loyalty ties in informal interaction networks to satisfy their basic needs.

Kıray focuses on the changing community in the rural context through her study of the changing patterns of patronage. In studying the social structure of Taşköprü village undergoing agricultural and economic change, she finds new types of patron/client relationships coming into existence which are not residues of an old system of relations, but which serve the same needs of security and protection. Specifically, with the end of the self-sufficient, agricultural economy and the disruption of its dependent, protective patron/ peasant relationships, basic needs remain unfulfilled, causing strain. As institutional support from the external environment is not available, new types of adjustment mechanisms emerge in the community. Thus, patron/client relations appear as "intermediary forms in social structures that change with external dynamics. They are buffer mechanisms and provide adjustment during change." In her chapter Kıray provides us with rich anthropological material illustrating the changing patterns of patronage in a village over a period of three decades, which substantiate her view of structural change mentioned above. It can easily be pointed out that the pattern she presents is not peculiar to Taşköprü, but is rather typical of many rural communities undergoing change in Turkey and in similar countries.

Part IV deals with problems both at the level of the family and at supra-family levels. The four chapters constituting the two subsections deal with different problems which reflect individual and family maladjustment in the face of changing environmental demands. The first subsection focuses on family crises reflected in family psychopathology and divorce.

Okman Fişek studies the Turkish family within the framework of Family Systems Theory and covers the areas of family structure, family dynamics, relations with the extended family and family pathology. She integrates available research findings on the Turkish family and the basic premises of Family Systems Theory into an analysis of the Turkish nuclear family. From this analysis, both the nuclear family and the social system surrounding it emerge with two contrasting characteristics. Both systems appear to be quite differentiated with regard to normative role expectations and the individual's position within a given status hierarchy. Such clear subsystem boundaries or rules as to who relates how, and to whom, facilitate the smooth functioning of individual family members as well as of the total system. However, the psychological experiences and emotional relationships of the individuals within these systems reflect a tendency toward lack of autonomy and blurring of identities, rather than differentiation.

The contrast between one's role expectations and psychological experience is not in itself pathological, as long as the larger social system is stable. However, rapid social change, which is weakening traditional role expectations without replacing them with new norms, is undermining the main locus of differentiation in the family system. Left without a guiding structure, the undifferentiated and highly charged emotional experience of the family could generate conflict and pathology. This outcome is illustrated in the case example Okman Fişek provides.

Levine investigates the nature of divorce in Turkey through social change, considering divorce as a "barometer of social change"; "a struggle against conservatism," and "an act of female emancipation." Reviewing national divorce statistics, he notes that divorce is associated more with urbanism and urban occupations; with a higher level of development; with changing women's roles; with developed agriculture rather than with full-scale industry; and with being barely literate (especially among women). Thus, it is the people "caught in the middle" of economic and structural change who are most vulnerable to divorce, as they are subject to most stress. In effect, the urban poor who are dislocated and economically vulnerable are more likely to get divorced. At the level of the family, Levine views the repressive, authoritarian, patriarchal family as a hindrance to the development of individual autonomy and initiative, as the needs of the family have primacy over those of its individual members. This family type, which may be a necessity in rural areas, is considered to be an impediment to economic and social development. Thus, divorce is seen as a liberating act.

In spite of Levine's positive orientation to divorce, his chapter is placed under "Family Maladjustment." This is because, even though divorce may have a liberating effect especially on the woman, it does bring with it serious problems of readjustment, especially for the woman in a society which does not condone it. Furthermore, from the perspective of the family, it represents a failure in adjustment, even though it may be "functional" in forcing the maladjustive family out of existence.

The second subsection of Part IV focuses on social problems which take the form of individual and collective violence. Özgür and Sunar examine the problem of homicide in Turkey. They attribute the generally high rates of homicide to the operation of a "subculture of violence": a traditional system of norms which condone and require a violent response to violations of personal honor. This normative system is also seen to entail the development of "under-controlled" personality types, social expectations of violent acts, and the availability of weapons, all of which may contribute to a higher incidence of homicide, even when honor is not at stake. This perspective, however, is seen to be valid only for male homicide offenders in the comparative survey carried out for the study. Female offenders are found, in general, to come from more disturbed backgrounds than their male counterparts, and to have committed murder under circumstances that are much more stressful. Male homicide is found to be more normative, i.e., to stem from more normatively approved motives, such as self-defense, property defense, or honor, while a greater proportion of female homicides stem from domestic quarrels, jealousy, and similar motives. It is also found that male homicides tend to be more spontaneous (not premeditated), less violent, and more regretted than female homicides. These differences are explained partly in terms of the apparently more pathogenic backgrounds of the female murderers, and partly in terms of the social pressures and tensions exerted on women in the patriarchal family context, especially as the traditional structures are subjected to the strains of rural-urban migration and other social changes.

In the last chapter of the volume, Magnarella studies the infrastructural, social and cultural foundations in Turkey of collective behavior in the form of civil violence. Utilizing newspaper reports as well as research findings and his own research and observations, he focuses on political terrorism in Turkey in the last two decades and especially in the last few years. Following Gurr's (1972) view that relative deprivation makes civil violence probable, Magnarella proposes a theoretical orientation to civil violence and terrorism, in which "the primary causal sequence is: first, the infrastructural and perceptual conditions leading to discontent; second, the acceptance of ideologies condemning those conditions and advocating violent action [to change them]; third, violent action." The infrastructural conditions, in turn, are considered to include too high a population, unequal income distribution, insecure economic situation (involving high inflation and unemployment rates), demand for, but limited access to, education and an inefficient government. In addition to the above conditions, which all exist in Turkey, certain traditional cultural themes are also considered to contribute to violence. Notable among these is condoning of violence in crimes of honor and blood feud (see also Özgür and Sunar in this volume).

NOTES

[1] *The Directory of Social Scientists*, prepared by the Organization for the Promotion of Social Sciences in the Middle East, lists Turkey as the country with the greatest number of social scientists (115 entries) and most research activity among the countries in the Middle East and North Africa.

BIBLIOGRAPHY

Abadan-Unat, N. "Implications of Migration on Emancipation and Pseudo-Emancipation of Turkish Women." Paper presented at Wellesley College Conference on Women and Development. June 2-6, 1976.

———. "The Modernization of Turkish Women," *The Middle East Journal*, 1978, 32, 3, 291-306.

———. "Toplumsal Değişme ve Türk Kadını" (Social Change and the Turkish Woman). In N. Abadan-Unat (ed.), *Türk Toplumunda Kadın*. Ankara: Çağ, 1979. pp. 15-43.

———(ed.). *Women in Turkish Society*. Leiden: E.J. Brill, 1982.

———, R. Keleş, R. Penninx, H.V. Renselaar, L.V. Velzen, L. Yenisey, (eds.). *Migration and Development*. Ankara: Ajans-Türk Press, 1976.

Arı, O. *Köy Sosyolojisi Okuma Kitabı* (Reader in Rural Sociology). Istanbul: Boğaziçi Univ. Publication, 1977.

Aswad, B. "Visiting Patterns Among Women of the Elite in a Small Turkish City," *Anthropological Quarterly*, 1974, 47, 1, 9-24.

Avcıoğlu, D. *Türkiye ' nin Düzeni* (The System of Turkey). Ankara: Bilgi Press, 1969.

Başaran, F.A. "A Psycho-Sociological Research About the Attitude Changes in Diyarbakır Villages." Ankara: Ankara Univ. Press, 1971. (Reprint from Research VII, 1969.)

Baysal, A. "Türk kadınının beslenme sorunları" (Nutrition Problems of Turkish Women). In N. Abadan-Unat (ed.), *Türk Toplumunda Kadın.* Ankara: Çağ, 1979, pp. 133-47.

Beck, L. and N. Keddie (eds.). *Women in the Muslim World.* Cambridge, Mass.: Harvard Univ. Press, 1978.

Beeley, B.W. *Rural Turkey: A Bibliographic Introduction.* Ankara: Hacettepe Univ. Publications, 10, 1969.

Benedict, P., E. Tümertekin, F. Mansur. *Turkey: Geographic and Social Perspective.* Leiden: E.J. Brill, 1974.

Bilgin, N. *Türk psikoloji bibliyografyası: 1928-1978.* (Turkish Psychology Bibliography: 1928-1978). Ege Univ. Publication, İzmir, 1979.

Bingöllü-Toprak, B. *Türk Kadını ve Din.* (The Turkish Woman and Religion). In N. Abadan-Unat (ed.), *Türk Toplumunda Kadın.* Ankara: Çağ, 1979, pp. 381-90.

Boserup, E. *Women's Role in Economic Development.* London: Allen and Unwin, 1970.

Bott, E. *Family and Social Network.* London: Tavistock Publications, 1957.

Cernea, M. "Macrosocial Change, Feminization of Agriculture, and Peasant Women's Threefold Economic Role," *Sociologia Ruralis,* 1978, 18, 2/3, 107-124.

Dubetsky, A. "Kinship, Primordial Ties and Factory Organization in Turkey: An Anthropological View," *International Journal of Middle East Studies,* 1976, 433-51.

_____. "Class and Community in Urban Turkey." In A.O. Van Nieuwenhuijze (ed.), *Commoners, Climbers and Notables: Social Ranking in the Middle East.* Leiden: E.J. Brill, 1977, 352-63.

Eberhard, W. "Change in Leading Families in Turkey," *Anthropos,* 1954, 19, 993-1004.

Emiroğlu, V. *Edilli Köyünün (Akçakoca) Kültür Değişmesi Bakımından İncelenmesi* (Investigation of a Village (Edilli, Akçakoca) Interms of Cultural Change). Ankara: Varol, 1972.

Erdentuğ, N. *Hal Köyünün Etnolojik Tetkiki* (An Ethnological Study of Hal Village). Ankara: Ankara Univ. Publications, No. 109, 1956.

_____. *Sun Köyünün Etnolojik Tetkiki* (An Ethnological Study of Sun Village). Ankara: Ankara Univ. Publications, No. 132, 1959.

Ergil, G. *Türk Köyünde Modernleşme Eğilimleri Araştırması, Rapor II* (Research on Modernization Tendencies in Turkish Villages, Report II). Istanbul: State Planning Organization Publications, No. 999-SPD: 226, 1971.

Fallers, L.A. and M.C. "Sex Roles in Edremit." In J. Peristiany (ed.) *Mediterranean Family Structures.* London: Cambridge Univ. Press, 1976, 243-60.

Frey, F.W. "Socialization to National Identification Among Turkish Peasants." Paper presented at the Advanced Seminar in the Social Sciences. Abant, Turkey, 1966.

Gökay, F.K. and S. Topçu. "Türk gençliğinin inanç ve tutumlarının dinamiği üzerine psiko-sosyal yönden bir araştırma" (A Social Psychological Study of the Dynamics of Beliefs and Attitudes among Turkish Youth). *50. Yıla Armağan* (Dedication to the 50th Year of the Republic). Ankara: Ankara Univ., Faculty of Education Publication, 1973, pp 63-77.

Gökçe, B. *Gecekondu Gençliği* (Gecekondu Youth). Ankara: Hacettepe Univ. Publication, c-15, 1976.

Gulick, J. and M.E. "An Annotated Bibliography of Sources Concerned With Women in the Modern Muslim Middle East." Princeton Near East Paper, Number 17, 1974.

Gurr, T.R. "Psychological Factors in Civil Violence." In I.K. and R.L. Feirabend, and T.R. Gurr (eds.), *Anger, Violence and Politics*. Englewood Cliffs: Prentice Hall, 1972, pp. 31-57.

Hart, C.W.M. *Zeytinburnu Gecekondu Bölgesi* (Zeytinburnu Squatter Area). Istanbul Chamber of Commerce Publication, 1969.

Helling, G.A. "The Turkish Village as a Social System." Los Angeles, Calif.: Unpublished Monograph, 1976.

Helmer, K. and J.F. Toth. "A Bibliography of Urban Change in the Middle East." In H.A.B. Rivlin and K. Helmer (eds.), *The Changing Middle Eastern City*. Binghamton: SUNY Publication, 1980.

Hinderink, J. and M. Kıray. *Social Stratification as an Obstacle to Development: A Study of Four Turkish Villages*. New York: Praeger, 1970.

Hyman, H.H., A. Payaslıoğlu and F.W. Frey. "Values of Turkish College Youth," *Public Opinion Quarterly*, 1958, 22, 3, 275-91.

Jacquette, D. and S. Erkut. "Operative and Representational Social Thought: Some Categories of Social Experience in the Turkish Village," *Hacettepe Bulletin of Social Sciences and Humanities*, 1975, 7, 1-2, 70-92.

Kâğıtçıbaşı, Ç. "Social Norms and Authoritarianism: A Comparison of Turkish and American Adolescents," *Journal of Personality and Social Psychology*, 1970, 16, 3, 444-51.

————. "Psychological Aspects of Modernization In Turkey," *Journal of Cross-Cultural Psychology*, 1973, 4, 157-74.

————. "Modernity and the Role of Women in Turkey," *Boğaziçi University Journal*, 1975, 3, 83-89.

————. *İnsan ve İnsanlar: Sosyal Psikolojiye Giriş* (Person and People: Introduction to Social Psychology). Ankara: Ankara Social Science Association Publication, No. 6-8, 1976.

————. "The Value of Children in Turkey: Perspectives and Preliminary Findings." Paper presented at the International Union for the Scientific Study of Population Seminar on Household Models of Economic Demographic Decision Making. Mexico City, Nov. 4-6, 1976.

_____. *Cultural Values and Population Action Programs: Turkey.* Istanbul: UNESCO Report, 1977.

_____. "Old-Age Security Value of Children and The Case of the Aged." Paper presented at the United Nations Seminar of Informal Action for the Welfare of the Aged. Copenhagen, Denmark, March 26-April 3, 1979.

_____. "Effects of Employment and Children on Women's Status and Fertility Decisions." Paper presented at IDRC Workshop on Women's Roles and Fertility. Ottawa, June, 1979a.

_____. *Çocuğun Değeri: Türkiye' de Değerler ve Doğurganlık.* (Value of Children:Values and Fertility in Turkey). Boğaziçi Univ. Publication, 1981.

_____. *The Changing Value of Children in Turkey.* Honolulu, Hawaii: East-West Center, 1982.

_____ and A. Kansu. "Cinsiyet Rollerinin Sosyalleşmesi ve Aile Dinamiği: Kuşaklararası bir Karşılaştırma" (Socialization of Sex Roles and Family Dynamics: An Intergenerational Comparison). *Boğaziçi Univ. Journal,* 4-5, 1976-77.

Kandiyoti, D. "Some Social-Psychological Dimensions of Social Change in a Turkish Village," *The British Journal of Sociology.* 1974, 25, 1, 47-62.

_____. "Sex Roles and Social Change: A Comparative Appraisal of Turkey's Women,"*Signs' Journal of Women in Culture and Society,* 1977, 3, 1, 57-73.

Karpat, K. *The Gecekondu: Rural Migration and Urbanization.* London: Cambridge Univ. Press, 1976.

Kazgan, G. "Türk Ekonomisinde Kadınların İşgücüne Katılması,Mesleki Dağılımı,Eğitim Düzeyi ve Sosyo-Ekonomik Statüsü" (Women's Labor Force Participation, Occupational Distribution, Education Level and Socio-Economic Status in Turkish Economy). In N. Abadan-Unat (ed.), *Türk Toplumunda Kadın* (Women in Turkish Society). Ankara, Çağ, 1979.

Kıray, M. *Ereğli, Ağır Sanayiden Önce Bir Sahil Kasabası* (Ereğli, A Coastal Town Before Heavy Industry). Ankara: Başbakanlık DPT Publication, 1964.

_____. "Values, Social Stratification and Development," *Journal of Social Issues.* 1968, 24, 2, 87-102.

_____. "Social Change in Çukurova: A Comparison of Four Villages." In P. Benedict, E. Tümertekin, and F. Mansur (eds.), *Turkey: Geographic and Social Perspectives.* Leiden: E.J. Brill, 1974, pp. 179-203.

_____. "Changing Roles of Mothers: Changing Intra-Family Relations in a Turkish Town." In J. Peristiany (ed.), *Mediterranean Family Structures.* London: Cambridge Univ. Press, 1976, pp. 261-71.

_____. "Küçük Kasaba Kadınları" (Small Town Women). In N. Abadan-Unat (ed.), *Türk Toplumunda Kadın.* Ankara: Çağ, 1979, pp. 359-74.

Kolars, J.F. "Community Studies in Rural Turkey," *Annals,* Asso. of American Geographers, 1972, 52, 4, 476-89.

Kongar, E. *İzmir 'de Kentsel Aile* (Urban Family in İzmir). Ankara: Turkish Social Sciences Asso. Publications, A-3, 1972.

Köknel, Ö. *Türk Toplumunda Bugünün Gençliği* (Today's Youth in Turkish Society). Istanbul: Bozak Press, 1970

Le Compte, W.A. "Some Recent Trends in Turkish Psychology," *American Psychologist*. 1980, 35, 8, 745-49.

Levine, N. "Value Orientation Among Migrants in Ankara, Turkey: A Case Study," *Journal of Asian and African Studies*, 1973, 8, 1-2, 50-68.

_____ . "Old Culture—New Culture. A Study of Migrants in Ankara, Turkey," *Social Forces*. 1973, 51, 3, 355-68.

Magnarella, P.J. *Tradition and Change in a Turkish Town*. New York: John Wiley and Sons, 1974.

_____ . *The Peasant Venture*. Cambridge, Mass.: Schenkman, 1979.

_____ and O. Türkdoğan. "Descent, Affinity and Ritual Relations in Eastern Turkey," *American Anthropologist*, 1973, 75, 5, 1626-33.

_____ and O. Türkdoğan. "The Development of Turkish Social Anthropology," *Current Anthropology*, 1976, 17, 2, 263-72.

Mardin, Ş. *Din ve İdeoloji* (Religion and Ideology). Ankara: Ankara Univ. Faculty of Political Science Publications, no. 275, 1969.

Meeker, M.E. "Meaning and Society in the Near East: Examples from the Black Sea Turks and the Levantine Arabs," Parts I and II *International Journal of Middle East Studies*. 1976, 7, 2 and 3, 243-70, 383-423.

Mernissi, F. *Beyond the Veil: Male-Female Dynamics in a Modern Muslim Society*. New York: John Wiley and Sons, 1975.

Öncü, A. "Uzman Mesleklerde Türk Kadını" (Women in the Professions). In N. Abadan-Unat (ed.), *Türk Toplumunda Kadın*. Ankara: Çağ, 1979, pp. 271-85.

Özbay, F. "Education and Labor Force Participation of Turkish Women as a Function of the Rural Property System." Paper presented at the 9th World Congress of Sociology, Uppsala, Sweden, 1978.

_____ . "Türkiye'de Kırsal/Kentsel Kesimde Eğitimin Kadınlar üzerinde Etkisi (Effects of Education on Woman in Rural/Urban Areas in Turkey). In N. Abadan-Unat (ed.), *Türk Toplumunda Kadın*. Ankara: Çağ, 1979, pp. 191-218.

Safilios-Rothschild, C. *Women and Social Policy*. Englewood Cliffs, N.J.: Prentice Hall, 1974.

Shorter, F. "Information on Fertility, Mortality and Population Growth in Turkey," *Population Index, 1968*. 34, 1, 3-22.

Smith, R.T. "The Matrifocal Family." In J. Goody (ed.), *The Character of Kinship*. London: Cambridge Univ. Press, 1973.

Spencer, R.F. "Aspects of Turkish Kinship and Social Structure," *Anthropological Quarterly*, 1960, 33, 1, 40-50.

Starr, J. *Dispute and Settlement in Rural Turkey: An Ethnography of Law*. Leiden: E.J. Brill, 1978.

Stirling, P. "Social Ranking in a Turkish Village," *British Journal of Sociology*. 1953, 14, 1.

_____. *Turkish Village*, London: Weidenfeld and Nicolson, 1965.

Suzuki, P. "Village Solidarity Among Turkish Peasants Underdoing Urbanization," *Science*, 1960, 132, 891.

_____. "Encounters With Istanbul: Urban Peasants and Village Peasants," *International Journal of Comparative Sociology*. 1964, 5, 208-16.

_____. "Peasants Without Plows: Some Anatolians in Istanbul," *Rural Sociology*, 1966, 31, 4, 428-38.

Şahinkaya, R. *Hatay Bölgesinde Köy ve Şehirde Aile Mutluluğu ve Çocuk Ölümü* (Family Happiness and Child Mortality in the Village and the City of Hatay Region). Ankara: Ankara Univ., Faculty of Agriculture Publications, no. 425, 1970.

Şenyapılı, T. *Bütünleşmemiş Kentli Nüfus Sorunu* (The Problem of Unintegrated Urban Population). Ankara: Middle East Technical Univ. Press, 1978.

_____. "A Proposal for a Comprehensive Framework for the Marginal Sector and Squatter Housing," *Studies in Development*. Middle East Technical Univ. Press, 1979, 6, 24-25.

Tanyol, C. "Peşke Binamlısı Köyü" (The Peşke Binamlılı Village), *Sosyoloji Dergisi*. 1960-61, 16, 17-58.

Tekeli, I. *Bağımlı Kentleşme* (Dependent Urbanization). Ankara: Chamber of Architects Publication, no. 18, 1977.

_____ and L. Erder. *İç Göçler* (Internal Migrations). Ankara: Hacettepe Univ. Publications, D-26, 1978.

Tezcan, M. *Türk Sosyoloji Bibliyografyası 1928-1968* (Turkish Sociology Bibliography 1928-1968). Ankara: Ankara Univ., Faculty of Education Publications, no. 6, 1969.

_____. *Kan Gütme Olayları Sosyolojisi* (The Sociology of Blood Feud). Ankara: Ankara Univ., Faculty of Education Publications, no. 24, 1972.

_____. *Türklerle İlgili Stereotipler (Kalıp Yargılar) ve Türk Değerleri Üzerine bir Deneme* (A Study on Turkish Stereotypes and Values). Ankara: Ankara Univ., Faculty of Education Publications, no. 44, 1974.

_____. "Türk Kadınının Sağlık Sorunları" (Health Problems of Turkish Women). In N. Abadan-Unat (ed.), *Türk Toplumunda Kadın*, Ankara: Çağ, 1979, pp. 73-87.

Timur, S. *Türkiye'de Aile Yapısı*, (Family Structure in Turkey). Ankara: Hacettepe Univ. Publications, D-15, 1972.

_____. "Demographic Correlates of Women's Education." Paper presented at the 18th General Conference of the International Union for the Scientific Study of Population. Mexico City, August, 1977.

Tinker, I. "The Adverse Impact of Development on Women." In I. Tinker and M.B. Bramson (eds.), *Women and World Development*. Washington, D.C.: Overseas Development Council, 1976.

Tugaç, A., I. Yurt, G. Ergil, and N.T. Sevil. *Türk Köyünde Modernleşme Eğilimleri Araştırması. Rapor 1* (Research on Modernization Tendencies, Report 1). Ankara: State Planning Organization Publications, D-20, 1976.

Turhan, M. *Kültür Değişmeleri: Sosyal Psikoloji Bakımından bir Tetkik* (Culture Change: A Social Psychological Investigation). Istanbul: Istanbul Univ., Faculty of Letters Publications, no. 479, 1951.

Türkdoğan, O. *Erzurum ve Çevresinde Sosyal Araştırmalar* (Social Research in Erzurum and Its Environs). Ankara: Atatürk Univ. Publications, no. 40, 1965.

_____. "Evlenmede Başlık Geleneğinin Sosyolojik Açıklaması" (Sociological Explanation of Bride Price in Marriage). *Proceedings of the First Folklore Congress.* 1976, 4, 315-63.

Yasa, I. *Türkiye' de Kız Kaçırma Gelenekleri ve Bununla ilgili Bazı İdari Meseleler* (Elopement Tradition in Turkey and Some Administrative Problems Related to Elopement). Ankara: TODAIE Village Publications Series, no. 3, 1962.

_____. "Gecekondu Ailesi", *Ankara Univ. Faculty of Political Science Journal,* 1970, 25, 4, 9-17.

World Fertility Survey. "Turkish Fertility Survey, 1978: A Summary of Findings." London, July, 1980.

DUOFOCAL FAMILY STRUCTURE AND AN ALTERNATIVE MODEL OF HUSBAND-WIFE RELATIONSHIPS

Emelie A. Olson

Anthropological and sociological discussion of husband-wife relationships in the Mediterranean littoral, Latin America, South and East Asia—regions that were traditionally "male-dominated" tends to rely heavily and uncritically on an evolutionary model of conjugal role relationships whose central dimension is dominance relations. As Marion Levy so aptly notes, this is partly attributable to the fact that, as part of that group of scholars who utilize the "membership unit" approach to the study of kinship and the family, they have tended to be "overwhelmingly concerned with the details of one interesting but peculiar case of societies in general—relatively modernized society and especially that form characteristic of the United States" (Levy, 1965, p. 11). My purpose in this paper is to question the validity of this model of conjugal role relationships for Turkey (and, by extension, for at least some other "male-dominated" societies) and to introduce an alternative model.[1]

A typical and influential description of this predominant model of conjugal role relationships is found in the seminal study entitled *The Family and Population Control*, by Hill, Stycos, and Back (1959). Here they posit a rather unilineal process of change from (1) a "traditional family structure" composed of an extended family which is headed by an authoritarian patriarch and characterized by a high degree of sexual segregation and feminine submission, to (2) a "modern family structure" composed of a nuclear family in which husband and wife have an egalitarian relationship, characterized by a high degree of communication and companionship between spouses and by joint decision-making. The "traditional family structure" is said to predominate in "traditional" societies: rural, non-industrialized, and technologically simple societies which are not highly differentiated in the occupational, social or political sense. As a society becomes "modern"—more urban, industrialized, technologically complex, and highly differentiated—it is expected that the "family structure" will also become more and more "modern."

The "Western" evolutionary model of conjugal role relationships has been applied to Turkey frequently, both by Western scholars (see Schnaiberg, 1968; Goldberg and Litton, 1969; and Magnarella, 1972) and by leading Turkish social scientists (see Yasa, 1957, 1960, 1966, 1969a; Kıray, 1964, 1976; Kongar, 1970, 1976). The use of Western models by the latter is not surprising, of course, since many of the educated elite in Turkey have tended to be active and self-conscious advocates of modernization and even Westernization, at least since the latter part of the nineteenth century. (See Magnarella and Türkdoğan, 1976, for a brief discussion of this tendency.)

Despite this acceptance by both Turkish and Western scholars, the application of this "Western"evolutionary model to husband-wife relationships in Turkey is inaccurate in two ways. First, the model posits that the patriarchal extended family was once and still is prevalent in Turkey, especially in rural areas. This is said to be true because, although formerly "male-dominated," Turkey is clearly becoming more "modern" in general. This process is relatively un-"advanced" among rural people, who still make up the large majority of the population. However, the evidence suggests that this description is at best an over-simplification of the actual situation in Turkey, and at worst highly inaccurate. First, as I have argued elsewhere, it appears that only a minority of Turkish families have ever been of the patriarchal extended type (Olson-Prather, 1976, p. 194-218). Further, according to a recent monograph by Timur, a national survey in 1968 revealed that less than a third of contemporary Turkish families are extended ones, even if one includes the 13% that Timur calls "transient extended" (geçici geniş) families (in which the son or son-in-law rather than the aged father is head of the household). Further, no more than 19% of all families are of the "patriarchal extended" type (ataerkil geniş). Thus the majority (60%) of all families are nuclear (çekirdek), 5% are "broken" or "incomplete" (*parçalanmış* or *eksik*) and 3% are "single" (Timur, 1972, p. 33).

Second, the "Western" model posits that the Turkish family is evolving into the familiar "modern" form with egalitarian, companionate husband-wife relationships and joint decision-making. However, there is little evidence to support this generalization, as Benedict has also urged (1976: p. 219-33).

In view of these shortcomings in the evolutionary model of conjugal role relationships defined primarily in terms of dominance relations within a husband-wife dyad, I will instead utilize a "social network" approach, drawing on the work of Elizabeth Bott. In her classic study of British families, *Family and Social Network* (1957), Bott isolates the dimension of segregation in conjugal role relationships. Describing variation in what she calls the "organization of familial activities," she defines two polar types: "segregated" and "joint" conjugal role-relationships, which represent the two extremes of a continuum. A "segregated conjugal role-relationship" is one in which "complementary and independent types of organization predominate. The husband and wife have a clear differentiation of tasks and a considerable number of separate interests and activities." A "joint conjugal role-relationship" is one in which "joint organization is relatively predominant." In turn, a joint organization is one in which "activities are carried out by husband and wife together, or the same activity is carried out by either partner at different times" (Bott, 1957, p. 53). A few pages later, she notes that families with a high degree of conjugal segregation are often described in the literature as ones in which the husband is "authoritarian." Bott regards this as too sweeping, and notes that this misinterpretation occurs because

> authors assign to the financial and sexual arrangements of these families the same psychological meaning as they would have to families where husband and wife are expected to have a joint relationship. This view is supported by the fact that authors also describe these families as "mother-centered" (Bott, 1957, p. 64).

Instead, she argues, what these arrangements really represent is a pattern in which each partner has authority and responsibility in his own sphere (*Ibid.*).

Integrally related to this concept of conjugal role-relationships is her second major concept, that of a network of extra-familial relationships. She conceptualizes each family she studied as a set of individuals, each of whom was the center of a network of social interactions rather than as a group which was part of a larger group, or even as a set of individuals, each of whom was necessarily part of the same group or groups: "External social relationships of all families assumed the form of a *network* rather than the form of an organized group" (Bott, 1957, p. 58). Further, there was "considerable variation in the 'connectedness' of their *networks*," with "connectedness" referring to the "extent to which people known by a family know and meet one another independently of the family." She characterized networks in which there are many relationships among the component units as "close-knit," and those with few relationships as "loose-knit." One of her major findings was that the degree of segregation of conjugal roles seems to be positively related to the degree of connectedness in the total extra-familial network. That is, the more segregated the conjugal role-relationship, the more "close-knit" the extra-familial network tends to be (Bott, 1957, pp. 59-60).

The Duofocal Family Structure

In applying Bott's approach to a description of Turkish families, I will revise it somewhat by using a concept I will refer to as the "focus" of social networks. My usage of the term "focus" is somewhat analogous to that of R. T. Smith in his discussion of the concept of "matrifocality," in which "focus" refers to the center of intra-familial relationships. In the group he is studying this is the mother, leading to his definition of these families as "matrifocal." In Smith's paper, "matrifocality" explicitly does not include a determination that the mother is "head of the household," but refers only to the degree to which she is the center, or *focus*, of relationships within the family. In the West Indies population which he is studying, families are largely "matrifocal," since the women tend to be the focus of both affective ties and of an economic and decision-making coalition with the children. Smith distinguishes between the various "spheres" of social life, making the domestic "sphere," in which women are the focus and are dominant, the central one in defining "matrifocality" (Smith, 1973, pp. 140-41).

In the majority of Turkish families, there is no strong single center of intra-familial relationships. Instead, each adult tends to be the focus of his/her own rather separate social network. Thus, in a "nuclear" family in which the conjugal role-relationships are highly segregated, there are two "foci"—the husband and the wife— a type of family structure which I will refer to as "duofocal." This concept is useful because it provides an alternative, on one hand, to the concept of unilateral dominance by the patriarch in an extended family, and on the other hand, to the concept of a married couple as the primary dyad in a nuclear family, especially of the ideal Western type.

It should be pointed out that the concept of duofocality in a Turkish family is not entirely parallel to the concept of matrifocality in Smith's model. Here, Yanagisako's distinction between Smith's *matrifocality* and her own concept of *women-centered networks* is useful. Yanagisako notes that *matrifocality* "emphasizes the centrality and power of the *mother* in relations within the household," while *women-centered kin networks* "refers to the centrality of *women* in the web of kinship linking together sets of households" (Yanagisako, 1977, p. 208). It will be argued that a Turkish wife is involved in a separate set of relationships more similar in some aspects to those found in the woman-centered kin networks of the Japanese-American families in Yanagisako's study than to the intra-(nuclear) family relationships of Smith's model. Similarly, a Turkish husband is also involved in a parallel man-centered network that reaches beyond nuclear family, household, and even kinship boundaries. The resulting "duofocal nuclear family" is shown to be defined less in terms of dyadic relationships between husband and wife than in terms of relationships which cut across nuclear family, household, and even kinship boundaries.[2]

For the sake of simplicity, the general descriptions of Turkish family and society presented below greatly exaggerate the homogeneity of Turkish society and culture and must be viewed as "ideal types" or "distillations" of some common features.[3] Specific examples following these general descriptions attempt to give some notion of the range and dimensions of actual variation. Unfortunately, the paucity of research in this area makes it impossible to define this variation precisely, or to indicate just how representative of Turkish society the existing studies are. Fortunately, the quantity and quality of ethnographic data are increasing greatly at the present time, and it is my hope that this introductory essay will make some contribution to the collective attempt to understand husband-wife relationships and the family in Turkey.

Domains of Action for Men and Women

In describing husband-wife relationships and the social networks of Turkish couples, it is useful to try to isolate some of the spheres or domains of action for Turkish men and women.

A common schema for defining these domains has been to use the dichotomy of public vs. private/domestic domains, as Schlegel noted in the lead chapter in *Sexual Stratification*:

> The domestic domain, the household or similar small corporate mixed-sex group, is the locus for a large portion of female activity, as it is indeed for male activity in many societies. The public domain includes those institutions and systems of activity that bring together members of different domestic groups into corporate groups or networks of relationship (Schlegel, 1977 b, p. 17).

Schlegel suggests that "a division into women-domestic/men-public may fit the facts of sexually segregated societies that exclude women from almost any decision-making beyond the household." However, despite the wide application of this dichotomy, she argues that it is "inadequate to describe most social action in many societies" (17). She continues:

> In place of the gross domestic-public distinction, it would seem more fruitful to consider the domestic institution as only one kind in which women participate and in which they can have important decision-making roles. An overview of any society reveals a broad range of institutional contexts; what is needed is a transinstitutional perspective that permits us to assess the roles and positions of women within these separate contexts. Furthermore, we must look at the larger systems within which these institutions operate (Schlegel, 1977b, pp. 17-18).

Despite a high degree of sexual segregation in Turkish society, this dichotomous schema does not help us understand the Turkish context, either. Instead, the total set of domains is complex, for they can be defined in terms of several dimensions simultaneously, and they vary over time and place. Thus, Schlegel's general injunction to look at multiple contexts and larger systems is relevant to Turkey as well, although it would be overly ambitious to deal with each of the sub-systems that she outlines, e.g., subsistence, political, military, religious systems (1977b, p. 18). Consequently, I will examine only a few of the dimensions which define the domains of action for Turkish men and women.

Sexual Separateness vs. Dominance

The predominance of segregated conjugal role relationships is a reflection of another social phenomenon in Turkish society: the sexual segregation already mentioned above.[4] As Bott also noted about studies of British society, this separation of the sexes in Turkey is often misinterpreted as simply a pattern of male dominance and female subordinance. Although there is some truth in this interpretation, especially for Turkish society in the past, it obscures the more significant factors of separateness and complementarity of the sexes. Second, sexual segregation can also provide certain freedoms denied women in non-sexually-segregated societies, as eloquently stated by the Fallers in their description of a Turkish town on the Aegean: "the women of this secluded world are in many respects more independent than the 'emancipated' women I know in Europe and America" (Fallers and Fallers, 1976, p. 246). Contrary to usual stereotype, the family in this segregated society allows women more autonomy, because it is easier for them to escape the dominance of men within it than within the joint nuclear family (1976, p. 255). Further, the two factors, dominance and separateness, operate rather independently, since even in situations where women have gained in power and social status relative to men, the separation of male and female spheres may continue to be very distinct.

Finally, it is the very existence of sexual segregation that allows the creation and persistence of what has been called the "myth of male dominance." This term, introduced by Rogers (1975), refers to a pattern of behavior which she suspects may exist in many reputedly male-dominated societies, though in varying forms (1975, pp. 733-37). In the French village she describes, this "myth" is acted out by both sexes: both sexes act publicly as if males were dominant in order to mask and maintain a "non-hierarchical power balance" between the sexes. This mutual fiction, which is more or less consciously recognized as such, is perpetuated in this village because each sex group "may maintain its power in this way" (1975, p. 746). In the village described by Rogers, the relative separation of male and female spheres helped perpetuate the myth of male dominance by preventing each sex group's role in the double subterfuge from becoming so conspicuous that they cannot maintain the fiction in interactions with each other. I would add that this sexual segregation may operate in yet another way to perpetuate another variant of the myth; in fact, it seems possible that both of them may operate within the same community. In the second variant, the myth is subscribed to mainly by men, while women are either unaware of it or pay mere lip service to it and then only on rare occasions. Relative segregation helps perpetuate the myth of male dominance in the second variant by keeping each sex largely ignorant of the actual behavior and attitudes of the other, thereby frequently preventing conflict between the sexes which their differing expectations would otherwise produce.

Data from the 1968 Turkish National Survey may be interpreted as providing some evidence for the existence of a "myth of male dominance" in Turkey, although the argument is somewhat indirect. The data on dominance relations at first suggests that the man is indeed dominant in most families, since both sexes are very likely to report that he is the decision-maker in general. However, this initial response may actually be an example of "acting out the myth" for public consumption (in this case the interviewer), for when married couples are questioned on specific issues, particularly domestic ones, the husband is much less frequently named as the decision-maker. This pattern suggests that the general question tends to tap a more superficial and public level of response, one where both husband and wife pay the customary lip service to the myth of male dominance. In contrast, the more specific questions are more likely to reflect actual behavior; for example, they may remind the wife that she actually decides domestic issues since just yesterday she had gone shopping or had replenished kitchen staples from the storeroom to which only she has a key (Olson-Prather, 1976, pp. 226-27).

A series of questions about the woman's social freedom provides evidence of a different sort. While other sources and my own observations suggest that women seem to be quite aware of patterns of social interaction among men, since these occur largely in public places like coffeehouses, clubs, mosques, places of work, etc., the reverse does not seem to be true. Instead, men appear to underestimate the autonomy, magnitude, and intensity of the patterns of social interaction among women; women tend to undercut the myth of male dominance. In particular, husbands and wives tend to differ in their perceptions of both the man's dominance and the woman's autonomy and social freedom within her own sphere. Thus, in comparison to their wives' perceptions, husbands tend to see (1) themselves as having more control over what their wives do and as being more restrictive in what they permit their wives to do, and (2) their wives as being either more acquiescent or more restive under these restrictions. In complementary fashion, in comparison to their husbands' perceptions, wives see (1) their husbands as intruding less into their lives and as being more permissive in what they allow their wives to do, and (2) themselves as being freer, and thus neither passively acquiescent nor oppressed. Husbands and wives are particularly likely to differ in their perceptions of two issues which are highly relevant to the separation of male and female spheres: the wife's freedom to visit friends and to shop alone (Olson-Prather, 1976, pp. 226-27).

Finally, the myth has created an obstacle which makes any attempt to describe male-female separateness more difficult: the myth keeps at least some Turkish men in ignorance not only of the dimensions of this separateness, but also of the character of the women's spheres and their activities. Since most ethnographies on Turkey have relied primarily on interviews with men, at least until recently, they reflect this ignorance as well and create a possible bias in the literature. Nevertheless, through a careful reading of the available ethnographies and drawing on my own observations, I will attempt to describe the major characteristics of male-female separateness in Turkish society, and its manifestation in husband-wife relationships in particular.

Spatial Segregation

One of the most conspicuous dimensions of the separateness of male and female spheres is the spatial or territorial one. In Ottoman times, the ideal was to keep women from having contact with men other than their fathers, brothers, husbands, and sons. This was actually accomplished among the elite by the use of several practices including the veiling and shrouding of women in public, the separation of the women's and children's quarters (the *harem*)[5] from the public part of the house where men would be entertained, the shuttering or latticing of those windows of the *harem* which opened on the street, the provision of eunuchs to supplement female servants in the *harem*, etc. Autobiographical works, novels, and descriptive narratives such as *Portrait of a Turkish Family* (Orga,

1950), *Haremlik*(Vaka, 1909), *Turkish Life in Town and Country* and *Home Life in Turkey* (Garnett, 1904, 1909), reveal that elite women enjoyed many amenities in their lives because of their spacious *harem* apartments, gardens, tutors, curtained coaches, summer houses, libraries, etc.

In contrast, women in less prosperous families who nevertheless tried to emulate the ideal of seclusion spent most of their lives indoors in dark, closed, cramped quarters, with little communication with the outside world except through their immediate male relatives and perhaps through small purchases from street vendors made from behind their shutters.[6]

However, in urban and village families so poor that they could not afford to forego the labor of their women to the extent that such seclusion entailed, the segregation of the sexes was not as complete. Nevertheless, when possible, each house would have a women's section or *harem*—perhaps no more than the kitchen area—and a public or "male" section. Although the women might spend much of their time out of the house, division of labor by sex was clear-cut, and no woman would work among strange men if it could possibly be avoided.

With the decay of the Ottoman regime in the late 19th and early 20th centuries came demands by reformists such as feminists and the Young Turks for the "emancipation" of women. By 1923, an American writer, Demetra Vaka Brown, raised as a "Greek" in pre-Republican Istanbul, could write a book entitled *The Unveiled Ladies of Stamboul* which included photographs of unveiled women street cleaners, teachers, salespersons, seamstresses, etc. (Brown, 1971). In it, she drew many contrasts to the earlier period she had described in her first book, *Haremlik* (Vaka, 1909).

Since the creation of the Turkish Republic in the 1920s, the participation of women in public has increased at an accelerated rate. Nonetheless, male and female spaces still tend to be separate in contemporary Turkey, and most women continue to lead less public lives than men.

Sex Differences in the Division of Labor

Another dimension of this male-female separation has to do with the definition of tasks and occupations considered appropriate to each sex. This dimension is frequently reflected in spatial separation, and the two reinforce each other both conceptually and behaviorally.

Sex differences in the division of labor and concomitant spatial segregation are quite marked in the domestic realm. For example, food preparation for the family, cleaning, childcare, etc., are almost exclusively women's work, to the extent that a single man is greatly pitied because it is assumed that he will be unable to take care of his own domestic needs.[7] Nonetheless, there is considerable contact between the sexes within the domestic circle. For example, in the large majority of families, unless there are strangers present, men and women do take their meals together despite a tradition called *gelinlik*, referring to the modesty and avoidance ideally expected of a *gelin* (son's wife) in some parts of Turkey (see Erdentuğ,1971, pp. 22-23; Timur, 1972, pp. 112-13).

Second, people of both sexes are very fond of children, and although babies are largely the responsibility of their mothers and other women, their fathers and brothers frequently fondle and play with toddlers and small children. Fathers will even take pre-schoolers of either sex with them when they go to visit their friends or to the coffeehouse, dandling them on their laps while they talk.

Within the extra-domestic realm of work, the differentiation of male and female tasks is more marked, but not total. It varies greatly according to occupation and social class. For example, sexual differentiation is virtually non-existent among highly-educated professionals, such as lawyers, doctors, teachers, university professors, etc. Particularly striking is the way it is taken for granted by Turks of both sexes that a highly-educated woman will pursue a life-time career just as a man would, and that she will be fully as professional as a man in that position.[8] For example, a professional woman usually exercises her legal right to a six-week maternity leave, but there is apparently no expectation that she will interrupt her career beyond this.

This lack of male-female differentiation in the professions was apparently recognized in other ways, to judge by my own experiences. For example, when either Turkish officials or our Peace Corps supervisors visited Güzelköy, the female schoolteacher and I would often be expected to join the delegation on its visits to prominent households in the village. On these "official" occassions, when we arrived at a house, she and I would be ushered into the guest room along with the men, even though we might be quite friendly with the women of the household. The latter would not enter the guest room, and the host or his son would brew the ceremonial tea or coffee and serve his guests, male and female alike. Somewhat similarly, if my husband and I went to a nearby town or village with a man from our village and visited the latter's friends, I would again be expected to join the men, while the women remained outside, except perhaps to greet us briefly. As a stranger, I was apparently defined in terms of my professional role, even though the occasion was primarily social.

In contrast, in nearly all non-professional occupations, male and female tasks are quite distinct and the sexes are usually spatially separate, even if they do similar or complementary work. Exceptions include small family stores in which members of both sexes are likely to wait on customers, and the most "modern" and elite establishments, such as department stores, record stores, tourist shops, some banks, travel agencies, etc., in which the lack of distinction between the sexes might even be symbolized by the wearing of unisex smocks (Fallers and Fallers, 1976, p. 252). However, workers in less prestigious service occupations are sexually segregated: waiters, *kapıcı* (literally "doorman," but usually translated as "janitor") and *odacı* ("room-man," who are assigned to offices to run errands for the official and his/her clients),[9] are usually male; only in restrooms and *hamamlar* (public baths) for women are the attendants female. Similarly, virtually all maids in homes—where contact is primarily with women—are female; if the dwelling is occupied by a single man, only an older woman would dare to work for him, for a younger woman's reputation would be ruined. In most factories which employ both men and women, attention is paid to segregating them by sex, even if they do the same work. Finally, many unskilled and skilled trades, such as construction, shoemaking, metalwork, etc., are male-dominated, while others like tailoring are done by each sex for its own members (Fallers and Fallers, 1976, pp. 252-53).

There is a definite division of labor by sex in agricultural labor as well. Although the criteria vary somewhat from one community to another, everywhere the inhabitants have a very clear notion of what is women's work, of what is men's work, and of the few areas in which they overlap, even though both sexes may work in the same field at the same time. In general, men do the plowing and the more skilled work, while women do much of the tedious, detailed, and heavy work. Often the small animals are the women's responsibility and the large animals the responsibility of the men. Butchering is men's work, since a Muslim is not supposed to eat anything killed by a woman. However, this division of labor breaks down at least partially when the men are absent from the village, which has been a common occurrence for generations in many villages. When the men are gone, the women do both men's and women's work, unless they can enlist the aid of one of the few men left in the village, especially for the traditionally male job of plowing. In the villages, construction may involve the complementary but not joint labor of both sexes, with the men doing the building and the women the toting of bricks, mortar, lumber, etc. (see Yasa, 1960, 46-49; Kolars, 1963, p. 69; Stirling, 1965, pp. 46-68; Erdentuğ, 1970, p. 37; Meeker, 1970, pp. 320-33.

Male and Female Spheres of Social Interaction

Sexual separation appears to be most marked on the dimension of social interaction. Even highly-educated professionals are much more likely to move within a uni-sex world during their leisure hours than during working hours (Fallers and Fallers, 1976, pp. 251-53). This social separation reflects the socialization of each individual into a male or female world, respectively, from childhood, and the development of his/her own largely uni-sexual social network (see Fallers and Fallers, 1976, pp. 252-58 for a description of this segregation in a small town).

Even within the family, the most initimate relationships tend to be among members of the same sex. For example, the relationship between a Turkish girl and her mother is usually very intimate (see Stirling, 1965, p. 108; Magnarella, 1974, p. 90; Kıray, 1964, pp. 118-19; 1976, p. 267; Yasa, 1960, pp. 60–61; Fallers and Fallers, 1976, pp. 252-53). The same is true of the relationship between sisters (see Bates, 1973, p. 117). This is both a result of and a reinforcement of the separation of male and female spheres. First, the female members of the family seek emotional support and companionship primarily from each other. Second, although it is said to be the father's ultimate responsibility to preserve the honor of each family member, it is the mother's immediate responsibility to see that the daughters develop the appropriate attributes and skills. Whether they are learning agricultural and domestic skills, pursuing a formal education, being taught how to manage "the enemy" (men) (Mansur, 1972, pp. 185-87), or learning social graces, the mother is intimately involved. As a result, most girls are in the company of their mothers and sisters almost constantly from the day of birth, except while they attend school.

In addition, a woman is typically part of a close-knit network of women, composed of kin, in-laws, neighbors, etc. This pattern also begins in childhood, for in many families the sundry aspects of "mothering" are shared by other women in the mother's network: the child's grandmothers, aunts, older sisters, older cousins, and neighbors. For example, this occurs in villages where women work in the fields and gardens, in urban families in which the mother has an outside job, in close-knit neighborhoods, etc. Although only a minority of Turkish families are truly extended ones, the social network of the mother typically has many of the same characteristics as the extended family, such as continuity of personnel over time, intimacy, mutual aid, etc.

As an adult, a women is likely to spend much of her time working in the company of women with whom she grew up. This is made possible by several factors. First, nearly two-thirds of village marriages are endogamous within the group of "kinfolk" (*akraba*) or within the village (Timur, 1972, p. 75). Second, the couple may reside with or near the wife's kin, either temporarily or permanently (Kıray, 1976, p. 269; Fallers and Fallers, 1976, pp. 246-50; Bates, 1975, p. 117). Third, even in communities where most of the women marry into patrilocal households as strangers, the women in the same and neighboring houses generally become very close; close cooperation and affection usually develop even between daughter and mother-in-law (Stirling, 1965, pp. 107-12). In fact, both in the villages and in the larger urban centers, a woman tends to regard long-term neighbors as being "like relatives," and they exchange gossip, advice, food, assistance, etc. (see Erdentuğ, 1971, p. 36; Star, 1970, pp. 113-15; Fallers and Fallers, 1976, pp. 252-53).

Magnarella's study of Susurluk, a town in northwestern Turkey, provides a good illustration of a close-knit, woman-centered neighborhood of this type, which he calls a "defended neighborhood." Despite the fact that these neighborhoods are characterized by enclosed courtyards, the "defended neighborhood" has many of the characteristics of an extended family.

> [The] immediate neighborhood is a shared extension of all the household, whose women and children participate in its use. . . . [Within this "defended neighborhood," there is a] female-dominated network of trust, cooperation and mutual aid linking its member households. . . . They also share in the consequences of any member's behavior, as there is a collective pride and guilt over one another's achievements and shortcomings (Magnarella, 1974, pp. 43-45).

Magnarella also notes that members of the neighborhood often address each other with kinship terms, and sexual relations between them are often regarded as incestuous.[10]

In the town of Ula, the *semt* and *mahalle* serve similar functions, though neither is exactly the equivalent of the "defended neighborhood" in Susurluk. Women within a single *semt* (a small group of neighboring households) work cooperatively as a group in a large number of domestic tasks, including work in tobacco fields, for reasons of efficiency and sociability (Benedict, 1974, p. 153). The *semt* is a subdivision of a *mahalle*, or quarter, of the town, the latter having not only an administratative, but also a social identity. Traditionally, women seldom left their own *mahalle*, and men entering a *mahalle* without the accompaniment of a resident would be immediately regarded with great suspicion (Benedict, 1974, pp. 39-44). The *mahalle* in Ula was also similar to the "defended neighborhood" in that boys within each *mahalle* shared a collective responsibility for all of the young girls within it, but unlike Susurluk boys in the "defended neighborhood," Ula boys would also likely choose their brides from their own *mahalle* (Benedict, 1974, p. 155).

Even immigrants to larger urban centers in Turkey tend to establish neighborhoods which are as homogeneous as possible, whether in terms of family and lineage, village, town, or even region if no closer identity is possible (Suzuki, 1960, 1964, 1966; Sewell, 1964, pp. 150-82; Dubetsky, 1976, pp. 437-40). When this is not possible, the loneliness of living among "strangers" is keenly felt. The importance of this social network in an urban migrant setting was poignantly illustrated for me by a middle-aged woman who had migrated to Ankara with her family several years previously. Immediately following a friendly conversation with the Kurdish women living next door to her, she turned to me and lamented the fact that she had no "friends" (*arkadaş*) near by in Ankara. Apparently, despite their long-term proximity and frequent contact, Kurds from eastern Turkey could not qualify as "friends" for a "Turk" from a town in central Anatolia. Instead, a small group of kin and non-kin from her home town were of much greater social and emotional importance to this woman, despite their residence in a rather distant *mahalle* of Ankara.

There are some exceptions to this sexual separation, for in addition to her participation in this unisexual network, a girl sometimes develops a very close relationship with a brother (see Bates, 1973, p. 117; Benedict, 1974, p. 194; Fallers and Fallers, 1976, pp. 250-58), especially one very near her age or a little younger, since an older brother may become a tyrannical guardian during his sister's adolescence (Magnarella, 1974, p. 91). In addition to guarding her honor before her marriage, a brother is expected to champion her interests throughout his lifetime. In urban areas a brother can often be relied on as an escort to social affairs, and a woman may ask him to do so even after she is married. Further, in contrast to lovers and spouses, brothers and sisters are allowed to express affection towards each other in public. In fact, if one observes a man and woman of about the same age kissing or embracing in public, almost assuredly they are brother and sister rather than lovers or husband and wife (Olson-Prather, 1976, p. 247).

A girl is very unlikely, however, to develop an intimate relationship with a boy who is a potential husband. Even though they attend coeducational primary schools in both the villages and the urban communities, girls in most social strata are expected to show modesty and to practice avoidance of boys as they approach adolescence. They may flirt from a distance with looks and gestures, but direct conversation is not proper. Although girls may have detailed knowledge of their fiances' reputation, social status, occupational potential, etc., many will not know their fiances personally at the time they become engaged, since parents play a major role in arranging marriages (Timur, 1972, pp. 71-73; Fallers and Fallers, 1976, p. 251).

Social distance between potential spouses is even found among the children of the elite in metropolitan areas, including those who attend coeducational high schools and colleges. This may seem surprising, since these young "moderns" of both sexes spend many leisure hours together in such public places as parks, tea gardens, *pastahane* (French-style cafes that serve fancy pastries, ice cream, hot beverages, soft drinks, etc.) and *kokteyl* (literally, "cocktail lounges," but more nearly a sophisticated and expensive version of a *pastahane* which also serves alcoholic drinks). However, they do very little "dating," since they visit such places in unisexual groups, not as heterosexual couples. Occasionally, the groups themselves consist of both sexes, and there are frequent verbal exchanges between members of groups who know each other, but there is little heterosexual "pairing off" either within or between the groups. Among this elite, a group of boys and girls in their pre- or early teens who know each other very well may express casual physical affection towards each other, rather irrespective of gender, but explicit sexuality is not acknowledged or expressed. Interaction of any type by girls with strange boys is inappropriate, and attention from boys of a lower social class is considered vulgar and insulting. Although girls might go in pairs or alone to meet friends at one of their familiar meeting places during the daytime, girls do not go to these at night or to large or unfamiliar public places except with an adult chaperone. And even if a girl and boy are dating each other, they are likely to do so in the company of friends rather than as a twosome. In sum, even these apparently "Westernized" children of the elite operate more within the context of their rather solidary unisexual groups than as individuals seeking intimacy with a particular person of the opposite sex, as in Western-style "dating."

Some incidents which I observed in 1970-71 in Ankara illustrate the character of an urban girls' social network in more detail. These involve Layla, a 16-year-old girl in our neighborhood. Although she was undoubtedly more lively and adventurous than most girls of her class, she nevertheless shared many of the attributes of the elite class described above, of which she was a member. Appropriate to her social class, she was a student in one of the private, coeducational English-language *liseler* (high schools), and was fluent in both English and Turkish. Layla dropped in to see us frequently, and we came to know her quite well.

Layla's relationship with her mother is a vivid example of the typically intense attachment between mothers and daughters. Layla was very close to her mother, even though she did not share her mother's conservatism, religious or otherwise, and did many things of which her mother disapproved. But Layla confided regularly in her mother, greeted her after a day at school with great affection—rather melodramatically at times, to be sure: "Oh, Mother, I missed you *so* much!", accompanied by exaggerated hugging and kissing—and occasionally had a vociferous, rousing fight with her in which Layla would yell and throw things, but which never seemed to impair the intensity of their relationship.

Layla was also an active participant in the activities typical of her peers. One day, at her invitation, we went together to an afternoon concert in the Atatürk Spor Salonu (the national sports arena) featuring the band of Barış Manço, a flamboyant folk-rock singer. We were accompanied by her best friend, a student at the same *lise*. Layla was a strikingly beautiful girl, and she capitalized on this by wearing false eyelashes, makeup, wigs, and clothes which very effectively drew attention to her and made her look older than her 16 years. Not only did she attract the admiring glances of virtually every strange male we encountered, but she also exchanged enthusiastic but brief greetings with a number of boys who were her classmates. She and her girlfriend, however, sat with my husband and me during the whole concert, nor were we joined by any of her male friends.

The crowd in the sports arena was composed mostly of small mixed groups of adolescents between the ages of twelve and fourteen, each group accompanied by an older sibling, parent, etc. There were also small groups of young men in their later teens and early twenties, some of them composed of high school or college students, others made up of single young working men, to judge by their clothes and manner. The audience included very few of the latter's female counterparts.

A boy's social network is also largely uni-sexual, with some important exceptions. The first exception, as noted above, arises out of the possibility that a boy will develop an intimate relationship with a sister. Second, it is likely that the most intimate cross-sex relationship he will ever have is the one he has with his mother both as a young boy and as an adult—a relationship which will probably be more intense and more important in several ways than the one he will develop with his wife. This relationship is very different from all others, moreover, since it is based on the gratitude he owes his mother for all the sacrifices she makes for him, including the pain of childbirth, nursing him, and the innumerable tasks and pampering undertaken to make his life comfortable and happy (Kıray, 1964, pp. 119-20; 1976, pp. 266-67). This debt is considered to be so great that no man can ever really hope to repay it, and it is traditionally the responsibility of the sons, especially the eldest, to see to their mother's well-being as long as she is alive.

Despite this debt of gratitude, however, as a boy enters adolescence he begins to identify more with his male peer group, and his emotional ties to his mother loosen somewhat while friendships with other boys become of central importance (see Magnarella, 1974, pp. 90-91, p. 168; Fallers and Fallers, 1976, pp. 256-58). In fact, a Turkish boy's relationships with his male peers are probably more central to him than are a girl's relationships with her female peers. One reason is that boys are free at an earlier age to join their peers outside of the house: boys can be seen roaming the streets and gardens in small groups from the age of four or five, while their sisters are already helping their mothers with domestic and agricultural tasks by that age.

Second, a boy must show rather formal respect towards his father in most families, which limits the development of intimacy between them. Further, when a boy becomes a *delikanlı* (literally, "one with mad blood," but used to refer to all boys in their teens and early twenties), it is assumed that he will want to play cards, smoke, drink, talk loudly, laugh, etc., and it is disrespectful for him to do any of these in his father's presence. Therefore, he and his father must socialize separately, or both will be highly uncomfortable. As a result, in order to enjoy themselves, most *delikanlı* will spend virtually all of their leisure time together in the exclusively masculine places recognized as appropriate for them, such as certain coffeehouses, the general sections of cinemas, tea gardens, etc. Only the elite class of young men is likely to frequent those public places where they can mix with or even exchange glances with young women (Kıray, 1976, pp. 263-64; Fallers and Fallers, 1976, pp. 255-58).

Not only do the young men spend a lot of time together, but they also develop intense emotional attachments to each other. For example, among my male acquaintances in Ankara, I was surprised at the warmth of their friendships with other men. They tended to have high expectations about the accessibility and loyalty of these friends, and responded with great heat and anger when their friends failed to meet these expectations. For example, after an argument, two friends might refuse to speak to each other for weeks or months before they or someone else patched up the disagreement and restored the friendship.

The intensity of friendship is also illustrated in the study of Susurluk by Magnarella, where he comments at some length on the importance of friendship for both sexes, noting that "true friends are loyal confidants; they share each others' joys, sorrows, and material possessions" (Magnarella, 1974, p. 168). He also describes an institution, *ahiret*, which I have not encountered elsewhere. Especially in the past, before the rapid growth of the town in the 1950s, it was said that close friends would establish "spiritual links" between themselves through the institution of *ahiret* kin.

> The word *"ahiret"* derives from a root meaning "other world" or "afterlife." *Ahiret* designates especially close friends, who are considered inseparable in this world and the next. If only one attains heaven, he has the right to intercede with Allah for the other. The institution which elevates friendship from the secular, worldly level to the sacred, spiritual level was customarily established in a simple ceremony following a communal meal. After all had eaten, the two friends rose and announced that they were entering an *ahiret* relationship. They exchanged gifts, and guests congratulated the two and offered best wishes (Magnarella, 1974, p. 168).

Today, friendships are still extremely important in Susurluk, but they remain secular (Magnarella, 1974, p. 168).

Husband-Wife Relationships in a Duofocal Family Structure

Given these patterns of socialization and the strength of the social networks in which each spouse is already involved at the time of marriage, it is not surprising that the relationship of a husband and wife in Turkey tends to be less a primary dyad than a bridge between the foci of two rather independent social networks. To expand the metaphor, this bridge, moreoever, is unlikely to have as much traffic as the major paths within each network. Thus, a Turkish marriage tends to be more nearly the juxtaposition of two networks than the uniting of two individuals, because, as was true of the couples in Bott's study, the "marriage is superimposed on these pre-existing relations" (Bott, 1957, p. 92).

After marriage, then, the couple 's respective networks of friends and/or relatives will expect each of them to continue cooperating and socializing separately with their old predominantly same-sex group, much as before their marriage, although their new responsibilities as a married man and woman are also recognized. This pattern seems to characterize most Turkish marriages, although the specifics vary. For example, because she is ten to fifteen years older, on the average, a highly-educated urban woman is likely to bring a more fully-developed social network to her marriage than her less-educated or rural counterpart. On the other hand, if a girl moves from her home community to a strange one at marriage, she will of course be largely cut off from her old social network. However, even here she will not expect her new husband to be her primary confidant and partner; instead she will build a new network involving primarily the female members of her new household and neighborhood with whom she will interact both while working and while socializing. The husband also frequently chooses to emphasize his affinal ties to his wife's male relatives (which may also be consanguinal ties, given the frequency of marriage between kin), thereby making additions to his existing network as well.[11]

This duality of networks--some overlap notwithstanding--was a conspicuous characteristic of the married couples whom I personally observed, both in rural and urban settings. For example, while we lived in Güzelköy in southwestern Turkey, Hasan, our landlord, arranged for the marriage of Fatma, his 16-year-old "adopted sister"[12] with the help of her biological father and brothers and other members of both families. It was agreed that she should marry someone from Güzelköy. During the process, she vetoed several choices suggested by her family, saying that she wanted an *usta* (a man with a skill). She finally married a 20-year-old man, probably the most desirable bachelor in the village except for his young age. He was an *usta* (a carpenter who had taken a vocational course and served as an apprentice in town), attractive, intelligent, good-natured, and hard-working. His father had died while he was young, and he lived with his mother and a sister in her early teens. Once contracted, this marriage took place immediately, despite the fact that his family had not wanted him to marry until he had completed his compulsory army service, and he left for a two-year stint a few months after the wedding.

After the wedding, Fatma moved into her mother-in-law's household, which was already familiar to her since the house next door was the one in which Fatma's "sister-in-law" (her "adopted" brother's wife) had grown up, and she had spent countless hours in both houses. Also, her "sister-in-law" continued to visit her parents' household regularly, and so Fatma saw her frequently. Her mother-in-law was a warm, gentle person, and Fatma seemed very happy every time we happened to see her at her new home. Before her husband's departure, she had become pregnant and soon produced a son, thereby adding to her happiness and her status. While nearly all of Fatma's time was spent working or visiting in the company of her female in-laws, "adopted" family, and neighbors, her husband spent most of his in the company of male friends, whether at work or during his leisure hours. If her husband was home, it was because it was mealtime or bedtime, or because he was entertaining a group of male friends in their guest room, and the women would ordinarily not intrude on them. In the evenings, the whole family might visit another family, probably kinfolk, and all sit in the guest room together, but the men and women would generally have separate conversations.

Among the urban elite, this bi-polarity or dual focus takes somewhat different forms, but it is no less striking. An example will help illustrate its urban dimensions.

One of my friends, Gülen, a 25-year-old professional woman, had been married about a year to a man 15 years her senior. One morning, I mentioned feeling guilty about having spent all the previous evening talking with my husband rather than "getting some work done." To my surprise, Gülen revealed her envy of my relationship with my husband, wistfully commenting that she wished her husband would spend an evening discussing something with her some time, but that they never did so. It was not that Gülen's husband did not think her capable of intelligent conversation; to the contrary, he was proud of the fact that she was a highly-educated, articulate, competent career woman. It was just that he had always found companionship and intellectual stimulation among a group of close male friends, and he expected to continue to do so after marriage. Further, he expected and encouraged Gülen to do the same among her network of friends.

Although he found this arrangement very convenient and satisfying, Gülen was unfortunately caught in a transitional state that in some ways gave her the "worst of both worlds," the "traditional" and the "modern" ones. First of all, the "modern" world: some of her best friends—former classmates and co-workers—were male, and the occasions on which she could see them socially were very limited. They could socialize somewhat at work, since the Turkish workday tends to be rather long but allows for frequent short social breaks during the day and includes a long 90-minute lunch hour. (See Magnarella, 1974, p. 96, for a more detailed description of the workday in a Turkish town.) Before she was married, she had frequented tea-gardens and other public places with this group of friends, and they had even met occasionally at someone's apartment to cook a meal for the whole group. However, after she married, the cooking sessions were discontinued and she joined the mixed group at public places after hours on only the rarest of occasions.

Second, the "traditional"factors: even in a "modern" city like Ankara, Gülen's mobility was much more restricted than her husband's. This was not because he wanted her to stay at home while he spent his evenings with his cronies at the club, coffeehouse, etc.; rather, he urged her to go out. However, he didn't seem to fully realize that she was not as mobile as he was. She could not even drop in for casual visits with family or friends as he could: her family lived in another city, and her friends lived in other sections of Ankara. Sometimes she would take her paperwork with her and walk the few blocks to her in-laws' apartment to "sit with her mother-in-law" for the evening. However, a woman alone at night on the street, in a share-cab, on a bus, etc., was likely to be perceived as "fair game" for insult and annoyance or even molestation, even in the respectable residential area where they lived, and she was frequently unwilling to take the risk.

Further, even if she or a woman friend had had a car, or if they had lived near enough to each other to go out together, there were virtually no appropriate places for them to go at night. Although older women might go to a *pastahane* or attend a cinema together, a pair of young matrons would hesitate to do so, because at their age it might look as if they were interested in meeting men. They could attend a "Western"-style concert or play, but this required elaborate planning and was expensive. There were virtually no feminine counterparts to their husbands' clubs and coffeehouses.

Instead, middle- and upper-class urban women traditionally met in each others' homes for religious gatherings, usually a *mevlud* (recitation of the famous poem on the life of Mohammed), to play cards, and on a regular schedule of week-day afternoons for rather elaborate teas (Olson-Prather, 1976, p. 268; Mansur, 1972, pp. 230-40), variously termed *kabul günü* (acceptance day) (Benedict, 1974, pp. 130-31), or *misafir günü* (visitors' day) (Fallers and Fallers, 1976, p. 252).[13]

However, the women in Gülen's social network had never established such a tea-time schedule. Although they now and then expressed a desire to do so, all of them were too busy with work and/or graduate school, plus a full load of housework with little or no domestic help to prepare the delicacies appropriate for such occasions. Even if they had been willing to defy tradition by purchasing pastries from the *pastahane* instead of making them themselves, most of them could not afford to do so on their modest government salaries or stipends. Moreover, some of them were so overburdened with work that even this more modest "tea" was too time-consuming. For Gülen, the weekend offered the best opportunities for socializing, and occasionally she would meet a woman friend or two on Saturday afternoon or Sunday to attend the cinema together, shop, go to a park, etc.

The importance of a chaperone, either male or female, is illustrated by two other anecdotes. While we were still in Ankara, Gülen's brother, a university student a few years her junior, moved in with his sister and brother-in-law for a few months. For a time, her social life and mobility improved dramatically, because her brother would escort her to places that were inappropriate or difficult for her to attend alone or with a woman friend. However, he later found separate lodgings, and became less and less accessible, until her mobility reverted nearly to its previous level. Later, her widowed mother came to spend a few days with her, and the two women went out nearly every evening together, taking immense pleasure in being together.

Male and female spheres are not completely separate, however, and it should not be thought that Turkish couples *never* socialize together. During the weekend or on a weeknight, urban couples occasionally joined friends and/or relatives in someone's home, or at a *pastahane*, a theatre, a park, etc. Urban couples with children are particularly likely to be found in family parks on weekend afternoons, often in a larger group including friends, neighbors, and/or relatives. Even the small cities in Turkey have "family" restaurants, cinemas, and *pastahane*, often with a special section at the back or upstairs reserved for the *aile* (usually translated "family," but referring primarily to women and children). In the villages and small towns, although formal social occasions like circumcisions and weddings are rather rigidly segregated by sex, informal occasions for mixed visiting among close relatives and friends frequently exist, as described for Fatma and her husband previously.

Romance and Sex in the Turkish Marriage

Despite the duofocality of family structure and the separation of male and female spheres, it should not be assumed that romance and passion between men and women do not exist in Turkey. To the contrary, there is a long historical tradition of secular poetry, epic stories, songs, etc., dealing with romantic love, though not always within the context of marriage by any means. This romantic tradition is continued in today's popular films, magazine serials, novels, etc. In mystical songs and poetry, moreover, the love of man for God is often couched in the metaphors of romantic and passionate love of a man for a woman.

Nor does the prohibition of cross-sex conversation necessarily preclude the development of passion between a boy and girl, even though they may communicate only through looks and body language (see Starr, 1970, p. 110). Not only are most of the elopements and some of the kidnappings a reflection of mutual romantic love (see Bates, 1973, pp.68-79; Sertel, 1969, pp. 96-104), but many of the "arranged" marriages are love-matches as well.

The family members who arrange their young people's marriages may also strive to create a situation in which romantic love can be expected to develop after marriage. For example, in an *Alevi* (Shiite) village in Anatolia, it was said that a couple should not be too familiar to each other, because this will make it impossible for them to "fall in love" with each other after marriage. In this same *Alevi* village, 20% of the marriages were by elopement, which required the cooperation of the girl and the boy and the help of some of their friends. There were also two cases in which married women had left their first husbands to live as the second wives of other men for the sake of "love," even though they had to live without the protection and status of legal marriage (Erdentuğ, 1971, pp. 27-28, p. 38). Admittedly these attitudes may not be representative of most Turkish marriages, since love is said to play a special role among the Alevi.

However, an example drawn from Güzelköy also seems to suggest the expectation of romance after marriage. In this case, it appeared that the husband took special care to nurture romantic love between himself and his young bride. He had insisted on marrying that particular girl and on marrying her that season, although she was a few months short of the legal age (15) for marriage, and the parents had at first been reluctant to have her marry so young. But he was personable, was from a respected family, and had a promising future because of his job with the highway department, and they finally consented. She was a very modest and pretty girl, about ten years younger than her husband. He did not build a new house for his bride, although he probably could have afforded it since he had worked for the highway department for several years. Instead, as the first son to marry, he brought his bride to live with his aging parents and his unmarried brothers. The wedding was held during the middle of his annual vacation, giving them a week after the wedding to get acquainted before he returned to working full-time.

His family's garden and orchard was just across the street from our house, which we shared with our landlord's family. Ordinarily his sisters (one of whom was our landlady) and their mother tended this garden, sometimes in the company of neighbor women as well. On their days off, the brothers might do some work there as well, but not very frequently. A couple of days after the wedding, I caught sight of the bride and groom working together in the garden, with the rest of the family conspicuously absent. The walls of the garden made it semi-private, since passers-by on the road did not have a clear view, though the couple were clearly visible from the second floor of our house. After a while I noticed that the husband had given up the pretense of working, and was coaxing his bride to sit down and chat with him. Still modest, she finally sat opposite him on the ground, and they spent the rest of the afternoon talking together. From a distance, the total impression left by the scene was that of a gentle, romantic young man wooing a shy young girl, trying to win her trust and overcome her timidity. I was also struck by the realization that he had obviously arranged the cooperation of his whole family, since ordinarily he would have been working or socializing with his brothers, and the women would probably have entered the garden to gather produce for a meal during the course of the afternoon. Since I have never encountered a written account of a similar phenomenon, I have no way of knowing how common this practice of post-wedding wooing is. However, when we visited the village about four years later, his younger brother had just married, and I chanced to see this young husband apparently wooing his bride in the same garden and in the same way as his older brother had done!

Nevertheless, most ethnographers report that romantic love is not generally associated with marriage, but that it did sometimes develop between a married couple. For example, Stirling wrote:

> women frequently said to my wife that they did not love their husbands—not only in specific cases, but as a general description of village life....More than once, men remarked to me in jest: "We love our wives at night" (Stirling, 1965, p. 113).

Yet he noted some cases of real affection between spouses (Stirling, 1965, pp. 109-13). Similarly, Mansur reported that while Bodrum women considered marriage a necessary stage of life, a partnership that is mutually advantageous to each side, the

> notion of romantic life does not enter into the matter, even though love often develops between the young couple as a result of intimacy and a happy coincidence of personalities....The Bodrum men will not waste time thinking about married bliss; a good wife is a good wife and the matter will rest there (Mansur, 1972, pp. 183-85).

In Edremit, marriage is not a sacred but a civil contract, but spouses sometimes do become affectionate, "though never demonstratively so until one of them dies" (Fallers and Fallers, 1976, p. 259). Starr describes a similar situation in Mandalinci Köy (1970, p. 115), while Magnarella reports that love is beginning to enter into the decision to marry in Susurluk as it becomes more an undertaking between two individuals rather than between two families. He sees the townspeople as being partly influenced in this by the immigration of Circassians and Georgians, for whom elopement has traditionally been very common (Magnarella, 1974, pp. 113-21).

While the expectation of romantic love within marriage appears to be relatively rare, it seems to me--and here I am being very speculative--that sexual satisfaction is deemed a conjugal right for both partners in a marriage, at least while they are young. I can cite very little evidence for Turkey to support this generalization, and what I do have is fragmentary, somewhat indirect, and impressionistic. However, with this qualification, I will elaborate upon my generalization.

First, it seems to me that the genitals of both sexes are greatly admired as organs of beauty and pleasure. Old women in Güzelköy delighted in snatching at the penises of little boys exposed by the loose shirts that were their only garment. Although there were obviously multiple motives in this action, since they would sometimes tease the boys that they were going to cut off their penises, I also interpreted this behavior as an expression of delight in the incipient virility of these tiny boys. When we lived in Ankara, we hired an older Turkish woman as maid and nurse. She and our two-year-old daughter adored each other, and "Aunt Miriam" expressed great delight in our daughter's *şeker kutu* ("sugar box," her pet name for a little girl's genitals).[14]

Second, it appears that sexual intercourse is generally viewed as being pleasurable for both sexes, although in some cases it is seen as a duty the wife must perform for her husband whether or not it is pleasurable for her. For example, Magnarella reports that the notion that wives must be able to satisfy the sexual desires of husbands throughout their lifetimes (as well as bear them children) is "still common throughout Turkey." He notes that the inability to do the former is called "losing one's womanhood," although he does not elaborate on the meaning of this phrase. More educated informants were said to disagree with this attitude, arguing further that a "man whose wife had already given him children and years of sexual companionship had no right to either a divorce or a second wife" (Magnarella, 1974, pp. 126-127). In the villages studied by

Stirling, although the women claimed not to "love" their husbands, as noted above, they were very open in their discussion of sex and reproduction, which were major topics of conversation among themselves (Stirling, 1965, p. 192). In Irfan Orga's autobiographical description of his turn-of-the-century Istanbul family, he recounts going at the age of five to the *hamam* (public bath) with his grandmother. There, his grandmother "looked at the naked young girls with the critical eye of a connoisseur." When she found one who met with her strong approval, she advised the girl's mother to "marry such a daughter as soon as possible to the strongest man that could be found. 'He will know how to delight her,' she would boom loudly, 'but make sure he is as strong as a lion—otherwise, with those fine legs of hers, she will kill him!' " (Orga, 1950, p. 21).

Further, conjugal sex is regarded as not only compatible with one's religious duties, but perhaps even as a part of them (Olson-Prather, 1976, pp. 280-281; Mernissi, 1975, pp. 23, 26, 63). A theologian at Ankara University declared that modern birth control methods are even more proper for Muslims than the traditional method of withdrawal (coitus interruptus), because they do not interfere with a woman's pleasure in sex (Ateş, 1968). Further, in another village where some Peace Corps friends of ours lived, it was considered a man's religious duty to have sexual intercourse with his wife Thursday night, the night before the Muslim holy day. Friday, the married men would come with dragging feet into the coffeehouse, apparently exhausted, and would be teased by the single men for being tired! Reportedly, they made no response, but sat sheepishly drinking their tea.

Starr's description of an incident in Mandalinci Köy, a Mediterranean village, also suggests not only the expectation that a woman will enjoy sex, but also the general opinion that it is her right to do so. In this incident, villagers expressed considerable sympathy for a particular young woman because it was said that her husband, 15 years her senior, was impotent, "had been for the last six months, and that his wife was frantic" (Starr, 1970, p. 273). When she secretly took a young unmarried man as lover, everyone eventually knew about it, and were both amused and sympathetic to the husband, but did not condemn the woman. Given the situation, the husband attempted to salvage his reputation by making a public scene when he discovered them together, but he did not divorce her. Instead, he spoke to the young man's father, insisting that he control his son. The young man kept away for some months, but eventually began visiting his lover again, but more discreetly this time, so that the husband was not publicly embarrassed (Starr, 1970, pp. 273-276).

My own observations also suggest that a Turkish woman expects to enjoy sex in marriage (Olson-Prather, 1976, pp. 281-284). In Güzelköy, I once observed a boisterous verbal exchange between an old woman and a young man, in which each playfully teased the other for having sexual intercourse with his/her spouse all the time, graphically demonstrating their meaning with hand gestures! In another case in the village, when the former *ağa's* son Ali temporarily separated from his wife to placate his father, her unmarried schoolteacher friend teased her, asking her whom she was "sleeping" with now that her husband wasn't with her—a "joke" which would be regarded as cruel in American culture, but which only produced a slightly embarrassed grin.

Similarly, my young urban friend, Layla, apparently regarded sex as something which both her parents enjoyed, even in their early 60's, since she regarded it as an appropriate target for teasing. Again, a close friend in Ankara initiated a matter-of-fact discussion with me one day about a minor difficulty in her sexual relationship with her husband which made it clear that both of them expected sex to be highly pleasurable, and that they assumed that everyone else they knew felt the same way.

On the other hand, my maid was rather contemptuous of a mutual friend of ours, a middle-aged woman with four children, and her husband, for their allegedly excessive interest in conjugal sex. According to her, whenever this woman's husband called for her, she would quite willingly disappear into the bedroom with him even if her friends were visiting her. My maid thought this showed lack of self-control, since the couple "already had enough children," and they were acting "just like dogs."

Finally, sex is often regarded as essential to good health. For example, Mansur notices that "mild nervous disorders" are more numerous among women and adolescents than among other groups in Bodrum. For the women, one cause is said to be the widespread practice of *coitus interruptus*, which reportedly has resulted in as many as 85% of the women going to the doctor for pills and tranquilizers. Mansur quotes the doctor: " 'In some cases,' says the doctor, 'I call the husband and explain the situation to him. He goes away contrite, but does not change his habits.' " Further, young men who suffer "repeated headaches, listlessness and such like debilitating uneasiness" are advised by the same doctor "not to wait until they get married," but to engage in premarital sex, presumably with prostitutes. It is assumed that this kind of nervousness will disappear when the young man marries (Mansur, 1972, p. 210).

Concluding Comments

In previous descriptions of husband-wife relationships in Turkey, the predominant model has been one in which the family is seen as evolving from a "traditional" form characterized by a patriarchal structure to a "modern" form characterized by an egalitarian structure. As an alternative to this model, in which dominance relations is the central concept, I have attempted to describe conjugal role-relationships in terms of a "duofocal" model of family structure. This duofocality of family structure is analyzed as a reflection of the sexual separation which characterizes Turkish society in general. According to this model, marriage for most Turks tends to be an arrangement which juxtaposes but does not merge two individual social networks, for the mutual advantage of the participants. Given the sharp division of labor and social roles by sex, this type of marriage appears to be a relatively efficient means for providing complementarity of skills and tasks within a single household. It also provides sexual satisfaction and a stable system for procreation and childbearing. It may even lead to romantic love between husband and wife. Marriage is not, however, likely to involve a unitary, highly "joint" relationship in which the spouses look to each other as a primary source of advice, companionship, emotional support, and entertainment as they do in the ideal "Western" relationship. Rather, to satisfy these needs, they continue to rely on the members of their own primarily uni-sexual social networks as they did before marriage.

So far, I have not dealt explicitly with the issue of change in conjugal role-relationships as a result of the rapid urbanization and "modernization" which is currently occurring in Turkey. According to the "Western" model, segregated conjugal role relationships should disappear with "modernization." However, this does not appear to be happening in the majority of cases. Instead, although the patterns vary in detail, the separation of male and female spheres and segregation in conjugal role relationships occur at all levels of urbanization and socio-economic status. There is even some evidence that the greatest segregation tends to occur among the middle classes and in medium-sized towns and cities, rather than among the lower classes and in rural areas as would be expected (Olson-Prather, 1976, pp. 285-288). Moreover, this pattern continues to characterize highly-urban families to a large degree, even among the elite. For example, as noted above, while members of the professional class tend to work with people of both sexes, they socialize in largely uni-sexual environments. Further, non-working urban women of the middle and upper classes move in spheres inhabited primarily by women (and children) during nearly every hour of the day.

An important exception is the class of highly-mobile civil servants and their wives, who sometimes spend considerably more time socializing in mixed groups. For example, in Susurluk, a town undergoing rapid change, a wide range of variation existed. The wives of the officials who were not native to Susurluk (whose numbers had greatly increased since the construction of a sugar beet factory in town) demanded the companionship of their husbands, even in the evenings. A group of them even wrote a letter to the subprovincial governor, their husbands' boss, complaining that the men were spending too much time playing poker in their clubs in the evenings, and demanding that the gambling laws be enforced and these clubs forced to close earlier so that the men would go home. They already participated in some public social interaction with their husbands, for these officials had made it a practice to take their families to the city's "Family Park," which had tea gardens that became casinos at night. However, these joint activities by husbands and wives were said to date only to the 1950s and 1960s, when the small town began urbanizing rapidly. Before that, there were virtually no exceptions to the segregated patterns which still characterized the majority of families at the time of the study (Magnarella, 1974, p. 49, pp. 96-98). Benedict describes a parallel set of patterns for Ula, a smaller town in southwestern Turkey (Magnarella, 1975, pp. 128-132), and Fallers and Fallers speculate about the possibility of such changes in Edremit, again due to the influences of the highly-mobile civil servants' families (Magnarella, 1976, pp. 254-255). These civil servants are repeatedly transferred from one strange city to another, thus severing the links of each spouse's social network.

This imposed mobility and the consequent isolation from natal family and friends may be a more important factor in explaining these women's demands for more interaction with their husbands than the diffusion of "modern" attitudes through education, mass media, etc., as is frequently suggested. These women also tend to be more "sophisticated" and highly-educated than the majority of local women, and thus feel like strangers in a second sense. Moreover, in small towns, their numbers are too small to compose a group of their own. The apparent result is to rely more on their husbands for companionship as the only constant individuals in their lives.

Within the villages, there is considerable variation in the degree of sexual segregation, as illustrated by these examples from the literature: (1) in a citrus-growing village in southern Turkey, men spent most of their leisure time in the coffeehouses and women at home, but husbands and wives apparently communicated freely when they were together (Kolars, 1963, pp. 69-84); (2) in an Alevi village in eastern Turkey, the men and women performed their separate tasks in the fields, but worshiped together, and the women were allowed to sit in (silently) on the men's group discussions, "so that they would profit from the men's knowledge" (Erdentuğ, 1971, p. 38); (3) in a village in central Anatolia, men spent as much time as possible away from their own houses, women joined men in their guest room only if no guests were present, and spouses were not expected to be companions, since it was assumed that there was no common ground for conversation (Stirling, 1965, pp. 98-101, p. 113); and (4) in an eastern Black Sea village which still showed some Pontic Greek influences, women were "restricted to the households in which they are wives or unmarried daughters," while men who were in their own hamlets too much were distrusted for solitariness and ridiculed for dependence on women (Meeker, 1970, pp. 320-332).

Nevertheless, contrary to the usual expectations, male and female spheres in the villages are in some ways less mutually exclusive than those in the more urban communities. In general, there are fewer highly-developed unisexual institutions in the villages in which each sex can participate than in the cities, and whole families may socialize in mixed groups with their families. Further, both sexes tend to be heavily involved in farming operations and to be aware of their mutual dependence. Further, although their tasks are more complementary than joint, husbands and wives come into relatively frequent contact with each other. As a result, it is my impression that husband-wife social interactions and discussion are perhaps more likely to be found among village couples than anywhere else except possibly among the self-consciously "Westernized" urban elite. Village spouses may even seek advice from each other, as our young village landlord and his wife, Hasan and Ayşe, seemed to do increasingly in the years that we knew them.

Paradoxically, of all the married couples I knew in Turkey, rural or urban, this young farmer and his functionally-illiterate wife came closest to exemplifying a joint conjugal role-relationship, largely because they seemed to confide in each other and make joint decisions. Their relationship was apparently evolving from a more typical sex-segregated one to a more companionate form as the family grew and the wife matured. The fact that Ayşe was so competent and fertile, and that Hasan had brothers-in-law and close friends (but no brothers) and a father who had retired long before from public life, are probably factors in this relatively "joint" conjugal relationship. Nonetheless, even their relationship was far different from the joint conjugal relationship idealized in "Western" culture.

This essay has just begun to outline some of the characteristics of segregated conjugal role-relationships and the duofocal family structure which are common patterns in Turkey today. Their precise definition and documentation remain to be done. Yet, their prevalence at the various levels of urbanization and "modernization," and the conditions which appear to be negatively associated with these patterns suggest a number of avenues for future discussion and research. In particular, it appears that the conditions under which a typical, less-segregated husband-wife relationship appear to develop, e.g., a high degree of geographical and social mobility, social isolation, involvement in small-scale agriculture, are similar to those under which the "joint" conjugal relationship developed historically in the United States; whether a similar process will occur in Turkey remains to be seen.

NOTES

[1]   Research for this study was supported by NIMH grants No. MH 10576 and MH 45984. The 1968 survey data reported in this paper were collected as part of the 1968 Turkish Social Survey on Family and Population Questions, conducted by the Nüfus Etüdleri Enstitüsü (Institute of Population Studies) at Hacettepe University in Ankara, Turkey. The author is grateful to the Institute for allowing her to use both the survey data and their facilities for sixteen months in 1970-71.

[2]   In a sense, "duofocal nuclear family" is a self-contradictory term, since the term "nuclear" itself denotes a unitary center and reflects the

ethnocentricity of the concept of "nuclear family" itself. In spite of this terminological ambiguity, rather than inventing additional neologisms here, I will follow conventional practice by using "nuclear family" to refer to the two-generational reproductive unit of mother, father, and their off-spring, which is typically the economic and residential unit in Turkey as well.

3 These general descriptions are based on three kinds of data: (1) Data from the 1968 Turkish Social Survey on Family Structure and Population Questions, and as presented by Serim Timur in her 1972 monograph, *Türkiye ' de Aile Yapısı* (Family Structure in Turkey), which is a slight revision of her doctoral dissertation. (2) Material from published ethnographies, in both English and Turkish. Although these ethnographies cover nearly a 30-year time span, include every major region except European Turkey (Thrace), and include communities of various types and sizes, it should be noted that they do not provide a random sample of Turkish communities. They also vary widely in methodology, depth, scope, etc. They do, however, provide many clues to the range of existing variation. (3) My own observations and experiences in Turkey as a Peace Corps volunteer from 1964-66 and while doing research for the dissertation from 1970-71. Although my own observations were rather unsystematic because I was not a trained anthropologist during the first period and because foreigners were not permitted to do systematic interviewing and observation in the second period (Olson-Prather, 1976, pp. 20-29), I feel that they complement the evidence from the other two types of sources, and compensate somewhat for the scarcity of in-depth contextual studies of family structure that are needed for interpretation of survey data. All Turkish names in my descriptions are pseudonyms.

4 The separation of male and female spheres is, of course, not unique to Turkish society. In fact, the separation of the sexes is probably less in contemporary Turkey than in many other Mediterranean societies, and according to one 19th century observer, was much less marked in Ottoman Turkey than in other Muslim societies (Woodsmall, 1936, p. 301). For descriptions of this phenomenon in other Mediterranean societies, see, for example, Friedl (1962) and Campbell (1964) for Greece, Rogers (1975) for France, Peristiany (1966 and 1976) and Sweet (1967) for articles on several Mediterranean societies, Mernissi (1975) and Dwyer (1978) for Morocco, and Fernea (1969) for Iraq.

5 The women's and children's quarters were referred to as the *harem* even when a man had only one wife; the common association of the word *harem* with polygyny and with a group of female concubines, in particular, is a distortion, since polygyny has never been widespread in Turkey. Generally, only the rich and leisured class could afford it, and not all of them exercised this privilege. In the villages today, the women's part of the house, even if only a single room in a two-room house, may still be referred to as the *harem* or *haremlik* although that does not necessarily imply

seclusion (see Kolars, 1963, pp. 58-59). It is, however, an area where strange men would not enter without the host's invitation.

⁶   Orga provides a vivid description of the contrast between the very different effects of the same ideal for the rich and less-rich in his book: while still young, Orga's father died and his mother had to make the transition from a life of luxury to one of relative poverty. Accustomed to light and fresh air, when she was forced to move to three small rooms without a garden, she unhesitatingly committed the shocking act of ordering that the heavy lattices be taken away from the windows so as to allow some air and light in, though no one else in the rundown neighborhood had the confidence or desire to do so (Orga, 1950, pp. 116-19).

⁷   A personal experience illustrates this vividly. For reasons which are still not entirely clear, but partly because I did not become pregnant, it was assumed for a time that my husband and I were not actually married to each other when we were living in a Turkish village as Peace Corps volunteers in 1964-66. We were somewhat shocked to learn that ours was regarded for some time as a temporary "marriage of convenience," necessary because both single women and single men are nearly helpless alone, given the exclusive but complementary nature of the sex roles.

⁸   If this seems unremarkable it should be remembered that such generalizations can still not be made without qualification about attitudes toward American professional women. Fallers and Fallers make a similar comment in their recent article (1976, p. 254).

⁹   The use of male *odacı* for female high-level officials and professionals again illustrates the non-sexual definition of the latter, who are not regarded as sexually vulnerable to men of this class. Conversely, *odacı* interact frequently among themselves, and should therefore be of the same sex, or the women among them would be seen as "exposed."

¹⁰   The use of kinship terms in addressing non-kin, even strangers, is very common in Turkey. Although Magnarella is certainly aware of how widespread this custom is, he does not mention this, nor describe exactly the forms of address in Susurluk. Presumably, he refers to a particular type of usage other than the casual forms used elsewhere.

¹¹   Spencer (1960) notes the "ambilineality" of the Turkish *aile* (family). According to Spencer, the aile is definable only in terms of ego, i.e., the husband's, and is the primary functional unit because no larger unit is stable enough for "concerted group action" (Spencer, 1969, p. 47). As a result, Turkish social structure is "highly flexible and permits readaptation to differing historical circumstance" (Spencer, 1960, p. 49), including, I would add, a variety of social, residential, and economic ties. However, I suggest that what Spencer characterizes as ambilineality also reflects duofocality, unrecognized because of the unwitting androcentrism of his analysis. He presents the structure only from male ego's point of view, and while he recognizes that the husband may emphasize affinal ties, he fails to consider the *aile* from the wife's perspective, thereby never seeing the dual

networks centering in the husband and the wife, respectively, which the duofocal model posits.

Links with affinals are found in Middle Eastern societies outside of Turkey as well. For example, see Peters (1976) for a discussion of what he terms "affinal sets" in a Lebanese Maronite village, though he explicitly places his analysis outside of network theory.

[12] She was not legally adopted, but had been taken in by Hasan's father at the age of three when her mother died.

[13] A remarkable exception should be noted: in 1972 a group of women started a women's coffeehouse in the small town of Keltepe on the sea of Marmara. This was undoubtedly the only women's coffeehouse in Turkey, and its establishment was an unusual enough event to make a stir in the national papers and to bring the (male) provincial governor to its official opening. The women annouced that men could accompany their women relatives and friends after 7 P.M., but that during the day it was for women only (*Milliyet*, February 7, 1972).

[14] I have seen no mention of this practice in the literature. However, another American researcher, Barbara Bilge, reports that this is a common practice among both recent and earlier Turkish immigrants now living in the Detroit, Michigan area. They use both the term *şeker kutu* and *fındık* (hazelnut), (Personal communication, November, 1978).

BIBLIOGRAPHY

Abadan, Nermin. *Social Change and Turkish Women*. Ankara: Ankara Univ. Political Science Publication No. 171, 1963.

Afetinan, A. *The Emancipation of the Turkish Woman*. Paris: UNESCO, 1962.

Aswad, Barbara. "Visiting Patterns Among Women of the Elite in a Small Turkish City," *Anthropological Quarterly*, 1974, 47, 9-27.

Ateş, Süleyman. "Azl Veya Doğum Tahdidi" (Prevention of Birth Limitation). *İlahiyat Fakültesi Dergisi (Journal of the Theology Faculty)* 1968, 16, 123-130.

Bates, Daniel G. *Nomads and Farmers: A Study of the Yörük of Southeastern Turkey*. Museum of Anthropology, Anthropological Paper No. 52. Ann Arbor: University of Michigan, 1973.

Benedict, Peter. "The Kabul Günü: Structured Visiting in an Anatolian Provincial Town," *Anthropological Quarterly*, 1974, 47, 28-47.

————. *Ula: An Anatolian Town*. Leiden: E.J. Brill, 1974.

————. "Aspects of the Domestic Cycle in a Turkish Provincial Town." In J.G. Peristiany, (ed.), *Mediterranean Family Structures*. London: Cambridge University Press, 1976, pp. 219-242.

Bott, Elizabeth. *Family and Social Network*. London: Tavistock Publications Limited, 1957.

Bradburn, Norman. "Interpersonal Relations within Formal Organizations in Turkey," *Journal of Social Issues,* 1963, 19, 61-67.
Brown, Demetra. *The Unveiled Ladies of Stamboul.* Freeport, NY: Books for Libraries, 1971.
Campbell, John. *Honor, Family, and Patronage.* London: Oxford University Press, 1964.
Dubetsky, Alan. "Kinship, Primordial Ties, and Factory Organization in Turkey: An Anthropological View," *International Journal of Middle East Studies,* 1976, 7, 433-51.
Dwyer, Daisy Hilse. *Images and Self-Images: Male and Female in Morocco.* New York: Columbia University Press, 1978.
Erdentuğ, Nermin. "Bazi Devrek Köy Toplumlarında Kadının Mevkii" (The Woman's Position in Some Devrek Village Communities). *Antropoloji.* Ankara,1964, 1, 8-20.
_____. *Hal Köyü ' nün Etnolojik Tetkiki* (An Ethnological Study of the VillageofHal).AnkaraÜniversitesiDilveTarih-CoğrafyaFakültesiYayınları No. 109. Ankara, 1968.
_____. *Sun Köyü ' nün Etnolojik Tetkiki* (An Ethnological Study of the Village of Sun). Ankara Üniversitesi Eğitim Fakültesi Yayınları No. 16. Ankara, 1971.
Fallers, Loyd A. and Margaret C. "Sex Roles in Edremit." In J.G. Peristiany (ed.), *Mediterranean Family Structures.* London: Cambridge University Press, 1976, pp. 243-260.
Fernea, Elizabeth Warnock. *Guests of the Sheik.* New York: Doubleday and Co., Inc., 1969.
Friedl, Ernestine. *Vasilika, A Village in Modern Greece.* New York: Holt, Rinehart and Winston, 1962.
Garnett, Lucy. *The Women of Turkey and Their Folk-Lore.* London: David Nutt, 1890.
_____. *Turkish Life in Town and Country.* New York: G.P. Putnam's Sons, 1904.
_____. *Home Life in Turkey.* New York: The Macmillan Co., 1909.
Goldberg, David, and Greer Litton. "Family Planning: Observations and an Interpretive Scheme." In F.G. Shorter and B. Güvenç (eds.), *Turkish Demography: Proceedings of a Conference.* Hacettepe University Publications No. 7. Ankara, 1969.
Hale, William M. (ed.). *Aspects of Modern Turkey.* London: Bowker, 1976.
Helling, Barbara.. *Child Rearing Techniques in Turkish Peasant Villages.* M.A. Thesis, University of Minnesota, 1960.
Hill, Reuben; J. Mayone Stycos, and Kurt W. Back. *The Family and Population Control.* Chapel Hill: Univ. of North Carolina Press, 1959.
Jennings, Ronald C. "Sakultultan Four Centuries Ago," *International Journal of Middle Eastern Studies,* 1978, 9, 89-98.
Kâğıtçıbaşı, Çiğdem. "Social Norms and Authoritarianism: A Comparison of Turkish and American Adolescents," *Journal of Personality and Social Psychology.* 1970, 16, 444-51.

————. "Psychological Aspects of Modernization in Turkey," *Journal of Cross Cultural Psychology.* 1973, 4, 157-74.

Kandiyoti, Deniz. "Social Change and Family Structure in a Turkish Village (Bachelors and Maidens: A Turkish Case Study)." In J.G. Peristiany, (ed.), *Kinship and Modernization In Mediterranean Society.* Hanover, N.H.: The Center for Mediterranean Studies, 1976, pp. 61-71.

Karpat, Kemal H. "Social Themes in Contemporary Turkish Literature, Part II," *Middle East Journal.* 1960, 14, 153-68.

————. *The Gecekondu: Rural Migration and Urbanization.* Cambridge: Cambridge Univ. Press, 1976.

Kemal, Yashar. *Memed, My Hawk.* London: Collins and Harvill Press, 1961.

Kerckhoff, Alan C. "Status-related Value Patterns Among Married Couples," *Journal of Marriage and the Family.* 1972, 34, 105-10.

Kıray, Mübeccel Belik. *Ereğli, Ağir Sanayiden Bir Sahil Kasabası* (Ereğli, A Coastal Town Before Heavy İndustry). Ankara: T.C. Devlet Planlama Teşkilatı, Devlett Karayolları, Matbaasında, 1964.

————. "The New Role of Mothers: Changing Intra-Familial Relationships in a Small Town in Turkey." In J.G. Peristiany (ed.), *Mediterranean Family Structures.* London: Cambridge Univ. Press, 1976, pp. 261-71.

Kolars, John F. *Tradition, Season, and Change in a Turkish Village* (NAS-NRC Foreign Field Research Program Report No. 15). Chicago: Univ. of Chicago Press, 1963.

Komarovsky, Mirra. *Blue-collar Marriage.* New York: Random House, 1967.

Kongar, Emre. "Türkiye ' de Aile: Yapısı, Evrimi ve Bürokratik Örgütlerle Ilikileri" (The Family in Turkey: Structure, Evolution, and Relationships with Bureaucratic Organizations). *Amme İdaresi Dergisi.* 1970, 3, 58-83.

————. "A Survey of Familial Change in Two Turkish Gecekondu Areas." In J.G. Peristiany (ed.), *Mediterranean Family Structures.* London: Cambridge Univ. Press, 1976, pp. 205-18.

Levine, Ned. "Old Culture—New Culture: A Study of Migrants in Ankara, Turkey," *Social Forces.* 1973, 51, 355-68.

Levy, Marion J., Jr., "Aspects of the Analysis of Family Structure." In A.J. Coale et. al. (eds.), *Aspects of the Analysis of Family Structure.* Princeton: Princeton Univ. Press, 1965.

Magnarella, Paul J. "Conjugal Role-relationships in a Modernizing Turkish Town," *International Journal of Sociology of the Family.* 1972, 2, 179-92.

————. *Tradition and Change in a Turkish Town.* New York: Schenkman Publishing Co., 1974.

———— and Orhan Türkdoğan. "The Development of Turkish Social Anthropology," *Current Anthropology.* 1976, 17, 263-74.

Mansur, Fatma. *Bodrum: A Town in the Aegean.* London: E.J. Brill, 1972.

Meeker, Michael E. *The Black Sea Turks: A Study of Honor, Descent, and Marriage.* Unpublished Ph.D, dissertation, Univ. of Chicago, 1970.

———. "Meaning and Society in the Near East: Examples from the Black Sea Turks and the Levantine Arabs (I and II)," *International Journal of Middle East Studies*, 1976, 7, 243-70.

Mernissi, Fatima. *Beyond the Veil: Male-Female Dynamics in a Modern Muslim Society.* Cambridge, Mass.: Schenkman Publishing Co., 1975.

Milliyet. "Vali, Kadınlar Kahvesini Açti" (The Governor Opened a Women's Coffeehouse). Istanbul, Feb. 7, 1972.

Olson-Prather, Emelie. *Family Planning and Husband-Wife Relationships in Contemporary Turkey.* Unpublished Ph.D. dissertation, Univ. of California, Los Angeles, 1976.

Orga, Irfan. *Portrait of a Turkish Family.* New York: The Macmillan Co., 1950.

Parker, Seymour and Hilda. "The Myth of Male Superiority: Rise and Demise," *American Anthropologist.*1979, 81, 289-309.

Peristiany, J.G. *Honor and Shame.* Chicago: Univ. of Chicago Press, 1966.

——— (ed.). *Mediterranean Family Structures.* London: Cambridge Univ. Press, 1976a.

——— (ed.). *Kinship and Modernization in Mediterranean Society.* Hanover, N.H.: The Center for Mediterranean Studies, 1976b.

Peters, Emrys L. "Aspects of Affinity in a Lebanese Maronite Village." In J.G. Peristiany (ed.), *Mediterranean Family Structures.* London: Cambridge Univ. Press, 1976, pp. 27-80.

Pohlman, Edward. *The Psychology of Birth Planning.* Cambridge, Mass.: Schenkman Publishing Co., 1969.

Quinn, Naomi. "Anthropological Studies on Women's Status," *Annual Review of Anthropology.* 1977, 6, 181-225.

Rainwater, Lee. *Family Design: Marital Sexuality, Family Size, and Family Planning.* Chicago: Aldine Publishing Co., 1965.

Rogers, Susan C. "Female Forms of Power and the Myth of Male Dominance," *American Ethnologist.* 1975, 2, 727-56.

Schlegel, Alice. *Sexual Stratification: A Cross-Cultural View.* Columbia Univ. Press, 1977a.

——— (ed.). "Toward a Theory of Sexual Stratification." In *Sexual Stratification.* New York: Columbia Univ. Press, 1977b, pp. 1-40.

Schnaiberg, Allan. *Some Determinants and Consequences of Modernism in Turkey.* Unpublished Ph.D. dissertation, Univ. of Michigan, 1969.

Sertel, Ayşe. "Kidnapping and Elopement in Rural Turkey," *Hacettepe Bulletin of Social Sciences and Humanities.* 1969, 2, 96-104.

Sewell, Granville H.*Squatter Settlements in Turkey: An Analysis of a Social, Political, and Economic Problem.* Unpublished Ph.D. dissertation, Mass. Institute of Technology, 1964

Smith, Raymond T. "The Matrifocal Family." In Jack Goody (ed.), *The Character of Kinship.* London: Cambridge Univ. Press, 1973.

Sönmez, Emel. "Turkish Women in Turkish Literature of the 19th Century," *Hacettepe Bulletin of Social Sciences and Humanities.* 1970, 2, 17-47.

Starr, June Oettinger. *Mandalıncı Köy: Law and Social Control in a Turkish Village.* Unpublished Ph. D. dissertation, Univ. of California, Berkeley, 1970.

Stirling, Paul. *Turkish Village.* London: Weidenfeld and Nicolson, 1965.

————. "Cause, Knowledge, and Change." In Wm. Hale (ed.), *Aspects of Modern Turkey.* London: Bowker, 1976.

Suzuki, Peter. "Village Solidarity Among Turkish Peasants Undergoing Urbanization," *Science.* 1960, 132, 1, 891-92.

————. "Encounters with Istanbul: Urban Peasants and Village Peasants," *International Journal of Comparative Sociology.* 1964, 5, 208-15.

————. "Peasants Without Plows: Some Anatolians in Istanbul," *Rural Sociology.* 1966, 31, 428-38.

Sweet, Louise (ed.). "Appearance and Reality: Status and Roles of Women in Mediterranean Society," *Anthropological Quarterly.* 1967, 40, 94-183.

Tewari, Laxmi. *Turkish Village Music* (Notes on the record jacket). New York: Nonesuch Records, n.d.

Timur, Serim. *Türkiye ' de Aile Yapısı* (Family Structure in Turkey). Ankara: Hacettepe Üniversitesi Nüfus Etüdleri Enstitüsü Yayınları No. 15, 1972.

Vaka, Demetra. *Haremlik: Some Pages from the Life of Turkish Women.* New York: Houghton Mifflin Co., 1909.

Woodsmall, Ruth F. *Study of the Role of Women, Their Activities, and Organization in Lebanon, Egypt, Iran, Jordan, and Syria.* New York: The International Federation of Business and Professional Women, 1936.

Yanagisako, Sylvia J. "Women-Centered Kin Networks in Urban Bilateral Kinship," *American Ethnologist.* 1977, 4, 207-26.

Yasa, Ibrahim. *Hasanoğlan, Socio-Economic Structure of a Turkish Village.* Ankara: Yeni Matbaa, 1957.

————. *Sindel Köyünün Toplumsal ve Ekonomik Yapısı* (The Community and Economic Structure of the Village of Sindel). Ankara: Public Administration Institute for Turkey and the Middle East Publication no. 17, 1960.

————. *Ankara'da Gecekondu Aileleri* (Gecekondu Families in Ankara). Ankara: Akın Matbaası, 1966.

————. *Yirmi-beş Yıl Sonra Hasanoğlan Köyü* (Hasanoğlan Village after Twenty-Five Years). Ankara: Ankara Universitesi Siyasal Bilgiler Fakültesi Yayınları no. 270, 1969.

THE SIGNIFICANCE OF FAMILY
AND KINSHIP IN URBAN TURKEY

Alan Duben

There is a commonly held myth in Turkey in which the population in the countryside is believed to live in large extended family households resembling those of the past, and people in the city in small nuclear family households increasingly like those of their peers in the West.[1] Believers in this myth, a very widespread one in the cities, especially among the educated, also hold that movement from countryside to city leads to a shrinking of the old rural family, bringing it closer to its diminutive urban counterpart. There is a second version of this myth in which the large rural extended family household is believed to have been transformed into a small nuclear one prior to its departure for the city under the impact of the rapid social changes that have taken place in recent years in the countryside. Adherents of both versions agree that once in the city, where nuclear families live separately, the significance of extended family and other kinship ties, or of kinship in general, decreases in direct proportion to the degree with which members of such families have become acclimated to and successful within the city. I shall try to show in this paper that most of these beliefs are indeed a myth, in fact a very powerful one, which may begin to explain why so important a subject has been so seriously neglected in this country.[2]

The question of the significance of family and kinship in urban Turkey revolves around two issues. Though related, they are often mistakenly collapsed into each other. The first is a statistical issue, one pertaining, that is, to changes in the numbers of various types of households[3] in urban areas, and to the frequency with which individuals in family and kinship groups interact with others in similar groupings for various purposes. The second is a cultural issue, which though related to the first, can be considered independently of it. There are two relevant aspects to the cultural issue. One concerns the significance of culturally-based preferences for various household types. The other aspect has to do with the code or codes governing interactions of individuals within or between such households and kinship groups, especially the extent to which social interactions (whether they be between kinsmen or not) are undertaken in what I refer to as a kinship idiom.

The statistical evidence is not as straightforward as one might assume it to be. Underlying most of the studies in relation to Turkey are certain well-known but questionable assumptions about the family, kinship, and social change in the city. The most prominent of these is that the size and form of the household and the frequency of interaction with and reliance upon family and kinsmen has been influenced either by certain aspects of the rural transformation of the past thirty years, by prolonged urban residence, or by the so-called exigencies of industrial society. Masses of statistics about family and kinship in the city are interpreted in light of these assumptions. Much potential evidence is ignored as a result of adherence to them. The cultural issue, as it relates to the significance of a kinship idiom in urban areas, is, to my knowledge, not even an issue. No such discussions of the cultural basis of social intercourse in urban Turkey have yet taken place.

Rural Transformation, Migration, and the Family

Turkey, like many countries on the capitalist periphery, has experienced a major population shift in the past thirty years. The result of this shift is that the balance between town and country has been irrevocably reversed. In 1950, 18.5 percent of the population lived in urban areas. By 1975, this figure had jumped to 42 percent. The preliminary results of the 1980 census reveal that nearly half of the country's population is urban (Genel Nüfus Sayımı, p. 5). Istanbul is now the third largest city in Europe, with a population of over 5 million inhabitants, while Ankara has over 2 million inhabitants.

This dramatic population shift is almost entirely attributable to the massive departure of people from the rural hinterlands of the central and eastern regions of Anatolia and the Black Sea Coast. By and large the migrants were poor peasant agriculturalists engaged in eking out a subsistence living on relatively small family farms in their natal villages, although some later became agricultural laborers. These family farms are often thought of as the embodiment of the most typical (and traditional) Turkish household structure.

In order to be able to make comparisons between rural and urban households and to discuss changes over time, it is important to look closely at these rural households. While I agree with Goody and others (Goody, 1972, p. 4) that an analysis of household (or family) form does not necessarily tell us about its functions, the fact is that much has been made of such form both in the international and Turkish literature. It is as a result necessary to address this issue. I must state at the outset that it is difficult to be precise about the structure of these households, or about rural-urban differences, particularly with regard to changes over time, since so little solid research has yet been done in this area. Furthermore, it must be made clear that statistics about household form often belie the very important fact that the domestic unit frequently undergoes a process of change in form as families move through the various stages of the life cycle. Such figures, taken as sociological snapshots at one point in time, cannot tell us what percentages of families at each stage have experienced living in a household of one type or another at some point in their life cycle, and whether there have been changes in these percentages over time or not. With these caveats, we can proceed.

A study by Serim Timur using data from a 1969 national survey, the most systematic and reliable evidence that we have in this area, indicates that there is a significantly larger percentage of households in rural areas that are extended[4] (25.4%), than in the three major metropolises in the country (4.6%), in which most of the migrants reside (Timur, 1972, p. 31). Kağıtçıbaşı's 1975 'Value of Children' study presents us with figures very close to Timur's (1981, p. 24). This clear contrast in household type may be qualified to a certain extent. Timur's study also reveals the fact that 12.4 percent of all metropolitan households that are not classified as extended are more complex than nuclear family households, that is, they contain either both parents, a single parent, or a sibling or other relative of one of the members of the married couple. The percentage for rural areas is very close to this, 13.3 percent. If we add these percentages to those for the extended family households, the figures for household types larger than the nuclear are 17 percent for the three metropolises and 38.7 percent for rural areas. Whether some or all of these can be classified as extended family households clearly varies with the definition of such households that various individuals use. My preference is for figures somewhat closer to the lower ones, as I believe they more closely coincide with my definition of the extended family household (see note 3).

Since Timur's study was carried out at a time when many of the present-day *gecekondu* (squatter settlement) dwellers had already left their villages, we must ask how we are to interpret the figures, she presents. Can the fact that roughly 25 percent of all rural households are extended be taken as an indicator of a long-term arrangement of household types in Anatolia? That is, can we generalize from this figure to the period prior to migration, say to the early 1950s? Can this figure then be used as a baseline against which we can measure the percentage of extended family households in the city and arrive at a (what I shall argue is a mistaken) index of social change? If not, what light, if any, does the figure shed on the processes of urbanization and on household and family structure? Rather than being an indicator of social arrangements of some historical depth, should the 25 percent figure be regarded as valid only for the period of Timur's survey? If so, is it a sign of certain changes that had taken place in household and family structure in rural areas prior to the study? In particular, can it be interpreted, as Kongar and others are inclined to do, as symptomatic of a decline in the so-called Ottoman patriarchal-patrilineal extended family household in recent years, as a figure supposedly lower than those of the past (Kongar, 1976a, pp. 401-02; Erentuğ, 1956, p. 31)?

Before attempting to answer this question, two related issues must be disentangled. We must be clear as to whether we are referring to the statistical frequency of extended family households in practice, or to the frequency of adherence to preferences for such households. The two kinds of data quite often do not give us figures that coincide. Even if we can assume that there was such an ideal in pre-1950 rural Anatolia, there is no guarantee that there was any correspondence between preference and practice. Given the fact that at any one time various households are at different stages in the domestic cycle of fission and fusion of conjugal units, Paul Stirling has estimated that it would in any case be quite impossible to find more than roughly fifty percent adherence to the ideal system (Stirling, 1965, p. 40). Furthermore, possible changes over time in the practice of the ideal may bear little relationship to possible changes in the preference for it. Recently, Peter Benedict has even called into question the uniform adherence to the ideal throughout Turkey, with particular reference to quite a different ideal in the southwest Anatolian area. The preference there is for early fission of new nuclear family units from the paternal household. However, he does note that his informants indicated an ideal type in the past more closely resembling the central Anatolian ideal (Benedict, 1976, pp. 222-30). While it is important and interesting to determine whether there is regional variation in preferences for various types of households and whether there have been significant changes in these over time, I shall not be concerned in this paper with that issue. My interest here is rather with changes in practice, as is the concern of most students of this subject in Turkey. In this light, I suspect that when Kongar and others refer to the Turkish household (or family) of the past, they are perhaps unwittingly referring to the ideal rather than the practice, comparing the ideal of the past with the practice of the present.

It is very difficult to get accurate information on the distribution of types of rural Turkish households of the past.[5] Those reliable studies that do exist are limited to two or three villages at a particular point in time. One of the best known village studies in Anatolia in the period prior to migration is Paul Stirling's 1949 study of two villages in Kayseri province. Although he is often remembered for stating that the patrilineal extended family household was the ideal at that time (1965, p. 38), it is often forgotten that his figures reveal that only 24 and 23 percent of all households in the two villages were actually extended in practice (1965, p. 38). He surmises that these figures are a bit lower than normal, as the generation of males that would have provided the grandfathers of many potential extended family households was significantly depleted due to large numbers of deaths in the wars in which their generation had been involved almost continuously from 1911 to 1922 (1965, p. 40). Indeed, a brief restudy of the villages in 1971 revealed that the figures had risen to 32 and 26 percent (1974, p. 201). In a study of three districts roughly 100 years earlier, in the 1840s one in Bolu, the other in Kastamonu in the western area, and the third in Rize in the eastern Black Sea area, Justin McCarthy indicates that an average of 31 percent of all households were extended (using criteria similar to mine) (1979, p. 314). If along with Stirling's qualifications for his villages, we take into account the fact that the Black Sea area is known to have a somewhat higher percentage of extended family households than other areas of the country (Timur, 1972, p. 33), is it possible to conclude that the percentages of such households in central Anatolia and the Black Sea region did not differ significantly from the 1840s to the present?[6]

When one examines the percentage of nuclear family households in contemporary rural areas (55.4%) as compared with that for the metropolises (67.9%), it is apparent that the rural-urban contrast is not terribly great (Timur, 1972, p. 31). Interesting to note is the fact that the *gecekondu* areas appear to have an even higher percentage of nuclear family households than the metropolises as a whole.[7] In rural areas, Timur discovered that the percentage of nuclear family households is highest among the poorest agriculturalists: 63.3 percent for sharecroppers, and as high as 79.3 percent for agricultural laborers, whereas it is only 33.8% for all farmers who own their own land (1972, p. 55). Furthermore, when one examines differences in the size of land tenure, it becomes apparent that there are corresponding variations in household types. The nuclear family household is most prevalent among the smallest landholders, those with less than five hectares, whereas the extended family household is associated with the largest landholders (Timur, 1972, p. 57; Tekeli, 1978, p. 322; Kandiyoti, 1976, p. 65).[8] Since the 1969 "Village Inventory Study" revealed that 74 percent of all rural households owned fewer than five hectares (Güriz, 1971, p. 98), it would not be unreasonable to say, in contrast to much popular belief, that the nuclear rather than the extended family household is, and, as far as we can tell, has for the past 140 years been by far the more prevalent household type in rural Turkey. The small size (4.9 persons per unit) of the households of small landowners (Tekeli, 1978, p. 322) compares favorably with Timur's metropolitan figure of 4.1. The average size of the rural household for all types of landholders is 6.1 (Timur, 1972, p. 38).

In 1952, when massive rural-urban migration was just beginning, 62 percent of all landowning families had fewer than five hectares, and 12.2 percent of all rural families were landless (Güriz, 1971, p. 91). Given the fact that most migrants to the cities come from among the ranks of the small landholders and of the landless Tümertekin, 1968, pp. 52-53), one must again conclude that, contrary to much popular belief and learned opinion on the subject (Şenyapılı, 1978, p. 84; Kongar, 1976b, pp. 208-11; Yasa, 1966, pp. 229-36; Kudat, 1975, p. 31), movement to the city in Turkey has probably not resulted in a shift in household type from extended to nuclear. Though Kongar expresses some doubt about the myth of the large rural household (1976b, p. 216), he structures his argument on family change on the assumption of such a household type (1976b, p. 208). If potential migrants were by and large already living in nuclear family units in their villages, then it is incorrect to use Timur's contrasting figures on percentages of extended family households in rural (25.4) and metropolitan (4.6) areas as an indicator of the negative influence of urban life on the traditional rural patrilineal extended family household. Since the migrants by and large began their urban married lives in nuclear family households, either arriving in the city in such families or coming unmarried and setting them up afterwards, we must conclude that the low percentage of extended family households amongst such new urbanites is basically independent of any influences of the city.

The low metropolitan figure for extended family households is, however, representative of more than the households of the newer residents. How can we explain the fact that so few of the older residents of the major metropolises also live in extended family households at the present? There are two possible conclusions: either there has always been a lower percentage of such households in cities than in rural areas (or possibly that we are at a low point in a cyclical process), or there has been a drop in the percentage of extended family households in the major cities in Turkey. Though I do not yet have figures to lend support to my argument, I have become convinced that there has been a significant drop in extended family residence in urban areas since the early years of the Republic, at which time there may have been an even higher proportion of extended family households in cities than there were in rural areas. I have come to believe that when people write or speak of the demise of the Ottoman extended family or household, it is to the urban or metropolitan, and possibly well-to-do metropolitan household, that they should refer. In light of this, my argument is that the low percentage of extended family households today, even among gecekondu dwellers, must be viewed as a phenomenon with different social roots than the changes which probably occurred among the older urban families. What we are confronted with, in other words, are similar structures of independent origin.

If we can generalize from Stirling's and McCarthy's data, it does not even appear as if household type shifted in rural areas *prior to* migration as a result of the fragmentation of landholdings from the 1950's on as Tekeli (1978, pp. 321-24) and Timur (1972, p. 118) claim, or for a variety of other reasons (Hinderink and Kıray, 1970, pp. 183-89; Kongar, 1976a, pp. 401-02; Erdentuğ, 1956, p. 31). Though Timur, like Hinderink and Kıray, asserts that family and household structures shift as a function of basic infrastructural changes in societies and that the transition to nuclear family structures in partricular is the result of an increase in opportunities for wage labor or, concomitantly, a decrease in the ability to survive on the family holding (1972, p. 117), the family history materials she has collected indicate that there has been no change since 1945 (the farthest back she can go) in the types of households in which each five-year cohort of her respondents began their lives (1972, pp. 49-50). Hinderink and Kıray claim that there is a positive relationship between agricultural development and the nuclear family (household) in their study of four villages in the Çukurova region in southern Anatolia (1970, p. 186).[9] However, the evidence they present does not support this assertion. I do not think that a synchronic cross-section of the kind they have undertaken revealing different percentages of nuclear versus extended family households in these villages, which are ranked in order of level of development, can be used as accurate indicators of common stages of development. Two of the villages they have chosen have different ethnic composition and different histories than the others and are located in quite different sorts of terrain, all of which may have significantly varying implications for agricultural development and family and household structure. We are presented with no diachronic evidence of change in family and household structure from any of the villages. We are, indeed, given no evidence of family and household structure prior to the major social changes discussed for those villages that have undergone the greatest change and that presently have the highest percentages of nuclear family households.

Timur observes that the departure of married sons early in the domestic cycle is a function of increasingly inadequate land resources for the whole household. While inadequate land resources can be an important factor in the fragmentation of households, the margin of adaptability to such a squeeze is in many cases quite wide. It is such a squeeze *combined* with opportunities for wage-labor that may be the factor in transforming an unpleasant but tolerable situation into an unpleasant and intolerable one. It must also be noted that plentiful land does not necessarily keep the extended family household together. The abundance of arable land prior to the post-World War II population explosion (Hirsch, 1970, p. 66) could have and most probably did provide opportunities for those who wanted or needed to establish independent nuclear family households, which the land squeeze from that period on has in fact largely precluded, except if combined with outmigration. In this light, Eric Wolf has argued that both scarcity and abundance of land resources can encourage the proliferation of nuclear families (1966, pp. 70-71). A situation of scarcity can lead to the fission of extended family households, often followed by migration, whereas abundance of land can encourage the same process without the necessity of a major residential move. While other factors, such as opportunities for wage-labor may have encouraged household fission in recent years, one could argue that in the past, the shorter life spans of family elders could have been a factor in the same process. Though there is truth to Kandiyoti's argument that there are factors leading to the fission of extended family households in recent years that did not exist in the past (1976, p. 64), one should not as a result automatically conclude that there were not factors in the past also leading in the same direction that may not exist today. In fact, our statistical evidence appears to lend support to that assertion.[10]

The Significance of Family and Kinship in the City

It is quite often assumed by those who posit a shift from extended to nuclear family residence either as an offshoot of rural transformation or as a product of migration to the cities, that such a shift is merely symptomatic of a more general decline in the significance of kinship ties on the whole. This, it seems, is part and parcel of the unquestioned application of a structural-functional logic, which sees rural transformation, urbanization and industrialization as somehow linked to, correlated with, or even causative of an eclipse of the significance of larger kinship ties, and of a shift in family and household structure. It is also a product of the now highly disputed interpretation of the historical relationship between industrialization and family change in the West in which a decline of extended family relations and a shift from extended to nuclear family households is viewed as emerging with the industrial revolution (Greenfield, 1961).

Historical demographers of the Cambridge Group for the History of Population and Social Structure and, most notably, Peter Laslett have amassed enough evidence to show that in certain areas of the West, most prominently in northwest Europe, in the major centers where industrial capitalism first emerged, households were nuclear in structure prior to the industrial revolution, as far back as the 17th, and possibly even in the 14th and 13th centuries (1971, pp. 93-95; 1977, pp. 14-25; 1980). They have shown that, despite our popular beliefs to the contrary, wider kinship relations were lax throughout that period, and that even before the industrial revolution social welfare was provided not by kin but by the collectivity, by the church, by charitable organizations, by the municipality, and by the nation (Laslett, 1980, p. 8).

While the percentages of extended ("multiple" in Hammel and Laslett's terminology) family households in Turkey have been and still are significantly higher than those for northwestern Europe prior to the industrial revolution (Laslett, 1977, pp. 22-23), there is, as I previously indicated, evidence that leads us to believe that as in Europe, the processes of rural transformation, urbanization and industrialization in Turkey have not greatly affected household structure, except possibly in relation to shifts in household type among long-time urban families. This does not imply that the significance of wider kin relations or by implication other sorts of particularistic ties resemble similar social relations in northwest Europe. It does not, that is, mean that the extent of such relations in public life is and has been as low as in northwest Europe, or that they will become transformed in that direction.[11] Though this issue has been discussed at great length in the literature on Turkish society, much of the evidence mustered in this area is contradictory, confusing, or even misleading. As we shall see, statistical figures indicating changes in the types of households or the frequency of family or kinship interaction in Turkey often foreclose just the issues that need to be opened for consideration, and most often do not answer the question of the larger significance of such kinship relationships. Furthermore, reliance on such statistics can obscure our understanding of the significance in Turkey of an immense sphere of relations with non-kinsmen transacted in what is often referred to in the anthropological literature as a kinship idiom.[12] The line between relations conducted by actual kinsmen in a kinship idiom and those conducted by non-kin in a kinship idiom is not nearly as clear as the distinction in the Turkish language between kin and non-kin.

Karpat, in his study of three Istanbul gecekondu neighborhoods, claims that old squatters are becoming dissatisfied with the obligations and responsibilities of kinship relationships, and that while such ties had been significant in the initial phase of migration and settlement, they have given way to what he calls "rational, interest-oriented relations with outsiders" (1976, pp. 151-52). Despite this, he indicates that nearly sixty percent of all personal relations of these people are with relatives and old village friends (1976, p. 152). Of new friendships initiated in the city, he claims that nearly seventy percent were between people who met on the worksite (1976, p. 155). Şenyapılı, in a study of another Istanbul gecekondu, also indicates that 45 percent of all the respondents met their new urban friends in the workplace, 37 percent in their neighborhood of residence (1978, p. 141). She notes that most friends were from the same occupational groups. What both she and Karpat fail to notice is that the large numbers of small factories and ateliers in which gecekondu men work are quite often staffed by people who share some personal linkage—if not kinship ties, then common regional origin, ethnicity, or the like. Two workers may not even have known each other prior to entry to the workplace, but the "routes" they have most probably taken to get their jobs have often involved the use of similar types of social apparatus—possibly the mobilization of parallel types of personalized ties with the owner of the atelier or with an older worker. Şenyapılı indicates that nearly 60 percent of the best friends of her respondents lived in the same neighborhood (1978, p. 147). We know that such neighborhoods are ethnically divided and often quite homogeneous in their subsections, and that it is unusual for close friendships to extend across ethnic boundaries among such people.

Şenyapılı found that whereas 59 percent of her respondents had access to their first jobs in the city through the assistance of relatives and acquaintances, only 31 percent have done so for their present jobs (1978, p. 151). Does this mean that fewer people have relied on such close ties and have begun to rely on themselves or on the state employment agency? The percentage of those who indicated they found their jobs by themselves was exactly the same in both cases, while there was a two percent increase in respondents who said they applied to the state employment agency—from 3 to 5 percent (1978, p. 151). The only significant shift was in the category "uncertain," which jumped from 11 to 39 percent between the first and present jobs. Could this not be the result of some categorical or conceptual confusion on the part of the respondents as to the nature of the "routes" they took toward their present jobs, that is, an indication of their unknowing mobilization of a kinship idiom?

Kongar claims that in his study of families in the city of Izmir, the gecekondu family is isolated from its relatives, citing the decline of reciprocal aid in housework among them (1972, p. 213). He argues that a shift from primary to secondary, that is, impersonal types of relationships, has taken place for those who have settled in the city as a result of the radical change in their social environment (Kongar, 1976a, p. 409). Karpat writes that "older squatters are becoming dissatisfied with relatives because of a series of obligations and responsibilities stemming from blood relatives" (1976, p. 151). Kâğıtçıbaşı, following a similar logic, states that "with economic and social growth this extended kinship support system may become less relevant in the everyday life of the people..." (1977, p. 27), though she carefully notes that such support may reemerge in periods of rapid socio-economic change and mobility, that is, as a counterbalance against possible personal and social dislocation.

In the final analysis, the eclipse of wider kin ties is viewed as an almost inexorable process in the literature on urban Turkey. To assume that such a "particularistic nexus," to use a characteristic referent of Talcott Parsons, becomes eclipsed with so-called modernization or urbanization is however neither logically nor empirically justifiable. The theoretical critique of the functionalist argument is sufficiently well-known at this point that I need not elaborate upon it here. Empirically speaking, there is significant evidence of the persistence of an institutionalized system of wider kin relations in Turkey of great historical depth, and certainly of the prevalence of a kinship idiom in cities. This does not mean that extended family residence is common. As we have seen, it was not at any one point in time for most of the migrants to the city either prior to or following their departure from their natal homes. Benedict rightly points out, in line with Goody, that evidence about patterns of residence may not tell us much about the extent of extended family functions (1976, p. 239). More specifically, high percentages of nuclear family residence in the past or at present do not necessarily tell us anything about the extent or importance of extended family relations. This view is reinforced when we consider the fact that more than two-thirds of all rural families and more than a third of all metropolitan families began the domestic cycle in an extended family household, and thus have had the experience of such relationships under the same roof for at least a short time during their married lives (Timur, p. 45). Hinderink and Kıray (1970, pp. 187-89) and Kongar (1976a, p. 404) note that significant economic and social cooperation persists in rural areas among the families of married siblings and their parents despite the prevalence of nuclear family residence. Let us look at the situation in the major cities.

The Significance of Family and Kinship Among Older Urban Families

I do not think that one can get far in unravelling the problem of extended family or wider kinship relations in the city solely by looking at gecekondu neighborhoods, as has usually been done. One must examine the social relations of the older metropolitan families as well. If indeed extended family and other wider kinship ties are transitory among the migrants, one might expect that they would be either virtually nonextistent or at best weak among actual older urbanites. I distinguish such urbanites from the hypothetical urbanites (living in a hypothetical urban world) who are supposed to bear some resemblance to their bourgeois peers in New York, Paris, or London, and who are often invoked as the ideal model toward which newer urbanites are aspiring. Taking such a look at these older families is not easy, since as I have indicated, so few systematic studies of this sort have been conducted in Turkey to my knowledge. I have made preliminary inquiries in this area recently, and I submit these observations as the basis for certain tentative conclusions.

Karpat's statement about the dissatisfaction with the obligations and responsibilities of blood relations that his respondents felt may be interpreted in quite a different way than I believe he would interpret them. That is, these dissatisfactions, to the extent that they exist, are (possibly) a state of mind of second generation migrants or of older urban residents, common to many people in Turkey with "modern" aspirations. Such dissatisfactions do not necessarily imply that such relations are not significant and that such ties are not maintained. A kinship nexus of this sort can after all be both a burden (at times) and significant (and in many cases highly beneficial) for the recipient of such services from a kinsman.

Since the western urban family and kinship systems are often viewed as the "measure" of social change, it is important to examine, if only cursorily, the situation in that part of the world. The limited role of extended family and wider kinship relations in the public sphere in the West cannot be adequately explained in terms of a breakdown of the so-called western preindustrial extended family household, but rather must be seen as a product of a shift, building up great momentum in the late 18th and early 19th centuries, of certain fundamental domestic activities, particularly economic production, from the domestic sphere to an increasingly expanded public sphere (Zaretsky, 1973, pp. 23-35). The state bureaucracy and the factory, a well-institutionalized legal code, and a developed sense of public morality, the morality of a "civil society," provided the normative and institutional underpinning for life in this expanded sphere outside of the traditional domestic world.[13] Western civil and criminal codes, a large state bureaucratic apparatus, and modern mechanized workplaces were transplanted to the newly founded Turkish Republic, onto a corpus of patrimonial traditions of much greater longevity (Mardin, 1969, p. 271). A public morality, an unspoken civil code never took root. Rather, the older patrimonial, personalistic codes continued to be effective at the level of the everyday life of people even in the public sphere. In their daily activities, where the law does not or cannot tread, people relied (and continue to rely) on this older "informal" system of justice, social security, interpersonal expectations and intimate reciprocities.

With this said, let us examine the significance of extended family and wider kinship relations in the lives of the older urban strata. While it is unusual for more than one nuclear family (or more than one nuclear family with an elderly parent) to live in the same flat in a city like Istanbul nowadays, there is evidence that middle income and well-to-do households in major Turkish cities in the 19th and early 20th centuries were quite large (Dirks, 1969, p. 56). The capacious size of most of the wooden houses in which families of these classes lived speaks for this. The households of two men of that period with whom the reader in English will be familiar provide us with a more personal glimpse into family life in those days. Ahmet Emin Yalman and Irfan Orga grew up in the late 19th and early 20th centuries in households that were very large indeed, containing grandparents, married uncles and aunts, nieces, and various servants (Yalman, 1956, p. 109; Orga, 1957, p. 1-10).

At present, despite separate residence, it is quite common for parents and their married children, uncles and their married nephews and nieces, and various sorts of married cousins to live with their nuclear families in separate flats in the same or adjacent apartment buildings or in the same neighborhood. From Kongar's study of the family in Izmir, we learn that 11 percent of all families have such close relatives in the same building, 35 percent in the same neighborhood, and a total of 64 percent have such relations at least within an adjacent neighborhood (1972, pp. 79-80). Significantly, it is middle income rather than gecekondu or upper income families that show the greatest desire to live close to these relatives (Kongar, 1972, p. 83). Such families visit each other with a remarkable frequency as compared with similar families in the West, and are deeply involved in each other's lives, with all the *gemütlichkeit* and conflict that that inevitably implies. Nearly a third of all the families in all classes in the Izmir study visit with close relatives every day, 60 percent at least once a week. In a study of the family relations of university graduates in the three major metropolises, Dirks found that 64 percent of all females and 68 percent of all males interviewed see their own parents at least once or twice a week (1969, p. 100). A quarter of the females see their parents daily. Blood, reflecting on this issue from the perspective of the American family, found that frequent contact (more than once a week) between relatives undermined the solidarity and autonomy of the nuclear family (1972, p. 214). My observation has been that no such clearcut autonomy exists even among families of university graduates in Turkey.

Close relatives from middle and upper income families share many important decisions, and seek support or advice in personal matters from each other. They regularly use their individual or joint personal social assets, personal and political contacts, to obtain favors for each other in the public sphere. Quite often the first and most sensible recourse in attempting to get something done in the public sphere is the mobilization of those obligations that emanate from the private one. The percentage of reciprocated and non-reciprocated financial aid is significantly higher amongst middle or upper income families than in the gecekondu (Kongar, 1972, p. 84). Sixty-two percent of all families interviewed in Izmir stated that the level of mutual aid among relatives had either stayed the same or had increased in comparison with that of their natal families (Kongar, 1973, p. 127-28). It is not unusual nowadays for wealthy parents to subsidize, directly or indirectly, the income of their married children in the early years of marriage, or even into the middle years, if their children have followed careers in various relatively low-income but prestigious professions, such as government service, university teaching, or the arts. In some cases, one may only contemplate such a career if he can be assured of such a family subsidy.

Nearly a third of all families in Izmir are involved with each other in some sort of mutual assistance or cooperative activity in relation to their work, the percentage of such assistance being directly correlated with the level of income (Kongar, 1972, p. 112). Family firms are very common in Turkey. The majority of manufacturing firms in the country are quite small, and there is a great tendency for them to be family-owned and run. It is not unusual to find close relatives, fathers and sons, brothers, cousins, uncles, working together in small and even some large corporations, universities, or other public organizations. While only six percent of all gecekondu families are engaged in business with their close relatives, nearly double the percentage of middle income and more than triple the percentage of all upper income families are involved in such activities (Kongar, p. 112). Kongar notes that success in business can often be attributed to the use of such kinship ties, and observes that this phenomenon is by no means limited to Izmir (1972, pp. 141-42).

In evaluating the data from his interesting study, Kongar, quite surprisingly, comes to conclusions that seem to contradict his own findings. His data reveal a tight weave of extended family relations, yet he concludes that families in Izmir are quite isolated from their relatives (1972, p. 137). It may be that he is using life in the Turkish village rather than in cities elsewhere in the industrialized world as his point of reference. He concludes that higher income families have a greater tendency to be nuclear than lower income families (1972, p. 136), and that there is a general tendency away from kinship coalitions as one moves up in income, though as we have seen, his statistics show that quite the contrary is true. I fear that it is with such conclusions that the reader is left.

Such social relationships of these older families are a far cry from the idealized impersonal utilitarian scenario that is sketched as the model toward which upwardly-mobile, second-generation, migrant working class or parvenu petty bourgeois families are moving. My earlier study of a gecekondu neighborhood revealed a situation *in forma vulgari* much like that among the older urbanites. Nuclear families tracing bilateral kinship ties to each other lived in close proximity, were intimately involved in each other's lives, often shared businesses, worked in the same shops, ateliers and factories, provided a constant source of support and aggravation for each other. And when they did not do so, it was because they could not, because they did not have many close kinsmen in the city (Dubetsky, 1973).

Social Relations in a Kinship Idiom

....if Fortes would make kinship a category of amity, we must observe with him, that non-kin amity loves to masquerade as kinship.

Julian Pitt-Rivers (1973, p. 90)

Family and even extended kinship ties, with the type of reciprocity they engender, can have only a limited scope in a densely populated, highly differentiated urban area. There are many social encounters where individuals must deal with those not related to them by blood or marriage. This is true for the migrants as well as for the older urban residents. It is in this realm, in the interstices somewhere between family, kinship and certainly inevitably impersonal encounters that individuals in Turkey try to place their interactions with each other in a kinship idiom, an idiom whose rules are familiar to them, rooted as they are in the kinship system and in a long history, and in place of which alternatives that we label the "public morality of a civil society" have not adequately developed. Before proceeding, we must be clear about what is meant by a kinship idiom. In order to do so, we must first make a detour through some of the anthropological arguments about the nature of kinship.

Bloch recently attempted to reconcile the arguments of Fortes about the essential "morality of kinship" with those of Worsley and Leach which emphasize the instrumentality which they claim underlies kinship relations in actuality. He did this by emphasizing the long-term adaptive value of such relations as well as the significance of subjective motives of the actors (Bloch, 1973, pp. 75-80). Pitt-Rivers, very much in the spirit of Fortes, argues that the essence of kinship is consubstantiality, or more precisely, the *notion* of consubstantiality (1973, p. 92). I would extend this to include affinity and the notion of affinity. The line between "true" kinship and "artificial" kinship is difficult to draw. A notion of consubstantiality or affinity can be created without actual biological and marriage ties, as the various modes of fictive kinship make clear. Furthermore, one encouters subtle gradations of sociability as one ranges out from the kinship realm. The contrasts are by no means black and white.

Fortes believes the essence of the morality of kinship to be "sharing" without "reckoning" (1969, p. 238). Sahlins refers to this code as one of "generalized" reciprocity (1973, pp. 193-94), a form of exchange wherein the obligation to reciprocate is diffuse, the stuff to be reciprocated often unspecified or unspecifiable, and the time-span of the process ill-defined. Bloch concludes that the effect of this altruistic moral code is particularly long-term reciprocity, and "the long-term effect is achieved because it is not reciprocity which is the motive but morality" (1973, p. 76).

Whether in fact the relationships so established are balanced or not in either the short term or even in the long term is an issue that must be examined, and which Bloch ignores. For it is not unusual, as Godelier points out (1978, p. 767), for exploitation to present itself in the guise of such reciprocity—of what appears to the actors as a fair exchange which may eventually balance out—or an exchange that is in fact so cloaked in the "morality" of kinship that the actors never even engage in such crass calculations. From the actor's point of view the exchange may be transacted in terms of "sharing," "hospitality," "help," "generosity," or even *noblesse oblige*, as Sahlins notes (1972, p. 194). From the observer's point of view the situation may appear in quite a different light.

While balance in many kinship relations is not sought in the short run because the relationship is assumed to endure, rooted as it is in a notion of consubstantiality, we should, as Bloch notes, be aware that there are many types of kinship with many types of commitments (1973, p. 77). At the outer limits of kinship, and into the realm of artificial kinship, though the motives may still appear altruistic to the parties involved, the expectation of a counter-presentation is greater, the obligation to return less diffuse. Here we begin to encounter Sahlin's less personal, more calculated "balanced" type of reciprocity. What may distinguish the balanced reciprocity of strangers and that of kinsmen or intimates is the pretension of altruism that lingers with the latter.

In referring to a kinship idiom I am referring then to a range of codes governing behavior: from genuine altruism to the pretension of altruism laid over a careful calculation of interests. What distinguishes such a "kinship" idiom from "non-kinship" idioms is the degree of morality, the extent of altruism that is present. I certainly do not mean to imply that altruism ends with the kinship idiom. I would only argue that altruism more clearly defines a kinship idiom than non-kinship idioms. Finally, it should be clear that a kinship idiom is by no means limited to actual kinship relations.

Issues such as these emerged in anthropology largely in relation to a consideration of actual kinship ties, which in the tribal societies that many anthropologists studied in fact meant rather extensive networks of people who were often related to each other quite distantly (in our terms). A kinship idiom in conjunction with actual kinship relations is, as Barnes notes, difficult to sustain on such a scale, as such kin-based societies have largely faded from existence. However, he observes that the idiom as an idiom may live on, though the actual kinship relations may not (1980, p. 296).

I shall argue in this paper that in highly dense and socially differentiated urban areas in societies like Turkey there is a significant spectrum of social relations falling somewhere between actual kinship ties and more impersonal formal relations. It is, I shall argue, in this vast interstices that a "kinship idiom," an idiom much like that actual kinsmen use, is called into play to order such social interactions. I shall explain why I think this is so. I do not claim that this phenomenon is uniquely Turkish,[14] though I would argue that certain characteristics of contemporary Turkish society provide the social structural underpinning for the extensive application of this idiom of interaction. I also think that there are elements in the structure of this idiom that are peculiarly Turkish, though I have not yet clearly isolated them. I confine myself to presenting the significance of the idiom.

Interactions utilizing this idiom involve individuals who in some cases share certain social attributes such as birth in a common sect or ethnic group, or the like. In others, a relationship of this type and in this idiom is mobilized as an intermediary link between two individuals who themselves do not share those attributes. In either case, these attributes can easily be translated into a basis for those individuals of relating to each other in terms that are not very different from the way they would have related if they were in fact actually kinsmen. Eickelman uses such a referent in discussing "closeness" in Moroccan society. Closeness he says involves acting *as if* ties of obligation with others are so compelling that they are expressed in the idiom of kinship, with the qualities of permanency that characterize kinship relations (1976, p. 96). Pitt-Rivers observes that the simulation of kinship is inspired by the concern "to borrow the qualities attached to 'real' kinship in order to cement a relationship initiated by nothing more than mutual agreement" (1973, p. 93). Oftentimes actual kinship terms are used in a classificatory sense to express and reinforce the significance of such relationships. And as I pointed out, the line between such relationships in terms of the rights and obligations they engender and actual kinship relations may often be blurred or nonexistent. It is also true that in urban industrial society, as C.C. Harris notes (1970, p. 11), recognition of kinship is often governed by less precise rules than in rural societies or societies of the past. To be sure, this does not mean that individuals confuse kinsmen and non-kinsmen, for that would be most unlikely, but rather that they chose to ignore the differences for many purposes.

I can only briefly illustrate the use of a kinship idiom in Turkey in the space of this paper. One of the most obvious examples of such an idiom is the very widespread classificatory usage of certain kinship terms outside the realm of "actual" kinship. It is very common for men (strangers or friends) of roughly the same age (or status) to refer to each other as *kardeş* (brother), or for a younger man to refer to an older man (or a man of lower status to one of higher status) as *abi* (older brother) or a man to a boy as *oğlum* (my son). Where these terms are used by individuals roughly within the same social class, they are, as in the actual kinship system, referents for age-status differentiation. Where they are used across class lines they refer to differential status by social class, regardless of the age of those using the terms. This means that the term *abi* is often invoked by an older man of a lower class in reference to a younger man of higher class. The term *kardeş* may be used by a man of higher class with reference to a person of a lower class, serving as a kind of status leveler.

Terminology of this sort is also frequently used across sex lines. It is common for men and women who are either not very familiar with each other or who are complete strangers to address or refer to one another by the use of certain kinship terms. A term often used by men of either lower class or rural or small town origin is *yenge* (female in-law). The use of this term places the female addressed or referred to under the moral and sexual constraints that would ordinarily apply to a man's actual *yenge* and is, in fact, the only legitimate recourse in a situation where a man of a certain class and background must refer to or address a woman who is not his kin.

I shall not dwell here on the particular rights and duties and expectations of these relationships in Turkish society. What is important to emphasize is that these relationships *do* have specific rights and duties and expectations rooted in a system that has at least the appearance of altruism. Outside of the realm of actual kinship, in the public arena, such terminology is used (though I am sure unbeknownst to the parties involved) for the purpose of evoking such a kinship morality or simulating it as much as is possible in the situation at hand, for there are often no other social rules upon which to establish such relationships. Sometimes this strategy works, sometimes not.

Where classificatory terminology is not directly invoked, or where, given the end result desired, it is clear that this method will not suffice, various intermediary devices are used. I would call this the *tanıdık* (mutual acquaintance) method. That is, the name of a relative of the recipient of the request or a mutual friend of the parties is invoked so that they will be obliged to relate to each other in other than formal, impersonal terms, so that the request, let us say, will be evaluated "as if" it were one coming from an actual kinsman. For to refuse to comply with such a request is just one step removed from refusing the actual *tanıdık* whose name was used. It is not at all difficult to mobilize such a *tanıdık* for most people in the city for most purposes, though these efforts are very often limited by, or more effective within, the bounds of one's own social class.

In sum, it is either through the direct introduction of kinship terms or the use of a kinship or kin-like intermediary that a notion of consubstantiality or affinity is generated, and it is in terms of such a synthetic kinship tie that a kin-like idiom can be invoked to structure social interaction.

Conclusions

There is significant evidence that leads us to believe that:
1. The percentage of extended family households in rural Anatolian Turkey may not have changed since the 1840s. In particular, it does not appear as if the transformation that has taken place in rural areas during the past 30 years has had any noticeable effect on household type.
2. The great majority of migrants to the cities in Turkey have come as nuclear families and have either migrated with such families or set up households in the city resembling their natal (rural) households. The evidence leads us to believe that as a result movement to the city has had little or no effect on household structure. That is, there is no evidence that the process of urbanization of migrants has been accompanied by a shift from the so-called rural patrilineal extended family household to the urban nuclear family household.
3. The most significant change in household type in Turkey in recent times has taken place in cities among the older middle and upper income groups. It is possible that a shift from extended to nuclear family residence among such groups began to take place in the early 20th century.
4. Extended family and wider kinship relations are extremely important in both rural and urban areas in Turkey among all social classes, despite the high percentage of nuclear family

residence in both these cases. The significance of kin relations seems not to be fading with increased urbanization or industrialization. Certain aspects of contemporary Turkish social structure provide the underpinning for such relations, which gain in significance the higher one's social class.

5. There is a significant area of social relations among non-kin in the city that is conducted in a kinship idiom, a code governing social reciprocities that is largely derived from (and also used in) the actual kinship system. The specific components of this code in Turkish society have yet to be analyzed.

NOTES

[1]   I thank Paul Stirling, Diane Sunar and İlkay Sunar for their very helpful comments and suggestions. They, of course, bear no responsibility for the final version.

[2]   With few exceptions, the only studies which have been undertaken in the area of family and kinship in urban Turkey have been those that focus on the *gecekondu* neighborhoods on the peripheries of the major cities. I shall discuss a number of these in the text.

[3]   There is much confusion in the literature about the usage of the terms "family" and "household." They are, in fact, often used quite interchangeably. This confusion is especially problematic in reference to the patterns of residence and the social relations of more than one related conjugal family unit. It is very often necessary to make a distinction between family and household in this context. Though certain activities such as economic cooperation or the preparation and consumption of food often take place among conjugal units living together, it is quite common both in rural and urban areas in many societies for such functions to be maintained despite the separate residence of such related conjugal units. It is important in such cases to emphasize the extended family character of such activities, and yet to have a way of differentiating residential unit from functional unit if necessary. I shall in this respect largely follow Wolf (1966, p. 61) and refer to the grouping together in one organizational (or functional) framework of more than one conjugal unit regardless of residence, as an extended family. I then follow the guidelines set out by Hammel and Laslett (1974, pp. 91-93) and refer to such an extended family which is actually living together as an extended family *household*. I should state that my usage of "extended" family household largely corresponds to their "multiple" family household, though occasionally it refers both to their extended and multiple family households (1974, pp. 92-93). In the Turkish context extended family households imply common consumption, often joint economic activities, and a common budget. The classic type is the three-generation patrilineal extended family household.

4   Timur subdivides extended family households into two types: patriarchal extended and "transitional" extended. She uses authority relations as the defining criterion. As a result, a three-generation household is considered patriarchally extended (the true extended family household from her point of view) only if authority rests in the senior generation. I find this criterion a bit narrow and idiosyncratic. It makes comparison difficult. Furthermore, I do not believe that authority can be so clearly or rigidly differentiated between generations in many cases. It is not entirely clear from Timur's data what percentages of the "transitional" extended family households are complete three-generation households, and in particular whether both members of the senior generation are present or not. Since it appears as if only a few percentage points would be added to her patriarchal extended family household figure from the relevant "transitional" extended family households in order to meet my definition (placing it somewhere between 25 and 30%), we can with this in mind use her statistic as a rough indicator of the extended family household as I have defined it.

5   Timur herslf comments on the difficulties of obtaining information of this sort (1972, p. 49).

6   Since it is generally accepted by demographers and others (Kunstader, 1972, p. 326; Coale, 1966, pp. 64-69; Levy, 1966, pp. 40-63; Stirling, 1965, p. 40 and Stirling, 1974, p. 218) that the relative size of the various age cohorts in a population can affect the possible percentages of extended versus nuclear family residence at any one point in time, it would ordinarily be advisable to examine such figures in order to evaluate the significance of the percentages of extended family residence when one is making comparisions over time or through space. Unfortunately, such statistics are not available for all the populations discussed in this paper, and as a result, this important comparative demographic dimension must necessarily remain unexamined.

7   The figures are 74 percent for Şenyapılı's study of Gültepe (1978, p. 85), 71 percent for my study of Aktepe (Dubetsky, 1973, p. 150), 72 percent for Yasa's study of Ankara gecekondus, as discussed in Dirks (1969, p. 90).

8   This association of extended families and the well-to-do is common in many parts of the world. Goody observes that the extended family was most commonly found among well-to-do Chinese, Arabs, and Indians. Most people lived in nuclear family households (1964, pp. 47-48). Goody confirms the same for Europe of the past and for the African continent (1972, pp. 26-27).

9   In the village with the highest percentage of extended family households (41.2%), which is at the same time the "least developed," nearly two-thirds of these households do not contain three complete generations. In more than a third of these the single parent is a female (1970, p. 185)). Since it is debatable whether these should even be classified as extended family households, the contrast in household types that the authors draw between the villages is actually somewhat more muted than they claim it is.

[10] Given the shorter life spans 140 years ago in Anatolia, one could speculate that the 1840 figures on extended family households might have been higher had there been more old men alive to head such households at that time, and that at present, with a larger percentage of older men alive, the figures we have might represent a movement away from the extended family household ideal for other reasons; in other words that the similar percentages of such households over a span of 140 years may carry quite different meanings at either end. Unfortunately, I am not able to develop this argument further in this paper.

[11] This is not to deny the significance of extended family and wider kinship networks for certain classes in the contemporary West, as Sussman and Burchinal argue (1971).

[12] See page 91 for my definition of a kinship idiom.

[13] I do not mean to imply that extended family relations are not or have not been significant, or that kinship or kin-like reciprocities do not exist in this sphere in the West, but rather that one can conduct a much greater range of "business" without them in that part of the world.

[14] See, for example, Kenna's discussion of a similar idiom in Greece (1976, pp. 360-61).

BIBLIOGRAPHY

Barnes, J.A. "Kinship Studies: Some Impressions on the State of Play," *Man*. 1980, 15, 293-303.

Benedict, Peter. "Aspects of the Domestic Cycle in a Turkish Provincial Town." In J.G. Peristiany (ed.), *Mediterranean Family Structures*. London: Cambridge Univ. Press, 1976.

Bloch, Maurice. "The Long Term and the Short Term: The Economic and Political Significance of the Morality of Kinship." In Jack Goody (ed.), *The Character of Kinship*. London: Cambridge Univ. Press, 1973.

Blood, R.O. *The Family*. New York: The Free Press, 1972.

Coale, Ansley J. "Appendix: Estimates of Average Size of Household." In Coale, et. al., *Aspects of the Analysis of Family Structure*. Princeton: Princeton Univ. Press, 1965.

Dirks, Sabine. *La Famille Musulmane Turque*. Paris: Mouton, 1969.

Dubetsky, A.R. *A New Community in Istanbul: A Study of Primordial Ties, Work Organization, and Turkish Culture*. Unpublished Ph.D. dissertation, Univ. of Chicago, 1973.

Eickleman, Dale F. *Moroccan Islam: Tradition and Society in a Pilgrimage Center*. Austin: Univ. of Texas Press, 1976.

Erentuğ, N. *Hal Köyünün Etnolojik Tetkiki* (An Ethnological Study of the Village of Hal). Ankara: Ankara Univ. Faculty of Languages, History and Geography Publication No. 109, 1956.

Fortes, Meyer. *Kinship and Social Order.* London: Cambridge Univ. Press, 1969.

Genel Nüfus Sayımı 1980: Telegrafla Alınan Geçici Sonuçlar (The 1980 Census: Preliminary Results Received by Cable). Ankara: State Institute of Statistics.

Godelier, Maurice. "Infrastructures, Societies, and History," *Current Anthropology.* 1978, 19, 763-71.

Goode, William J. *The Family.* Englewood Cliffs, N.J.: Prentice Hall, Inc., 1964.

Goody, Jack. "Domestic Groups." Addison-Wesley Module in Anthropology. 1972.

Greenfield, S.M. "Industrialization and the Family in Sociological Theory," *American Journal of Sociology.* 1961, 67, 212-22.

Güriz, Adnan. "Kir Yerleşmelerinde Mülkiyet" (Land Tenure in Rural Settlements). In E. Tümertekin, F. Mansur, and P. Benedict (eds.), *Türkiye: Coğrafi ve Sosyal Araştırmalar* (Turkey: Geographical and Social Research). Istanbul: Istanbul Univ. Institute of Geography, 1971.

Harris, C.C. "Introduction." In C.C. Harris (ed.), *Readings in Kinship in Urban Society.* Oxford: Pergamon Press, 1970.

Hammel, E.A. and Peter Laslett. "Comparing Household Structure over Time and Between Cultures: A Suggested Scheme for Representation and Classsification with a Provision for Handling by Computer," *Comparative Studies in Society and History,* 1974, 16, 73-103.

Hinderink, Jan and Mübeccel B. Kıray. *Social Stratification as Obstacle to Development: A Study of Four Turkish Villages.* New York: Praeger Publishers, 1970.

Hirsch, Eva. *Poverty and Plenty on the Turkish Farm.* New York: The Middle East Institute of Columbia Univ., 1970.

Kâğıtçıbaşı, Çiğdem. *Cultural Values and Population Action Program: Turkey.* Istanbul: UNESCO Report (mimeographed), 1977.

_____. *Çocuğun Değeri: Türkiye ' de Değerler ve Doğurganlık* (The Value of Children: Fertility and Values in Turkey). Istanbul: Boğaziçi Univ., Faculty of Administrative Sciences, 1981.

Kandiyoti, Deniz. "Bachelors and Maidens: A Turkish Case Study." In J.G. Peristiany (ed.) *Kinship and Modernization In Mediterranean Society.* Rome: The Center for Mediterranean Studies, 1976.

Karpat, Kemal. *The Gecekondu: Rural Migration and Urbanization.* London: Cambridge Univ. Press, 1976.

Kenna, Margaret E. "The Idiom of Family." In J.G. Peristiany (ed.), *Mediterranean Family Structures.* London: Cambridge Univ. Press, 1976

Kongar, Emre. *İzmir ' de Kentsel Aile* (The Urban Family in Izmir). Ankara: Turkish Association for the Social Sciences, 1972.

_____. *Imparatorluktan Günümüze Türkiye ' nin Toplumsal Yapısı* (The Social Structure of Turkey from the Empire to the Present). Istanbul: Cem Yayınevi, 1976a.

_____. "A Survey of Familial Change in Two Turkish *Gecekondu* Areas." In J.G. Peristiany (ed.), *Mediterranean Family Structures*. London: Cambridge Univ. Press, 1976b.

Kudat, Ayşe. *Stability and Change in the Turkish Family at Home and Abroad: Comparative Perspectives*. Berlin: International Institute for Comparative Social Studies (mimeographed), 1975.

Kunstadler, Peter. "Demography, Ecology, Social Structure, and Settlement Patterns." In G.A. Harrison and A.J. Boyce (eds.), *The Structure of Human Populations*. London: Oxford Univ. Press, 1972.

Laslett, Peter. *The World We Have Lost*. New York: Scribner's Sons, 1971.

_____. "Characteristics of the Western Family Considered Over Time." In *Family and Illicit Love in Earlier Generations*. London: Cambridge Univ. Press, 1977.

_____. "Characteristics of the Western European Family," *London Review of Books*, 1980, 2, (20), 7-8.

Levy, Marion J. "Aspects of the Analysis of Family Structure." In A.J. Coale, et. al. (eds.), *Aspects of the Analysis of Family Structure*. Princeton: Princeton Univ. Press, 1965.

Litwak, E. and I. Szelenyi. "Kinship and Other Primary Groups." In Michael Anderson(ed.), *Sociology of the Family*. London: Penguin Books, Ltd., 1971.

Mardin, Şerif. "Power, Civil Society, and Culture in the Ottoman Empire," *Comparative Studies in Society and History*, 1969, 11, 258-81.

McCarthy, Justin. "Age, Family, and Migration in Nineteenth-Century Black Sea Provinces of the Ottoman Empire," *International Journal of Middle East Studies*, 1979, 10, 309-23.

Orga, Irfan. *Portrait of a Turkish Family*. New York: The Macmillan Co., 1957.

Pitt-Rivers, Julian. "The Kith and the Kin." In Jack Goody (ed.), *The Character of Kinship*. London: Cambridge Univ. Press, 1973.

Sahlins, Marshall. *Stone Age Economics*. London: Tavistock Publications, 1972.

Şenyapılı, Tansı. *Bütünleşmiş Kentli Nüfus Sorunu* (The Question of an Unintegrated Urban Population). Ankara: Middle East Technical Univ. Publications, 1978.

Stirling, Paul. *Turkish Village*. New York: John Wiley and Sons, Inc., 1965.

_____. "Cause, Knowledge, and Change: Turkish Village Revisited." In J. Davis (ed.), *Choice and Change*. London: The Athlone Press, 1979.

Sussman, M.B. and L.G. Burchinal. "The Kin Family Network in Urban-Industrial America." In Michael Anderson (ed.), *Sociology of the Family*. London: Penguin Books,Ltd., 1971.

Tekeli, İlhan. *"Türkiye Tarımında Mekanizasyonun Yarattığı Yapısal Dönüşümler ve Kırdan Kopuş Süreci"* (Structural Transformations Caused by the Mechanization of Agriculture in Turkey and the

Process of Leaving the Land). In İlhan Tekeli and Leila Erder (eds.), *İç Göçler* (Internal Migrations). Ankara: Hacettepe Univ. Publications, 1978.

Timur, Serim. *Türkiye'de Aile Yapısı* (Family Structure in Turkey). Ankara: Hacettepe Univ. Publications, 1972.

Tümertekin, Erol. *Türkiye'de İç Göçler* (Internal Migrations in Turkey). Istanbul: Istanbul Univ. Publications, 1968.

Wolf, Eric. *Peasants*. Englewood Cliffs, N.J.: Prentice-Hall, Inc., 1966.

Yalman, Ahmet Emin. *Turkey in My Time*. Norman: Univ. of Oklahoma Press, 1956.

Yasa, İbrahim. *Ankara'da Gecekondu Aileleri* (Gecekondu Families in Ankara). Ankara: Ministry of Health and Social Assistance, 1966.

Zaretsky, Eli. *Capitalism, the Family, and Personal Life*. New York: Harper and Row, 1973.

URBAN CHANGE AND WOMEN'S ROLES
IN TURKEY: AN OVERVIEW AND EVALUATION

Deniz Kandiyoti

Women and the Urban Context

We will start by noting the relative scarcity of studies on women in urban contexts, not only in Turkey, but more generally in developing countries. Part of this neglect may be due to the fact that the societies under consideration have indeed moved from a predominantly tribal, nomadic or peasant subsistence base to integration with the international market through either colonialism proper or the work of world market forces. It is perhaps not surprising, therefore, that many studies on women and development concern themselves primarily with analyzing how women have fared through the process of integration of the rural sector into the market economy. In addition, the methodological and material requirements for the study of urban patterns are harder to meet than those applying to the study of nomadic tribes or rural communities since these latter are more readily amenable to anthropological scrutiny and have a greater degree of internal homogeneity (Kandiyoti, 1977). Nevertheless, with the notable exception of essentially demographic studies of women's labor force participation (Collver and Langlois, 1962; Durand, 1975; I.L.O., 1973; Safilios-Rothschild, 1971; Sinha, 1965; Youssef, 1974), even works dealing directly with Third World urban patterns concern themselves with women only peripherally (see, for example, Bromley and Gerry, 1979). Yet, as the emphasis moves away from dualisms such as rural/urban, formal/informal sector to more concrete analysis of mechanisms of surplus transfer, and interdependencies between economic sectors, the specificities of women's place and their contributions are being increasingly highlighted.

The aim of this paper will be to provide an overview and critical evaluation of studies dealing with women's place in the Turkish urban context in order to highlight the dynamic nature of current patterns and their potentiality for change.[1] The scope and importance of the contemporary phenomenon of urbanization in Turkey has received enough separate attention so as not to need elaboration in this paper. Its significance will be discussed from the point of view of women's roles only. The challenge presented to women by rapid urbanization has been succinctly put within a Turkish demographic context by Erder (1982). According to her projections, a conservative estimate of Turkey's female population will be 35.6 million in the year 2000 (Turkey's current total population is on the order of 45 million). If the urbanization rates foreseen in the Third Five-Year Development Plan materialize and women close the gap, evening out the sex ratios of cities, 26.7 million women, as many as Turkey's total rural population today, will be living in cities. The change in women's age structure, namely a projected decline in the proportion of girls under 15, an increase of women in the working ages and a rise in the proportion of women over 65 years of age, are likely to have serious implications for women's demands for jobs, child care and health services in urban areas.

If work opportunities in the city to replace women's productive roles in rural areas fail to materialize, as they are most likely to do, problems are bound to arise. Competition for a slot in organized urban jobs is likely to become more intense and the relatively low participation of women in "marginal" activities today (see the section below) is likely to change. In addition, predictions of decline in fertility may fail to materialize if rural fertility patterns are "imported" to cities, if urban families continue to rely on addional land income and use child labor in marginal activities. If, on the other hand, more organized jobs were to become available to low-income urban women, this would drastically alter the opportunities of middle or upper middle class women who rely on the availability of a pool of low paid domestic servants to pursue careers relatively unfettered by domestic obligations (Kandiyoti, 1978, p.11). Thus, the urban situation is an extremely dynamic one, both from the point of view of women within different classes and from the point of view of the inter-relationship, symbiotic or antagonistic, between women of different classes.

It should be clear from the foregoing that in contrast to the relative homogeneity of women's status in nomadic and peasant communities, it is impossible to discuss women in the urban context without explicit reference to urban stratification. Likewise, what is meant by the "urban context" may vary from provincial town to metropolis. The metropolitan urban environment may again range from the shanty towns to the upper middle class districts. The literature will therefore be reviewed keeping these distinctions in mind. Rather than providing a separate discussion of metropolitan and provincial patterns, they will be treated as the occasion for making such a distinction arises. Women's condition will be discussed with reference to three categories of urban women: (1) women in the shanty towns, (2) lower middle class and "traditional" middle class women, and (3) educated middle and upper class women. These proposed subdivisions should be considered simply as a convenient means of classifying a complex and varied phenomenon rather than as rigid stratification categories.

Women in the Shanty Towns

A prevalent feature of the Turkish metropolis is the existence of the shanty town or *gecekondu*, harboring rural-to-urban migrants. As such, this setting for women's roles can be considered a typically metropolitan phenomenon. Şenyapılı's study (1982) of the *gecekondus* of Istanbul and Ankara indicates a generally young population. The average age of the male head of household is 40.1 and the average age of wives is 35.3. Nuclear families predominate (72% in Istanbul, 77% in Ankara). Women marry at eighteen to twenty years of age, giving bith to their first child at age twenty-two on the average, with a reproductive cycle of about ten to fifteen years. Both in terms of their labor force participation and their social lives, these women exhibit distinct patterns.

As far as labor force participation is concerned, Kazgan (1982) notes that women occupy a relatively unimportant place in Turkey's urban labor force (approximately 11%) and that the distribution of this labor force exhibits a peculiar form, quite characteristic of many Middle Eastern societies, i.e., a heavy base of non-qualified women, a relatively heavy top of qualified, professional women, and an indentation in the distribution of the semi-qualified category. This presents a clear contrast to the distribution of female employment in industrialized countries where semi-qualified working women weigh heavily in the labor force. Even allowing for the possibility that some so-called "informal" sector activities may have escaped statistics althogether, the Turkish case exhibits characteristics distinguishing it from urban patterns of developing countries at comparable levels of development, such as Latin American countries, through the conspicuous absence of women from small trade, vending or peddling jobs, which require spatial mobility and exposure in public places. Nonetheless, the heavy base of non-qualified women referred to above does exist and its reservoir is to be found in the shanty towns. In terms of temporal variations in participation trends, a distinction needs to be made between early waves of migration in the 1950s and later ones in the 1960s and 1970s. In the 1950s the only opportunity for illiterate, uskilled women was to work as maids for middle-class women. This put one class of women in an exploitive relationship. (This is a prevalent phenomenon in many societies with surplus rural population.) Later, as more jobs opened up for male migrants and as more middle-class women entered the labor market, the *gecekondu* women withdrew to their homes or entered unspecialized branches of the urban service sector. In the *gecekondus* of Istanbul and Ankara respectively, only 5.5% and 6% of gecekondu women in the age group fifteen through sixty-four were working in 1976-77. Those who work are engaged in low-paid, low-prestige, unorganized jobs which discourage enthusiasm for further work. The highest position a woman can reach in the urban employment scale is that of teacher. It is gecekondu women who swell the ranks of female factory workers.

The heaviest concentration of women in Turkey's labor force is in agriculture, the next category being light manufacturing industry, i.e., tobacco, textiles, apparel, food, beverages, packing operations of chemicals, etc., and certain subdivisions of the service industries. Women in industry work in sectors which produce Turkey's major export products and are open to competition on the world market. This contrasts with the well-protected domestic industries which produce import substitutes and employ male workers. From 1955 to 1974, wages of female employees have varied between two-thirds to four-fifths of male employee wages (Kazgan, 1982). In addition, only about 9% of the workers covered by social security are women. Women in the more competitive, low-wage sectors are normally not unionized. Female minors are often employed clandestinely and escape statistical records altogether. The concentration of working women in the twenty-five and less age cohort suggests that it is mainly single women who enter and then leave the work force upon marriage. A survey carried out among male industrial workers who are mainly rural-to-urban migrants in the towns of Istanbul and Izmit (Kandiyoti, 1977) showed that only 2% of their wives were engaged in any form of employment. Factors reinforcing this trend include: the relatively stable income of blue-collar workers, early marriage for women, a high proportion of pre-school children, the absence of any child-care facilities, and inadequate support from female kin.

However, despite the cultural ideal of keeping wives at home and the intrinsic unattractiveness of the jobs available to lower-class women, more and more married women are joining and will have to join the urban work force just to meet the soaring costs of urban living. The withdrawal of gecekondu women, especially married women, from the urban labor market may thus be a temporary phenomenon followed by an increase in their tendency to enter unorganized, low-paying, unspecialized jobs which confer bargaining power. Especially in a period of economic recession, the response of low-income households to economic pressure may be greater reliance on the supplementary earnings of secondary workers, namely, women and children. Thus, the future most likely holds increasing levels of exploitation and a heightened sense of relative deprivation for these women.

In terms of their social lives, gecekondu women generally keep within the confines of their immediate neighborhood. In her study of migrants to Cairo, Abu-Lughod (1961) pointed out that while informal associations are available for male migrants, no such associations exist for women. In villages and small towns, religious festivals, births, deaths and the like are important occasions when women have major roles to play. Within the city these events become more "private," with the result that women's lives become confined to a narrower and more immediate environment. However, Maher's (1974) work on Morocco suggests that migrant women keep a network of female relationships alive, cutting across the boundaries of town and countryside. These women continually revitalize such links, returning to their home region to have their children, visit their mothers, celebrate weddings and funerals and look for prospective brides for their sons. There is also a network of mutual support in the form of a constant flow of money and goods from richer to poorer women, against a reverse flow of services and visiting. The efficacy of such female networks may be expected to vary with the amount of mobility women are allowed, and the rigidity of patriarchal controls. Although there are no studies specifically dealing with this issue in Turkey, indices such as a relatively low divorce rate and the low incidence of female-headed households as compared to Morocco would tend to suggest that women may not be as strongly connected in female networks and may be more tightly controlled by male kin.

Another important issue with regard to shanty town women is that of generational differences. There is a considerable educational differential between generations. The majority of mothers are illiterate (48.7% in Istanbul and 50.5% in Ankara) or have attended primary school (Şenyapılı, 1982). On the other hand, almost all of the daughters attend primary school and some enter higher educational institutions up to the high school level (five to eight years of education). However, this formal education has no direct relevance to the life styles in their environment. It is the popular mass media, such as television and simple reading materials like photocomics and women's magazines that have an influence on women. The culture that permeates the mass media, exploiting women's basic desires in simple, understandable terminology, symbols and images, is more effective than the alien bourgeois culture promoted in public schools.

The messages transmitted by the popular media can be characterized as a constant stimulation to more extensive consumption and the achievement of upward mobility through marriage. As a result, consumption, as the only channel of mobility and integration into urban life, finds the female population of the gecekondu eager and willing participants. However, the goal of upward mobility is never fully realized by these women who are segregated in social space and bound by their social and economic affiliations. Meanwhile, the television and simple reading material which penetrates the socially hungry gecekondu environment, "effectively imposes a consumption-oriented value system which leads to needless cravings, unsatisfied desires, and alienation from one's own class and consequent unhappiness to women" (Şenyapılı, 1982, p. 295).

Feelings of relative deprivation, generally absent from the first generation of women migrants are also likely to become exacerbated for the second generation as they increasingly enter jobs such as manicurists, hair dressers' and dressmakers' attendants, salesgirls, petty clerics, which afford them increased opportunity to come into contact with classes other than their own. This generation is also more likely to avoid entering domestic service despite the intrinsic limitation of their educational attainment and skill levels. Mernissi's

(1977) study of young domestic servants in Morocco accurately reflects the feelings of degradation and resentment experienced by these women. Unless their numbers are replenished by new recruits migrating from rural areas and with lower aspiration levels, the decline of domestic labor is likely to be a factor that middle-class women will have to contend with.

Lower Middle-Class and "Traditional" Middle-Class Women

Lower middle-class women, whether they are the wives of small entrepreneurs or lower-ranking civil servants, are undoubtedly the most under-researched category of women in Turkey. There is good reason to believe that the wives of small entrepreneurs, some of whom can be considered as part of the traditional urban middle class, may exhibit different patterns from those married to state-employed men. Thus, their being grouped under the same heading can hardly be justified on grounds other than the paucity of data. These women are literally the least visible in the sense that they are the most home-bound and secluded, the most restricted in their movements and the least prominent in terms of employment. There is no parallel among them to the Cairene *bint-al-balad* or so-called *baladi* women who retain some measure of autonomy through independent trading and business activities (El-Messiri, 1978; Early, 1978). Maher notes that in Morocco it is the petty bourgeois women, dependent on state-employed men, who are most secluded and whose ties with their own female kin have been most severed. This observation may well hold in the Turkish case too, where the greater geographical mobility of state employees through appointments may produce similar effects. When such women contribute to family income in Turkey, this may easily take the form of home-based jobs, such as sewing and embroidery, which may escape statistics altogether. While their daugthers may be going to high school, vocational schools or even universities, the older women in this category tend to have little education and few marketable skills outside traditional feminine crafts, such as sewing and knitting, learned from their mothers and female kin while preparing their own trousseaux.

Little would be known about the social lives of these home-bound women if it were not for a wealth of information derived from studies of provincial towns (Kıray, 1976, 1981; Fallers and Fallers 1976; Benedict, 1974; Mansur, 1972; Aswad, 1974; Magnarella,

1974). Provincial towns exhibit certain characteristic features and can be said to harbor three categories of women: the "locals," who are the wives of traders and local notables (the *ashraf*); the "outsiders," who are the wives of government-appointed civil servants and professionals; and poorer townswomen, who work in agriculture and services. Studies of the women of the provincial middle class, a group clearly not assimilable to their metropolitan counterparts, provide us with interesting insights into their life styles.

In her study of the women of Ereğli, a coastal town in the Black Sea region, Kıray points out that, despite their exclusion from public life and work, women perform delicate, crucial roles, which generally go unnoticed. The whole burden of tension management within the family rests on the women's shoulders. She is virtually the only one to whom every family member has independent access. Thus, she occupies a very central role, mediating between father and son, generally easing the tensions of the new role demands created by social change (Kıray, 1976, 1981).

Another important feature of women's place is their position vis-a-vis consumption. Women spend their time at home, whereas men are very seldom there. This gives men and women differential access to consumption. Women have to make do with the housekeeping money allocated to them, and this results in a diet of starchy, non-fancy foods. Men often eat out and have protein-rich diets. This inequality in terms of consumption also pertains to the choice of clothes; men generally wear market-bought, stylish clothes, whereas women more often wear home-made, unfashionable clothes. Thus, it is seen that it is men and not women who carry a conspicuous consumption function in traditional settings. The women are not on display; the men are on parade and enjoy higher consumption standards while women have to fight at home to make ends meet (Kıray, 1976, 1981).

Women's movements are greatly restricted and their presence outside the home must be established as harmless and legitimate. Thus, activities carried out in the open air in the company of children and gatherings of a religious nature, i.e., recitations of the *mevlut* prayer, offer legitimate grounds for activities outside the home (Kıray, 1981). However, the restrictions imposed by such a narrow range of options and their incompatibility with professional life are clear. It is very difficult to see how these small town women can break out of their home-bound status and use their interpersonal skills in a broader framework.

On the subject of leisure and social lives, all students of the field note that men and women live in separate social worlds, the latter in a female network of relatives and neighbors segregated from male networks. The Fallers' study of Edremit, a small coastal town in Western Anatolia, suggests that this separation provides women with greater psychological independence from men. This independence becomes apparent when such women step into public roles and their sexual identity does not interfere with their professional self or behavior. It would seem that the confusion or conflict between sexual and professional identity is most likely to occur in societies or parts of societies where women are in free competition with each other on the marriage market. Where the sexes are segregated, family control over female sexuality stricter, and marriages arranged, the concern over femininity does not appear to be as acute. In fact, powerful external constraints seem to take the place of psychological barriers or more subtle mystification. Such views on the effects of sex-segregation are also shared by other students of the Middle East (Nelson and Olesen, 1977; Papanek, 1973), but await further investigation of a comparative nature.

As a by-product of segregated urban female leisure activities, special visiting patterns create networks which are different both in function and composition from the rural domestic and neighborly networks. Studies of the reception day or *kabul günü* (also referred to as *istiqbal* in other parts of the Middle East) when women receive guests on a regular, almost rotational basis, suggest that structured visiting among women serves important extra-domestic social functions. In Tütüneli, a small town which gained a cadre of non-local professional civil servants in 1954, the *kabul günü* was initiated by the non-local women, wives of the non-local civil servants who felt alienated in their new social surroundings. However, within the first couple of years, the circle was widened to include the wives of local landowners (*ağas*) and those of wealthy merchants who were influential at the level of town and provincial politics (Benedict, 1974). The more cosmopolitan wives of civil servants transmitted their cultural tastes to the local women. Not only was the social gap between the town notables and non-locals bridged, but a considerable amount of male influence on the kinds of information transmitted at these gatherings was apparent. Men can use their wives to transmit knowledge about local events to other men when it would be improper to communicate such information face-to-face. Moreover, since the wife's position in the kabul is determined by her husband's standing in the community, the female hierarchy mirrors the ranking in the male world (Benedict, 1974).

It would be an over-simplification to imagine that these visiting patterns take the same form or perform the same functions regardless of class. In fact, the visiting patterns among the traditional elite families in Antakya serve to retain the cohesion of this group (Aswad, 1974). Visiting takes place mainly among persons who are considered kin, and new women enter this network through marriage ties. Nonetheless, the kabul also serves to extend the power of the elite, since women from a lower socioeconomic background may be invited and patronized by wealthier female relatives. Within the Antakya elite which dominated both of the leading national political parties at the time, half of the marriages were across party lines. Thus, the party alignments which divide the male members of the elite were crossed by marriage and, subsequently, by the kabul, which established important cohesive lines within the elite, as well as vertical ties of a patron-client type. In contrast, the middle-class kabul patterns were confined to people of the same political party. Mansur's study of Bodrum (1972) suggests that female leisure is more unstructured in lower socioeconomic groups, while the town's elite women, mainly the wives of civil servants and rich locals, follow the more rigidly defined kabul. Ceremonial occasions, especially religious feasts, seem to offer another focus for female gatherings, in contrast to rural areas where formal religious and ceremonial participation is more clearly in the male domain. In small towns, the women's involvement in formal ceremonies not only invests them with knowledge and learning, but provides them with legitimate grounds for social gatherings. There is good reason to assume that such patterns of entertainment are also valid for the lower-class women of larger urban centers and metropolises.

Women's associations may exhibit considerable variation both within Turkey and as compared to other countries in the Middle East. For instance, Good's (1978) comparision of Turkish and Iranian provincial patterns suggests that in provincial Iran the status-group hierarchy of women is flatter and less differentiated than that of men. In Turkish provincial society, the status-group hierarchy of women tends to be more sharply differentiated and to duplicate the patterns of male stratification. Good relates these differences to the extent to which traditional associations are maintained, the degree and manner to women's participation in the public world, and the impact of national ideologies. She predicts that associations based on female solidarity will increasingly be replaced by those based on status. This trend is most readily apparent in metropolises where there are virtually no women's associations cutting across class lines. Even within similar income groups, the cultural cleavage is deep between women whose life styles are modern in terms of education, dress, entertainment and conjugal patterns, and those women whose outlook and lifelstyles are more traditional and less secular. The former represent the educated middle class to which we shall now turn our attention.

Educated Middle and Upper-Middle Class Women

The literacy differential between men and women is great throughout the Middle East. The interesting point about Turkey is that its literacy differential of 35% is the highest in the world. In 1970, 40% of the women were literate as opposed to 75% of the men; in 1975, 48% of the women were literate as compared to 80% of the men (Timur, 1978). The important fact to note is that educational facilities are available to some degree, but they are unequally available to the two sexes. Latin American and Far Eastern countries of about the same level of development do not display such enormous differentials as Turkey. Against this background it seems important to point out what may at first sight seem like an anomaly, namely, the high participation rates of women in the professions. In her study of women professionals in the fields of law and medicine, Öncü (1982) points out that one in every five practicing lawyers in Turkey is female, and one in every six practicing doctors is female; 28.5% of the members listed in the Istanbul Bar Association for 1978 are women and the estimated proportion of female physicians on the labor market in 1970 was 21%. These figures indicate that the access Turkish women enjoy to the prestigious professions of law and medicine is equal to, if not wider than, the access of their counterparts in such highly industrial-ized countries as the U.S.A. or France. Turkey is not unique in this respect. Safilios-Rothschild (1971) has demonstrated that there is a curvilinear relationship between the level of development and the range of professional career options open to women in capitalist countries where a higher proportion of women in the professions work at intermediate levels rather than at either extreme.

Öncü (1982) offers a provocative analysis of this phenomenon with special reference to Turkey. Aside from the classic argument that working women in Turkey may rely on wider support systems in the form of cheap domestic labor or the extended family network, Öncü points out that their entry into the professions is primarily a function of class inequalities and the initial mode of cadre recruitment under conditions of rapid expansion. While the existence of support systems is certainly a facilitating and necessary condition, it is not sufficient in the sense that it creates supply but not demand. The growth of demand is more readily traceable to the differential evolution of the professions in industrialized and Third World countries. In the latter, a major aim of governments has been the rapid creation of trained cadres to supervise the introduction of advance industrial techniques into previously "underdeveloped" countries. Such rapid expansion of elite cadres with specialised and technical education would necessitate the recruitment of individuals from manual or peasant origins, if upper and middle class women did not begin to enter professional schools. Thus, women's entry into the professions is part and parcel of an elite recruitment pattern. Despite the rapid expansion of professional education over the last fifty years, relatively few university students are drawn from manual or peasant backgrounds. Therefore, it can be said that the recruitment of the elite into the most prestigious and highly renumerated professions is maintained through the admission of women from the upper reaches of the social hierarchy. These women pose less of a threat than upwardly mobile men from humbler origins. It would seem that the education of women is not so much a means for mobility as for class consolidation. Given the historical specificity of women's entry into the professions in Turkey, one may well wonder if this trend is a temporary one which will be followed by a period of stabilization or decline. However, the entry of women into these professions has created a momentum of its own and avoided the sex-typing of jobs. Devoid of any overtones of "masculinity" or "deviancy," the professions have retained their appeal for female students. Papanek (1971) further suggests in her analysis of Pakistan that a sex-segregated system may actually be functional in the establishment of certain professions for women. She shows that, in the case of medicine and teaching, sex-segregation reinforces the need for women specialists to serve the special needs of a female clientele. This may have applied to Turkey at a much earlier stage, as in the initial establishment of teacher training colleges for women in the 19th century.

Despite evidence of the high entry rates of women into the professions and the relatively unimportant sex-typing of professions, we have little evidence of how they actually fare in their professional lives in terms of achievement and advancement. Çitçi's study (1982) of women government employees shows that they are typically concentrated in sex-typed jobs at the lower echelons of the civil service. There has been a steady increase of women in civil service jobs between 1938 and 1975. Whereas 9.5% of government employees were female in 1938, this figure had risen to 25.3% in 1977. Thus, while the number of men working in the civil service has increased sixfold over forty years, the number of women has increased nineteenfold in the same time period.

Women employees are far from being evenly distributed among government agencies; 69.1% are concentrated in the Ministries of Education, Health, Welfare, and the Post Office Directorate. Women employed as teachers and attached to the Ministry of Education constitute 40% of all female civil servants. The only case of actual "feminization" of civil service is among health personnel where 61% of the employees are female. However, 73% of the female employees are concentrated in sex-typed occupations, such as nursing and midwifery, while there is a much higher proportion of doctors among males. Thus, while the number of female government employees has increased steadily and massively, they have typically remained in "feminine" occupations, such as secretarial work, switchboard operating, nursing and teaching. They have remained low in the bureaucratic echelons, in adjunct rather than autonomous positions, and with fewer opportunities for advancement than men. Çitçi's sample survey (1982) in the public sector indicates that personnel directors perceive women employees as unfit for jobs requiring responsibility and travel, and as having more unstable working lives. They are valued, on the other hand, for their submissiveness and dependability. Sex segregation is less apparent in hiring practices and more apparent in granting administrative responsibility and managerial positions; 59% of the managers interviewed admitted that neither male nor female employees enjoyed working under a female boss. As a complementary finding, the same author indicates that women employees view themselves primarily as wives and mothers and experience their jobs as a hindrance to the performance of these roles. The majority of women employees indicated that economic necessity was the major factor prompting their search for employment. A comparison of the findings on female professional and civil servants clearly indicates their different class extractions. The former are typically of an elite, middle or upper middle class background, while the latter tend to be of middle or lower middle class origins. The latter are restricted by lower levels of education and enter less skilled occupations with little chance of promotion. They also have fewer options in terms of support systems which require higher purchasing power. For women professionals, we may properly talk about "careers," whereas in the case of civil service employees, we are speaking of mere "jobs."

Compared to other categories of women, relatively little is known about the lives of upper class or elite women. An intergenerational study of mother-daughter pairs in Istanbul (Kandiyoti, 1978) provides some insights into this question. The mothers in the sample are quite typical of the first Republican generation of women whose urban extraction and high socioeconomic status meant that they could benefit from the educational advantages afforded by Atatürk's reforms. 30% of these women had completed a university education as compared to 1.2% in their mother's generation. Nonetheless, only 23% are employed. Only 12% have been able to sustain an uninterrupted work life, and the rest had to stop working when they had children.

These women may also be considered a transitional generation with regard to their way of entering marriage, their conception of their roles as women and their leisure activities. Some met their husbands as the result of traditional arranged marriages, while others had mutually consented to marry schoolmates or colleagues; 68.3% of the mothers found mates by using intermediaries, either directly through arranged marriages or more indirectly through arranged "chance" meetings; 31.7% seem to have made independent choices. It is interesting to note that 46% of the university graduates were married in the traditional, arranged manner, despite their increased opportunity for contact with the opposite sex.

It is clear that these women define their roles in predominantly domestic terms. When asked what attributes they considered a "successful" woman to possess, 32.9% defined the successful woman in exclusively domestic terms as a "good mother and wife"; 23.2% stressed the importance of being socially active and useful to the community along with being an accomplished housewife; 25.6% believed that the ability to combine a career with household duties was a criterion of success. Finally, 12.2% stressed being self-sufficient and self-fulfilled persons as the ultimate goal. Apart from this last exception, all mothers insisted on not compromising their qualities of being a good spouse and mother, whatever their other achievements might be. Thus, it is possible to conclude that mothers have developed new role strivings without making any fundamental changes in their traditional domestic expectations.

Women's leisure activities have been evaluated along two axes considered to be of theoretical significance. The first is the degree to which leisure is spent within primary groups or secondary organizations, such as clubs and associations; the second is the degree to which leisure is sex-segregated or shared with husbands. It is possible to see specific combinations of these two dimensions in different cultures and social classes. Both the traditional lives of women in Turkey and those of the Western working class present intense primary group, sex-segregated socializing. In contrast, the Western middle class presents a picture of greater participation in voluntary associations as well as a higher gravitation toward the husband's work connections. Indeed, where the social and geographical mobility of the couple is high, it may be harder for women to sustain their own primary ties, such as family, schoolmates and old neighbors. They become automatically more dependent on the husband's network of social relations and on the secondary organizations of the comnmunity in which they live.

The position of the mothers in our study may be considered an intermediate one with regard to the axes defined above. Membership in voluntary associations exists to a certain degree (38%); however, the prestige function of such memberships seems to be more salient than the actual social funtion. Unlike the traditional sex-segregated model, women do share many social activities with their husbands. However, these shared activities remain limited to evenings and weekends. In no way do they impede the independent cultivation of social circles and primary groups by women in a manner that would tend to lend support to Olson-Prather's (1976) definition of the Turkish family as being "duo-focal." The geographical mobility profile of middle and upper class women was found to be rather low. Hence, it is possible for them to maintain a network of social relations which predates their marriage. In fact, when mothers were asked with whom they spent most of their time, 87.8% mentioned family, relatives, neighbors, and former classmates. Those who mentioned their husbands' social circle remained at a low 3.7%, and 8.5% mentioned their own professional circle as their source of most frequent social contact.

It is increasingly suggested in the literature that women whose self-definition is not dependent on their husbands or other males may have greater psychological freedom and clearer ego boundaries. If that is a criterion to be taken seriously, upper middle class women seem to be at the crossroads since they keep a delicate, but so far, an advantageous balance between traditional prerogatives and more modern participation patterns.

As for the daughter generation, currently university students, there is evidence that their socialization has been sufficiently different from their mothers' to produce new expectations and demands. The combination of several factors, i.e., their new demands, the persisting rigidity of male role definitions, declining informal support systems and the absence of any planning to cater for women's needs, holds an unprecedented potential for conflict and may constitute the structural underpinnings for a social movement that were lacking when Turkish women were granted legal emancipation.

Conclusion

Our overview of studies on women in urban Turkey indicates a dynamic situation and the existence of precarious equilibria which may create sources of stress and change. A common feature of the social and economic adjustments urban women have to make across social categories is that they do not in any way challenge the male role, disrupt expected norms of family functioning or put into question male prerogatives. This result is achieved through the operation of different mechanisms in each case. In the case of low-income urban women, the evidence indicates that they retreat into domesticity to the extent that economic conditions allow. When they enter the labor force, they often treat their work as a temporary, sometimes shameful, expedient to tide their families through difficult times. The fact that this temporary situation may last for years or that the wages earned by women may constitute a substantial part of family income does not affect their primarily domestic role definition or decrease any of the burdens that go with it. Typically, the only household members who can be relied upon to share tasks are daughters or daughters-in-law. Even with very limited resources, the basic living comforts of the family are created by women at the expense of women. There is also evidence of considerable inter-generational continuity of socialization in the domestic/nurturant role by women (Kâğıtçıbaşı and Kansu, 1976-77).

In the case of lower-middle class women, who were referred to as the most secluded and least likely to enter employment especially in the context of small towns, male prerogatives are amply apparent in the sphere of budget control. Exclusive control over monetary resources by men and the seclusion of women may lead to extremes such as the creation of a double standard of consumption in matters ranging from nutrition to leisure. Here, the subordination of women takes the concrete form of drastically limited access to the outside world, this to a greater extent than in the case of poorer women whose husbands and fathers are in a more unfavorable position with regards to being the sole providers.

Even in the case of professional women the strains inherent in combining work and domestic responsibilities are seldom allowed to reflect on men who continue to be sheltered from new role demands. This shelter is largely secured through the help or exploitation of other women who act as "buffers," absorbing the effects of change for the couple; these women range from maids and nannies to poorer relatives and mothers. In all the cases discussed, the male role seems to have been least affected by change, bolstered as it is by socialization practices, ideology and structural supports.

If anything, the future seems to hold further difficult choices and adjustments for all the women discussed, albeit for different reasons. For poorer urban women, economic recession, with high unemployment and falling real wages, will increase the pressure on their families and will require their increased involvement either in unpaid family labor in the petty production and distribution sectors or in low wage employment, on a more or less permanent basis. The household will be forced to absorb the stresses created by low wage employment and this will effectively mean that patriarchal control will be tightened rather than relaxed, as men become more economically dependent on women (Kandiyoti, 1980). In extreme cases, if relocation or investment policies create stable employment for women, as in optics and electronic industries in some countries, failing to provide similar job or migration outlets for men, a further erosion of the economic role of men is likely to ensue, with serious implications for family formation and functioning.

The extent to which the home-bound, secluded existence of lower middle class women will reproduce itself in their daughters' generation is very questionable. The higher level of education of the second generation will give them increased access to at least white collar and service occupations and their likelihood of entering employment will be higher, although admittedly competition for jobs will also be tougher. Nonetheless, state-employed men and even small entrepreneurs will need the extra income generated by their wives, and a woman's capability to enter employment will be an asset rather than a liability on the marriage market. This will influence matters such as budget control, access to consumption and patterns of leisure, although, in the first instance, this influence may take the form of greater marital conflict. Finally, highly educated women aiming at professional careers will be at a clear disadvantage compared to their mothers, who, as the first Republican generation, benefited from a greater demand for trained cadres in a situation of relative scarcity. Their daughters will have to face not only much fiercer competition from men, both of their own and other classes, but will feel the pinch of the decline in quasi-traditional support systems (from kin to domestic workers) at a time when satisfactory planned alternatives to cater for their needs are almost nonexistent. We had already pointed out that their relative level of welfare and autonomy is inextricably linked to the fate of lower-income urban women; to the extent that the minimum wage represents a significant portion of middle class incomes and as job alternatives are created outside the domestic sector the availability of domestic labor will tend to decline. This may act as a further impetus for these women to become more organized and make increased demands for services at their workplaces and in their communities. Ultimately, the whole issue of the division of labor within the household, successfully avoided so far, may have to be confronted. Clearly, the future of women in Turkey is fraught with uncertainty and challenge.

NOTES

[1]   A first version of this paper was presented at the workshop on "Processes and Consequences of Urban Change in the Middle East," held at the State University of New York, Binghampton, July 9-20, 1979. The author wishes to express her gratitude to the participants for their valuable comments and suggestions.

BIBLIOGRAPHY

Abu-Lughod, J. "Migrant Adjustment to City Life: The Egyptian Case," *American Journal of Sociology.* 1961, 67, 22-23.
Aswad, B. "Visiting Patterns Among Women of the Elite in a Small Turkish City," *Anthropological Quarterly.* 1974, 47, 9-27.

Benedict, P. "The Kabul Günü: Structured Visiting in an Anatolian Provincial Town," *Anthropological Quarterly*. 1974, 47, 28-47.
Bromley, R. and C. Gerry (eds.). *Casual Work and Poverty in Third World Cities*. London: John Wiley and Sons, 1979.
Çitçi, O. "Turkish Female Civil Service Employees." In N. Abadan—Unat (ed.), *Women in Turkish Society*. Leiden: E.J. Brill, 1982.
Collver, H. and E. Langlois. "The Female Labour Force in Metopolitan Areas: An International Comparison," *Economic Development and Cultural Change*. 1962, 10, 367-85.
Durand, John. *The Labor Force in Economic Development*. Princeton: Princeton Univ. Press, 1975.
Early, E. "Entrepreneurship Among Lower Class Egyptian Women." Paper presented at the Ninth World Congress of Sociology, Uppsala, Sweden, August, 1978.
Erder, L. "The Women of Turkey: A Demographic Overview." In N. Abadan—Unat (ed.), *Women In Turkish Society* . Leiden: E.J. Brill, 1982.
Fallers, L. and M. Fallers. "Sex Roles in Edremit." In J.G. Peristiany (ed.), *Mediterranean Family Structures*. London: Cambridge Univ. Press, 1976.
Good, Del Vecchio M.J. "A Comparative Perspective on Provincial Iran and Turkey." In L. Beck and N. Keddie (eds.), *Women in the Muslim World*. Cambridge, Mass.: Harvard Univ. Press, 1978.
International Labour Office. "Labour Force Projections, 1965-1985," Part VI, Methodological Supplement. Geneva: 1973.
Kâğıtçıbaşı, Ç. and A. Kansu. "Cinsiyet Rollerinin Sosyalleşmesi ve Aile Dinamiği: Kuşaklararası bir Karşılaştırma," *Boğaziçi University Journal* (Social Sciences Series). 1976-77, 5, 35-48.
Kandiyoti, D. "Sex Roles and Social Change: A Comparative Appraisal of Turkey's Women," *Signs*. 1977, 3, 57-73.
_____. "Characteristics of Industrial Workers in the Istanbul-Izmit Complex," *Amme Idaresi Dergisi* (Journal of Public Administration). 1977, 10, 1.
_____. "Intergenerational Change Among Turkish Women." Paper presented at the Ninth World Congress of Sociology, Uppsala, August, 1978.
_____ . "Rural Transformation in Turkey and Its Implications for Women's Status." Paper presented at the Meeting of Experts on Research on the Status of Women, Development and Population Trends, UNESCO, Paris, November, 1980.
Kazgan, G. "Labor Force Participation, Occupational Distribution, Educational Attainment and the Socio-Economic Status of Women in the Turkish Economy." In N. Abadan-Unat (ed.), *Women in Turkish Society*. Leiden: E.J. Brill, 1982.

Kıray, M. "Changing Roles of Mothers: Changing Intra-Family Relations in a Turkish Town." In J. Peristiany (ed.), *Mediterranean Family Structures.* London: Cambridge Univ. Press, 1976.

————. "Women in Small Towns." In N. Abadan-Unat (ed.), *Women in Turkish Society.* Leiden: E.J. Brill, 1982.

Magnarella, P. *Tradition and Change in a Turkish Town.* New York: John Wiley and Sons, 1974.

Mansur, F. *Bodrum: A Town in the Aegean.* Leiden: E.J. Brill, 1972.

Mernissi, F. "Les Bonnes," *Al Asas.* 1977, 5.

el-Messiri, S. "Self-Images of Traditional Urban Women in Cairo." In L. Beck and N. Keddie (eds.) *Women in the Muslim World.* Cambridge, Mass.: Harvard Univ. Press, 1978.

Maher, V. *Women and Property in Morocco.* Cambridge: 1974.

Nelson, C. and V. Olesen. "Veil of Illusion: a Critique of the Concept of Equality in Western Thought," *Catalyst.* 1977, 1, 10-11; 2, 8-37.

Olson-Prather, E. "*Çocuk Doğurma* [Natality] is Women's Business." Paper presented at the 75th Annual Meeting of the American Anthropological Association. Washington, D.C., 1976.

Öncü, A. "Turkish Women in the Professions: Why So Many?" In N. Abadan-Unat (ed.), *Women in Turkish Society.* Leiden: E.J. Brill, 1982.

Papanek, H. "Purdah in Pakistan: Seclusion and Modern Occupations for Women," *Journal of Marriage and the Family.* 1971, 517-30.

————. "Purdah: Separate Worlds and Symbolic Shelter," *Comparative Studies in Society and History.* 15, 3, 289-325.

Safilios-Rothschild, C. "A Cross-Cultural Examination of Women's Marital, Educational and Occupational Options," *Acta Sociologica.* 1971, 14, 93-113.

Şenyapılı, T. "A New Component in the Metropolitan Areas—The 'Gecekondu' Women." In N. Abadan-Unat (ed.), *Women in Turkish Society.* Leiden: E.J. Brill, 1982.

Sinha, J.N. "Dynamics of Female Participation in Economic Activity in a Developing Economy." Document WCP/285, Session A5 (mimeo), United Nations World Population Conference, 1965.

Timur, S. "Determinants of Family Structure in Turkey." Paper presented at the seminar on "Women in Turkish Society." Istanbul, May 16-19, 1978.

Youssef, N.H. *Women and Work in Developing Societies.* Population Monograph Series No. 15. Berkeley: Univ. of California, 1974.

DUALISM IN VALUES TOWARD EDUCATION
OF TURKISH WOMEN

Sumru Erkut

We start out with three observations on the educational status of Turkish women. (1) Relative to men, women display substantially lower levels of educational attainment. (2) Again relative to men, women who go on in school beyond the primary level show more persistence and achieve greater success. (3) Despite the low levels of educational attainment for women in general, substantial numbers of Turkish women obtain professional degrees and practice in what are considered in the West to be male-dominated occupations. The thesis of this essay is that these three phenomena are not isolated curiosities. Rather, they are functionally interrelated such that the educational and occupational successes of an elite group of Turkish women is made possible by the lack of opportunities for the majority.[1]

In a nutshell, the process works as follows: A select group of women are able to pursue educational and career goals without opposition from men because they do not pose a threat either to men's privileged status or to their traditional role. Husbands and fathers of career women are able to maintain their status as heads of households while continuing not to share in the daily tasks of running the house which has traditionally been women's role. The daily chores of keeping house and caring for children are performed by other women with minimal education who can be hired at relatively low wages to work as domestics, cooks, laundresses, and governesses. If men can enjoy the enhanced family prestige and income that a career woman can bring without having to take much more responsibility at home, why should they object to educating their daughters and allowing their wives to pursue careers outside the home? Indeed, the urban elite place a high value on women's education.

The inevitable irony is that the high value the elite place in education is translated into action only for their own womenfolk. It remains at best an abstract ideal for the rest of Turkish women; at worst it is nonexistent. That there is a lack of adequate educational opportunities for the majority of Turkish women is a living testimony to the Turkish power elite's dualistic value system regarding women's education. Thus, it appears that Turks are of two minds when it comes to valuing education for women. They encourage and support it for some, but do not provide educational opportunites for the majority of women.

Sex Differences in Overall Educational Attainment

At the level of official ideology there is no discrimination against women in education. Primary education is compulsory for both girls and boys. Beyond primary school, merit rather than gender determines who gets an education. The emphasis on merit is most conspicuous in admission to universities where the entrance examination score is the only criterion for admission.

As soon as one goes beyond stated ideology, however, to enforcement of policy, one can see that women are at a disadvantage. Whereas primary school is compulsory for all, this policy is not enforced with equal vigor for girls and boys. In 1974-75, for example, girls made up only 43.1% of the enrollment in rural primary schools. In urban primary schools girls made up 46.3% of the enrollment, which is still less than half. Thus, in rural areas and to some extent in urban areas, some families are able to keep their daughters out of primary school in defiance of the law with impunity.

Beyond primary school where school attendance is not compulsory but based on merit, one can see the detrimental effect of certain policies working against women. The vast majority of secondary institutions are located in urban centers, but there are fewer dormitory facilities available for women than for men. Lack of dormitory facilities automatically excludes many rural and small town women from secondary education. The same is true for facilities available to women in higher education.

Educational opportunities available for Turkish women must also be set into the perspective of what is available to men. There is no doubt that opportunities are limited. Not every village has a primary school, despite the compulsory nature of primary school attendance. Secondary schools are located in urban areas and are limited in number. But the largest scarcity is in higher education. In 1974-75, for example, there was only room for 16% of applicants in institutions of higher education (Çavdar, Tümay, and Yurtseven, 1976).

Limited educational facilities tend to favor selection based on rural-urban residence and socio-economic status such that children of urban, financially better-off families become the beneficiaries of the limited educational opportunities that do exist. Gender also plays a major role, however. At every level of education, women are underrepresented relative to men (see Table 1). Moreover, rural-urban residence and socio-economic status have a greater impact on women's educational attainment than on men's.

Table 1

Sex Differences in Educational Attainment:
Literacy and Highest Level Completed
Among Population Over 6 years of Age in 1975

Educational Attainment	Women	Men
Illiterate	51.8	24.9
Attended but did not graduate	14.1	19.7
Primary	27.7	42.0
Middle School and equivalent	3.2	6.5
High School and equivalent	2.6	4.9
Higher Education	0.4	1.6

Source: Devlet Istatistik Enstitüsü.
1975 Census of the Population, 1 percent sample.
Results, 1976 (Başbakanlık: Ankara).

Çavdar, Tümay, and Yurtseven (1976) point out that fewer women than men of rural origin apply for admission to universities, and fewer female than male applicants are children of fathers engaged in agriculutrual or blue-collar occupations. On the other hand, more women than men applicants have fathers who are professionals or white-collar workers.

Educational Successes of Elite Women

The greater lack of opportunities for women's education than for men's which favors women of urban, middle and upper-class origin has a curious effect. Few women achieve more than a primary education, but those that go on in school are more successful than men in general. That women do better than men beyond primary school can be seen by comparing women's representation in total enrollments at a given level with their representation among graduates at that level (see Table 2). At every level and for almost every year for which figures are available, the percentage of women among the graduates is higher than their representation in the total enrollment. These comparisons indicate that women have lower attrition and higher completion rates than men.

There is no doubt that the minority of women who go on with their education beyond primary school are a select group in that they are mostly women of urban origin from families with economic means. Çavdar, Tümay, and Yurtseven (1976) have documented the overrepresentation of urban women from professional families in colleges and universities.We can speculate that they are a select group in terms of academic qualities as well. Perhaps their greater success relative to men beyond primary education can be attributed to women being a more select group on the basis of academic qualities. That is, only the very talented women may be the ones who go on beyond primary school. In reality, however, academic achievement and socio-economic status are highly interrelated. Families with financial means are often more materially and emotionally supportive of their children's education than families with limited means. Thus, it is hard to tell whether it is native intelligence or parental support which makes the urban, well-to-do women succeed in school.

In effect, the official ideology of merit being the determinant of who receives a post-primary education probably holds true for children from urban, well-to-do families. That urban, well-to-do women are able to pursue their education based on merit has made it possible for these women to specialize in fields of their choice. Many have chosen to receive training in previously male-dominated fields such as medicine and law. They have been able to choose these fields without much opposition from their parents because an interesting aspect of attitudes toward women's status in Turkey is that many previously male-dominated occupations are now considered appropriate for women. In the following section comparative data on sex typing of occupations in the U.S. and Turkey will be presented as an illustration of the support elite Turkish women receive in pursuit of their educational goals.

Table 2

Women's Persistence in Secondary and Higher Education:
Enrollment and Graduation Rates

	Academic Middle Schools		Academic High Schools		Secondary Level Vocational and Technical Schools		Universities and Other Institutions of Higher Education	
	Enroll.	Grad.	Enroll.	Grad.	Enroll.	Grad.	Enroll.	Grad.
1970-71	27.3	28.5	28.9	30.5	34.0	35.9	20.6	21.5
1971-72	27.6	28.8	29.7	30.2	34.2	36.9	19.8	22.5
1972-73	28.2	29.6	31.0	30.4	34.9	34.8	20.2	22.7
1973-74	28.4	n.a.	31.7	n.a.	35.3	35.8	20.6	21.4
1974-75	n.a.	n.a.	n.a.	n.a.	33.6	n.a.	21.2	24.0

Source: Devlet İstatistik Enstitüsü. Statistical Yearbook of Turkey. Ankara: Başbakanlık, 1977.

Positive Attitudes toward Turkish Women's
Advanced Training in the Professions

It is well known that economic development has an inverse relationship with the availability of educational opportunity in general, and specifically for women. Whereas developed countries closely approximate universal literacy for both men and women, many more women than men remain illiterate in the third world. For example, while the illiteracy rate is only 1% for men and women in the United States (*Current Population Report*, 1971, p. 2), in Turkey approximately 25% of the men, but as many as 50% of the women are illiterate according to 1975 Census definitions (*Statistical Yearbook of Turkey*, 1977, p. 42). What is less well known is that this phenomenon of limited educational attainment among third world women is often accompanied by a seemingly paradoxical abundance of professionally trained women in the third world (see Safilios-Rothschild, 1974).

In Turkey also, high levels of illiteracy among women coexist with significant numbers of women educated in the free professions (see Öncü, 1979). In fact, there are proportionally more women physicians and lawyers in Turkey than in the U.S. (see Table 3). Where female literacy is almost universal, as in the U.S., one might expect that many more women would be available for advanced training in the professions; where female literacy is low, as in Turkey, one might expect fewer women to persist in the education system to complete professional education. But statistics show the opposite to be the case. In Turkey, as in many other third world

Table 3
Women as Percentage of Total
Number of Physicians and Lawyers
In Turkey and the United States

	Turkey	United States
Physicians	14.1%[1]	10.1%[3]
Lawyers	18.69%[2]	5.0%[3]

Sources: [1] Estimate for 1970 cited in Öncü (1979). [2] Figures for 1975, Turkish Bar Association cited in Öncü. [3] *1970 Census of the Population, Characteristics of the Population, United States Summary*, Vol. 1, Part 1, Section 2, U.S. Department of Commerce , Government Printing Office, 1973.

countries, women who receive an education beyond primary school find relatively few obstacles in their way to completing advanced training, while many American women's entry to professional education appears to be blocked. One manifestation of this blockage is sex typing of occupations whereby some occupations are deemed inappropriate for women.

Feldman (1974) surveyed 352 undergraduate men and women in five different colleges and universities in the U.S. on sex typing of occupations. Subjects rated occupations on a 7 point semantic differential scale on the polar types masculine-feminine. His results show that occupations such as medicine and law are perceived to be very unfeminine. They received ratings of 2.50 and 1.94, respectively, out of a possible 7 rating. Erkut conducted a similar study with 95 Turkish students in two universities in 1973 on whether selected occupations were seen as appropriate for women. The results show that Turkish students viewed medicine and law to be less appropriate for women than teaching or nursing. Still, 81% of Turkish students considered medicine and 78% considered law to be an appropriate occupation for women. It appears that there is a much more favorable attitude toward women's entry to these occupations in Turkey than in the U.S. This more favorable attitude to women's participation in medicine and law is ultimately reflected in the larger percentages of women in these occupations in Turkey than in the U.S. The question which remains to be answered is why Turkish elite are less restictive of women's educational/occupational choices than their American counterparts.

The Failures of Many Allow the Few to Succeed

Safilios-Rothschild (1974) and Öncü (1979) suggest that the greater educational and occupational choices accorded elite women in the third world is a direct function of the large numbers of uneducated women who can be hired at low wages to perform the household functions educated women cannot perform due to professional employment outside the home. Thus, the rise of a few women is made possible by the expoitation of many.

This argument has general merit, but it needs to be expanded to show who actually benefits from the status quo. The analysis of who benefits from the availability of domestic labor at low cost is germane to understanding attitudes towards women's education in Turkey.

A number of factors are associated with the educational and

career successes of a select group of Turkish women. Many of these pertain to benefits which accrue to the fathers/husbands of these women. Above all, there is the income professional women bring to their family. As the ravages of inflation wipe away earning power, it is no longer possible for one-career families to maintain the standard of living to which they were accustomed 10 or 20 years ago. Thus, the earning power of women allows families financial means to maintain and perhaps to enhance their standard of living.

Secondly, there is the status enhancement/ status demonstration component of women's employment as professionals. The free professions are viewed as highly prestigious occupations in Turkey (Aral, 1977). Employment as a professional in fields such as medicine and law enhances not only the individual woman's social standing within the community but also her family's. Even in cases where the family's prestige is already well established, the professional employment of a wife or daughter serves a status demonstration function (see Papanek, 1979). Such employment underscores the elite standing of families for whose female members professional employment is often the only socially appropriate career outlet.

Both of these benefits are "rational" considerations; they lead to a positive valuation of education for women because they enhance the income and prestige of the family. If they are rational means of improving a family's social standing, why aren't they universally valued? The answer is not a simple one. In part, it has to be sought in the costs a family may incur when wives, mothers, and/or daughters work outside the home. Outside employment curtails the hours and energy women have traditionally spent maintaining the home and rearing children. Absence from home, hence, from housewifely duties, has been viewed as such a cost to the family that some groups in America claim women's employment is a threat to family life and consequently to the very fabric of society. Curiously, such an outcry is seldom heard in Turkey. This is not because Turks do not place a high value on home life. On the contrary, family and childrearing values are central to Turkish life (Kâğıtçıbaşı, 1979). One reason there has not been a movement to limit women's educational and career opportunities is that in Turkey, working women can hire other women to take over their household responsibilities. Hence, family life can go on with minimal disruption. The men of these elite groups are the primary beneficiaries of this situation. They enjoy improved income and prestige without incurring the cost of taking over household responsibilities. In the United States, however, the prohibitive cost of domestic help puts such services out of the reach of all but a few wealthy families. Lack of readily available domestic help places a burden on American men that they ought to help out around the house. Whereas time-use studies repearedly show that American men do little housework even when their spouses have outside employment (Pleck, 1979; Walker and Woods, 1976), the expectation that men should help is widely shared. It is this unfulfilled expectation that men should do housework, which is the real burden, not that men actually do the work. That men do not share in housework, but leave working women with outside as well as household responsibilities, is often a source of family conflict. The conflict arises because, while the expectation that men ought to help out around the house is widely shared, that men should feel good about doing housework is a relatively new value, espoused only by a minority of American men. The average American man is at best ambivalent about participating in household tasks. Even if he feels some sense of responsibility, he feels no moral support for doing such work from his social network of male peers (Lein, 1979). The net result is often little, if any, actual sharing of household responsibilities, accompanied by a resentment of the situation which created the expectation that they should help out, namely, women's outside employment.

In Turkey, on the other hand, no such conflict exists. The easy availability of domestic help does not create a need for men to share in housework. Consequently, there is no expectation that men will do housework. Indeed, there is a widely shared expectation that they will not help around the house. An interesting finding by Holmstrom attests to the lack of conflict over husbands not helping with domestic tasks. She found that not helping around the house was *least* often mentioned by upper-middle-class and lower-class women living in Istanbul as a trait in their husband that bothered them strongly (Holmstrom, 1973). Thus, women's employment outside the home does not threaten the internal status and role distribution within the family. Men's privileged position in the home is not threatened in any way. Consequently, Turkish men have little reason to oppose the professional training and employment of their women.

Conclusions

The basic thesis of this essay is that elite Turkish women are encouraged to engage in educational pursuits which lead to professional employment outside the home, not in spite of, but because of, the large numbers of nonelite women who have limited educational, hence occupational, opportunities. In other words, the successes of the few are made possible by the failures of many. The multitudes of illiterate or semiliterate women can be hired at low wages to take over the domestic tasks a working professional woman has neither the time nor energy to perform. The easy availability of domestic help maintains the status quo of division of labor within the family. The men remain household heads with little if any responsibility of household tasks. Yet they enjoy the added income and prestige a professionally employed woman brings to the family. The women enjoy the freedom to pursue careers outside the home with minimal disruption of domestic stability. Nonelite women, on the other hand, not only receive low wages for hard labor, but they must perform their own households' tasks after performing someone else's.

The exchange relationship among elite men, elite women, and domestic workers is such that, given the balance of powers, it is unlikely to lead to changes due to any internal dynamics. This is for the simple reason that the more powerful parties in the relationship—elite men and women—benefit from the relationship as it exists. They will be reluctant to initiate changes which will disrupt the system whereby inexpensive domestic labor becomes scarce. Hence, it is quite apparent that the elite will not be the ones to promote educational opportunities for the nonelite women, which would improve their employment status.

Domestic workers have much to gain if their relationship with the elite were altered in such a way that they could get a better education, more secure employment or higher wages, but they are powerless to effect these changes. The sheer numbers of illiterate and semi-literate women in need of employment makes it difficult, if not impossible, for this group to push for changes that would improve their lot at the expense of the benefits which accrue to the elite. Consequently, any change in the relationship must originate outside the relationship.

There are two external sources of change that can impinge on the relationship among elite men, elite women, and domestic workers. These are a drop in the buying power of elite families and an increase in employment opportunities for domestic workers. In only one of these cases—in the case of an increase in alternative employment opportunities—can one reasonably expect that the domestic workers' lot will be improved.

If the first impetus for change occurs, that is, if the buying power of elite families is eroded due to excessive inflation or general economic depression, their effective demand for domestic help will be lowered. Families that once could afford domestic help at relatively low wages will no longer be able to spare that money. Such a situation will create widespread unemployment among domestic workers. Unemployment among domestic workers is not likely to have anything but a deteriorating effect on the lot of non-elite women's general status in society and their educational opportunities.

The second external impetus for change would come about if employment opportunities outside of domestic work were created, such as factory work, for example. An increase in demand for the labor of illiterate or semi-literate women would certainly put an upward pressure on their wages as domestics. With the siphoning off of excess labor to other sectors, domestic workers can find themselves in a situation where they can bargain not only for higher wages but may be able to organize to achieve more formalized employer/employee relationships, benefits, and improved working conditions. Only then will they be in a position to influence educational policy to their advantage. Only then will serious attempts to overcome the dualism in educational values be made.

Unfortunately, the prognosis for the near future is not bright for eliminating the dualism in values related to the education of Turkish women. If the status quo *does* get disrupted, it is likely to take the form of a lower demand for domestic labor due to an erosion of buying power among people who used to be able to afford household help. The increase in unemployment among domestic workers this situation will create will not be conducive to improving educational opportunities for nonelite women.

It is interesting to note in conclusion that when families can no longer find inexpensive household help, for whatever reason, there are implications for elite men and women. One implication is that women will assume a role overload. They will continue to work outside, and they will also be the ones to carry out the daily tasks at home. The second implication is that elite women will come to expect the men in the family to share in household responsibilities. However, in the short run, at least, it is unlikely that this expectation will become transformed into a behavioral norm, that men should help with family chores when their womenfolk work outside the home. Rather, the more likely scenario is that the unfulfilled expectation will become a source of conflict among working couples, perhaps galvanizing men to oppose women's outside employment.

NOTES

[1]   This essay is a revised version of a presentation made to the Seminar Series on the Critique of Scientific Milieu in Turkey, held in Montreal, Canada, in March, 1977. I wish to thank the seminar participants for their feedback emphasizing the effect of elite status on the formation of attitudes toward women's education. Sevgi Aral made comments on an early draft and pointed out that men are the true beneficiaries of women's professional employment. I am grateful to her for sharing her insights with me. Finally, I wish to thank Pamela Perun for commenting on the final draft. The original data reported in the essay was collected as part of a study supported by grant #73-01-02-100 from the Middle East Technical University.

BIBLIOGRAPHY

Aral, S. *Occupational Prestige: An Empirical and Theoretical Analysis.* Ankara: Middle East Technical University Publications, 1977.

Çavdar, T., D. Tümay, and T. Yurtseven. *Yuksek ogretime basvuran ogrenciler, 1974-1975: sosyoekonomik çözümleme.* Ankara: D.P.T., Yayin No. 1496, 1976.

Feldman, S.D. *Escape from the Doll's House: Women in Graduate and Professional School Education.* New York: McGraw-Hill, 1974.

Holmstrom, E.I. "Changing Sex Roles in a Developing Country," *Journal of Marriage and the Family.* 1973, 546-53.

Kâğıtçıbaşı, Ç. "Türkiyede çocuğun değeri, kadının rolü ve doğurganlığı." In N. Abadan-Unat (ed.), *Türk toplumunda kadın.* Ankara: Türk Sosyal Bilimler Derneği, 1979.

Lein, L. "Male Participation in Home Life: Impact of Social Supports and Breadwinner Responsibility on the Allocation of Tasks." *The Family Coordinator.* 1979, 26, 489-95.

Öncü, A. "Uzman mesleklerde Türk Kadını." In N. Abadan-Unat (ed.), *Türk toplumunda kadın.* Ankara: Türk Sosyal Bilimler Derneği, 1979.

Papanek, H. "Family Status Production: The 'Work' and 'Non-Work' of Women." *Signs.* 1979, 4, 775-81.

Pleck, J."Men's Family Work: Three Perspectives and Some New Data." *The Family Coordinator,* 1979, 26, 481-88.

Safilios-Rothschild, C. *Women and Social Policy.* Englewood Cliffs, N.J.: Prentice-Hall, 1974.

Walker, K and M.E. Woods, *Time Use: A Measure of Household Production of Family Goods and Services.* Washington, D.C.: American Home Economics Asso., 1976.

WOMEN'S EDUCATION IN RURAL TURKEY

Ferhunde Özbay

It has often been argued that the almost universally lower status of women is related to their ineffective participation in production and low level of educational attainment. Marxist writers have long emphasized the importance of female participation in production as a condition for the equalization of the sexes (e.g., Engels, 1942), while education has been considered as the most decisive means to achieve this aim and higher status (Buvinic, 1976). For some time, it was thought that modernization in Third World countries would increase women's educational opportunities and hence access to the organized labor market. However, recent studies have increasingly shown that modernization and development do not necessarily facilitate these outcomes (Boserup, 1970; Chaney and Schmink, 1977). It is consistently argued that labor force participation of women in developing countries is not accompanied by economic independence and hence higher status. Sanday (1973) claims that labor force participation is a necessary but not sufficient condition of female status. It is, therefore, clear that the relationship between labor force participation, education and status needs close scrutiny. The aim of this paper is to discuss first the overall trends in labor force participation as related to educational level in Turkey, and second, to propose a model of the relationship between education and labor force participation, understood within the context of property relations in contemporary rural Turkey.[1]

Overall Trends of Labor Force Participation and Education Among Turkey's Female Population

According to the population censuses between 1950 and 1975, there are two trends clearly observable with regard to labor force participation. The first is that female labor force participation (LFP), which is still relatively high (about 37% in 1975), is steadily decreasing (see Table 1). The second, which is corollary to the first, is that the difference in LFP between males and female is widening. As far as literacy is concerned, on the other hand, women's literacy rate is still low (about 48% in 1975), but increasing (see Table 2). However, the trend is in the direction of a widening gap between men's and women's educational attainment. Thus, interestingly, women's increasing literacy rates coincide with a decrease in female labor force participation, and, in any case, both the LFP rates and educational attainment of men and women are getting further apart, to the detriment of women. Therefore, it seems important to look at the relationship between LFP and education in Turkey more closely.

The greatest proportion of the female labor force consists of uneducated women (67%). However, when educational level is controlled for, it is women with university degrees or vocational training whose LFP rates are higher (see Table 3). It is well to remember that the numbers of women with such qualifications remain low (3%). This relationship between LFP and education is well illustrated by the occupational distribution of the economically active female population (see Table 4). As can be seen in Table 4, the majority of women in the labor force are engaged in agriculture (89%). Furthermore, Ergil (1977) points out that about 83% of the female labor force in Turkey worked as unpaid family labor in 1970. These figures clearly suggest that the majority of female labor force participants in Turkey consists of uneducated women, participating in agricultural production as unpaid family laborers.

A nation-wide survey carried out in 1973 by Hacettepe University gives us separate rural-urban estimations which we are unable to get from the recent census tabulations. While this survey confirms the above trends, it also shows that the proportion of employed women in urban centers is about 9% among the uneducated and increases to 28% among those who graduated from secondary or higher level schools, whereas in the rural areas employment decreases with the increase in educational attainment. There is an

Table 1
Labor Force Participation of the Population
(Ages 15 and Over)

Years	Male	Female	Total	Difference
1950	95.3	81.5	88.4	13.8
1955	95.6	72.2	83.9	23.4
1960	93.9	65.5	79.8	28.1
1965	92.1	56.7	74.5	35.4
1970	74.9	45.3	60.1	29.6
1975	66.6	37.0	51.8	29.6

Source: Kazgan, 1979, Table 11.

Table 2
Literacy Rates by Sex in Turkey, 1927-1975
(Ages 6 and over)

Census Years	Percent Literate		Difference
	Male	Female	
1927	17.4	4.6	12.8
1935	29.3	9.8	19.5
1940	33.9	11.2	22.7
1945	41.9	18.1	23.8
1950	47.1	20.1	27.0
1955	55.6	25.6	30.0
1960	53.6	24.8	28.8
1965	64.0	32.8	31.2
1970	69.0	40.0	29.0
1975	75.1	48.1	26.8

Source: SIS, 1973, p. XXXVIII; and SIS, 1975, p. 6-7.

inverse relationship between the degree of education and the rate of agricultural labor participation in the rural sector: participation in agricultural production is 92% among the uneducated female labor force, 84% among the primary school graduates, and 5% among the secondary or higher level school graduates (Özbay, 1979).

In sum, two different patterns are observed in the relationship between LFP and education in rural and urban areas of the country. In the urban areas, where women mainly participate in non-agricultural occupations, the proportion of LFP is low, but there is a positive relationship between educational attainment and LFP. In the rural areas, on the other hand, the female LFP is concentrated in agricultural activities and the proportion of employed women is relatively higher than those in the urban areas. The relationship between LFP and education is somewhat problematic in the rural areas, however, since labor force participation does not increase by educational attainment, but, on the contrary decreases. As can be concluded from the above discussion, the problem of the relation between LFP and education is basically the problem of rural women, which is reflected heavily in the nation-wide trends. While there have been studies on the effect of development on rural LFP of women, there is a lack of detailed analysis of the interaction between LFP and education within different rural property systems.

Our aim is to provide an analysis of the changing rural social structure in Turkey and to examine the LFP-education relationship within this context.

Table 3
Distribution of Female Population by Last School
Graduated From and Employment Status, 1975 Turkey
(Ages 12 and Over)

School	Employed	Unemployed	Total	N
Non-Graduate	50.1	49.9	100.0	7,913,364
Primary	36.4	63.6	100.0	4,454,068
Junior High	15.4	84.6	100.0	521,594
Vocational at Jr. High Level	34.0	66.0	100.0	13,530
High School	32.1	67.9	100.0	239,475
Vocational at H.S. Level	57.2	42.8	100.0	192,331
College	71.4	28.6	100.0	67,093
Total	44.1	55.9	100.0	13,401,455

Source: SIS, 1976, pp. 6-7, 24-25.

Table 4
Distribution of the Population by Sex
and Occupation (in the previous week) 1970 Turkey

Occupation	Male%	Female%
Professional & Technical Personnel	4.7	2.4
Managers & Entrepreneurs	0.9	0.1
Administrative Personnel	2.3	1.3
Trade & Sales Personnel	4.9	0.3
Private Service Work	5.7	0.8
Agriculture	53.3	88.7
Non-Agricultural Producers (artisans and workers)	11.9	4.5
Others	16.4	2.0
Total	100.0	100.0

Source: Ergil (1977), p. 40, Table II.

The Social Structure of Rural Turkey

Rural areas, which before the 1950s were engaged in the cultivation of some form of subsistence crop, using primitive technology and family labor, have since been fundamentally transformed by the spread of cash crops, mechanization, and integration into the market economy. An important consequence from the point of view of the rural stratification system has been land polarization, wherein land resources have been concentrated into fewer households, the rest of the producers increasingly being pushed into marginal categories (Kandiyoti, 1974). The outcome of this process has been the creation of at least four distinct types of rural social structure:

Type 1) Large agricultural enterprises, using mechanized and agricultural wage workers.

Type 2) Medium size agricultural enterprises. This type of enterprise is the most heterogenous group in terms of the type of technology used and the kind of crops cultivated. In this type, labor elements are drawn predominantly from the family.

Type 3) Small agricultural enterprises. These are enterprises incapable of using all their family labor capacity in agriculture production. These may be either small producers whose land income is insufficient for their subsistence and who have to use additional income sources, or producers of labor intensive crops.

Type 4) Landless wage laborers. These are seasonal workers who are all in family labor and have no means of subsistence aside from their wages.

Another phenomenon in rural areas is the existence of rural inhabitants whose means of livelihood is in nonagricultural occupations. Although there is a certain proportion of such occupations (e.g., teacher, grocer, barber, *imam*, etc.) in most villages, the numbers of people in this category reach their maximum in rural areas adjoining town centers where there are possibilities of salaried work.

The types outlined above have different implications regarding the labor force participation of women:

In Type 1, where agriculture is mechanized, the existence of wage workers employed in non-mechanized areas indicates that women are not kept out of labor force participation because of underemployment, but because of voluntary non-employment related to their socio-economic status (Tekeli, 1977).

In Type 2, men are the main producers, female family labor being complementary. The degree of female participation in production is a function of the crops produced and technology used.

In Type 3, women are principally in charge of agricultural production, either because men have to seek non-agricultural income elsewhere or because they leave the menial manual tasks, such as tea picking, hazel nut gathering, etc., to women and land is not large enough to use the family labor force to full capacity. It is interesting to note that while it is women who perform the actual production tasks, it is men who monopolize dealings with merchants, cooperatives and the commercial world in general. Some men also go to urban centers to work for several years, leaving their families in the village.

This type of rural family emerges due to the modernization of agriculture and has attracted the attention of several authors with regard to other modernizing societies. Boserup (1970) gives examples of such families in Africa. Deere (1976) discussed the "semi-proletarianization" of small farmers in most of Latin America. Castillo (1977) similarly gives examples of studies in Poland, Yugoslavia and Romania which discuss the increasing "feminization of agriculture" where industrialization, collectivization, mechanization of agriculture, and rural-urban migration have involved mostly male peasants.

The Type 4 families do not have any other means but their labor for subsistence and women in this type of family are not in an unpaid labor force status. Both men and women work in seasonal wage occupations like cotton picking. But still women do not have their economic independence since wage distributors (elçi) give the wages of women and children to the household head.

Four Case Studies

Hacettepe University conducted a rural survey in 1975, where all the households in the selected villages were interviewed, and observation schedules about general village life were produced. Four villages are selected here as case studies, where the majority of the families in each village represent one of the four structural types defined above.

These villages are in different geographical regions; however, they have some common characteristics: their populations are similar (the range being between 810 to 1220); they are located near town centers (15-20 minutes by car); and they all have a primary school (Özbay and Balamir, 1977).

Type 1: A village of *Kırşehir* in Central Anatolia is selected as an example of the large agricultural enterprise type. The mean land size in the village is about 293 Ha. Agriculture is mechanized, and seasonal wage laborers come there to work with their families in agricultural production requiring manual labor. The laborers stay in the village for about 2-3 weeks. Over one third of the families are landless (see Table 5). The majority of landless families work in a factory in the town nearby. They, thus, represent the working class of the urban area. In the village there are some smaller agricultural enterprises as well. Hence, families which are engaged in both agriculutural and non-agricultural activities can be seen. The village as a whole is prosperous and urban-like. In the village, there are about 50 migrants who have returned from Europe and about 30-50 migrants who are still living abroad. Seventeen percent of the families in the village have some relatives living in town (Özbay and Balamir, 1977). It is most likely that contact with other cities in Turkey and outside Turkey has an impact on the general prosperity of the village.

Type 2: A village of *Kirklareli* in Western Turkey is more homogeneous in terms of representing one type of enterprise: The majority of the villagers have medium-sized agricultural enterprises as in Type 2. The mean size of land holding is about 90 Ha., and agriculuture is mostly mechanized. In this village there are very few landless families who are engaged only in non-agricultural work (see Tables 5 and 6). Some families, on the other hand, have enterprises larger than the mean size, and hence need wage laborers from outside the village. The need for wage laborers, however, is comparatively less in this village than in the one previously mentioned (Type 1). Wage laborers are all men and they come to the village on a daily basis. Migration to urban cities is increasing. 22% of the families have indicated that they have at least one member living in a large city. Although there are migrants who live abroad or have returned, they constitute only about 2-3% of the village population (Özbay and Balamir, 1977).

Type 3: A village of *Trabzon* is a good example of the Black Sea villages in which the majority represents Type 3 enterprises. In this village most of the families produce tea in their gardens which are about 5 Ha. on the average. Besides tea, hazel nut and vegetable production, a little animal husbandry is being done. In addition to this cash cropping, in about 61% of the households some additional non-agricultural work has to be done (see Table 5). One is likely to see people who are tea garden owners working as butchers, grocers or policemen in near-by towns, but seasonal wage earners are the majority. The migration rate to Europe is low (about 3%), whereas it is higher to large cities; 15% of the families have indicated that they have at least one member living in a large city (Özbay and Balamir, 1977).

Type 4: A village of *Mardin* is selected to represent Type 4 families. It is located in South-East Anatolia, near the Syrian border. The villagers by no means consist of wage laborers only. In fact, in this village, economic inequalities among the families are remarkable. More than half of the families do not own any land, yet the average size of land holdings is well over 100 Ha. Besides agricultural work there is some animal husbandry. Non-agricultural work is about 7%. In the village of Mardin, Type 1 (large land owners) and Type 4 (agricultural workers) households coexist in a somewhat complementary fashion. These two types are very different in terms of women's participation in the labor force. Most landless families work in the large agricultural enterprises in and outside the village. Although the villagers have a low standard of living, the migration rate is very low, and there is no migration to Europe (Özbay and Balamir, 1977).

Table 5

Percent Landless and Mean Size
of Land Holdings in Four Villages

	Percent Landless	Mean Size of Land Holdings (Ha)
Mardin	54.3	184.3
Trabzon	10.1	05.0
Kırşehir	36.4	292.6
Kırklareli	06.8	89.7

Source: The 1975 Hacettepe Rural Survey Data

Table 6

Distribution of Families by Economic
Activities in Four Villages

	Total	Agriculture	Agriculture + Non-Agriculture	Non-Agriculture
Mardin	100	81.0	12.0	07.0
Trabzon	100	35.4	60.6	04.0
Kırşehir	100	37.8	37.8	24.4
Kırklareli	100	80.1	16.3	03.6

Source: The 1975 Hacettepe Rural Survey Data

Women's Labor Force Participation and Education in the Four Villages

In the village of *Mardin* most landless families work in large agricultural enterprises in their villages (wheat fields) or as seasonal wage earners in September or October when they go to *Çukurova* or *Nusaybin* as cotton pickers. While in about half of the households women participated in agricultural production as wage laborers, the other wealthy half are unemployed. Women at other times look after the animals, take care of the children and do household work. According to the observation of researchers, women work more than men.

There are very few large landowners in the village, and small landowners let their lands to large agricultural enterpreneurs, to work as agricultural wage laborers to increase their income. One of the researchers to work in the area reported that the villagers were happy to let their lands to large agricultural enterpreneurs, since they were able to get more products within less time by the use of mechanized technology. Although the economic status of the villagers does not change because of the share the large agricultural enterpreneurs get, they save time and labor, so they can work as seasonal wage earners.

Large agricultural enterpreneurs prevent development of the village; they try to carry on the unequal power structure in the village, discouraging education and the emergence of governmental institutions such as a post office or police station.

Girls are not educated in the village. Between ages 12-19 there were only two girls and over 20 only one women who had primary education. As the education services in the village are not adequate, boys' education level was also low. Children are also used as wage laborers. During the cotton picking season there were only one or two students in classes. Indeed, among the four villages the lowest education level was in the village of Mardin.

In the village of Trabzon, where the majority are small labor intensive cash crop producers (Type 3), a high concentration of female labor in agriculture is observed. Most women work as unpaid family workers. They work very hard in the tea gardens, in the forest collecting wood for heating, in the house preparing food and taking care of the children, and also, in carrying water, for the source of water supply is far from the houses. Women consider carrying loads as women's work and when asked why men were not carrying loads they replied that it would be beneath men's dignity, as men were intelligent and superior. On the other hand, men considered women to be physically stronger. A tea factory in the village is open for 6 months a year during which most of the men are hired, though not permanently.

The sex differential in education has notably decreased in the younger generations. There were no women over 40 years who had completed primary education, but 87% of the girls and 97% of the boys were attending primary school. It is also wide-spread for men to continue their education after primary school, they are even encouraged. It is not a common practice among girls since they participate in agricultural labor after primary school.

The educational gap between men and women is very significant at higher levels of education. In Type 3 households, where men are underemployed or unemployed, seeking a higher level of schooling seems to be a logical alternative pattern for them, as social mobility requires skilled non-agricultural occupation. Agricultural land is limited, and with modern technology the maximum production level has been reached. This is another reason for men to seek higher levels of schooling and thus achieve social mobility.

Higher levels of education result in the alienation of men from village life and village women, thus leading to higher migration rates. Studies on migration have shown that migration to cities, especially to large cities, is very common in the Black Sea region where the socio-economic structure is homogeneous (Tekçe, 1975). This outcome is also obvious in the village of Trabzon where the majority of migrants are men.

In the families of large agricultural enterprises and non-agricultural occupations, women do not participate in the labor force. In the village of Kırşehir, where the majority of families are in these two categories, women generally show very low LFP (see Table 7). The difference between men and women is important not only because men work and women do not, but also because men go to school while women are kept at home as housewives. However, in the village of Kırşehir women are relatively more educated than those in Mardin and Trabzon. About 98% of the children (both boys and girls) attend primary school since they do not participate in the agricultural labor force at early ages and also the educational facilities are more advanced in Kırşehir compared with the other villages discussed before (Özbay and Balamir, 1977). Frequent relations with large cities contribute to the education of girls, but after primary school education is again for men. This was also seen in the village of Trabzon.

Even though women in the villages of Trabzon and Kırşehir have similar education levels, their labor force participation and labor loads are quite different. These differences derive from the differences in their rural strata.

The fourth village is the village of *Kırklareli* in Western Anatolia, where medium size agricultural enterprises are in the majority. Although the labor force participation of women in agriculture is high, their work load in production is not as heavy as men's, who are the principal producers.

Mechanized technoloogy in agriculture has been practiced since the 1950s, which has decreased the need for labor force in agriculture, causing migration to large cities. This situation has increased the already existing tendency towards education.

As one of the researchers reports, the village is an old emigrant village. Emigrants of 1923 are now the local inhabitants of the village. In 1939-1951 new migrants came into the village, and the local Greeks departed and migrated to Greece (through the agreement on exchange of Turkish and Greek populations). During wars, the villagers were engaged in animal husbandry, later turning to agriculture.

Villagers stress the importance of education and economy, as they fear their village might be one of the first to be invaded in war. Governmental officials indicate that the villagers are modern and easy-going people who are eager to get the maximum out of the facilities provided for them such as education. The literacy rate among men and women is very high. The sex differential is very low (almost none) in primary education, though it increases slightly at higher levels.

Villagers deal with their problems by themselves and try to find possible solutions—a rare practice among the other villagers discussed above.

In this study a scale for the evaluation of women's status in the family and society has not been constructed; however, women's educational level and the sex differential in education can be considered as indicators of women's status as compared to men's.

Figures I and II, drawn from Table 8, illustrate the relative educational attainment of the sexes across four villages discussed. It is seen that the lowest educational attainment of women is in the village of Mardin followed by Trabzon, Kırşehir and Kırklareli, respectively.

The relation between LFP and women's status indicates an interesting pattern. In the villages of Mardin and Trabzon where the level of education is the lowest, woman's LFP and labor load are the highest. In the village of Mardin, women are seen as property. Girls are not counted as children and are not educated. Men beat

Table 7
Female Labor Force Participation in Four
Turkish Villages (Ages 12 and Over)

| | Unemployed | | Employed | | |
| | | | | Wage | Family |
	Total	Unemployed	Total	Laborer	Laborer
Mardin	100	54.9	45.1	(36.1)	(09.0)
Trabzon	100	13.9	86.1	(09.2)	(76.9)
Kırşehir	100	52.1	47.9	(16.5)	(31.4)
Kırklareli	100	16.1	83.9	(06.2)	(77.7)

Source: The 1975 Hacettepe Rural Survey Data

Table 8
School Attendance in Four Turkish Villages
(Ages 12 and Over) (Figures in Percent)

| | Primary Graduates | | | Secondary Attendance or Higher | | |
	Male	Female	Diff.	Male	Female	Diff.
Mardin	38.7	01.6	37.1	07.9	0.8	07.1
Trabzon	73.1	28.9	44.2	19.3	1.5	17.8
Kırşehir	80.8	48.1	32.7	17.5	3.5	14.0
Kırklareli	75.9	61.2	14.7	08.8	7.3	01.5

Source: The 1975 Hacettepe Rural Survey Data

women frequently and this is considered natural.. All these observations clearly indicate that women's status is very low. In the village of Trabzon, similar observations are reported. Women do heavy labor, and men are busy playing cards in coffee-houses or drinking most of the time.

Type 3 and Type 4 families are in the majority in the villages of Mardin and Trabzon where women are in charge of agricultural production. Men are either unemployed or engage in temporary work, so they try to overcome the gap by greater physical force, showing off, and overvaluing themselves. In the villages of Kırşehir and Kırklareli, however, men's role in society is more defined and their relations with women are not as authoritarian as in the other two villages. In the village of Kırklareli women's appearance and behavior are similar to those of urban women.

Figure 1.   Attendance in Secondary or Higher Level Schools

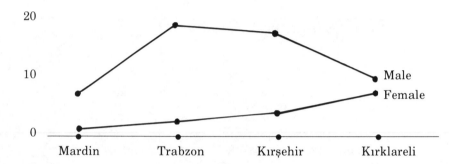

Figure 2.   Primary School Graduates

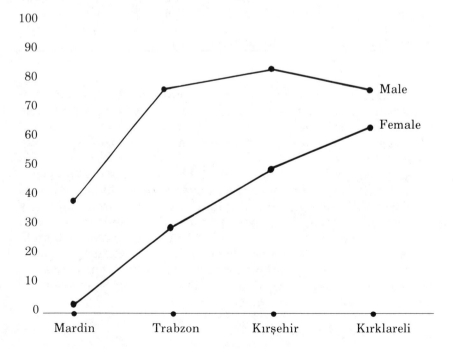

Conclusions

It may be concluded that education *per se* does not have an impact on female LFP in the four villages. On the contrary, certain kinds of land ownership and agricultural production which necessitate a heavy involvement of women in agricultural work create obstacles for their education.

The proportions on the national scale of the rural types referred to above were estimated by the author from land distribution and rural occupational data derived from the 1973 Hacettepe University Survey.[2] According to these estimates, the distribution of the types is as follows: 9.7% of the households are in the landless wage laborers category (Type 4); 39.9% are small producers or rural marginals (Type 3); 28.4% are in the medium size independent producer category (Type 2); 8.4% are large land enterprises (Type 1); and finally 13.6% are rural-dwelling but primarily non-agricultural employees.

A critical issue from the point of view of women's status is how these types will evolve through social change. The current trends suggest that independent producers on land will decline and join the ranks of landless laborers, become marginal, or migrate to town centers (Tekeli, 1977). The implication of this is that the division of labor between the sexes in agricultural production will increasingly resemble the pattern we now observe for "feminized agriculutural production." This will mean that the educational gap between the sexes in rural Turkey is likely to increase despite the overall increase in the level of rural education (both male and female). Furthermore, this will not increase women's status. As noted previously, women's participation in the labor force is associated with low status.

A shift in agricultural production, on the other hand, will mean an overall drop in female LFP with continuing migration to large cities and spreading of non-agricultural occupations.

Our data suggest that it is misleading and even impossible to discuss the relationship of education and labor force participation of women outside the context of property and the agricultural production of the rural areas. The proportion and composition of rural types is primarily a function of the capitalization of agriculture of any society. Hence an analysis of rural women's status depends essentially on the correct identification of the structural properties of the developing country under consideration.

NOTES

[1] This essay is based to a large extent on a paper delivered at the 9th World Congress of Sociology, Uppsala, Sweden, 14-19 August, 1978.

[2] Varlıer (1978) published the tabulations on which the estimations are based.

BIBLIOGRAPHY

Boserup, Ester. *Women's Role in Economic Development*. New York: St. Martin's Press, 1970.

Buvinic, Mayra. "A Critical Review of Some Research Concepts and Concerns." In *Women in Development: An Annotated Bibliography*. Overseas Development Council, 1976, pp. 1-20.

Castillo, Gelia T. "The Changing Role of Women in Rural Societies: A Summary of Trends and Issues." In *A/D/C Seminar Report*, No. 12. The Agricultural Development Council, Inc., 1977.

Chaney, Elsa M. and Marianne Schmink. "Women and Modernization: Access to Tools." In June Nash and Helen Icken Safa (eds.), *Sex and Class in Latin America*. New York: Praeger, 1977, pp. 160-82.

Deere, Carmen D. "Rural Women's Subsistence Production in the Capitalist Periphery." In *The Review of Radical Political Economics*, 8, 1, 9-17.

Engels, Frederick. *The Origin of the Family, Private Property and the State in Light of the Researches of Lews H. Morgan*. New York: 1942.

Ergil, Gül. *Toplumsal Yapı Araştırması: Nüfus ile İlgili Gelişmeler*. Ankara: State Planning Office, 1977.

Kandiyoti, Deniz. "Social Change and Social Stratification in a Turkish Village," *The Journal of Peasant Societies*, 1, 4.

Kazgan, Gülten. "Labor Force Participation, Occupational Distribution, Educational Attainment and the Socio-Economic Status of Women." In Nermin Abadan-Unat (ed.), *Women in Turkish Society*. Ankara: Turkish Social Science Association Publication, 1979.

Özbay, Ferhunde. "The Impact of Education on Women in Rural and Urban Turkey." In Abadan-Unat (ed.), ibid.

―――― and Nefise Balamir. "School Attendance and its Correlates in Turkish Villages." Mimeograph presented to Hacettepe Institute of Population Studies International Development Research Center, 1977.

Sanday, Peggy R. "Toward a Theory of the Status of Women," *American Anthropologist*. 1973, 75, 1682-1700.

Statistical Year Book. Ankara: State Institute of Statistics, 1973.

The 1975 Population Census, 1% Sampling Results. Ankara: State Institute of Statistics, 1976.

Tekçe, B. *Türkiye'de Şehirlere Göçler 1955-60 ve 1960-65 Dönemlerine Ait Tahminler*. Ankara: DİE Publications, 1975.

Tekeli, İlhan. *Bağımlı Kentleşme: Kırda ve Kentte Dönüşüm Süreci*. Ankara: Chamber of Architectures, 1977.

Varlier, Oktay. *Türkiye Tarımında Yapısal Değişme, Teknoloji ve Toprak Bölüşümü*.

SEX ROLES, VALUE OF CHILDREN AND FERTILITY

Çiğdem Kâğıtçıbaşı

The child is the core of the family and society, through whom they perpetuate themselves. Therefore, understanding the value given to the child and the role he/she is assigned in the family teaches us a great deal about a society. The place of the child within the family reflects both family structure and social structure and is, therefore, affected by any changes in them. This essay examines the values attributed to children and their relation to fertility in the context of social change in Turkey. The family and sex roles will be focal points of interest as they inherently affect the perceived values of children and, consequently, fertility behavior. The chapter reports on the findings of the Turkish Value of Children (VOC) study,[1] conducted by the author.

The concept of the value of children has entered into various conceptualizations of fertility in the past few decades. A focus on the value of children has been noticeable especially in the economic and social-psychological orientations to fertility.[2]

The economic interpretation views the individual as trying to maximize his satisfactions. In this context children are considered to be a particular type of good. The study of fertility in the developing countries has focused mainly on the production function of children, and thus has emphasized their economic value—so much so that the value of children has been equated with their economic value for the family. Within the social psychological framework, however, the value of children for parents assumes importance in terms of the motivational dynamics underlying fertility. As various needs may be satisfied by children, a variety of values may be attributed to them. Theoretical frameworks for a social psychological approach have been provided by Fawcett (1972), Hoffman and Hoffman (1973), and Berelson (1973). Based mainly on the Hoffman and Hoffman scheme, the VOC study has contributed to further theoretical development in this area (Arnold, et al., 1975; Fawcett, 1976; Kağıtçıbaşı, 1979, 1981 and 1982; Bulatao, 1979a and 1979b).

The concept of the value of children (VOC) is used in the VOC study as a key causal variable that is postulated to change along with social change and to affect fertility accordingly. It is conceptualized as the perceived benefits minus costs that parents obtain from having children. These benefits and costs, in turn, are viewed as multidimensional, complex variables, including three dimensions, namely, psychological, social and economic. The VOCs are further conceptualized as intervening between antecedent background and social psychological variables and the consequent fertility-related outcome. Figure 1 presents the conceptual framework underlying the Turkish VOC Study. Thus, a further refinement is brought to the commonly observed (causal) relationship between socio-economic development and decreased fertility by introducing the concept of the perceived value of children. The understanding is that, with social change and development, the needs are satisfied by children; thus, functions of children change. This is reflected in modifications in the values attributed to children, and consequently in the numbers of children desired, eventually affecting fertility.

An implicit decision-making model is being used here, as there is an underlying assumption that advantages and disadvantages of having children are weighed against each other. However, a lot of uncontrolled variation may enter this model. Especially in the traditional context, restrictive social norms, fatalistic tendencies, ignorance, etc. can interfere with personal preferences. Such variation would preclude prediction, and it is indicated by the element of uncertainty in Figure 1. However, this does not mean that people do not have any choices or preferences or that they are not aware of alternatives in such an important matter as child-bearing. Alternatives do not have to be rationally and explicitly calculated in order to enter into some form of a decision-making process, and especially *not* to have a child requires an active choice. Thus, even though rational explicit decision-making may be lacking, at least an implicit decision-making is assumed.

Figure 1: Theoretical Model of The Turkish VOC Study

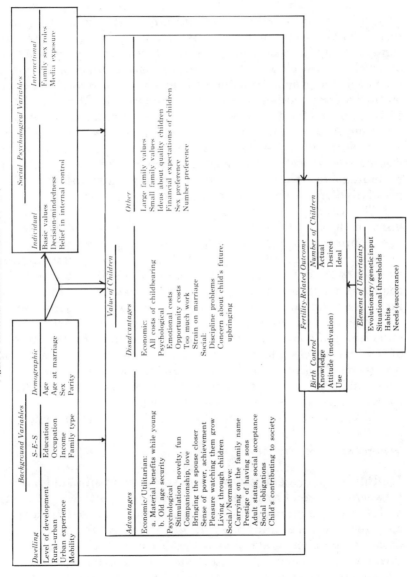

Method

In the Turkish VOC study lengthy interviews were conducted in 1975 with a nationally representative sample of 2305 married respondents, 1762 females and 543 males.[3] Multi-stage stratified random sampling was used, with stratification being done in terms of levels of development. Three different groups of provinces, namely developed, intermediate and less developed, were delineated on the basis of composite socio-economic indices (D.P.T., 1972, pp. 12-15 and 54-59). In addition, the three metropolitan areas of Istanbul, Ankara and Izmir were treated as a "self-representative area." Within the three levels of development the urban populations were further stratified into four strata in terms of their populations, excluding again the three metropolitan areas. Rural areas having a population of less than 2000 comprised the fifth stratum.

The criteria for eligibility included being married, the upper age limit of 40 for the wife and the spouses living together. The questionnaire used in the national survey was developed on the basis of experience with the previous Turkish pilot questionnaire as well as with the questionnaire applications in the other VOC countries. A core questionnaire was thus developed in order to allow for cross-national comparisons. In final form the questionnaire contained 103 questions. The topics covered were: parity, desired and ideal numbers of children, values and costs of children, number of sex preferences, ideas about "quality children," general values, financial expectations from children, birth control (attitudes, knowledge and use), decision contexts (belief in internal vs. external control of reinforcement), sex roles, education and occupation, mobility, mass-media participation, family type and income.

General Characteristics

Fifty-two percent of the women respondents had married between the ages of 15 and 17. Twenty-nine percent were between 18 and 20 at first marriage and 16% married either at less than 15 years of age or between 21 and 23. Marriages at 24-26 were only 2% and all those at later ages totaled a mere 1%.[4] These figures, pointing to the predominantly early age of marriage for women in Turkey, have significant implications both for fertility and for women's status in Turkey.

Education levels were found to be quite low, a finding substantiated by other national survey results as well (e.g. Tuncer, 1976, p.

106). Forty-six percent of the females and 13% of the males had no formal schooling. Twenty-eight percent of the females and 45% of the males were primary school graduates. Only 6% of the females and 13% of the males had a high school education or more. The mean number of school years attended was 2.87 for women and 5.27 for men. Urban–rural differences in mean school years were marked: 6.18 and 4.03 years, respectively, for men; 3.6 and 1.77 years, respectively, for women. Those who never attended school were 38% of women in the urban areas and 58% in the rural areas, the corresponding figures being 10% and 17% for men. The marked sex differential in education, a common finding in the Middle East (Timur, 1977), has obvious implications for the status of women.

Seventy percent of the women were not working;[5] of these 52% had worked some of the time since marriage. Of those who were working, 54.6% were family workers, not earning money, but contributing to the family income. Thirteen percent of the women and 18% of the men were unskilled laborers. A higher percentage of women was working as landless agricultural laborers (9.5%), compared with men (2.8%); more men, on the other hand, were industrial workers (10%) than women (1%). Greater percentages of men were entrepreneurs, salaried skilled workers and government employees. However, some professions demanding university education were similarly distributed among men and women, though both rated very low.

In line with low levels of education and professionalization, low family incomes were reported, the mean income corresponding roughly to the subsistence level. This probably reflects only actual cash income and not additional income in goods.

Three main family type categories were delineated with subcategories within each. These are nuclear, patriarchally extended, and transient extended (Timur, 1972). Whether a family is of the patriarchally extended or transient extended family types depends on whether the household head is the married son or his father. The latter case is typically a patriarchally extended family, whereas the former is a transient extended family which is on its way to becoming a nuclear family. Patriarchally extended families comprised 12.9%, and transient extended, 8.5% of the families; nuclear families were 78.6%.

Over half of the respondents showed no mobility or linear mobility (57.3%). Thirty-seven percent were rural peasants without any urban experience, and 37% were urban residents without any rural experience.

The number of living children (parity) ranged from 0 to 13, the mean being 2.9. Sixty-nine percent of the respondents had 1 to 4 children, while only 18% had more. Those without children comprised 13% of the total. Forty-three percent of the female respondents had children who died after live birth and 36% had pregnancies not resulting in live birth. Marked urban–rural differences were found, the mean parities being 2.58 and 3.16, respectively.

Mean desired number of children was found to be 3.2 (3.1 for women and 3.3 for men) and ideal number of children was 2.7 (2.6 for women; 2.9 for men). Even though Turkey is a high fertility country, with a crude birth rate of 39 per thousand in 1976 (as indicated by Population Reference Bureau, 1976), the above figures indicate small family norms and values closer to those in moderate fertility countries, as also noted by others (Bulatao, 1979; Berelson and Mauldin, 1978; Özbay and Shorter, 1970).

The above descriptive characteristics draw a general picture of social change together with widespread problems especially of low education and income levels. Women are further disadvantaged due to their even lower education and young age at marriage. Early marriage interferes with education and increases the child-bearing period of the woman, which contributes to her high fertility. Having many children, in turn, keeps the woman tied down and thus unavailable for non-child-bearing functions outside the home. Also, mere young age of the bride contributes to her low status in her husband's household, thus reinforcing the traditional intra-family status hierarchy.

General Values and Family Dynamics

General life orientations were assessed in the VOC Study by presenting a number of basic values to the respondents and asking about the importance of each (Table 1).

The most important sex difference was found in "being close to spouse," which is highly important for women but not for men. This indicates that women value their relationship with their spouses more than men do. It has been noted in anthropological observations, also, that men's most valued relationships are with people outside the home (Stirling, 1965), especially with their male kin. Indeed, men stress values implying social recognition, such as "achievement" and being "accepted by others," more than women do (Table 1). Men also endorse more traditional values related to fertility, such as "to be remembered after death" and "continuation of family name," the latter implying a preference for male offspring.

Table 1
Most Important Values*

	Men %	Women %	Relative Weight
To Have a Happy Home	43.1	57.3	51
To Be Close to Spouse	19.2	62.5	40
Financial Security	32.5	28.7	30
Carry on Family Name	28.8	15.7	23
To Be Remembered After Death	22.0	15.7	19
To Achieve Something, To Succeed	18.0	05.7	12
To Be Accepted By Others	21.8	06.3	14
Not To Be Alone, To Have Friends	09.5	04.9	07
To Have Fun and Entertainment	04.9	03.4	05

(x^2 significant at beyond the .001 level)

* In this table and the following ones, more than one response was coded for each respondent; thus, percentages may add up to more than 100.

Thus, together with generally held widespread values, such as "having a happy home," there are also sex differences in general values, reflecting differences in outlooks on life and experiences of men and women.

A clear cut sex difference also appeared in belief in internal versus external control of reinforcement,[6] women demonstrating greater belief in external control. This finding replicates an earlier one with high school girls in Turkey (Kâğıtçıbaşı, 1973). These sex differences are probably due to the different socialization environments of boys and girls where more external control is in fact exerted on girls and where boys enjoy more freedom of action. The implication of this finding for varying degrees of individual modernity and differences in world views and roles of men and women are obvious. The emerging picture, at the national level, reflects the adverse condition of women both in terms of their low levels of autonomy and self-perceived efficacy and also in terms of the values they attach to their relations with their spouses.

Some aspects of family dynamics were assessed, namely decision making, role sharing and communication between spouses (Table 2).

The consistently high frequency with which both men and women report greater male decision making at home is noteworthy and fits in with the findings mentioned above. Low levels of role sharing and communication between spouses complete the picture.

Table 2
Family Dynamics and Sex Roles
Intra-Family Decision Making:
  1. Who decides about buying something expensive?
  2. Who decides about how many children to have?
  3. Who decides about using birth control?

	Women %			Men %			General %	
	Woman Decides	Together	Man Decides	Woman Decides	Together	Man Decides	Woman Decides	Together	Man Decides
1.	09.5	17.3	73.1	03.2	13.5	83.4	06	15	78
2.	16.0	33.2	50.7	05.8	32.1	62.2	11	33	56
3.	28.2	35.7	36.1	17.2	44.2	38.6	23	39	37

Communication and Role Sharing:
  1. Have you talked with your spouse about how many children he/she wants?
  2. Do you do things together with your spouse outside the house?
  3. Does your spouse help with the housework?

	Yes %			No %		
	Women	Men	General	Women	Men	General
1.	63.8	56.0	60	36.2	44.0	40
2.	61.8	61.8	62	38.2	38.2	38
3.	54.7	77.5	66	45.3	22.5	34

Spouse Assistance:
  How often does the spouse help?

Never %			Rarely %			Sometimes %			Regularly %		
Women	Men	General	Women	Men	General	Women	Men	General	Women	Men	General
45.3	22.5	34	12.5	17.3	15	32.1	53	43	10.1	7.3	09

Among all the nine VOC countries, the highest levels of male decision making and lowest levels of communication and role sharing are found in Turkey (Kâğıtçıbaşı, 1979). It would not be correct to attribute this situation to the influence of Islam, per se, as great inter-spouse communication and role sharing are found in Indonesia, also a Muslim nation. Middle Eastern and Mediterranean historical/cultural influences are also important for the situation in Turkey.

These findings describe the family context in relation to which other findings of the Turkish VOC study should be interpreted. They reflect the traditional intra-family sex role segregation and low status of women in Turkey, and they concur with previous research and observations (e.g. Kâğıtçıbaşı, 1973, 1975, and 1979; Kandiyoti, 1977; Abadan-Unat, 1976; Kıray, 1976; Fallers and Fallers, 1976; Meeker, 1976; Magnarella, 1974).

Values of Children (VOCs)

Within the conceptual framework of the VOC Study, perceived values of children underlie fertility behavior. Thus, it is important to understand which of these values are more prevalent and how they relate to background variables and to the fertility outcome. Two open-ended questions about the advantages and disadvantages of having children produced a great variety of spontaneous answers grouped into the categories indicated in Figure 1.[7] Advantages are presented in Table 3 in a coded form.

The spontaneously expressed advantages of having children comprise economic/utilitarian, psychological and social/normative values, in line with our hypotheses deriving from the theoretical conceptualization of the VOC Study (Figure 1). Both economic contribution at young ages and support in the future are very important values. Psychological value is perceived in children providing companionship, love and joy and strengthening the marital bond. The social/normative value, which is not stressed as much, is mainly reflected in children continuing the family name and contributing to society, with implications for preference for sons. The very high salience of old age security value of the child when combined with material contributions at young ages reflects a general utilitarian outlook. This utilitarian approach to children involves heavy demands and expectations of support put on them in a context of interdependent family ties, as will be discussed later.

A similar pattern of multidimensional values also appears in reasons given for wanting another child (Table 4).

Here, again, the "old age security" value of the child is stressed. As this value is emphasized for wanting additional children, it appears to be associated with high numbers of children and high fertility. An important sex difference emerges for wanting another child "to bring the spouse closer to self," being of much greater

Table 3
Advantages of Having Children

	Relative Weight %	Male %	Female %
Help from Children	145		
Help in housework	19	16	25
Help in old age	79	70	91
Financial and practical help	47	50	40
For Family, God and Country	48		
Family name, family line	20	24	15
Religious and social obligations	28	38	13
For Our Marriage	21		
Marital bond, home life	21	17	25
To Show People	24		
Adult status, social norms	24	24	23
Companions, Playmates	78		
Companionship, love	29	19	41
Play, fun, distraction	49	53	42
Living Through Children	6		
Living through children	6	6	5
Children Are an Accomplishment	20		
Achievement, power	20	18	26
Character, Fulfillment, Experience	10		
Incentive to succeed	2	3	0
Fulfillment	8	7	9
Miscellaneous	49	52	43

importance for women than for men. This finding is in line with the previously discussed basic values and orientations. Thus, in the traditional context where the relationship with the husband is more valuable for the woman, she finds an additional child functional in "bringing him back home." Indeed, some women expressed the wish to bring the husband back from the coffeehouse to the home, thus stressing the separateness of men's and women's worlds. A new baby could possibly bring these worlds together. This appears to be an important function of childbearing which does not find much recognition in fertility literature.

Wanting another child to carry on the family name and to have a (another) boy are fertility-prone traditional social/normative

Table 4

Most Important Reasons for Wanting Another Child

	Male	%	Female	%
1. To have someone for you to love and care for.	05.7	(13.1)*	04.9	(10.6)*
2. So that there will be one more person to help economically	12.8	(25.7)	12.9	(22.8)
3. Because you want to have a [another] boy.	12.1	(22.1)	15.5	(22.8)
4. To provide a companion for your child [children].	03.2	(06.5)	03.6	(08.6)
5. Because another child would give your husband/you more reason to succeed in his/your work.	02.9	(06.5)	01.2	(02.8)
6. To be sure that in old age you will have someone to help you	14.3	(31.6)	22.0	(39.8)
7. To have a child to help around the house.	01.8	(08.8)	02.4	(11.9)
8. Because of the pleasure you get out of watching children grow.	07.4	(15.9)	04.0	(11.6)
9. To bring your husband/wife and yourself closer together.	09.4	(18.5)	17.7	(32.3)
10. Because you want to have a [another] girl.	03.6	(06.7)	05.7	(10.5)
11. To help carry on your family name.	22.2	(31.3)	06.3	(14.4)
12. Because it is fun to have young children around the house.	04.6	(13.2)	03.8	(12.0)

* Combined frequency of first and second most important reasons.

values stressed more by men. The preference for male children is equally important for women also, [but not so much for preserving the family name]. For women, the status value of bearing a son is probably more salient. This would be the case especially in the traditional context where a woman's status is defined mainly by her age and (male) children, as has been substantiated by much anthropological research in Turkey (e.g., Stirling, 1965; Meeker, 1976).

A related closed-ended question inquired into the reasons for not wanting *less* than the expressed desired number of children. The most relevant reason for women is that children strengthen the marital bond (52%; 29% for men), and for men, their providing financial and other help (47%; 29% for women). This sex difference is in line with the different sex roles and the corresponding needs of men and women. The greater importance of the marital bond for the woman reflects her inferior position within this bond; thus she needs to attribute to her children the value (function) of strengthening this bond.

Fear of child loss and replacement value of the child are of high relevance for both men (37%) and women (35%). This fear may be realistic in view of the high infant mortality rate in Turkey (119%).[8] The concern to have some surviving children in old age was expressed often in the interviews.

The multi-dimensional nature of VOCs as proposed in our model (Figure 1) was also reflected in the results of a factor analysis done on the reasons given for wanting another child.[9] Three factors were clearly differentiated from one another, as indicated below.

a) Economic/utilitarian VOC factor:
   2—"to have one more person to help family economically"
   6—"to be sure to have someone to help you in old age"
   7—"to have a child to help around the house"

b) Psychological VOC factor:
   8—"because of the pleasure you get out of watching children grow"
   9—"to bring your (husband/wife) and you closer together"
   12—"because it is fun to have young children around the house"

c) Social/normative VOC factor:
   11—"to help carry on your family name"
   3—"because you want to have (another) boy"

Thus the validity of our multidimensional conceptualization of the value of children found empirical support in various findings of the study. Accordingly, a simple view of the child's value as, for example, being only economic, would seem unwarranted. The multidimensional nature of the VOC becomes especially important in terms of its relations with other variables. This is because the relations to be expected between economic VOC, development and fertility variables should be different from those between psychological VOC, development and fertility.

Socio-Economic Development and VOCs

One of the basic hypotheses of the VOC study is that with socio-economic development, economic VOC would decrease and psychological VOC would increase. In the analyses designed to test this hypothesis, various indicators of development were used.

One indicator is the sampling criterion used, as explained before, to differentiate least, medium and most developed areas and metropolitan centers. The results based on simple cross-tabulations indicate that as the level of development increases, the salience of "old-age security" value of children decreases (100% in least developed; 73% in medium developed; 61% in developed; 40% in metropolitan areas), but companionship value of children (psychological value) increases (20% in least; 26% in medium; 32% in developed; 51% in metropolitan areas). The sense of accomplishment derived from children shows a similar increase in salience with development (16%, 18%, 20% and 43% from least to most developed areas, respectively). The "material help" value of children, on the other hand, decreases in salience as development increases, mainly at the metropolitan level (45%, 61%, 45%, 18%, respectively). When only women's responses are considered, the above relationships are intensified, indicating that women are affected by socio-economic development even more than men. (From least to most developed, "old age security": 100%, 89%, 74%, 47%; "companionship" value: 33%, 32%, 50%, 63%; "sense of accomplishment": 12%, 34%, 20%, 42%; "material help": 59%, 44%, 29%, 18%.)

Education as another indicator of socio-economic development also related differentially to the VOCs. Specifically, economic/utilitarian values such as "helping with housework" and "material help" decrease with education (28% and 56%, respectively, at no education level; 22% and 54% at primary school level; 11% and 15% at high school level; and 0% and 20% at university level). The "old age security" value, on the other hand, keeps its very high salience up to the high school level (above 80%), dropping drastically (to 16%) at the university level. University education seems to play a key role in changing other values as well, specifically in increasing such psychological values as providing "companionship," "accomplishment," "character and responsibility development" (from 33% to 43%, from 23% to 51% and from 12% to 29%, respectively, from high school to university level).

When women's education is considered separately the relationships are again intensified. For example, the "old-age security" value loses salience for women at the high school level, as well, and the "companionship" VOC gains greater salience with women's education (94%, 100%, 50% and 38%, and 33%, 41%, 64% and 69%, respectively, from no education, through primary school, high school to university levels). As the general level of education is very low for women, having some education makes more of a difference for them than it does for men.

Unpredicted relationships were obtained between women's work and VOCs. Specifically, working women, more than non-working, stress economic/utilitarian values, such as "old-age security," "financial help" and "help in housework" (95%, 57%, 31%, respectively, for working women; 65%, 36%, 8%, respectively, for non-working women). Psychological values of children, on the other hand, are emphasized more by non-working women. (The respective figures for working and non-working women are 24% and 37% for the "companionship" value and 48% and 54% for the "joy, enjoyment" value.)

Women's work is usually considered to be an indicator of development and modernization. Yet these results point to the need to consider the *type* of work women do. This is because, as indicated before, what constitutes "work" in the case of women is not clear (even though more than half of women work, only 30% are cash earners). Furthermore, as female education and consequently occupational specialization levels are low, women's work often reflects economic necessity rather than socio-economic development. Thus, for most working women, their work brings neither status nor adequate remuneration, thus it is not a social mobilizer. Professionalization of women, however, involving both education and economic autonomy, does make a difference (see Kâğıtçıbaşı, 1981). In this context, the above findings make sense. Indeed, among women, the "old-age security" value of children is stressed most strongly by unpaid family workers (100%) and then by small shop owners and artisans (91%) (a typically "traditional" group) but is found to be less important by wage-earners (around 50%) and least important by white collar workers (19–37%). This finding shows that when employment provides old-age security, the contribution of children to satisfy this need loses importance. A similar pattern appears for men, also.

In addition to the general VOC discussed above, specific values associated with preference for boys were also predicted to change with socio-economic development. Specifically, the importance of reasons for wanting a boy—especially economic/utilitarian reasons—are hypothesized to decrease with development, and this is found to be the case. (From least developed areas to metropolitan centers, "material help" reasons decrease from 100% to 56%.) The "old-age security" reason shows a similar decrease with development for men (from 65% to 23%) but not for women, indicating that in spite of development, women have less guarantee of old age support than men.

The "old-age security" and "material help" values of sons also lose importance with education. Women's education again is a stronger "modernizer" ("old-age security" drops from 63% at no education down to 9% at university for women, compared with 46% to 12% for men). Conversely, the "companionship" value of sons (a psychological value) increases in salience with women's education but not with men's; it also gains importance with development of the area, again especially for women. Carrying on the family name, a social value of sons, keeps its high salience for men through different development levels (above 80%). Thus different reasons for wanting sons are differentially related to sex of the parent and to development. As predicted, economic/utilitarian values of sons lose importance whereas their psychological values of sons have greater salience for women, whereas sons' social/normative value is more important for men.

Further analysis of the relation between VOCs and development variables used empirically derived VOCs (obtained by the previously-mentioned factor analysis). Considering first the urban–rural dimension, the economic/utilitarian value factor is found to be of much greater importance in rural than in urban settings. The psychological value factor, however, is of greater importance for women than for men regardless of the setting; for men it is higher in urban areas. These findings fit with the ones previously discussed. Similarly, it is found that as development increases, the importance of economic/utilitarian values for wanting another child decreases, especially for women. By contrast, the importance of psychological values *increases* with development. For men the social/normative value does not change with development, though it decreases for women. These findings, showing meaningful relations in the expected direction between development/urbanization and VOCs, support the basic hypothesis of the VOC Study, namely, with development economic VOC decreases and psychological VOC increases.

Finally, correlations between VOCs and various development indices were also done. The results generally concur with the previous ones and support the basic hypothesis. Specifically, the negative correlations between social/normative and especially economic/utilitarian VOCs and development indices and education are noteworthy and fit our expectations.

Thus, it is clear that through social change and development the way children are perceived and the values attributed to them change in a systematic way. This change is not a general decline in the value of the child as claimed by those who consider the value of the child to be mainly economic (e.g. Youssef makes such a claim for the Middle East, 1978, pp. 95 and 97). It is, rather, a qualitative change in the total value attributed to the child, mainly as a result of a decrease in the economic value and an increase in the psychological value of the child.

Parity and VOCs

Another hypothesis of the study claims a positive association between parity (number of living children) and economic/utilitarian VOC and a negative association between parity and psychological VOC. It was found, indeed, that both "old age security" and "material help" values gain in salience with parity (50% and 28%, respectively at parity of 1; 69% and 49% at 2; 68% and 47% at 3; and 100% and 60% at 4 or more parity levels). Thus, economic/utilitarian VOC appears to be cumulative, in the sense that each additional child is a source of additional income especially at high parity levels. "Companionship" or psychological VOC, on the other hand, loses importance with parity (40% at parity of 1; 31% at 2; 22% at 3; and 23% at 4 or more). In other words, 1 or 2 children may provide just as much satisfaction to parents as 4 or more children. Indeed, the reverse is found to be the case as the worry and burden of many children may interfere with the psychological satisfaction they provide. Thus, for example, the "play, fun and distraction" value of children drop drastically with 4 or more children (from 71% at parity of 3 down to 33% at parity of 4). Also negative correlations obtain between parity and psychological VOC (r=-.19) and psychological reasons for wanting another child (r=-.31), whereas positive correlations are found between parity and economic/utilitarian VOC (r=.14) and social/normative VOC (r=.12).

Values Attributed to Sons and Daughters

The perceived contribution of sons to basic values (discussed before) was found to be greater than that of daughters (Table 5).

Table 5

Contributions of Sons and Daughters to Important Values

	Women %			Men %		
	Daughter	Same	Son	Daughter	Same	Son
Financial security	03	18	80	06	15	79
To be accepted by others	18	36	44	02	20	78
To have fun and entertainment	(22)	(49)	(24)	(10)	(48)	(38)
To be close to spouse	11	42	47	34	40	26
Not to be alone, to have friends	36	36	31	(20)	(37)	(46)
To achieve something, to succeed	16	58	27	10	31	61
To be remembered after death	27	45	28	10	35	55
To have a happy home	11	54	36	05	53	43
Carry on family name	04	18	78	04	11	85
All values	12	42	46	10	34	56

The figures in Table 5 provide insight into the respective places of boys and girls in the family; they also throw light on the reasons for son preference.

Sex differences are also apparent in desired future qualities of children. Specifically, "be good to parents, respectful and loyal" is more highly salient and desired for boys (52%, 34% for girls). This utilitarian value reflects dependence on sons as the main source of support, especially in old age. "To be a good spouse, to have a happy marriage," on the other hand, is desired more for girls (58%; 12% for boys), reflecting widespread acceptance of the home-making role of women. Indeed, even though education is desired for both sons and daughters (58% and 50%, respectively), professional achievement is aspired to much more for boys (51%; 20% for girls). Thus expressed aspirations for girls do not imply drastic changes in traditional sex roles. This may underlie the endurance and stability of sex roles and stereotypes noted in other research results (e.g. Kâğıtçıbaşı and Kansu, 1976-77).

Specific expectations of help from boys are also greater than those from girls, in line with the above. Sons more than daughters are expected "to give part of their salary to parents when they start to work," "to help support their younger brothers and sisters through school," "to contribute money in family emergencies," and "to support parents financially when they grow old." Only "household help" is expected more of girls than of boys.

Thus where social security is lacking and social welfare institutions are inadequate, their functions are undertaken by adult-age children, especially sons. Together with this objective situation go high values put on closely knit interpersonal ties and interdependence, rather than independence, which is valued in the context of high level of economic development where adequate institutional support is available in old age, as found in Germany and the U.S. among the VOC countries.

This interdependence first takes the form of the child's dependence on parents and then, in old age, the parents' dependence on the grown-up offspring. The child's dependence, rather than independence, is valued, as apparent from a question asking about the desired attributes of children. Sixty percent of the respondents endorsed "the child's obeying his parents" as the most (or second most) desirable attribute of a child, compared with 18% who endorsed "the child's being independent and self-reliant." When this is considered together with the highly salient future desired attribute of "being good and loyal to parents," we see a home environment conducive to the socialization of familistic and communal values of mutual support rather than individualistic achievement. This is reflected in various expressions of respondents, such as, "if my son is worthy of his family and his family name, *of course* he will take care of us when we get old," "a loyal son would never let down his parents." Interdependence is, thus, a requisite for family honor as well as for family survival in the context of underdevelopment, whereas in the highly developed technological society with its social welfare institutions, independence is so valued that it would be hard to admit one's dependency on one's children.[10]

A high level of material expectations from children, furthermore, is associated with sex differentiation and son preference in the traditional context because males are usually the "breadwinners," and thus more dependable sources of financial support. Indeed, among the VOC countries differential expectations from sons and daughters are most marked in Turkey and Korea, countries where son preference is widespread.

On a forced-choice question, son preference was found to be 84%, as contrasted with a daughter preference of 16% (92.5% among men; 75% among women). Such a strong son preference is understandable in terms of what has been discussed before and in terms of reasons for wanting a son or a daughter (Table 6).

Table 6
Reasons for Wanting a Son or a Daughter

	SONS		DAUGHTERS	
	Men %	Women %	Men %	Women %
1. Help in housework	06.4	09.1	85.2	87.9
2. Caring for other children	01.0	01.1	—	—
3. Help in old age	54.1	56.1	—	—
4. Financial and practical help	70.6	77.2	—	—
5. Family name, family line	48.2	26.5	05.0	01.0
6. Religious and social obligations	39.3	20.2	06.1	01.2
7. Marital bond, homelife	00.4	01.2	11.7	04.2
10. Companionship, love	35.9	52.4	99.0	144.5
12. Play, fun, distraction	—	—	—	03.8
13. Companion for child	—	2.4	03.8	01.6
14. Living through children	04.5	07.9	22.9	11.2
15. Achievement, power	16.6	15.5	—	03.2
18. Fulfillment	00.9	00.6	06.4	01.0
19. Less expensive	—	—	02.4	08.2
20. Easier to raise	13.2	19.1	04.9	09.2
22. Miscellaneous	09.1	10.7	52.3	23.2

Spontaneously given reasons, presented in a coded form in Table 6, show that sons are wanted for numerous reasons, whereas there are fewer reasons for wanting daughters.

Sons are wanted in spite of their higher emotional and economic costs. Forty-four of the respondents indicate that sons cost more economically, compared with 20% claiming higher costs for daughters. The respective figures are 33% and 18% for emotional costs. The higher costs of sons can be seen as greater indulgence in sons, or as higher investment for higher expected returns, as discussed before.

The companionship value of the daughter for the mother is expressed often by the respondents and reflects the importance of the emotional support function of the daughter for the mother. Such support from her daughter and from other close women relatives and friends may help the woman endure her low status and hard work within the traditional family context (Kâğıtçıbaşı, 1980; Stirling, 1965; Olson-Prather, 1976).

These findings all show clear cut differences in expectations and preferences indicating sex role differentiation. They point to the different values attributed to sons and daughters and provide insight into the social-psychological context in which male and female children are socialized. It is this differential socialization which creates, justifies and perpetuates the hierarchical and separate worlds of men and women within the family.

VOCs, Family Dynamics and Fertility

It is found that boy preference and expectation of financial help from children decrease with increased intra-family status of the woman (r=-.12 and r=-.19, respectively). Woman's intra-family status, in turn, increases with socio-economic development (.14). Woman's status is also found to relate positively to belief in internal control (.16); and the latter, in turn, is negatively associated with boy preference (-.18), economic expectations from children (-.35), economic/utilitarian VOC (-.30) and social-normative VOC (-.36).

Similarly, ideal number of children and boy preference decrease among men with increased role sharing in the family (-.12 and -.11). Furthermore, male decision making in the family correlates positively with desired (.14) and ideal (.23) numbers of children and negatively with use (-.37) and approval of birth control (-.21) among men. Communication between spouses relates negatively to desired (-.11) and to ideal number of children (-.18); whereas it relates positively to birth control practice (.17) among women (among men, the correlations are -.15, -.16, and .22, respectively).

Thus, as intra-family relations become more egalitarian, fertility and fertility desires decrease. Furthermore, male decision making and low intra-family status of women are associated with economic/utilitarian VOC. As the economic VOC is, in turn, associated with high fertility, this VOC may be an explanatory link between family dynamics and fertility. In the context of egalitarian family relations, then, women have greater autonomy, efficacy and self-sufficiency; they are less dependent on their children and especially on their sons for economic support, hence the low salience of the economic VOC and the resultant low fertility. Authoritarian relations within the family, on the other hand, appear to be conducive to higher fertility.

VOCs and Fertility

One of the key hypotheses of the study is that values attributed to children explain some of the variance in fertility even when socio-economic development variables are held constant. Specifically, it is predicted that the economic VOC and boy preference are associated with high fertility, and psychological VOC is associated with low fertility. This hypothesis is the core of our social-psychological model focusing on the effect of values on fertility behavior, both in their own right and as intervening variables.

Among the variables used as indicators of fertility attitudes and behavior, parity, desired and ideal number of children, and approval and use of birth control entered various analyses. Relations between VOCs and wanting another child (for women) are presented in Table 7.

At different parity levels (number of existing children), VOCs are differentially related to wanting another child. Specifically, those women who stress economic/utilitarian VOC want another child even if they already have four or more children. By contrast, those who stress the psychological VOC want another child if they have few children (parity of one or two), but do not want more if they already have three or four. This finding, in itself, clearly shows the difference between economic and psychological VOCs in relation to fertility attitudes. Economic VOC appears to be closely associated with child numbers, whereas psychological VOC is not, as also discussed before. Here we find an explanatory link between two other findings: one, discussed before, is the decline of economic VOC and to some extent the increase of psychological VOC with development. The other, to be discussed later, is the common finding of

Table 7

VOC's and Wanting Additional Children

(Women %)

Parity:	0		1		2		3		4 or more	
Wanting additional children:	No	Yes	No	Yes	No	Yes	No	Yes	No	Yes
Econ./Utilitarian VOC Factor		N=220		N=283		N=344		N=325		N=546
Not important	48.2	29.9	50.5	38.4	69.1	34.2	60.1	37.3	46.7	10.4
Important	51.8	70.1	49.5	61.6	30.9	65.8	39.9	62.7	53.3	89.6
	x^2=.94		x^2=3.26		x^2=28.13		x^2=6.43		x^2=10.98	
	—		—		(p <.001)		(p <.02)		(p <.001)	
Psychological VOC Factor		N=220		N=283		N=344		N=325		N=546
Not important	26.7	10.8	49.7	31.5	65.0	45.4	63.9	61.4	64.2	50.7
Important	73.3	89.2	50.3	68.5	35.0	54.6	36.1	38.6	35.8	49.3
	x^2=1.33		x^2=8.00		x^2=8.42		x^2=.01		x^2=1.30	
	—		(p <.01)		(p <.01)		—		—	
Social/Normative VOC Factor		N=220		N=283		N=344		N=325		N=546
Not important	38.1	26.2	52.1	46.2	82.4	44.6	72.7	43.7	67.4	35.1
Important	61.9	73.8	47.9	53.8	17.6	55.4	27.3	56.3	32.6	64.9
	x^2=.29		x^2=.65		x^2=41.00		x^2=12.25		x^2=9.38	
	—		—		(p <.001)		(p <.001)		(p <.01)	

increased birth control and decreased parity with socio-economic development. In other words, at least to some degree, it is because economic and psychological VOCs are differentially affected by development and are also differentially related to desired child numbers that a decrease in fertility is seen with development. Our conceptualization and findings, thus, bring an explanatory refinement into this generally observed phenomenon, on which the "demographic transition theory" is based (Notestein, 1945; Caldwell, 1977).

Social normative VOC is similar to economic VOC (Table 7). Factor analysis indicates that this value is composed of son preference and carrying on the family name, so this finding is to be expected.

Further evidence for the proposed relationships between VOCs and fertility is provided by correlations utilizing indices. Economic/utilitarian VOC and social/normative VOC have positive correlations with parity (.14 and .12, respectively), desired number of children (.31 and .29) and ideal number of children (.20 each); they correlate negatively with approval of birth control (-.14 and -.11). On the other hand, psychological VOC correlates negatively with parity (-.19) and does not related to the others. Thus, though the correlations are not strong, they show systematic relations between different VOCs and fertility. Furthermore, when the effects of education and socio-economic development are controlled through partial correlations, negative relations between psychological VOCs and various fertility variables appear or become even greater, whereas the opposite effect is obtained for economic/utilitarian and social/normative VOCs. Thus, VOCs show predicted relations with fertility variables, independently of socio-economic variables.

Multiple regression results also provide support for the hypothesis that VOCs contribute to the variance in fertility when socio-economic variables are held constant (Tables 8 A-D).

In parity, together with the positive contribution of boy preference, VOC indices explain .08 of the variance (.16 of the explained .53). Among these, only the negative contribution of the psychological VOC reaches significance, explaining .06 of the total variance in parity (.12 of the explained .53). The fact that the psychological VOC has a negative effect on parity when other variables are controlled is an important finding that is in line with our theoretical approach. In other words, an increase in this value does not lead to high child numbers but rather has the opposite effect. Thus, the unidimensional conceptualization of the value of the child (as economic) and the

Table 8

A.) Multiple Regression Analysis Including Indices For Women
(Dependent Variable: PARITY)

Independent Variables	b	SE	R^2
Economic/Utilitarian VOC	not sig.	—	.009
Psychological VOC	-.059	(.016)**	.068
Social/Normative VOC	not sig.	—	.078
Development-Population	-.063	(.020)*	.093
Marriage duration	.166	(.009)**	.496
Husband's education	-.069	(.022)*	.511
Woman's status	.048	(.022)	.514
% Urban experience	-.003	(.001)	.519
Son Preference	.078	(.020)*	.534
TOTAL			.534

B.) Multiple Regression Analysis (Dependent Variable:
PRESENT USE OF BIRTH CONTROL)

Independent Variables	b	SE	R^2
Parity	.072	(.017)**	.031
Economic/Utilitarian VOC	-.035	(.011)**	.110
Psychological VOC	.017	(.007)	.119
Social/Normative VOC	not sig.	—	—
Education	.023	(.009)	.152
TOTAL			.163

C.) Multiple Regression Analysis (Dependent Variable:
DESIRED NUMBER OF CHIDLREN)

Independent Variables	b	SE	R^2
Parity	.323	(.034)**	.296
Economic/Utilitarian VOC	.077	(.019)**	.351
Psychological VOC	-.073	(.013)**	.374
Social/Normative VOC	.094	(.021)**	.400
Development-Population	-.045	(.016)*	.407
Woman's status	.064	(.018)	.424
Son Preference	.047	(.016)*	.435
TOTAL			.435

D.) Multiple Regression Analysis (Dependent Variable:
IDEAL NUMBER OF CHILDREN)

Independent Variables	b	SE	R^2
Parity	.100	(.029)**	.109
Economic/Utilitarian VOC	.047	(.017)*	.140
Psychological VOC	not sig.	—	.142
Social/Normative VOC	not sig.	—	.149
Marriage duration	.017	(.008)	.154
Expectation of economic help	.020	(.009)	.158
Son preference	.046	(.014)	.178
TOTAL			.178

Explanation: In every regression equation the three VOC indices are given
regardless of whether their b values are significant or not. Other
than these, all the b values presented in tables 8 A–D are significant
at least at $p \le .05$ level.
In every equation:
* $p \le .01$
** $p \le .001$

assumption of an automatic positive relationship between the value
of the child and parity is being challenged here.

Total explained variance in birth control practice is not high,
but the greatest contribution to this is made by the VOC variables
(Table 8 B). As expected, economic/utilitarian VOC has a notable
negative effect on birth control (.08 of the total variance, and .50 of
the explained .16 is accounted for by this variable). Though of lesser
magnitude, psychological VOC has a significant effect in the
positive direction, as expected.

VOC variables contribute significantly to the variance in
desired number of children (Table 8 C). Economic/utiliarian VOC,
in particular, assumes importance, (accounting for .05 of the total
variance; .11 of the explained .44). Again as expected, the contribution of psychological VOC to desired number of children is negative
whereas the economic/utilitarian and the social/normative VOCs
have significant positive effects, indicating that the psychological
VOC is not a fertility-prone value, whereas economic/utilitarian
and social/normative VOCs are. This result shows the explanatory
value of VOCs for fertility attitudes even when socio-economic
structural variables are controlled. Together with boy preference,
values related to children explain .11 of the total variance (.25 of the
explained .44) of the desired number of children.

The last dependent variable considered is ideal number of children (Table 8 D). VOCs also assume importance here. Specifically, the economic/utilitarian VOC, economic expectations from children and boy preference altogether explain .06 of the total variance in ideal number of children (.18 of the explained .33).

Thus, regression results show that VOCs' independent contribution to the variance in fertility variables is substantial when socio-economic and demographic variables and education are controlled. Furthermore, in all regression equations, the contribution of VOCs surpasses that of socio-economic development variables. This finding provides additional support to the theoretical model of the VOC study and generally to a social-psychological orientation to fertility. The multidimensional conceptualization of the VOCs and their differential relations with fertility outcome are validated by these results. Specifically, economic VOC and boy preference are associated with high fertility and psychological VOC with low fertility.

Development and Fertility

In line with our hypotheses and numerous research results from all over the world, our results indicate that with socio-economic development, fertility attitudes are affected, and fertility decreases. It is found, for example, that among women with two children the percentage of those wanting additional children decreases with increased development level at each population stratum. Specifically, within rural areas, 38% of women with 2 children in least developed rural areas want more children whereas only 10% of those in most developed rural areas want more.

Sixty-nine percent of women know of modern birth control techniques in rural areas, whereas 82% have such knowledge in urban areas ($X^2 = 33.76$, p<.001). The corresponding figures are 68% and 84% for men. ($X^2 = 15.43$, p < .001). It is apparent from these figures that urban-rural differences in knowledge and use of contraception are substantial, thus the difference between rural and urban parities (3.16 and 2.58, respectively).

"Modernizing" exposure to mass communication, education and husband's education are negatively associated with parity (-.20, -.41 and -.37, respectively), desired number of children (-.20, -.37 and -.33), ideal number of children (-.14, -.26, -.22) and boy preference (-.19, -.33 and -.29), whereas they show positive relations with approval (.16, .10, .11) and use of birth control (.12, .15, .13). Furthermore, development variables such as development-population index, urban standing, percent of urban experience and income also show the expected negative relations with the above-mentioned fertility variables.

Multiple regression analyses also point to the negative effect of socio-economic development on fertility variables (Table 8 A, B, C). These findings are in line with numerous research results around the world and fit the "demographic transition theory." They complete the sets of findings supporting our theoretical orientation.

Conclusion

The Turkish VOC Study has shown that socio-economic-cultural factors affect people's perceptions and values and are reflected in intra-family relations. Perceptions, values and family dynamics, in turn, as social-psychological mechanisms, affect fertility behavior. In this context the perceived value of children (VOC) forms the missing link, at the individual level, between two socially observed phenomena—development and fertility decline. Specifically, it has been found that with socio-economic development and especially with education, the economic VOC decreases whereas the psychological VOC increases, at least in relative terms. The total perceived value of the child, thus, probably does not change much. However, as the economic VOC is cumulative with child numbers whereas the psychological VOC is not, the result is lowered fertility. In other words, fertility decreases with development because economic and psychological VOCs are differentially affected by development and are differentially related to desired child numbers.

In the socio-economic context, where economic VOC assumes great importance, there is also widespread son preference. This is because sons, both while they are young and as the main future breadwinners, satisfy the needs for material support and old-age security. In this socio-economic context the dependent, inferior status of the uneducated woman is crucial. Woman's dependency is an inherent part of a general pattern of interdependent relationships appearing first as dependency of the child on the parents and then as the reversal of this relationship. Such a pattern of intrafamilial relations and corresponding values is associated with high child numbers. The reverse pattern, however, entails low levels of dependency on children and low parity in the developed socio-economic context.

Thus, the needs which assume importance for people in particular socio-economic contexts and the values corresponding to these needs help us understand why social structure and development affect fertility. With development, the changing needs and motivations reinforce the emergence of different values and resulting behavior. This study has sought on the one hand to define the socio-cultural context in which this change takes place, and on the other hand to understand the dynamics of this change in Turkish society.

NOTES

[1]   The Turkish VOC Study is one of the nine country studies comprising the total VOC Project. The principal investigators and the countries participating were Russel Darroch and Masri Singarimbun (Indonesia); Sung Jin Lee (Korea); Rodolfo Bulatao (Philippines); Tom Sun and Tsong-Shien Wu (Republic of China); Betty J. Chung, Eddie Kuo and Peter S.J. Chen (Singapore); Chalio Buri-Pakdi, Visid Prachuabman and Nibhon Debavalya (Thailand); Çiğdem Kâğıtçıbaşı (Turkey); Lois Hoffman, James T. Fawcett and Fred Arnold (U.S.A.); and Brian Flay, Adrejs Urdze and Esther R. Mechler (Germany). The Turkish VOC Project was supported by the International Development Research Centre of Canada.

[2]   These conceptualizations and orientations have been presented in detail elsewhere (e.g. Fawcett, 1976, pp. 94–97; Kâğıtçıbaşı, 1981; Kâğıtçıbaşı and Esmer, 1980).

[3]   Various aspects of the cross-national VOC research procedures, including the Turkish VOC Study, are presented in detail in a number of Technical Notes prepared by the East–West Population Institute, Hawaii, and are available from that organization. Of special relevance are Technical Notes No. 4 (Sampling Procedures); No. 5 (The Questionnaire); and No. 6 (Survey Procedures). The detailed procedures of the Turkish VOC Study are presented in Kâğıtçıbaşı (1981 and 1982).

[4]   Since national representation is sought in the Turkish VOC study, all the figures given in this paper are weighted population figures.

[5]   A reason for the low percentage of female work could be the fact that in the rural context most women who work in the family consider themselves to be "not working" (Kâğıtçıbaşı, 1977, p. 42).

[6]   According to Rotter's conceptualization (1966), belief in internal control implies autonomy and a tendency to assume responsibility for one's actions and lot in life. The opposite tendency, belief in external control, is to attribute this responsibility to outside agents, such as God, fate, other people, etc. On the three items measuring this variable, t–tests were found significant at beyond the $p < .001$ level.

⁷ These questions were asked at the beginning of the interview in order to obtain spontaneous answers, unaffected by the subsequent interview content. In this essay only advantages (values) of children will be dealt with. Disadvantages are covered elsewhere (Kâğıtçıbaşı, 1981 and 1982).
⁸ Among the VOC countries this figure is the highest after Indonesia.
⁹ This analysis was carried out by Dr. Yılmaz Esmer, and detailed information is provided by him (Esmer, 1979).
¹⁰ Especially on one's children, according to Lois Hoffman (personal communication, 1979). A detailed analysis of this issue is given in Kâğıtçıbaşı, 1979b.

BIBLIOGRAPHY

Abadan-Unat, N., *Implications of Migration on Emancipation and Pseudo-Emancipation of Turkish Women*. Paper presented at The Wellesley College Conference on Women, June 2-6, 1976.
Arnold, F., et al. *The Value of Children: A Cross-National Study*, Vol. I. Honolulu, Hawaii: East-West Population Institute, 1975.
Berelson, B. "The Value of Children: A Taxonomical Essay." In *The Population Council Annual Report of 1972*. New York: Population Council, 1973, pp.17-27.
Bulatao, R. A. *On the Nature of the Transition in the Value of Children*. East-West Population Institute, no. 60–A, 1979a.
————. *Further Evidence of the Transition in the Value of Children*. East-West Population Institute, 60–B, 1979b.
Caldwell, J. C. "Towards a Restatement of Demographic Transition Theory." In J. Caldwell, (ed.), *The Persistence of High Fertility*, pp. 25-123. Family and Fertility Change Series 1, Part 1. Canberra: The Australian National University, 1977.
DPT — *İllerin Gelişmişlik düzeylerinin saptanmasında bir yöntem denemesi* (A methodological study for establishing cities development levels). Ankara: DPT Publications, No. 152, SPD 250, 1972.
Esmer, Y. "Classifying the Value of Children: An Empirical Approach." Unpublished monograph. East-West Center, 1979.
Fallers, L., and M. Fallers. "Sex Roles in Edremit." In J. Peristiany (ed.), *Mediterranean Family Structures*. London: Cambridge University Press, 1976, pp.243-60.
Fawcett, J. T. (ed.). *The Satisfactions and Costs of Children: Theories, Concepts and Methods*. Honolulu: East-West Center, 1972.
————. "The Value and Cost of Children: Converging Theory and Research." Paper presented at the annual meeting of the American Psychological Association, Washington, D.C., September, 1976.
Hoffman, L. W., and M. L. Hoffman. "The Value of Children to Parents." In J. T. Fawcett (ed.), *Psychological Perspectives on Education*. New York: Basic Books, 1973, pp. 19-76.

Kâğıtçıbaşı, Ç. "Psychological Aspects of Modernization in Turkey," *Journal of Cross-Cultural Psychology.* 1973, 4, 157-74.

———. "Modernity and the Role of Women in Turkey." *Boğaziçi University Journal.* 1975a, 3, 83-93.

———. "Value of Children." Paper presented at the 2nd Demographic Conference, Çeşme, İzmir, Sept. 29, Oct. 1, 1975b.

———. "Some Social Psychological Correlates of Fertility in Turkey." IUSSP General Conference Spontaneous Paper, 1977.

———. "Effect of Employment and Children on Women's Status and Fertility Decisions." Paper presented at The International Development Research Center Workshop on Women's Roles and Fertility. Ottawa, Canada, June 25-27, 1979a.

———. "Old Age Security Value of Children and the Care of the Aged." Paper presented at the United Nations Seminar on Informal Action for the Welfare of Aged, Copenhagen, Denmark, Mar. 26-April 3, 1979b.

———. *Çocuğun Değeri: Türkiye'de değerler ve doğurganlık* (Value of the child: values and fertility in Turkey). Boğaziçi University, Istanbul, 1981.

———. *The Changing Value of Children in Turkey.* Honolulu: East-West Center, 1982.

———. *Value of Children.* Honolulu: East-West Center, 1981b.

——— and Y. Esmer. *Development Value of Children and Fertility: A Multiple Indicator Approach.* Istanbul: Boğaziçi University, 1980.

——— and A. Kansu. "Cinsiyet rollerinin sosyalleşmesi ve aile dinamiği: Kuşaklararası bir Karşılastırma" (Socialization of sex roles and family dynamics: an intergenerational comparison).*Boğaziçi University Journal.* 1976-77, 4-5.

Kandiyoti, D. "Sex Roles and Social Change: A Comparative Appraisal of Turkey's Women," *Signs: Journal of Women in Culture and Society.* 1977, 3, 1.

Kıray, M. "Changing Roles of Mothers: Changing Intra-Family Relations in a Turkish Town." In J. Peristiany (ed.), *Mediterranean Family Structures.* London: Cambridge Univ. Press, 1976, pp. 261-71.

Magnarella, P. J. *Tradition and Change in a Turkish Town.* New York: John Wiley and Sons, 1974.

Mauldin, W. P. and B. Berelson. "Conditions of Fertility Decline in Developing Countries, 1965-75." *Studies in Family Planning.* 1978, 9, 5, 89-148.

Meeker, M. E. "Meaning and Society in the Near East: Examples from the Black Sea Turks and the Levantine Arabs," *International Journal of Middle East Studies.* 1976, 7, 243-70, 338-423.

Notestein, D. "Population: the Long View." In T. W. Schultz (ed.), *Food for the World.* Chicago: Univ. of Chicago Press, 1945, pp. 36-57.

Olson-Prather, E. "An Alternative Model of the Family in Turkey." In *Family Planning and Husband-Wife Relationships in Contemporary Turkey*. Unpublished Ph.D. dissertation, UCLA, 1976.

Özbay, F.and F. C. Shorter. "Türkiye'de aile planlaması uygulamalarında 1963 ve 1968 yılları arasında görülen değişmeler" (Changes in Family Planning Applications in Turkey Between 1963 and 1968). *Hacettepe Sosyal ve Beşeri Bilimler Journal*. 1970, 2, 2.

Population Reference Bureau, 1976 World Population Data Sheet, Washington, D.C., 1976.

Rotter, J. B. "Generalized Expectancies for Internal Versus External Control of Reinforcement," *Psychological Monographs*. 1966, 80, 1, 1-28.

Stirling, P. *Turkish Village*. London: Weidenfeld and Nicolson, 1965.

Timur, S. *Türkiye'de aile yapısı* (Family Structure in Turkey). Ankara: Hacettepe University Publications, D-15, 1972.

————. "Demographic Correlates of Woman's Education." Paper presented at the International Union for the Scientific Study of Population, 18th General Conference, Mexico City, Aug. 8-13, 1977.

Tuncer, B. *Ekonomik gelişme ve nüfus* (Economic Development and Population). Ankara: Hacettepe University Publication, D-20, 1976.

Youssef, N. H. "The Status and Fertility Patterns of Moslem Women." In N. Keddie and L. Beck (eds.), *Women in the Moslem World*. Cambridge, Mass.: Harvard Univ. Press, 1978, pp. 69-99.

THE EFFECTS OF FEMALE LABOR ON POWER RELATIONS IN THE URBAN TURKISH FAMILY

Nilüfer F. Kuyaş

As long as the central institutions and relations of social organization at all levels of development continue to recruit and affect men and women differentially, there will be an incentive for the conceptualization of the division between the sexes as a separate theoretical issue and, with it, of the family as the locus of this division.

The family is an economic or *value* relation, both produced by and itself reproducing the fundamental economic relations within society at large, with their accompanying socio-cultural sanctions. No doubt the economic aspect of the family historically has undergone vast alterations; just as this economic aspect is integrated with the dominant mode of production, the same can also be said about its effective and ideological content and control over its members.

It has by now become a well-established hypothesis in the literature, however, that there usually is a time lag between these structural and ideological levels of transition in the family, especially where these intersect in individual behavior and consciousness. Men and women are affected by this time lag differentially. The particular and individual forms of interaction between these levels depend on what sort of economic change and cultural background a researcher has to deal with. And it is a fact that they are nowhere as full of contradictions and peculiar deviations as in specific instances of transition to dependent capitalist industrialization as in , for example, the case of Turkey.

As a society undergoing quite radical transformations, Turkey presently offers rich opportunities for investigating this interaction at the individual level, especially across class lines. There has been considerable progress, albeit formal, towards legally raising the status of women, for example, in terms of their autonomy in exercising their rights, in the decision to marry, choice of spouse, time of marriage, divorce, education, economic independence through work and wider participation in public life. Many valuable studies have been done on such effects of the changing social, economic and family structures on women, although it has been questioned whether this process of change has really been reflected in the behavior, attitudes and consciousness of women.

On the other hand, however, it is quite difficult to encounter in the literature questions as to what extent the changes in social and family structures are in effect in different social classes; to what extent women of different class origin *and* membership have internalized or perpetuate ideologies of male dominance; and to what extent older values are still inseparable from the internal dynamics of different types of household and individual male/female relations, representing different variants of the bourgeois family ideal.

Any consideration of the reasons for women's specific sexual subordination in the urban family, and the avenues open to them for changing this reality inevitably leads to the formulation of the division between the sexes as a *power* relation. At the foundation of the contractual family bond, there is an inequality of social power which determines its terms. Approaching the changes in this power structure and its terms, as well as in women's perceptions of them, raises basic questions of how social relations are reflected in individual values or, more specifically, when and in what manner their immediate class, family and household dynamics affect women's perceptions of and expectations about their sex-roles.

Such an approach would have to be carried out in light of certain theoretical hypotheses which dominate current family and women studies. Chief among these is the expectation that the increasing participation of women in social production, as opposed to the exclusive allocation of their labor power to domestic subsistence, challenges the economic and ideological basis of their subordination in the family in all strata of society.

Parameters of Modernization

In their proposed answer to these questions, theories of so-called modernization are prone to see emerging forms of family organization as marking historical turning points in the perpetuation of gender-linked hierarchies of power (Reiter, 1977). Since they usually analyze social structure through a scale of increasing complexity, change is interpreted as a process from traditional patriarchy to capitalist modernity. The problem of the changing status of women and the differences of power between the sexes in the family context, therefore, becomes one of changes in family interaction in response to processes of modernization such as industrialization or urbanization.

On the ideological side of this process, Goode (1963) declared that a world-wide change is occurring in the direction of the conjugal family characterized by a radical ideology: rights of the individual, emphasis on desires and abilities, romantic love, liberty of personal decision, equality of the sexes and egalitarian power structure. Research in this area does indeed suggest that there is a high correlation between egalitarian family patterns and industrialization, as the two seem to implicate each other. Cross-cultural comparisons of family authority patterns in five differentially industrialized nations showed that the extent of male authority in these societies is inversely related to the degree of industrialization and urbanization (König, 1957; Michel, 1967; Rodman, 1967; Buric and Zecevic, 1967; Safilios-Rothschild, 1967; Lupri, 1969). The same studies documented that patriarchy in the family prevails more in rural than in urban areas and the extent of rural to urban differences varies with the level of industrialization.

There remains the double task, however, of explaining both why male authority/power persists in some cases in the urban areas and where or how change occurs towards less powerlessness for women. In dealing with these questions, modernization theories and studies drawing from them depend more and more on the resource or exchange model. First stated by Blood and Wolfe (1960), the resource theory of marital power constitutes an alternative to, or rather, a modification of the theory that tradition is the major basis of family power structure. In their United States survey, they found that men's mean authority scores increased with higher levels of education, income, or occupational status, which were then conceptualized as resources which give individuals leverage in marital decision making and interaction, in a manner similar to theories of exchange and reciprocity in social interaction (Homans, 1961; Thibaut and Kelley, 1959). The wife's employment, for example, is formulated as a crucial resource affecting her relative power within the family in this theoretical framework.

Comparative data from studies carried out in this framework showed that the more often women work outside their homes, the more often the husband's authority is low. Employment is thus a resource which permits women to increase their decision making power in the family. Generally speaking, higher level of education and occupational prestige also increase the individual's weight in marital interaction, mostly in the husband's case. It was found that the husband's income level was an even more sensitive indicator of his power than occupation (König, 1956; Blood and Wolfe, 1960). These trends were especially marked in the husband's power in deciding whether or not the wife should work outside the home. It was seen that in cases where the wife had either higher education or higher income than her husband, her power in personal decision, especially concerning her employment, increased (Michel, 1967).

According to Michel's analysis, the values of these couples are also the values or norms of modern industrialized urban society, where money (exchange value), education and qualification in occupational hierarchy are basic elements of power and authority, not only in the family but in all of public life as well. She warns, however, that this is reflection by the family of social structure and values which are by no means universal, since in "developing" countries values related to educational and job qualification may be less important for individual status than in highly industrialized nations. Sexual and/or generational values, together with kinship status, may be more important in still "traditional" societies.

Indeed, further duplication of these studies in two less developed countries, Greece and Yugoslavia, produced quite different results; it was found that over all, lower social status in combined terms of education and occupation meant more authority for the husband (Safilios-Rothschild, 1967; Buric and Zecivic, 1967). In contrast to highly industrialized countries, husbands' power in Greece and Yugoslavia was inversely related to education, occupational status and income.

It can be concluded that in countries where the social organization under which the relation of the sexes is determined has not reached a level of considerable differentiation and where the boundaries of class have not been stabilized in terms of uniform economic gradations, the application of similar hypotheses is problematic and calls for certain modifications or alternative ways of accounting for the specific form of male domination through the institutional mediation of the family.

Thus, modernization theory presents us with a view of societies and individuals changing towards more differentiated and increasingly egalitarian relations or values, in the sense of equal opportunity or competition, in which the differential participation of subgroups, minorities, sexes, or social strata is seen to be determined by their varying states of preparedness to adopt these modern values and behavior norms, as opposed to states of "embeddedness" in past experiences and previously learned cultural values and norms, with states of transition in between.

This is thought to be the reason that in developing counties, for example, lower class men are able to still maintain their objectively non-legitimized, but subjectively unquestioned marital power, although they are clearly not able to live up to the ascribed role of unique provider required for this status. Upper class men, in contrast, while they do live up to this role to a much greater extent, seem more willing to share their power with women on an egalitarian basis, chiefly because education has exposed them to more liberal sex-role standards (Safilios-Rothschild, 1967).

There is some reason to think, however, that this division of industrial, as opposed to developing, societies is not altogether to the point. Many studies carried out within advanced industrialized societies emphasize the fact that the transition is more subtle, towards "quasi-egalitarianism" (Holter, 1975). It is pointed out that the social participation of women is quite different from that of men. Even in cases where women are employed outside the home, they tend to be concentrated in predominantly "female" occupations and move within narrow limits of social action. Other considerations opposing the hypothesis that employment generally increases women's status and power include the fact that even if the wife works outside the home, she is usually seen as a junior partner to her husband and still has less power. She complements the husband's legitimate role of unique provider, since she is seen as being interested in a job or in contribution to the family budget, rather than a career (Scanzoni, 1972; Blake, 1974; Stevens, 1975; Papanek, 1976). Furthermore, this derived status is also reinforced by the very poor employment and/or education options that are usually available to women as a group.

More and more studies, thus, have confirmed the counter hypothesis that even substantial economic contributions to the family budget by women need not result in higher status or power. This has more to do, it seems, with the degree to which women are socially controlled and have internalized, or perpetuate, ideologies of male dominance (Chinas, 1973; Sanday, 1973). This is paralleled to a certain extent by the fact that most women tend to see the housewife/mother role as their primary vocation in life and work seldom becomes an integral part of their personality. This ideological and, in the final analysis, psychological internalization or "false consciousness" informally sanctions deviations from the accepted sex-role standards. The maintenance of the division of labor and task differentiation between the sexes becomes more and more dependent on different personality formation of men and women.

At this point, it becomes necessary to bring in the basic problem of the reflection of the ideology concerning women's proper place to the actual mechanisms of every day life whereby this is imposed on individual consciousness. On this score, theories of alienation also have been influential in challenging the "female labor" hypothesis regarding power relations in the family. It has been argued that false consciousness or, in other words, precapitalist familistic attitudes, are maintained predominantly in cases where there is a continuing responsibility for production in the family. The degree of integration of different families into the changing economic structure and the actual standards of living under which this occurs constitute the basis of the relations between the sexes. As long as women's labor in the home preserves its importance, their participation in the labor force has limited effects on the specific patriarchal power relations in the family, whose alleged economic function of subsistence and reproduction, social and biological, relegates women to positions of powerlessness and alienation from their own development as individuals (Meszaros, 1970; Israel, 1971; Ollman, 1971; Sanday, 1973; Rowbotham, 1973; Sacks, 1974; Saffioti, 1975; Papanek, 1976; Nash and Safa, 1976; Kudat, 1977; Young, Harris, Edholm, 1977).

On account of these considerations we face conflicting theoretical views on the structure and the psychological dynamics of female powerlessness in the family and the effects of female labor outside the home. On the one hand, participation in the labor force is a resource that increases women's status and power in relation to men, towards egalitarianism in the family. On the other hand, however, there is the consideration of economic, ideological and psychological conditions under which the same factors fail to have the same effect, and may even accentuate patiarchy and the subordination of women in traditional or at least quasi-egalitarian forms. It is also the case that the relative weight of these elements depends for the most part on internal socio-economic factors specific to each country.

The Case of Turkey: An Overview

Studies on the changing power structure of the family and the consciousness of women related to modernization in Turkey are of a nature to confirm the continuing existence of sexual stratification and division of labor by sex, alongside the increasingly class-determined formation of Turkish society in the process of dependent but rapid transition to capitalist industrialization and urbaniza-tion. Parallel to this is the striking plurality of co-existing economic forms and cultural values concerning marital ideology and women's role (Timur, 1972; Kâğıtçıbaşı, 1977a; Kâğıtçıbaşı and Kansu, 1977b;; Kandiyoti, 1977a; Kandiyoti, 1978; Kazgan, 1979; Çitçi, 1974, 1979; Şenyapılı, 1979).

The differences in family structure and function in the social and economic sphere as an antecedent to the transition to quasi-egalitarian marital ideology has been a continuing focus of interest. There are clear indications that the transition forced by moderni-zation and new economic relations affect the actual dynamics of family making and intrafamily relations as well. On the whole, however, predominantly male decision making in the family, a sign of traditional sex-role relations, has been observed in two national surverys carried out in 1968 (Timur, 1972) and 1975 (Kâğıtçıbaşı, 1977a, b). The findings of these surveys clearly show that Turkish society still offers rich opportunities for ideological type moder-nization theories, aiming to isolate the parameters of social change as they produce corresponding changes in values, or conversely, fail to dissolve resistant traditional norms. And indeed this has been the general trend in research done on the family or on women as a separate issue.

The problem of women's increasing employment outside the home is also a major theme of these approaches. There is, however, some reason to think that the role played by employment in changing marital power structure has been overestimated in view of the social barriers facing women's emancipation in Turkey. It is impossible not to agree with the argument that most researchers have set themselves rather modest standards in evaluating the dynamics of the Turkish family and changing sex roles by adopting the western model of conjugal union as egalitarian or modern (Kandiyoti, 1977a), giving us very little insight into the discrepancy between liberal ideology and the actual level of women's potential for flexibility and change, faced with the conditions of their everyday struggle.

The literature seems to suggest that in order to use a resource theory approach to marital power or the powerlessness of women, certain assumptions need to be made. Chief among these is the dyadic conception of the marital relationship, instead of an "institutional" conception. According to the former, the family relation is a voluntaristic, contractual arrangement where increasing status in relation to expansion of roles outside the family system enables partners to be potential competitors with each other for power. This in turn involves attitudes towards decision power and autonomy that necessitate, on the part of the women, a high consciousness of the need to develop their own personalities in order to be more competent in relation to their husbands and to favor their own emancipation in external roles which are very important for individual performance in an industrialized society based on achievement (Hoffman, 1960; Blood and Wolfe, 1960; Lupri, 1967; Lamousé, 1967).

According to data available in Turkey, such an attribution of competitive and highly conscious personalities to Turkish women seems unwarranted. The familism still dominant in Turkish society prevents a coherent usage of the dyadic conception. In view of the fact that the majority of marriages are still more or less traditionally arranged even in the urban middle classes, it would be futile to conceive of women as entering a voluntaristic, contractual relationship, especially since most women get married at an age at which it is nearly impossible to have individual goals and achievement orientations, independent of family responsibility.

The family conception more appropriate for Turkey's present level of "modernization," therefore, seems to be the institutional approach, because, at least as far as women are concerned, there are as yet no alternatives to the family mode of social reproduction, and non-married life (celibacy, co-habitation, etc.) is on the whole considered to be anomalous. In the terms of exchange theorists, therefore, our thesis is that in institutional settings where women have a very low "comparison level of alternatives" (Thibaut and

Kelley, 1959) within the family relation as well as outside it, we cannot conceive of them as real competitors for power.

The above assessment is especially true in the case of our present concern, namely whether or not women's participation in the labor force constitutes the basis for such an alternative within the family relation itself. We need to recognize the fact that employment outside the home, as such, is not an adequate variable on which we could build a paradigm of change in family power structure, from the standpoint of female psychology and social status. The reasons for this are manifold and interdependent.

First of all, we can never sufficiently emphasize the fact that labor force participation is a dimension where both the sexual stratification and the class hierarchy of a given social formation are salient. In other words, the deep differences of class among women, as well as their relatively low social status as a group, stand out most clearly in the case of employment. We should therefore be more interested in what it means for an urban woman to be employed outside the home in terms of her status within it, as well as the changes this meaning undergoes with social class.

Secondly, the discrete socio-economic factors used by resource theories such as status, income, and occupational prestige, in short, the stratification variables of social hierarchy, might prove to be unwarranted for an emergent class society like Turkey. Stratification in a post-industrial society involves a high level of social differentiation where the family has transferred to other social structures many of its functions. This is over and above the essentially industrial transition of the economic functions from the family to the occupational structure (Stevens, 1975). There is evidence that even these economic functions are to a large extent served by the family and women's domestic work in developing countries, as a sort of 'pre-capitalistic' or secondary family economy.

This immediately suggests a hierarchic form of social reproduction in the urban sector, divided along class lines, restricting the access of different strata to the limited socialized means of reproduction such as inexpensive and/or free child care or education, health services and social security, as well as the commodity form of reproduction through modern conveniences and consumer goods (Kudat, 1977). Since class boundaries also affect the exchange value of female labor power in the labor market, as well as employment and training opportunities for both men and women, social class seems to be a more unifying and explanatory antecedent to household dynamics in Turkish society, and it is impossible to expect employment to have a similar effect in all social strata.

It has been observed, in fact, that Turkish women's participation in the labor force is inversely related to socio-economic status (Kazgan, 1979), indicating a strong sexual division of labor in the sphere of market production. There is evidence that in conformity to certain predictions of dependency theory, capitalist industrialization is dislodging workers from agriculture faster than they are being absorbed into industry, with a sex differential: the women are adversely affected. Labor force participation in economically recognized sectors declines with development, while a corresponding growth in the female-concentrated service sector is observed (Çitçi, 1979).

Labor force statistics show that social division of labor by sex is a very dominant reality in Turkey, where only 37.8% of the entire active female population and 11.0% of the urban female population in the three largest metropolitan areas are actually employed, excluding the unpaid family workers in the rural sector (70.0% of all the rural labor force) (Kazgan, 1979). Service occupations and unskilled/semi-skilled labor in light industry are the categories with the highest concentrations of female labor, changing between 20-35%. Among economically active women, 4% are in light industry and 8% are in service occupations. Due to the low level of women's education and skilled training, as well as the uneven expansion of the economy, this concentration of female occupations is likely to increase over time as well. Usually, female-concentrated occupations are also low paid. Together with agriculture (Kazgan, 1979), this is especially true of manufacture and light industry, which produce Turkey's main export goods.

Within such changing economic relations, marked by the increasing emergence of nuclear family units where more than one member is employed in the labor market, it is clear that the mostly "proletarian" female urban labor force (the lower, working classes and the "new" middle class) finds very little or no motivation for work except out of economic necessity. Aside from exceptions among upperclass career women, most women work because they have to, and they derive very little status from their low exchange value on the labor market.

There is considerable evidence that in Turkey women's work is seen as primarily a source of extra income needed, and in cases where economic necessity ceases, the women themselves do not find much incentive to go on working (Çitçi, 1974). This makes their employment status highly precarious and creates a corresponding ambivalence in normative expectations, reinforcing a value system in which not having to work and being a well-to-do housewife seems to be considered as a privilege and the indicator of a gain in social status. This is incidentally a trend which is also widely observed in the working classes of advanced industrialized countries (Young, Wilmott, 1957; Rainwater, Coleman and Handel, 1962; Komarovsky, 1967; Lamousé, 1969).

Overall, it can be ventured that many conditions must be fulfilled over and above mere employment in order to be able to speak of a positive move towards more economic and psychological freedom for women in the family. Especially in cases where autonomy in decisions concerning one's own labor power and the control of economic assets are at a low level, this alleged effect becomes quite negligible indeed, the more so since the most difficult thing is to change the socialization patterns of the female population which are inclined towards other-directedness, or familism. This perpetuates the vicious circle of lower education, low status job opportunities, and preference for the home. We must therefore expect:

a) factors such as socialization, work experience before marriage, level and quality of employment, type of marriage and family to be more important in determining women's family power than employment as such;

b) the effects of employment to vary with social class;

c) the class factor to be more important than the employment factor in determining the powerlessness of women in the family relation.

A Case in Point: Women and Social Classes in a Turkish Metropolis

After thus reviewing the main theoretical considerations on the subject, we are now in a position to summarize the relevant results obtained in an empirical study conducted to test the hypotheses outlined above. This was a small scale field research based on an interview-type questionnaire administered in Istanbul during the summer and fall of 1979.

Women from the lower and middle classes residing in the Istanbul metropolitan area constituted the sampling population. Sixty women were interviewed in each class, who were further divided equally between employed women and full time housewives. Access to the subjects was established through purposive sampling throughout. The criteria for determining the social class of the subjects were largely intuitive, based on more or less rooted categories of social consciousness in urban settings, such as district of residence or type of occupation.

The entire population mentioned in the category of "lower class" lives in fairly established squatter districts of Istanbul. The main characteristics of this population, aside from predominantly rural origins, are high physical mobility (Kandiyoti, 1973), internal stratification (Kıray, 1971), usually according to level of urbanization and type of occupation (Kongar, 1973a), which ranges from unemployment and work in "marginal" sectors to the relatively organized mass of the urban working class, and a realistic desire to acquire property or to set up small private entrepreneurial-type business Şenyapılı, 1977, 1979). It can be characterized as a semi-proletarian population, with strong values of "embourgeoisement" (Levine, 1973), but increasingly developing towards wage labor only, either in industry or the service sectors, and with very restricted opportunities for the upward social mobility desired (Kongar, 1973a, 1976; Keleş, 1972; Şenyapılı, 1979). This population composes the lower stratum of the large metropolitan centers, with potentially high labor power and consumption implications for the internal market.

The population classified as "middle class," on the other hand, consists of even more nebulous and inter-related sectors in terms of occupation and cultural background. There are two major groups constituting the middle strata, regardless of the relative changes in income or life style: the first group consists of families who either possess small means of entrepreneurial production or of commercial exchange, but not on a scale to appropriate the labor power of others. It is the group traditionally called the small bourgeoisie. The second group are people who have sufficient education or training to enable them to provide skilled bureaucratic, technical or service-type salaried labor to either the public or the private sectors. This is the group called the "new" middle class, most of whom are also either of rural petty bourgeois or of peasant origin.

Intuitively at least, these considerations indicate that the usage of "middle" and "lower" corresponds to real categories of social class in the present social structure, although they are not too clearly defined. It is not surprising, therefore, that the different social classes chosen for the study according to these intuitive criteria statistically yielded highly significant differences in most of the socio-economic status indicators used in the classical stratification model.

The objective of the study was to observe the effects of employment on women's perceptions and consciousness related to urban household dynamics and power structure in two social classes differing considerably in terms of life style, expectations, and potential for social or political change. This was done through measuring: (1) the division of decision power and control between spouses, as perceived by the wife; (2) their corresponding normative preferences related to this sphere.

An overview of the results showed that there is a striking uniformity and parallelism between the classes in the findings, although in opposite directions: In very general terms, middle-class women who perceived overall mutuality or sharing in their marital interactions also expressed normative preferences for such a state of affairs. This was further reflected in their values on femininity, which were divided between traditional, home-centered motives for achievement or success, and more progressive views on proper spheres of fulfillment for women in general, such as employment, social activities and public responsibilities.

Lower class women, on the other hand, consistently perceived themselves to be under almost total male control, and reflected this situation in their normative preference for such a reality and further defined achievement, success or fulfillment for women in other-directed and instrumental (vicarious) terms. The most important finding, however, was the fact that being employed made no ostensible difference in these patterns. (See Table 1).[1]

Telescoping on certain aspects of this picture yielded some interesting results. First of all, the marked decrease in male control in the middle class was accompanied by an increase in sharing or

Table 1
Class Differences in Male and Female Control (Means)

| | EMPLOYED WOMEN | | | |
	Middle Class N=30	Lower Class N=30	t	(two tail) p
Male Control	.24	.40	-3.40	.001
Female Control	.34	.30	.63	—

| | HOUSEWIVES | | | |
	Middle Class N=-30	Lower Class N=30	t	(two tail) p
Male Control	.28	.40	-2.78	.007
Female Control	.34	.30	.81	—

joint decision. Alongside the lower class reality where perceptions of sharing are almost non-existent and where a clear male/female polarity prevails, there is the middle class reality where this polarity or division of power (usually asymmetric) is increasingly taken over by syncratic sharing, i.e., conferences on most matters. Aside from certain unquestioned domains of male control, we observed in our sample that in areas where male control is overriding in the lower class, middle class women consistently perceived sharing much more often, and the same pattern was duplicated in the normative sphere as well.

Telescoping still further, we observed that there were important exceptions to this pattern. Detailed examination of the factors involved in family decision revealed that certain areas of marital interaction and resources are still tabu and under male control regardless of social class, such as the women's physical mobility, their employment decisions, autonomy in birth control or family planning, and sexuality; in short, all of those individual capacities or powers which are "expropriated" from women upon their marriage. Aside from these contexts, decisions in other areas concerning children, family activities, and financial matters, conformed to the pattern mentioned before, except for decisions on expensive purchases, which were mostly male-controlled in both classes.

Middle class sharing was syncratic in budgeting, shopping, and family activities, as well as the education, discipline and upbringing of the children, while in the lower class these were divided between the spouses, women making the decisions concerning child care and education, as well as routine shopping, while men decided on how to bring up or discipline their children, and how much to spend and where regarding major expenses.

In all of these areas taken together, either in male control or in female control and autonomy, employment did not make any significant difference. Whatever effect working did have on women's powerlessness in discrete contexts was found to be always dependent on the class factor. One such case is the autonomy of the women in disposing of their own labor power independently of the husband's control. A significantly larger number of employed middle class women perceived themselves as autonomous in the decision to work or not. Among middle class housewives, sharing was predominant, while in the lower class, women perceived male control more often, employment making very little difference between the two groups.

The findings mainly showed that employment has more subtle effects on family organization and women's powerlessness than meets the eye at first in an overall view. It has more negative effects than positive, and what positive effect there is clearly shows a class difference.

Working removes the woman somewhat from her traditional feminine domain where she controls daily expenses within the given division of labor, and sometimes she probably also shares in major decisions of money allocation, but has little say in the purchase of expensive items or the control of the family's economic assets in general. The women in our sample were not relieved to any large extent of their daily domestic responsibilities through employment, while they were in turn divested of their "privelege" of regulating routine budgeting. They lost what little financial autonomy they had as housewives. Employment apparently had little effect on their power over expensive purchases, which was a domain that remained masculine in both classes. Only middle class women were seen to reach a relatively egalitarian status in major expenses due to employment, while for lower class women this advantage was not available either.

Except for certain changes in financial matters of family organization, therefore, employment does not bring women more power in their marital relations. It is in one sense normal that woman's labor does not bring her any real resource in the power relation, since she has very little control over it and its products to begin with, and since the exchange value of her labor never reaches a sufficient level for her to appropriate it as a means towards social emancipation, especially in the lower classes.

The same class differences were also observed in the results on women's norms about male power or dominance in the family, which indicate a slight normative change in the middle class towards a more egalitarian marital ideology. As a matter of fact, we found an even deeper class difference in norms than in actual relations.

The difference of means across classes was enormous in male-control attitude scores, lower class women preferring male domination to a significantly higher extent than middle class women who had a very low group mean, whereas employment made almost no difference in the normative preferences of women about marital power in either class. (See Table 2.)

When considered separately, the only normative variable which was affected by employment was the decision to work, in conformity to the finding on actual decision power for this variable. Significantly more employed women said that a woman should decide herself

Table 2
Class Differences in Norms about Male/Female Control (Means)

	EMPLOYED			
	Middle Class N=30	Lower Class N=30	t	(two tail) p
Preference for Male Control	.27	.50	–4.04	.0001
Preference for Female Control	.34	.24	1.76	.08

	NON-EMPLOYED			
	Middle Class N=30	Lower Class N=30	t	(two tail) p
Preference for Male Control	.22	.57	–5.79	.000
Preference for Female Control	.33	.25	1.46	.05

whether or not to work. Even this variable, however, was not exempt from the general class differential observed in the study. When class was controlled, this employemnt effect was seen to be much stronger in the lower class, that is, non-employed lower class women were much more conservative in their normative preferences concerning the decision to work. In the middle class the employment effect was not so strong.

We can say that the most important result emerging from this general discussion is the surprising correspondence or parallel between women's perceptions of their actual powerlessness, and their normative preferences related to this powerlessness. Where we expected to find discrepancy, there was none, and the only cases of discrepancy observed between actual situation and normative values was one for the worse, e.g., in sexuality where middle class women preferred male control and initiative, despite the relative autonomy they perceived in their actual relations.

For example, of the lower class women who said a woman should not be free to move about as she pleases, 87% were actually not free themselves. Among employed lower class women, 81.8% of those who said the decision to work should depend on the husband, actually had no autonomy in this respect, while among those who preferred to be in control of their own labor power, 80% were actually in control. Lower class housewives had very conservative attitudes on women's work, and 95.2% of those who said working should depend on the husband's permission were actually dependent in this context, and these latter were in the majority.

A striking example of lower class conservatism, or false consciousness, is the fact that whenever lower class women experience a discrepancy between values and behavior, they consistently have values that *negate* whatever positive gain they have made in the actual marital power structure and autonomy. In birth control, for instance, about 50% of lower class women who said that men should be in control in fact perceived either autonomy or joint decision in this respect. When employment was controlled, this finding did not change, since the same pattern prevailed both among housewives and working women, although among housewives it was the majority who perceived sharing, but preferred male initiative in birth control decisions.

Employment also had very little effect on discrepancy between attitude and behavior in the middle class. Among middle class housewives, 81% of those who preferred male control in sexual matters, as opposed to 100% of those who preferred female control, perceived themselves as autonomous in this respect, while among working women, 85% of those who preferred male control actually perceived no such control or inhibition in their sexual relation with their husband. In birth control, on the other hand, sharing was uniformly higher in both actual fact and in subjective attitudes for all women, regardless of the employment factor. Concerning labor power also, the majority of middle class women were concordant in their values and actual perceptions, without any discrepancy.

These results show that, relatively independent of employment as a factor, discrepancy between values and behavior is stronger in the lower class, but where it exists in either class, such as in the case of sexuality, values are more conservative than behavior. In general, however, the interaction between values and behavior is more or less unilateral in both classes, in the sense that women's objective conditions—as perceived by them—are surprisingly well reflected in their normative values. An interaction pattern where values were more progressive than behavior in defining normative guidelines was rarely encountered in our sample, even though in the middle class the category of "sharing" carried the day. This fact does confirm to a certain extent our expectation of liberal value change in middle class marital ideology and practice, albeit still determined by economic factors. It does not, however, support the resource theory hypothesis that the learning of modern, progressive values changes actual behavior, especially in upper social strata, since our findings nowhere indicated such a causal modernization effect independent of the actual constraints of family organization and maintenance on the women in our sample.

Liberation versus Alienation through Labor

The findings show that women's work cannot be interpreted as a positive resource *per se*, independent of related factors through which it serves either as a further means for the economic and social control over women or as a means to their relative independence and autonomy. As for the specific contexts in which these different patterns are determined, they are the function of a specific interaction between socialization structures and socio-economic factors.

For example, the crucial variable of marriage type was effective in the domain of women's expressed values, non-traditional marriage being associated with expectations of female autonomy. Perceived male control was also significantly higher in traditionally arranged marriages than in modern ones established through personal choice. The same difference was also found in female control scores, though to a lesser extent: female control or autonomy in various family or personal decision areas was higher in modern marriages by choice, as opposed to different types of traditional marriage such as family-arranged marriages or marriage with close kin. Also, among women who never worked before marriage, male control was perceived significantly more often. (See Table 3.)

Our findings consistently showed that among other socialization factors, women's employment before marriage is much more important in relation to their power status than labor force participation after marriage. This is apparent in both actual powerlessness

Table 3
Marriage Type and Women's Decision Power and Norms (Means)

	Traditional Marriage N=61	Nontradtional Marriage N=59	t	(two tail) p
Male Control	.38	.28	3.07	.003
Female Control	.28	.36	-2.52	.01
Male Control Preference	.43	.36	1.44	.15
Female Control Preference	.25	.33	2.10	.03

and in related norms. Women who did not work at all before marriage (mostly lower class) had significantly higher male control preference, while the fact of having worked while single significantly increased attitudes favoring female control or autonomy. (See Table 4.)

Table 4
Premarital Employment and Decision Power and Norms

	Unemployed N=69	Employed N=51	t	(two tail) p
Male Control	.35	.29	1.70	.09
Female Control	.31	.33	—	—
Male Control Preference	.45	.51	2.98	.004
Female Control Preference	.24	.35	-2.91	.004

An important parallel finding concerned wage control for those women who worked prior to marriage. In the lower class, the earnings of most women who worked before their marriage were completely appropriated by their families. This factor seemed to be correlated with preference for male control in work-related matters, since 60% of such women expected that men should decide or control their wives' employment patterns. This relation was also observed in the middle class, but in the opposite sense. Almost all of the women who worked prior to marriage controlled their own wages and spent them mostly on themselves. Again 60% among them thought that women should have liberty of personal decision to dispose of their own labor power.

This is a crucial finding which shows that not even early participation in the labor force and social production is enough for a relatively "liberal" socialization of women, as long as their labor is appropriated as a family resource rather than an individual one. Their wages are completely turned over to the head of household, and this trend changes little upon marriage, as the women mostly turn their wages over to the husband even in cases where incomes are ostensibly pooled. In terms of emphasizing what different meanings and consequences labor may have for women, these considerations are very important. They also reveal the major weakness of the resource theory when it is applied to differentially developed societies: as long as women are controlled and denied autonomy in their relation to production, or in the appropriation of the exchange value of their labor power, the extension of their traditional roles to the labor market cannot be interpreted as a genuine resource. It thus does not determine their marital status or power, nor could it be expected to produce any positive change in their values, except in isolated, individual cases.

The integration of women into the labor market is thus a function of the kind of economic *and* ideological (cultural) basis of family life into which they are socialized. The rural/urban difference is, of course, pivotal here, but it is articulated to a genuine class difference once the context of comparison becomes the urban area. Although patriarchy, already present in legal, social and sexual relations, does constitute a defensive ideology in these families' integration into the urban, capitalist cash nexus in both classes, the mechanism works differently in each case, determining whether or not employment will work as a positive resource for the women.

In the middle class, the ideology is one of a better understanding between spouses with less conflict, since both men and women have clear-cut ideas about what their respective areas of control should be, and which perpetuates the cultural ideal for the role of the male as the chief breadwinner, who must provide and dominate. This balance largely depends on the family's income. In our study, we found that quite independently of women's employment as a factor, the husband's occupational status made significant differences in family power as perceived by the women. In the middle class, wage-earning husbands were perceived to be more powerful than self-employed husbands, whereas the opposite was the case in the lower class. (See Table 5.)

Table 5
Effects of Husband's Relation to Production, According to Class

| | MIDDLE | CLASS | | |
	Wage Labor N=24	Self Employed N=36	t	(two tail) p
Male Control	.29	.24	1.24	.22
Female Control	.27	.39	-2.91	.005
	LOWER	CLASS		
	Wage Labor N=29	Self Employed N=27	t	(two tail) p
Male Control	.35	.42	-1.35	.20
Female Control	.32	.30	—	—

In the middle class, if the husband is a wage earner, it is usually the case that income is low and this probably necessitates more effort and responsibility for the woman in transforming this income into use values for the family's physical subsistence. In such cases, where their domestic labor is a basic condition of the family's reproduction, the labor power and activities of women are especially contolled. If they work due to economic necessity their wages are a fundamental contribution to the family budget and this presupposes their being controlled.

It is only in cases where the family income is high, which is mostly possible if the husband is a self-employed professional or entrepreneur, that the relatively higher buying power frees women from domestic burdens to some extent through easier access to conveniences demanding less labor. It is also in such a setting that women's employment is in fact a resource providing them with some degree of independence, since their earnings are no longer a vital part of the family's subsistence and therefore do not presuppose their control to a comparable extent. A remarkable finding that parallels this was in the case of over-all family income. Female control was significantly higher in families whose monthly incomes were above 20.000 T.L., while male contol was much higher in families where monthly income was below this number.

In the lower class, on the other hand, the ideology is not only patriarchal as in the middle class but feudal as well. Due to the more or less recent rural origin of this population, which moreover generally retains its economic relations with the rural sector, the patriarchy experienced is based on peasant labor, where women were a means of production, "owned" by men, and where they could not have individual interests or resources not included in those of the men, as heads of housefold, or those of the family economy. Thus, the lower class women in our sample had an increasing range of liberal values in direct relation to the duration of their stay in the metropolitan area.

In the lower class a wage-earning husband usually has a more stable income than a self-employed one. The slightly increased female power observed in lower class families where the husband is a wage worker might be the counterpart of a phenomenon also observed in the higher-income working classes of industrialized countries, where as soon as economic necessity ceases, women do not find much incentive to work themselves and tend to dominate the household. This is mainly because lower class women universally derive neither the social prestige nor the material benefits usually associated with employment for middle class women.

Although the majority of the employed women in our lower class sample were industrial wage laborers themselves, their work status was not found to provide them with much advantage in their actual conditions. It is clear, moreover, that contrary to the assumptions of modernization theories, moving into the labor market does not necessarily mean attitude or value change in the domestic sphere. This can be also assessed in the case of the middle class population in our study.

Here too it was seen that a job was not the answer for women who mostly identify with their homes, or with their husbands or children. Even for most middle class women, working does not mean having money or social resources that are really their own, and it is only in cases where the women's earnings are not to be considered as an important component of the family budget, as we have seen, that they are much more free to dispose of their wages and have much more influence over matters of family organization and maintenance.

Concluding Remarks

The persistent powerlessness of women and the patriarchal, familistic values that accompany these are a function of the level and mode of their continuing responsibility in the family. The contradiction between the subordinate family mode and the prevalent rationalization of major social relations will continue to be resolved in women's consciousness in favor of the former, as long as this continues the dominant reality in their lives. The expectation that integration to the labor market will gradually lead to the permeation of this consciousness by individualistic, self-directed and achievement-oriented values of industrial societies can not be realized unless economic development and social organization admit all women into public life and production.

The implications of such a move in terms of the "socialization" of the family and the transformation in dominant cultural values are enormous, but they show us that the conditions of women's powerlessness and alienation, both economic and ideological, cannot be meaningfully questioned without at the same time questioning the totality of social relations which divide the sexes within the ostensible unity of the family. We have attempted to throw light on the intricate social/psychological factors involved in such a task in the specific conjuncture of Turkey's developing social and economic conditions.

NOTES

1   For a more detailed account of these and following findings, as well as the major arguments presented in this section, see Nilüfer Kuyaş, *The Family As A Power Relation, A Comparison Between Two Social Classes.* Unpublished master's thesis, Social Sciences Department, Boğaziçi Univ., İstanbul, October, 1980.

The author is indebted to Professors Çiğdem Kâğıtçıbaşı, Hamit Fişek and Deniz Kandiyoti for their invaluable help in this study.

BIBLIOGRAPHY

Blake, J. "The Changing Status of Women in Developed Countries," *Scientific American*, 1974, Sept., 137-47.

Blood, Robert O., Jr., and D.M. Wolfe. *Husbands and Wives: The Dynamics of Married Living.* New York: The Free Press, 1960.

Buric, O. and A. Zecevic. "Family Authority, Marital Satisfaction and the Social Network in Yugoslavia," *Journal of Marriage and the Family.* 1967, 29, 2, 325-36.

Chinas, B. *The Isthmus Zapotecs: Women's Roles in Cultural Context.* New York: Holt, Rinehart and Winston, 1973.

Çitçi, O. "Kadın ve Çalışma" (Women and Work), *Amme Idaresi Dergisi*, 1974, 7, 45-75.

_____. "Türk Kamu Yönetiminde Kadın Görevliler" (Women in Turkish Public Administration). In N. Abadan-Unat (ed.), *Türk Toplumunda Kadın* (Women in Turkish Society). Ankara: Turkish Social Science Association Publication, 1979.

Elliott, C.M. "Theories of Development: An Assessment," *Signs*, 1977, 3, 1.

Goode, W.J. *World Revolution and Family Patterns.* New York: The Free Press, 1973.

Hoffman, L.W. "Effects of the Employment of Mothers on Parental Power Relations and the Division of Household Tasks," *Marriage and Family Living*, 1960, 22, 1, 27-35.

Holter, H. "Sex Roles and Social Change." In Martha T.S. Mednick, S.S. Tangri, L.W. Hoffmann (eds.), *Women and Achievement: Social and Motivational Analyses.* London: Hemisphere Publishing Corp., The Halsted Press, 1975.

Homans, George C. *Social Behavior: Its Elementary Forms*. New York: Harcourt, Brace and World, 1961.

Israel, J. *Alienation: From Marx to Modern Sociology*. Boston: Allyn and Bacon, 1971.

Kâğıtçıbaşı, Ç. *Cultural Values and Population Action Programs: Report on Turkey*. Prepared for UNESCO, 1977a.

―――― and A. Kansu. "Socialization of Sex Roles and Family Dynamics: A Cross-generational Comparison," *Boğaziçi Univ. Journal Social Science Series*, 1977b, 5, 35-48.

Kandiyoti, D. *Mobility Among the Industrial Workers of Istanbul, A Working Report*. Istanbul: Marmaris Social Sciences Asso., 1973.

―――― . "Sex Roles and Social Change: A Comparative Appraisal of Turkey's Women." In *Women and Development: The Complexities of Change*. Chicago: Univ. of Chicago, Wellesley Editorial Committee, 1977a.

―――― . *The Dimensions of Psycho-social Change in Women: A Cross-generational Comparison*. Unpublished thesis, Boğaziçi Univ., 1978.

Kazgan, G. "Labour Force Participation, Occupational Distribution, Educational Attainment and Socio-economic Status of Women in the Turkish Economy." In N. Abadan-Unat (ed.) *Türk Toplumunda Kadın*. Ankara: Turkish Social Science Association Publication, 1979.

Keleş, R. *Urbanization, Housing and Gecekondu in Turkey*. Istanbul: Gerçek Yayınevi, 1972.

Kıray, M. "Modern Şehircilik Gelişmesi ve Türkiye'ye has Bazı Eğilimler," *İstanbul Mimarlık Fakültesi Şehircilik Kürsüsü Yayınları*, 1971.

Komarovsky, M. *Blue Collar Marriage*. New York: Vintage Books, 1967.

Kongar, E. "The Altındağ Gecekondu Area," *Amme İdaresi Dergisi*, 1970, 3.

―――― . *The Social Structure of Turkey*. Istanbul: Cem Yayınevi, 1976.

König, R. "Family and Authority, the German Father in 1955," *The Sociological Review*, 1957, 5, 107-27.

―――― . "Changes in the Western Family," *Proceedings of the Third World Congress of Sociology*. International Association of Sociology, 1956, 4, 63-64.

Kudat, A. "Family and Reproduction," *Toplum ve Bilim*. 1977, Summer.

Lamousé, A "The Family Roles of Women: A German Example," *Journal of Marriage and the Family*. 1969, 31, 1, 145-52.

Levine, N. "Divorce in Turkey." Paper presented at the Second Conference of Demography. Çeşme Izmir, 1975.

Lupri, E. "Contemporary Authority Patterns in the West German Family: A Study in Cross-National Validation," *Journal of Marriage and the Family*. 1969, 31, 134-44.

Meszaros, I. *Marx's Theory of Alienation*. New York: Harper and Row, 1970.

Michel, A. "Comparative Data Concerning the Interaction in French and American Families," *Journal of Marriage and the Family*. 1967, 29, 2, 337-44.

Nash, J. and H. Safa. *Sex and Class in Latin America.* New York: Praeger Publishers, 1976.

Ollman, B. *Alienation: Marx's Conception of Man in Capitalist Society.* London: Cambridge Univ. Press, 1971.

Papanek, H. "Women in Cities: Problems and Perspectives." In I. Tinker, B.M. Bramsen, and M. Burinic (eds.), *Women and World Development.* New York: Praeger Publishers, 1976.

Rainwater, L. and R.P. Coleman. *Workingman's Wife.* New York: McFadden-Bartell, 1962.

Reiter, R. *Toward an Anthropology of Women.* Monthly Review Press, 1975.

Rothschild, C.S. "A Comparison of Power Structure and Marital Satisfaction in Urban Greek and French Families," *Journal of Marriage and the Family,* 1967, 29, 2, 345-52.

Rowbotham, S. *Woman's Consciousness, Man's World.* London: Penguin Books, 1973.

Sacks, K. "Engels Revisited: Women, the Organization of Production and Private Property." In M.Z. Rosaldo and L. Lamphere (eds.), *Women, Culture and Society.* Palo Alto: Stanford Univ. Press, 1974.

Saffioti, H.B. "Female Labour and Capitalism in the United States and Brazil." In R. Rohrlich-Leavitt (ed.), *Women Cross-Culturally: Change and Challenge.* The Hague: Mouton and Co., 1975.

Sanday, P.R. "Toward a Theory of the Status of Women," *American Anthropologist,* 1973, 75, 1682-1700.

Scanzoni, J. *Sexual Bargaining: Power Politics in the American Marriage.* Englewood Cliffs: Prentice Hall, 1972.

Stevens, D.I. *Cohabitation Without Marriage.* Unpublished Ph.D. dissertation, Univ. of Texas, Austin, 1975.

Şenyapılı, T. "Women in the Face of Political Power," *Toplum ve Bilim,* 1977, Fall.

_____. "A New Factor of Metropolitan Areas: The Gecekondu Women." In N. Abadan-Unat (ed.), *Türk Toplumunda Kadın.* Ankara: Turkish Social Science Association Publication, 1979.

Thibaut, J.W. and H.H. Kelley. *The Social Psychology of Groups.* New York: Wiley, 1959.

Timur, S. *Family Structure in Turkey.* Ankara: Sevinç Matbaası, 1972.

Young, K., O. Harris, and F. Edholm. "Conceptualizing Women," *Critique of Anthropology.* 1977, 9-10.

Young, M. and P. Wilmott. *Family and Kinship in East London.* London: Penguin Books, 1957.

THE EFFECT OF INTERNATIONAL LABOR MIGRATION ON WOMEN'S ROLES: THE TURKISH CASE

Nermin Abadan-Unat

International Migration: A Brief Historical Perspective

Over the course of history, migrations of various kinds have been nearly universal. Three main patterns of migration can be discerned: group migration, free individual migration, and restricted migration (Thomlinson, 1976).

Group migration, or large scale population displacements, may spring from various causes, including invasion, conquest, forced labor, colonization, war, etc. In recent centuries (with some exceptions), migration has tended to be in smaller units: a single person or a nuclear family unit, sometimes accompanied by other relatives. This free individual migration has been defined as "a spontaneous movement of individuals, relatively free. . . from legal restrictions, sometimes aided by the land policies of some leading countries of immigration" (Fairchild, 1925, quoted in Thomlinson, 1976, pp. 285-86).

Especially after World War II, however, rules regulating external migration increased in number and restrictiveness, resulting in the present pattern of restricted migration. The migratory movements of today take place within the framework of carefully designed bilateral agreements, as governments adopt deliberate policies toward migration, even embedding such policies in their development plans. Rather than individual decisions, migration is now a function of government plans for "manpower import" or "export of excessive manpower." Thus migration has become an inherent element of the prevailing economic system, supplying a new army of reserve labor.

International Migration: Current and Future Perspectives

Today, international migration flows mainly towards the highly industrialized countries—to Europe, the U.S. and Canada, and the oil-rich countries of the Middle East. There are regional movements as well to the more developed countries of Africa and Latin America. All of these migratory movements have been subjected to policies based on one or another of three models: a) the immigrant or integration model; b) the guest worker or rotation model; or c) the selective migration model. As the Turkish case has been subjected, at different times, to all three types of policies, a short analysis is in order.

The first model has been adopted by countries which are or have been underpopulated, or have experienced a sharp demographic decline, so that foreigners are invited for both economic and demographic reasons. Thus, countries such as the U.S., Canada and Australia, and more recently, France and the Federal Republic of Germany, have accepted foreigners not only as economically productive manpower, but also as potential citizens, and have, therefore, made efforts to integrate immigrants and their families into their own economy and society. These countries, however, have been quite selective, often on cultural or racial grounds. Most recently the criteria for selecting immigrants have focused on both the qualities of the immigrants (level of skill, education) and the country of origin.

The guest worker or rotation model is basically a product of the economic expansionism of the highly industrialized countries of post–World War II Europe. Most important in spearheading this model were Switzerland, Federal Germany, and the Netherlands, but in the second half of the 1960s, it was generally accepted by almost all the EEC countries. During this time, essential structural changes affecting the Common Market countries, such as the attainment of a high level of concentration and centralization of capital, the internalization of capital, and the tendency of this capital to move to peripheral areas, led to the invitation of foreign workers for primarily economic (not demographic) reasons, as cheap imported labor fed economic growth by holding down or at least stabilizing wages and maintaining high rates of profit, investment and expansion (Abadan-Unat, 1976; Paine, 1974).

The migrants of the new "European South" (at first predominantly male, later increasingly also female) from the Mediterranean countries such as Portugal, Spain, Italy, Greece, Yugoslavia, Turkey and the Maghreb, permitted the worker class of the host country to move up into skilled or semi-skilled jobs (Nikolinakos, 1973). Given the fact that these foreign workers were considered to be employed for a limited period of time and potentially dischargeable in periods of recession, efforts towards integration were not undertaken. The host countries were much less selective as to the occupational, national and racial backgrounds of the foreign workers.

The Turkish external migration concept was built upon this model. The Turkish economists and administrators who designed the first Five Year Development Plan assumed that Turkish migrant workers would sign contracts of one year's duration, acquire during this period new skills and experiences, gain the possibility of saving and sending home remittances and, after the completion of their turn, return home in order to make room for a second group. The spirit of the Turkish-German bilateral agreement of October 31, 1961 reflects these ideas. However, events took another course. The demand for additonal manpower in Europe was so acute and intensive in the 1960s that very soon the duration of the working contracts was prolonged, first for two years, later for an indefinite period of time. Furthermore, many migrant workers bluntly refused to return home. Employers, too, were reluctant to undertake new efforts and expenses and to lose time in order to receive replacements for their work force. Finally, arguments based on human rights began to exert pressure on public opinion, labelling the rotation model as unjust and unfair. These developments prepared the ground for the transition to the third model, which became dominant after the energy crisis of 1973 (Abadan-Unat, 1976; Weber, 1970).

In the third model, called *mixed or selective integration,*some foreigners are invited for demographic and economic reasons and are encouraged to become citizens of the host country, while others are invited only for economic reasons and are encouraged to return to their home countries after a given number of years. This policy was developed by France, followed by Belgium. France, for instance, encourages Portuguese and Spanish migrants to settle, but attempts to induce North Africans to return home.

Following the energy crisis of 1973, all European countries totally stopped any further recruitment, thus bringing the remnants of any rotation practice *de facto* to an end, and replaced it with the model of selective integration. This significant change of policy had most important consequences with regard to family reunion, employ-ment of women migrants and education of the second generation. It affected not only the Turkish migrant population in Europe, but indirectly also the demographic structure of some regions within Turkey with a high rate of external migration, such as Yozgat, Sivas, Şereflikoçhisar, Denizli, etc.

In addition to these three major types of post-war migration, a new form of selective migration, applied mainly in the Middle East, deserves special attention. Migratory workers in this area are exclusively male and handled as "package deals" between governments and entrepreneurs of large projects (Choucri, 1977; Adler, 1975). Thus, instead of granting migrant workers the right to work for a given period of time, the work permit is only given for the duration of the project.

In all cases of present day migration, the major "pull" factors have been: economic expansion, unfavorable demographic situations in both the sending and receiving countries, and a steady upward mobility of indigenous workers. On the other side, the major "push" factors in the sending countries have been unemployment, poverty, economic underdevelopment, and retarded industrialization (Castles and Kossack, 1973).

These processes lead, as Galtung rightly points out, to asymmetrical interaction relations between nations and create a new form of dependency (Galtung, 1971). Thus "center nations" tend to require a higher level of skill and education, knowledge and research, whereas "periphery nations" continue to supply raw materials, markets, and surplus labor force.

Since the abrupt halt in recruitment to all EEC countries in 1973, new forms of illegal migration have emerged as a logical consequence of the asymmetrical dependency. So-called "tourist" workers from Turkey continue to intrude into West European and oil-rich countries, hoping to find some employment. Furthermore, increasing requests for asylum for alleged political persecutions are creating new political conflicts, since most of these demands are actually economically motivated. This desperate search for new job opportunities has resulted in further restrictive policies, such as the decision of Federal Germany, followed by other European countries, to require entrance visas from citizens of Turkey, Pakistan and Sri Lanka.

To sum up, Turkish migration has undergone four major phases. Each of these phases has affected both these migrant women who went abroad as well as those who were left behind. The first phase represents "predominantly single exodus, husbands leaving wives at home." The second phase contains "family reunion under special conditions," implying a minimum term of two-year employment abroad. During the third phase, which coincides approximately with the recession of 1966-67, "priority in recruitment of women workers" is accorded. This phase marks the sudden rush of Turkish migrant workers to Europe. The fourth phase, which follows the energy crisis of 1973, is marked by "consolidation of the numbers of existing migrant workers, encouraged family reunion, opening of work possibilities to women migrants, acceleration of male migration to oil-rich Arab countries."

During all these phases, migration has posed problems very different from those arising from internal movements; problems such as longer absences, greater distances, uncertainty of remittances, significant wage differentials, the necessity of mastering a new language, difficulties in communication with authorities, longer separation of family members, and cross-cultural conflicts. It is in the light of these special problems that we endeavor to analyze the impact of international migration on women with special reference to Turkish empirical data.

Women in International Migration

Contrary to prevalent opinion, significant numbers of women join the international labor migration movements autonomously, though they also accompany their families and join the labor force in the receiving country. Between 1960 and 1974 in the U.S., 53% of the 1,977,400 immigrants from Latin America, 56% of the 933,800 immigrants from Asia and 56% of the 1,753,300 immigrants from Europe were women. In Africa in 1973, 43% of all the emigrants leaving for residence in another country were women (Youssef, Buvinic and Kudat, 1979). In 1978 there were about 215,000 Turkish migrant women employed in Europe. Their distribution was as follows: Austria, 31,800; Federal Republic of Germany, 134,342; Switzerland, 12,979; Belgium, 5,175; the rest being scattered over France, Holland, and the Scandinavian countries (OECD, 1979).

During the initial phases of the labor movement from one country to another, female participation is often low. It increases during subsequent phases, owing both to autonomous and to dependent female immigration, but is predominantly controlled by explicit migratory policies of the host country. The sudden flux of Mediterranean excessive population was at the beginning almost exclusively male.

However, due to economic factors such as the continued usage of out-dated industrial equipment, lower wages, and technical need for manual dexterity, etc. right after the recovery from the recession of 1966–67, there has been a growing demand for the employment of female migrant workers (Abadan-Unat, 1977). This situation produced a brand new challenge not only to Turkish women, but even more so to Turkish men. Due to the fact that at that period over 1 million Turkish men were registered for work permits and contracts at the Turkish Labor and Employment Office, the possibility of sending one's wife or daughter ahead, thus creating the legal ground for family reunion, created in the mentality of a great number of traditional-minded Turkish men revolutionary concepts. Women of rural background, traditionally socialized, totally unprepared mentally and to a considerable extent unwilling, were strongly urged by their fathers, husbands or other relatives to take up industrial or service jobs in foreign countries in order to secure for their male relatives the possibility of obtaining lucrative jobs with higher income possibilities in the near future. Thus, a great number of Turkish women entered industrial jobs with no knowledge of city life, highly disciplined working hours or production norms.

Meanwhile, new recruitment has come to an end, and most of the European receiving countries are elaborating comprehensive sets of policies in order to smooth family reunion. The only exception to this trend is the position of the immigration countries in the Middle East. At present, Libya, Saudi Arabia and the Gulf States have adopted a very restrictive immigration policy. Accordingly, Saudi Arabia permits only professionals, experts and the staff people of those corporations with a minimum of 300 million dollars capital to bring their families with them.

Typologies of Migrant Women

Because there are so many different types of international migration (seasonal, temporary, permanent), an attempt to develop some criteria for classifying migrant women may be useful.

One classification may be based on the type of instigation to leave the home country. Three basic types may be distinguished. a) *Accompanying migration:* in this case the woman or girl leaves her country of origin together with the male head of the family. b) *Induced migration:* in this case the woman's migration is imposed by a husband or father in order to facilitate his own exodus or that of other male members of the family. c) *Autonomous migration:* in this case the woman's migration represents an individual decision and should be accounted as the product of an emancipatory process.

A second classification may be based on degree of experience in urban settings in the home country. Again, three categories may be distinguished. a) *Urban background:* in this case, the woman was born in the city, or has lived in the city for an extended time prior to migration. b) *Transitory urban background:* in this case, the woman has spent time in the city only as the first step in a two-phase out-migration process. Here familiarity with urban structures remains extremely limited, and there is little change in the rural life style. c) *Rural background:* in this case the woman has no urban experience in the home country prior to migration. This situation represents the most abrupt transition from peasant culture to Western urban culture.

A third typology, based on the duration of stay abroad or at home, may be suggested. Once again, three groups may be differentiated: a) migrant women, who after a period of waiting join their husbands and take up permanent *residence abroad;* b) migrant women or girls, who after a lengthy stay abroad, are *repatriated;* and c) female members of migrant workers' families who *stay behind in the home country.*

Depending on the nature of the questions to be analyzed, one or all of these three typologies may be of relevance.

Characteristics of Turkish Migrant Women

- Turkish migrant women represent a relatively young population group; more than half (56%) are in the age group of 25-30. Similar to other migrant women in Europe, 76% of the Turkish migrant women are less than 35 years old.
- More than two thirds of the employed Turkish women are married (64%), 58% live with their husbands in Europe.
- The highest fertility rate belongs to Turkish families, the lowest to Greeks. Generally 50% of the Turkish workers have 2 children, 21% have 3-5, and 10% have more than 5 children.
- The educational level of migrant women reflects two distinct groups. Those who have not attended school at all are slightly more numerous than among the male migrants (10% vs. 7%). The same difference is also reflected among the groups that only attended primary school: while 70% of the men attended 3-5 years in primary school, this percentage is 61% for women. The second group of women represents those who attended secondary or professional schools. Among this group the ratio

is opposite. More women have a higher educational level than men (38% vs. 21%).

• The occupational training of women is considerably less than that of men. In 1974 there were 16% of women versus 34% of men who benefitted from school or enterprise-furnished occupational training. Even so, Turkish women abroad are more skilled than their counterparts in Turkey (Maehrlaender, 1974).

• Most are employed in jobs requiring no qualification (50%). Out of 81% engaged in production jobs, 26% are employed in the metal branch, 19% in textiles, 9% in the food industry, and another 9% in the chemical industry; the remainder work in the service sector, in which 11% work in cleaning jobs. In Scandinavian countries the majority of Turkish migrant women are employed only in part-time jobs.

• As their primary motivation for migrating abroad, 55% of the women surveyed indicated the desire to join their families, while another 45% indicated the desire to save money.

• Turkish women workers are receiving noticeably lower wages than men. In 1977, 66% of the women workers in Germany were receiving a monthly net income between 500 and 800 DM, while 63% of the men received an income of 900–1500 DM or more.[1]

Economic Activity, Occupational Roles, and Outlook for Future Employment

Migration has a more positive effect on men than it does on women. Female migrants experience lower occupational status, longer working hours, lower earnings and worse living conditions. Discriminatory practices are bound to affect women migrants because they are restricted from the outset in terms of opportunities, types of work, and work conditions available to them.

Although migrant women in general are aware of the lower wage scale they are paid and the limited opportunities for promotion they are given, their adjustment to industrial life is totally negative. This is partly due to the fact that while "female" occupations are underpaid, work in sectors with heavy female employment such as textile, clothing, and food packaging is not exhausting. Although the nature of the work is relatively simple, repetitive and monotonous, it is not particularly hazardous.

The basic source of dissatisfaction among migrant women workers seems to be the open discrepancy of wages. According to Abadan's 1963 survey, only 36% were satisfied, the dissatisfaction rising with increased education. While only 44% of primary school graduates expressed critical attitudes, the rate went up to 58% among secondary school graduates (Abadan, 1964). This tendency has been confirmed in another comparative survey (Maehrlaender, 1974), in which 64% of the Italian, 64% of the Turkish, 68% of the Greek, 54% of the Yugoslav and 41% of the Spanish women workers evaluated their wages in regard to meeting the cost of living as "bad."

On the subject of chances for promotion, a significant proportion (48%) of migrant women had no opinion. This reflects the failure to inform migrant workers about the possibilities of social mobility. Among those who saw no chances (20%), 32% cited as the major obstacle ignorance of the language, 15% lack of professional training, and 14% prejudices and discrimination on the part of Germans (Maehrlaender, 1974).

Lack of previous working experience, belonging to different social strata together with unaccustomed spatial arrangements in dormitories seem to be factors contributing to a high degree of isolation and alienation among migrant women, preventing the development of an "esprit de corps." This reflects itself in situations requiring mutual assistance and group integration. In the Abadan survey of 1963, while 25% of the migrant women claimed not to be able to receive any help during working hours, this proportion reached only 15% for men. Similarly, 80% of the men rated group cohesion as highly favorable while 65% of the women expressed the same degree of satisfaction (Abadan, 1960).

The frustration encountered during working hours due to isolation seems, however, to be compensated for by increased friendship ties after work hours. While only 41% of the men met their colleagues outside of work, this rate went up to 60% for the women. Especially among women with vocational education there seems to be a higher degree of communication. Fifty percent of the workers with such background meet their work colleagues also outside the factory.

Another interesting point is related to preferences for fraternization with other contingents. While both men and women seem to prefer the citizens of their host countries for friendship forming, men cited in second place Italians (9%), while women preferred Greeks (6%). This preference shows that negative stereotypes are losing their effectiveness if similar social conditions of the respondents help to create common frames of reference. This observation was reconfirmed by a recent study in Federal Germany, in which migrant women emphasized the same preferences (Abadan, 1964; compare also Teber, 1980).

It is possible to conclude that the entrance of foreign women workers into complex industrial enterprises of developed countries should not be looked upon as an unsuccessful venture. In spite of migrant women's difficulties in terms of adjustment, industrial jobs and even menial ones expose migrant women to factory work, discipline, awareness of time, punctuality, trade union activity, and access to social security, all of which were unknown to most of them prior to their departure from their home country. In addition, environmental conditions in satisfactory housing, life in big cities, and increased exposure to mass media prepare the ground for emancipatory actions. This process also explains why unemployed migrant housewives in Federal Germany are eagerly waiting for an opportunity to work outside their homes (Table 1).

Table 1
Intention of Foreign Housewives to Enter the Labor Market (Figures in Percent)

Nationality	Yes	No	Perhaps
Greeks	52	36	12
Italians	48	36	16
Yugoslavs	72	16	12
Turks	80	08	12
Age			
Under 25	90	10	—
25–35	48	35	17
35 and over	66	18	16

Source: Bundesministerium für Jugend, Familie u. Gesundheit, Situationsanalyse nichterwerbstaetigen Ehefrauen auslaendischer Arbeitnehmer in der BDR, 1977, Tabelle: 11.

Occupational Opportunities for Migrant Women

One of the fundamental characteristics of the labor market in all industrialized countries is the marked degree of segregation by sex: women are concentrated in a limited range of occupations and industries. Occupation or industry thus divides the male and female labor force effectively into two different and relatively noncompeting labor markets. Hence labor market segregation has important implications for adjustment to technological change.

The labor market is also segmented, with a primary sector employing so-called "advantaged workers" and a secondary sector employing "disadvantaged workers." Disadvantaged workers are employed in enterprises where wages are low, working conditions poor, employment often unstable, and opportunities for further on-the-job training limited. A great many of the "female" occupations referred to above are in the so-called "secondary sector." Technological changes are worsening this situation.

As reported by ILO and other UN specialized agencies, the decline in female employment in particular industries such as the metal trades, clothing, leather footwear, food and beverages may be attributed in large part to the extent and nature of modernization methods. Industries which have adopted a higher capital-intensive technology resulting in displacement of labor have found it easier to displace women than men. They have justified this on the ground that women lack skills, are illiterate, and are unwilling to learn new processes. This argument hits mostly migrant women workers, who fit in these categories and due to language barriers are unable to improve their qualifications (Beneria, 1978; Tadesse, 1979; UN Decade for Women Conference, 1980).

In textile industries, ILO found that when new machines were installed, the tendency was to substitute male workers for women workers and to keep women workers on the older, non-automatic machinery. In postal and telecommunication services too, new technical equipment resulted in the abolition of temporary or part-time jobs. Such posts were frequently occupied by women and it was the female staff who were most affected by the adoption of new techniques (ILO, 1977).

A recent report of the UN stresses that "in the absence of full employment, rapid and thoughtless technological change can only exacerbate social problems, especially through the displacement of workers—particularly minorities and women who are just beginning to achieve job levels which permit them to enjoy the benefits of technology" (UN Decade of Women Conference, 1980).

The estimation of employment chances for women in the 1980s indicates that automation of manufacturing processes has tended to diminish much of the routine work typically done by women (light assembly, conveyor belt work, packing). The general pattern in such technical developments seems to be to reduce or downgrade the openings for routine work, but to enlarge the opportunities for more highly qualified people (UN Seminar, 1969).

This tendency obviously leaves only domestic service as a future outlet for female employment (aside from low status industrial jobs). This is especially well documented in Latin America and France for those migrants who are young and have arrived recently in the capital city areas. In 1970 in Buenos Aires, 62% of migrants coming in from neighboring countries found employment in domestic service (Jelin, 1977). In France, of 210,000 active migrant workers, 76,000 were employed in industry, and 73,000 in domestic services (Secretariat d'Etat, 1975). In the case of Turkish women workers, those who enter domestic jobs are opting for such an occupation as a supplementary income source. They usually perform domestic work on weekends and are predominantly widows or divorced women with heavy family charges. However, looking closer at the salaried work, a great number of Turkish women are performing in the service sector; we may detect that a great majority are cleaning jobs, especially with municipal institutions in large cities.

Many employed migrant women are not only confronted with the problem of handling the double burden of work and housework, but, in order to secure an additional source of income, are shouldering a third type of work, the illegal "black work." This accumulation of stress due to overwork, of course, results in physical exhaustion. In 1976, 44% of Turkish women (versus 38% of men) were ill longer than 10 days (Nolkensmeier, 1976).

Spending, Saving and Investment Tendencies

For migrant women, the basic motivation in taking up any type of work is economic. The tendency of migrant women to spend more and remit less money than men is quite sharp. A Turkish survey on spending and saving habits of Turkish migrant workers revealed that 47% of women are not sending any money back. Lack of confidence in complex organizations and inadequate information on banking facilities seem to induce women to keep large sums at their temporary homes. While men are more eager to invest in agricultural enterprises or land, women prefer houses or flats in the home country. Women seem to prefer safe, riskless and passive investment forms. The irresistible impact of advertisements, mass media, and especially TV, encourage Turkish women migrants towards excessive purchase of clothing and durable household goods. A belief in the superiority of commodities produced abroad leads them to pronounced conspicuous consumption (Abadan-Unat, 1977).

However, freedom for consumption does not necessarily mean the liberty of choosing a different way of living. If one looks at many of the houses built in Anatolia by migrant workers who have returned or are still working abroad, one may see that in these brightly painted, large (five or six room) houses, most of the rooms are left unused. Thus we may ask whether economic affluence and the cult of foreign consumer goods can serve as a criterion for emancipation. It seems that these new habits represent more pseudo-emancipation than deep and lasting change in mentality (Yenisey, 1976). Marginalization as a minority group in an alien society at large probably leads to compensation by means of showing off. Women in this respect appear to be especially vulnerable and open to consumerism-oriented advertisement.

In Turkey, as in other Mediterranean countries, among the urban, lower income groups, husbands are as a rule the principal breadwinners. Even in rural areas, where women bear an equal share with men in terms of participating in agricultural production, the husband is the sole middleman between the household and the market. This unchallenged position becomes shaky if women are the first to migrate. This sudden role reversal became particularly visible during the third phase of Turkish migration to Federal Germany, when women workers were preferred over men and large contingents of psychologically unprepared rural women were, so to speak, catapulted abroad when they entered a world they were unable to comprehend (Abadan-Unat, 1977).

Thus, one of the most important sources of dispute among working spouses has been and still continues to be the allocation and control of household income, the establishment of separate bank accounts and the authority to decide on these subjects. Dispute also arises very frequently over the use of joint savings and the type of investment (Kudat, 1975).

Whether or not migrant women will be willing to make greater use of educational opportunities in order to be able to compete in the face of dwindling work opportunities depends to a large extent on the attitude of the husbands. The likelihood that more free time will be made available to women through a kind of partnership marriage arrangement is not very high, due to the overwhelmingly traditional orientation of the Turkish migrant group abroad. This strong social control prevents the growth of belief in internal control of reinforcement, meaning a tendency to assume full responsibility for one's actions. The existence of large ethnic groups in foreign countries generally means that the individuals there, especially the women, are more "other-oriented" and less prepared to develop an autonomous, self-reliant, active behavior tendency (Akpınar, 1977).

Psychological Consequences of Migration

At first glance the entrance of migrant women without industrial work experience into the labor market, or their joining their husbands abroad, seems to take place without particular friction or conflict. Since a great number of migrant women have been brought up in a traditional way, the assumption is that in their childhood they were already prepared to adjust themselves at any time to totally different environments (e.g. Kıray, 1979). Yet very soon it becomes evident that confrontation with a highly different environment and the resultant steadily growing nostalgia create much psychological change and stress which may lead eventually to behavioral disturbances. The effects are as follows:

- Multifaceted abruptness

  Women who for the first time in their lives have to undertake a long journey alone or are obliged to commute to their work place by themselves are prey to serious frustrations. Similarly, unexperienced women are suddenly introduced into a complex industrial system where they work for wages with an intricate tax deduction scale on the payroll, which needs detailed explanation to be understood. Some of these examples clearly indicate the unpreparedness to which many migrant women are exposed. The crucial point in this process is that when all this exposure occurs simultaneously, it creates among an important segment of the migrant population acute anxiety and alienation.

- Discontinuity

  For many migrant women the change of work participation appears to be limited to their stay abroad. Since they consider their new occupational role to be temporary and assume that they will have little or no chance of using their working experience, they are not very highly motivated to learn new skills or the indigenous language.

  A significant change occurs also in their self-image. Women suddenly measure almost all their actions from the point of view of being a breadwinner, a money maker, a capital accumulator. Thus the entrance of migrant women into the labor market means generally not to become an "industrial worker," but to "make money, and accumulate savings." This monetary orientation has a deep effect both on the wives and children who accompany their husbands and those who are left behind (Gürel and Kudat, 1978).

- Easing Up of Social Control

The total change of environment means generally that migrants from rural or small town origins are no longer subject to the permanent control of the family, especially the father, relatives of the father, and later the husband. Migration causes changes in the composition of the family structure and the acceptance of new frames of reference. Instead of submission, passivity and lack of initiative, migrant women are psychologically ready to accept new patterns of behavior. This is a healthy development if it is also supported by the environment, which is often not the case.

- Impact of Migration on Mental Health

The extraordinarily fast transition from traditional to industrial life has produced mental disorders. A recent survey of migrant women workers in the Ruhr region of Federal Germany indicates that particularly migrant women workers from rural areas who were obliged to move directly from their home villages to large cities abroad and to be separated from their husbands and/or children without any knowledge of a foreign language were subject to psychosomatic diseases. Out of 77 female patients, 53 were treated for conditions such as "uprootedness syndrome," "atypical depression," "neurosis," "depressive reaction" and "nostalgia reaction." The most common symptoms of these patients were intense anxiety accompanied by heart or chest pains, stomach ulcers, sleeplessness, lack of appetite, physical deficiency, sexual problems, and head and back aches. These symptoms generally appeared after an incident such as a traffic accident, discharge from work, or bad news from home. The average age of these 53 Turkish women patients was 30; their duration of stay abroad, 6.2 years. A second important group of disorders were of a more serious nature, such as schizophrenia, paranoid syndrome and fatal melancholy. Among this group, too, women were in the majority. These recurrent patterns have resulted in the acknowledgement in medical circles of a new type of disorder, labeled the "guestworker syndrome" (Teber, 1980; Benhert, Florn and Fraistein, 1974; Melon and Timsit, 1971; Özek, 1971). In general women migrants, once faced with serious challenges, seem to be less able than men to overcome unfavorable conditions.

Impact of Migration on Familial Roles: Instability of Family Structures

Important changes take place in the composition of migrant households as a result of out-migration and settlement in urban areas. In contrast to the relative stability of rural or small town households, the make-up of the migrant urban household tends to be more temporary in nature. Migrants often need to exercise not only paternal bonds, but also those of kinship, neighborhood, fellow townmanship, friendship and affinity. According to T. Parsons the isolated nuclear family is a response to the demands of an industrial economy. However, much of the recent sociological research on urban social organizations in Western societies has demonstrated the significance of extra-household kinship ties and the supportive functions of the kin group. Litwak, Sussman and Leske (1965) assert that among industrial urban groups, modified extended family structure consists of a coalition of nuclear families in a state of partial dependence. This interaction is situational and takes place according to the needs of the moment.

This general observation is particularly true for the family structure of migrants. Although the basic rule is to have a nuclear family, important changes may take place as a result of out-migration and settlement in urban areas. This is equally true for families left behind. As Kıray correctly states (1976), the major characteristic of the migrant family is the change in its composition. The migrant family may split itself into various parts and compose itself in many ways with other kin as the conditions and possibilities of job, money and accomodation change for the migrant himself during his stay abroad. Thus the choices for migrants are quite varied. They may live as married or single residents in dormitories (Heim); with their wives, some or all of their children, and/or with paternal or maternal relatives; they also may share flats with previously unrelated couples or several singles. Any given household of migrants throughout its existence abroad or at home may assume multiple configurations as each arrival and departure affects the network of relationships. Its temporary nature is attributable to the over-all high turnover rate among the migrant population. Even in cases of prolonged stay abroad or definite settlement, the unbroken ties with the home country due to intensive physical mobility, maintain this structural instability (Kıray, 1976).

Fragmentation

The families involved in the migratory movement are eager to accept employment abroad; try to secure employment also for the marriage partner if possible; and for financial, cultural or personal reasons to leave dependents in the home country. As a result, family fragmentation becomes almost a rule. It has become normatively acceptable for a family unit to remain separated for years. In Turkey such a practice was traditionally widely accepted for men, while wives and children would be entrusted to the care of relatives. The big change has been triggered by external migration. Not only unmarried and married women without their families were permitted in recent years to leave in order to secure jobs abroad, but women heading households also became acceptable for the families left behind (Abadan-Unat, 1977). These families could choose between joining either spouses' families or leading an independent existence in their own homes. Kıray considers heading the separate house in the village to be one of the most important functional changes in the role of women brought about by migration in Turkey, a change which no law of the republican era could have brought on such a scale (1976).

Thus one may conclude that a temporary, independent lifestyle due to migration might eventually reinforce emancipatory efforts at home or abroad, yet fragmentation of family life produces a great number of serious inconveniences too. The most essential ones are as follows: separation of spouses may result in very long absences, causing alienation within marital life. This might be especially detrimental to women, considering the "machismo" value judgments or the "double standard" accorded to men. Furthermore, due to various reasons such as the desire to educate children in the home country, unemployment, bad housing, or maladjustment, women are more likely to return to their home country. Fragmentation in such cases increases mistrust among partners, fears of divorce, neglect of children, and deprivation of affection.

Familial Responsibilities and Division of Work

Migration provokes a rapid change with regard to familial responsibilities and work division. The degree of change strongly depends on whether the man or the woman has migrated first, in what kind of milieu the migrant family settles, and to what extent their social network acts as a buffer mechanism to overcome the hardships of adjustment. Generally, even in cases of family reunion in countries placing a strong emphasis on egalitarian values and norms between marital partners, the married migrant woman worker remains attached to the values of her traditional upbringing. The pressure of the in-group tends to reinforce this attachment. Thus, working wives are expected to carry a "double burden," which may become extraordinarily heavy under tiresome work conditions in industrial settings, household chores and poor housing conditions. Even in cases where the woman acted as vanguard and was the first to obtain a work permit, thus acting as the head of the family and being the main breadwinner, reunion seldom produces an equal sharing of tasks. On the contrary, the economic independence achieved by migrant women almost inevitably leads to sharp conflicts.

Another factor which influences women's independence in decision making is the social and economic status occupied by the migrants in their home country previous to migration. An anthropological study of Turkish migrants of rural background in Sweden indicates that the social background of the migrants influences decision making (Engelbrektsson, 1978). Thus the social networks which link migrants at home and abroad has an impact on their capacity for making independent decisions and determines whether they can become "architects of their own destinies" (Magnarella, 1979). This last item is crucial in regard to whether or not women of rural background are permitted to take up employment outside the home.

For those migrant women who by choice or legal restriction are confined at home, other problems gain relevance. For women from cultures where the daily life of the sexes is well separated, such as in many Mediterranean countries, the only way to overcome loneliness is in groups of the same sex. Thus, for instance, the much-criticized Turkish residential ghettos like Kreuzberg and Wedding in West Berlin, Rijkoberg in Stockholm, Feijenoord in Rotterdam, etc., actually provide a tightly structured community life, which represents the only means to escape total isolation. Integration in such communities decreases problems of daily life; however, by reinforcing traditional behavior, the chances for an emancipatory process within the family are blocked. (See Baumgartner-Karabak and Landesberger, 1978; although the picture this book presents of Turkish migrant women is grossly exaggerated, it nevertheless gives some insight into the social control exercised in these ghetto districts.) Taking into consideration the fact that migrant women— employed or not—are confronted with serious handicaps such as uprootedness, lack of language, isolation, and prohibitions against going out alone, the interaction of the micro-community they belong to and the macro-community they live in affects basically only their behavior as consumers. While daily shopping is more or less acceptable, any further exploration in community life becomes an absolute taboo, especially for housewives. As revealed by a comparative study with a group of Greek, Italian, Yugoslav and Turkish housewives, 80% never went to a swimming pool, 63% to a movie, 55% to a restaurant, or 51% to a coffeehouse by themselves (Johansen). This prohibitive code of behavior explains the relatively weak usage of the adult educational opportunities offered. Aside from radio and weekly TV programs in their respective national languages, very few modernizers seem to be able to touch the non-employed migrant women living abroad. To sum up, the change of intra-familial roles takes a longer time than the change of the individual migrant women abroad or the females left behind at home.

Decision Making and Authority

The growth in size of fragmented families due to migration affects authority patterns and decision making within the family both abroad and left behind in Turkey and almost forces women to act independently. Those who are abroad have their own bank accounts, and feel free to invite their own relatives or friends to their homes for lengthy periods, sometimes without even consulting their husbands. In the home country, wherever women act as head of the family in the absence of their husbands who are migrant workers abroad they are obliged to carry on a number of previously unknown transactions such as cashing remittances from the post office or bank, requesting credit for crops or building, choosing the place and type of schools for their children, organizing social functions such as engagements, weddings, etc.

Generally speaking, women migrants who have acquired economic independence abroad or those who are leading an independent life at home in Turkey increasingly handle their income, savings and investments more autonomously.

In nuclear or transient extended families abroad where the migrant woman's authority is not strongly challenged by the husband or other relatives, the new role assumed makes the woman more aware of the importance of literacy, schooling and family planning.

However, migration does not inevitably enlarge the horizons of women in terms of participating more in decision making and sharing authority with the husband. The dominant pattern for husbands and fathers still seems to be to retain as long as possible their traditional privileges based upon inequality within the family and to attempt to transmit these values through socialization. Nevertheless, migration imbues participants with an increased awareness of change. The reaction against these drastic changes depends much on the environment, the background of the family and no doubt to an important degree on the type of personality.

In this context, dominant values cherished by the public opinion of the Turkish community abroad also play a decisive role. Liberalizing tendencies are deliberately counterbalanced by fundamentalist, traditional moral values diffused through various socializing institutions such as Koran courses, cultural programs, films and some press organs. A review of a considerable number of Turkish films shown in Federal Germany indicates that in 90.5% of them traditional male–female roles continue to be depicted. Women in all these films were subordinate to men and women were shown either as housewives or in less than flattering occupations, such as prostitutes, belly dancers, etc. In every instance, decision-making roles were in the hands of men. As the author of this content analysis points out, sexism persists in contemporary Turkey (Suzuki).

The least consulted persons in migrant families are daughters of marriageable age. Those who were born abroad or who joined their parents at an early age may have enjoyed professional training. However, the family head, under the influence of the social control exercised by the ethnic group to which they belong, particularly in urban centers of high concentration, may advocate abrupt cessation of school attendance and force upon the girls the acceptance of pre-arranged marriages, many times in exchange for bride prices. Torn between two cultures, not strong enough to resist, not old enough to achieve economic independence, these girls face grave problems. They tend easily to become drop-outs, to acquiesce in the choices of their families, or sometimes to desert them.

Ambivalence in Fertility Patterns and Sex Relations

Contrary to expectations, migration does not affect the fertility pattern of migrants, especially among the families left behind in rural areas. No matter how much they may be the mistresses of their own homes, the wives left behind do feel lonely because of long years of separation from their husbands. Reunion is the only hope for both sides. One solution is to have children with great frequency. To be pregnant or to be breastfeeding infants helps to keep the women emotionally satisfied (Kıray, 1976).

An interview carried out with a midwife within the Boğazlıyan survey in the village of Çalapverdi revealed that although as a rule there are one or two births each month, in March there is an abundance of births, because the migrant workers who come back on vacation in July almost invariably impregnate their wives. In 1975, as many as 30 women in the village were expecting babies in that month. According to this midwife, these women were not at all interested in birth control methods. The most common reason for childbearing is that they have enough money and property to feed their children, so why not? Reconsidering that according to the Boğazlıyan survey, 65% of the family members left behind were illiterate, 11% were only able to read and write, 7% had attended primary school and only 3% had completed primary school, it is not surprising that in an underdeveloped rural setting a proper evaluation of the nature of the husband's employment abroad and its estimated duration cannot be expected from these women. Here only age seems to be relevant. Among newly married couples since 1970 on, there is some interest in family planning, particularly the pill. There are some 40-50 women in the village in this category. However, they have difficulty in sticking to a daily schedule (Yenisey, 1976).

Turkish migrant women employed abroad are less eager to raise a large family. As far back as 1963, 57.3% of the migrant workers did not want a family larger than three children. The preference of women for no more than two children (38.7%) was slightly higher than that of men (31.5%). Similarly, readiness to make use of family planning methods was quite high (65%). However, important factors may cause an almost total rejection of these intentions. The decision of the government of Federal Germany to extend the maternity leave up to eight months and support it through financial incentives in order to overcome the steady decline in the growth of Federal

Germany's population, exercised its most important effect on migrant workers. Turkish families especially did not hesitate to take advantage of this new right and to produce larger families despite the crowded and unfavorable housing conditions a great majority have to endure (Seidel, 1979).

Migration obviously has also brought about some significant changes in the relations between men and women. Although the majority of Turkish migrants, being aware of their minority position, are generally strongly committed to projecting a profile of strict puritan values, there are many who lean toward the more permissive rules of conduct of Western countries. It should not be forgotten that migration by its very nature leads to a lengthy separation within the family. This very fact produces a consequent exposure to a more liberal social environment. There are quite a few reports in the Turkish press testifying about migrant heads of families who bring with them during their yearly leave their "German wives," even requesting that their legal wives serve and entertain these important "guests." In other cases, local rumors or letters from local inform-ants about the alledged misdemeanor or unfaithfulness of a female family member (wife, sister or daughter) have induced some Turkish migrants to return home in order to save the "honor" of the family by divorce or homicide.

It can be assumed that even in the future, as the incidence of separation may be reduced and the sex composition of the popula-tion adjusted, the drift to a more liberal social environment and the changing economic status of women will perpetuate a higher rate of adultery and even bigamy (Kudat, 1975). Parallel to this tendency, the number of children born out of wedlock may continue to increase.

Education of Children, Childraising Function of Female Teenagers

The most crucial issue for fragmented families is the problem of the children either left in their home countries or raised abroad. The decision of how many children should remain abroad depends largely on the migratory policy of the host country. Although Turkish families in Federal Germany had the largest proportion of large families in 1971 (18% two children, 29% three children, 16% four children, 10% five children, 6% six or more children), they kept the least number of children with them abroad (Maehrlaender, 1974, p. 206). In 1971 only 5% of Turkish migrant workers had three and 3% had four children living with them. This situation changed drastically when Federal Germany implemented a revised tax law and entitled for family allocation only those families, both German and foreign, who kept their children living with them. This legislative amendment provoked a "childrush." Another legislative amendment mentioned above concerning a prolongation of maternity leave with financial assistance also resulted in the growth of family size. Thus it seems realistic to state that decisions in regard to family reunion are taken more on the basis of regulatory policies than individual preferences.

In those cases where all or most of the children are brought into the country of immigration a special role falls upon the shoulders of the eldest daughter of the family, who becomes a surrogate mother, although she is not emotionally ready for the task of raising small children. In addition, these girls—usually in their teenage years—are deprived of school attendance and left deliberately without formal education and professional training (Abadan-Unat, 1977; Meister, 1975; GED, 1979; Berger and Mohr, 1975).

In those families where the mother remains at home, the language barrier prevents these migrant women from helping their children with their homework, and similarly they are unable to establish any contact with school authorities. Neither are they able to transmit adequately to their children the culture, customs, religious values or language of the home country. Wherever bilingual education has not become a part of the immigration policy of the host country, the problem of severe inter-generational cultural gaps and conflicts preoccupies educators and social workers.

The socialization process within migrant families as contrasted with the institutionally guided socialization efforts shows important differences. In regard to child discipline, for instance, there are diametrically opposed values between German and Turkish families. In Turkish families it is predominantly the father who disciplines the children, while in German families discipline problems and educational matters are considered to be the province of the mother. In almost all Turkish families, the father also acts as mediator between the outside world and the family. Thus one can say that within the Turkish family, as in other southern Mediterranean families, the power structure leans more toward patriarchal attitudes, while in about two-thirds of German families, a model of equal partnership is more dominant.

Another important source of differences of opinion is related to the anticipated goals of education. A comparative survey among the major migrant groups living in Germany yielded a juxtaposed picture. For German families the most important goal for their children was to help them become more self-sufficient, independent and responsible, and to develop an autonomous personality, while for the Turks learning aspiration for achievement, obedience and adherence to order occupied the first place (Holtbrügge, 1975).

Another relevant trend seems to be the high importance placed by Turkish migrant families on loyalty toward the state and identification with religious and national identity. Parents attempt to transmit these goals through a patriarchal value system, which very often is rejected by the adolescent second generation. Young boys, especially, in order to achieve full integration, conform to the dominant ideas of their indigenous peers (Neumann, 1977; Ronneberger, 1976; Wilpert, 1976; CIME, 1979).

The temporary migration syndrome in Europe thus compels people to belong to two worlds. Wherever a pluralistic cultural approach towards the migrant child is provided—at present West Berlin has started such a curriculum in districts with heavy concentrations of Turkish children—a balance can be achieved between the culture of the receiving society and that of the country of origin. However, where such a compromise school model is not pursued, institutions performing an "ersatz" (support) function are appearing, such as the numerous Koran schools in Federal Germany. These private schools escape any public control. They emphasize recitation and memorization, and they practice physical punishment. Such schools no doubt represent serious obstacles to the child's development and to his integration into the receiving society. Yet almost all of the pupils of such schools attend them under the strong pressure of their parents (Abadan-Unat, 1975, 1979).

The ambivalent position of parents toward their children in migrant families is very important. The clash between different civilizations, cultures and religions creates in the minds of these youngsters confusing pictures. Having grown up in family settings where little importance is placed on personal communication and where mass media takes up the majority of free time available, youngsters are practically deprived of linguistic means of expression. The pattern of communication is reduced to simple conversation focused on errands of daily life. On the other hand, second generation children are often ostracized by their peer groups in the indigenous population. Since they have little affinity with their home country, they do not feel themselves at ease anywhere and become obsessed by the norms of the affluent society, which all tend towards conspicuous consumption.

With regard to the position of migrant women as mothers, two different models seem to emerge. Women of predominantly rural background with very little or no education, whether employed or not employed, are virtually unable to fulfill their maternal roles after their children outgrow babyhood. Not knowing any foreign language, they are dependent on their children for any communication. This situation often causes children to look down upon their mothers, considering them useless and ineffective.

This first category represents a rather large group. The acute isolation to which these women are subject not only severs them from the accustomed network of their neighbors, relatives and peers, but also undermines their emotional relationships within the family, shaking their personal and psychic stability, contributing to an increasing alienation between mother and children.

The various types of assistance offered by social services exercise only a limited influence. Initiatives taken in favor of women migrants usually originate from voluntary, nongovernmental associations, which, instead of helping the growth of awareness and consciousness, reinforce the traditional roles of women by offering courses in tailoring, sewing, cooking, etc. Thus, for these women migration does not necessarily mean emancipation, understood as individual independence, self-realization, and liberation from repressive social influences. However, women migrants with slightly higher educational levels or satisfactory professional training, who display an eagerness to learn the local language and are aware of the benefits of social security, may improve their status in regard to equality and responsibility.

The second group of women, representing the family members left behind, should be evaluated in two categories. The first one embraces those women who have been entrusted by their husbands/fathers to stay at home within the family of the male migrant. Living with parents-in-law in the patriarchal and patrilocal extended household seems to delay the process of a bride's establishing herself as second-in-command to her husband. This becomes particularly relevant when the husband is out of the country. In the second category, representing semi-complete nuclear households, where the wife left behind is acting as plenipotentiary head of family, the long separation and deprivation of marital companionship may create some problems. But by and large those women belonging to the second category seem to handle the situation with greater vigor and energy. As a result of the challenge, they are obliged to deal autonomously with many questions previously left to the discretion of the male head of the family. This situation permits them to develop in a relatively short period a strong, independent, self-reliant character. Female heads of migrant families are showing—as in the survey of Boğazlıyan—that migration can play a decisive role in accelerating emancipation.

Summary and Conclusions

Present day migration represents a planned exchange of manpower subject to complex governmental policies and bilateral agreements. This situation plays an important role in decisions concerning the choice of working place, family reunion, family size, children's education, etc. The alternatives adopted by migrant women at home or abroad are not exclusively taken on the basis of individual preferences, but as a by-product of the policies shaping the international migration process. Structural changes within migrant families have to be evaluated also under the light of rotation, integration or selective integration policies.

Problems of adjustment depend largely on the type of migration such as accompanying, induced or autonomous. Other criteria related to residential background, duration of stay in various settings, and interaction between networks connecting the home country to the migrant's living place, as well as the prevailing family structure (fragmented, reunited or repatriated), also influence the status of migrant women workers and the structure of their families.

Turkish migrant women are generally employed in "feminine" industrial jobs and the service sector. Considerably lower wages than those of their male counterparts, little or no opportunity for acquiring new skills, lack of awareness of existing labor legislation and limited participation in trade-union activity are the dominant traits of Turkish migrant women employed abroad. Their economic participation substantially changes the family pattern of saving, investing and spending. Conflicts due to financial questions are frequent. A strong move toward conspicuous consumption is noticeable.

The psychological impact of migration on migrant women both at home and abroad is noticeable. Abroad, alienation and isolation create significant psychic disturbances. Stress situations deeply affect sex roles within the family, often leading to psychosomatic diseases. Monetary concerns overshadow traditional loyalties.

Structural changes within the migrant's family are characterized by constantly changing dimensions of fragmentation. Migration causes intrinsic changes in decision making and authority, ambivalence in fertility patterns, and polarization in regard to heterosexual relationships, ranging from archconservative traditional behavior to permissive, liberal attitudes.

Major inter-generational conflicts due to clashing value systems in the socialization of migrant children create a permanent source of serious conflicts. The "surrogate mother" function, imposed upon a great number of teenage girls, along with prearranged marriages leading to forced repatriation, increases stress situations within the family. The school attendance of girls both abroad and at home remains a serious problem, closely related to the educational level of the parents, especially the mother, the impact of social control, life in ghettos, religious indoctrination and duration of stay abroad.

Migration does not logically lead to emancipation of women, understood as liberation from social pressures hindering individual independence and self realization. Emancipation requires increased redistribution of roles and role-sharing within the family and during leisure time. It also requires a grasp of the interrelationship of structures related to production, power structures, social norms, and value judgments. Looking ahead, one might wonder whether the rigid policies concerning visa requirements for Turkish citizens with migrant relatives abroad will not lead to an increasing fragmentation of the migrant family or the family left behind.

NOTES

[1]   Data in this section are drawn mainly from empirical research material of the author (see Abadan, 1964); data relevant to the 1970s are drawn from a comprehensive German survey and another comparative survey carried out in Federal Germany on behalf of the Friedrich Ebert Foundation by U. Maehrlaender (Maehrlaender, 1974).

BIBLIOGRAPHY

Abadan, N., *Batı Almanya'daki Türk İşçileri ve Sorunları* (Turkish Workers and Their Problems in West Germany). Ankara: DPT, 1964, p. 125.

Abadan-Unat, N. "Educational Problems of Turkish Migrants' Children," *International Review of Education.* special issue, 1975.

———. *Turkish Workers in Europe, 1960-1975.* Leiden: E.J. Brill, 1976.

———. "Implications of Migration on Emancipation and Pseudo-Emancipation of Turkish Women," *International Migration Review.* 1977, 2, 1, 32-33.

———. "Die politischen Auswirkungen der turkischen Migration in In- und Ausland," *Orient,* 1979, 1, p. 23.

Adler, S. "People in the Pipeline." Unpublished Ph.D. dissertation, Massachusetts Institute of Technology, 1975.

Akpınar, Ü. "Angleichungsprobleme türkischer Arbeiterfamilien." In G. Mertens and Akpınar (eds.), *Turkische Migrantenfamilien.* Sonderheft 2. Bonn, 1977, pp. 135-300.

Baumgartner-Karabak, A., and Landesberger, G. *Die Verkauften Braeute: Türkische Frauen zwischen Kreuzberg und Anatolien.* Hamburg: Reinbeck, 1978.

Beneria, L. "Production, Reproduction and the Sexual Division of Labour." ILO Working Paper, series WEP 10 (WP .2), July 1978.

Benhert, H., Florn, L., and Fraistein, H. "Psychische Störungen bei auslaendischen Arbeitnehmer," *Nervenarzt.* 1974, 45, pp. 76-87.

Berger, J., and Mohr, J. *A Seventh Man, The Story of a Migrant Worker in Europe.* New York: Penguin Books, 1975, pp. 150-51.

Bundesanstalt für Arbeit. *Repreasentativuntersuchung '72.* Beschaeftigung auslaendischer Arbeitnehmer, 1973, pp. 14-26.

Bundesministerium für Jugend, Familie und Gesundheit. *Situationsanalyse nichterwerbstaetiger Ehefrauen auslaendischer Arbeiternehmer in der BDR.* 1977, pp. 180-81.

Castles, S., and Kossack, G., *Immigrant Workers and Class Structure in Western Europe.* London, 1973, p. 67.

Choucri, N. "Migration Processes among Developing Countries: The Middle East." Paper for Meeting APSA, September 1-4, 1977, pp. 3-4.

CIME, *Fourth Seminar on Adaptation and Integration of Permanent Immigrants.* Geneva: May 8-11, 1979. (17, 1-2, 1979).

Engelbrektsson, U. *The Force of Tradition, Turkish Migrants at Home and Abroad.* Acta Universitatis Gothoburgen sis, 1978, p. 249.

Fairchild, H.P. *Immigration.* New York: The Macmillan Co., 1925.

Galtung, J. "A Structural Theory of Imperialism," *Journal of Peace Research.* 1971, 8, 81-117.

Gürel, S., and A. Kudat. "Türk Kadınının Avrupa'ya Göçünün Kişilik Aile ve Topluma Yansıyan Sonuçları," *SBF Journal.* 1978, 33, 3-4, 115-18.

Holtbrugge, H. *Türkische Familien in der BDR, Erziehungsvorstellungen und familiale Rollen und Autoritaetsstruktur.* Verlag der Sozialwissenschaftlichen Kooperative, 1975, p. 116.

ILO. *The Effects of Technological Changes on Conditions of Work and Employment in Postal and Telecommunications Services.* 1977.

Jelin, E. "Migration and Labor Force Participation of Latin American Women: The Domestic Servants in the Cities." In Wellesley Editorial Committee, *Women and National Development: The Complexity of Change.* Chicago: Illinois University Press, 1977, p. 133.

Johansen, U. "Die guten Sitten des Essens und Trinken," *Sociologus,* 23, 1, 41-70.

Kıray, M., "Küçük kasaba kadınları" (Women in Little Towns). In N. Abadan-Unat, (ed.), *Türk Toplumunda Kadın* (Women in Turkish Society). Ankara: Çağ, 1979.

————. "The Family of the Immigrant Worker." In N. Abadan-Unat (ed.), *Turkish Workers in Europe, 1960-1975.* Leiden: E.J. Brill, 1976.

Kudat, A. "Structural Changes in the Migrant Turkish Family." In R.E. Krane (ed.), *Manpower Mobility Across Cultural Boundaries: Social, Economic and Legal Aspects.* Leiden: E.J. Brill, 1975, p. 88.

Litvak, E. "Extended Kin Relations in an Industrial Democratic Society." In E. Shanas and G.F. Streib (eds.), *Social Structure and the Family: Generational Relations.* Englewood Cliffs, N.J.: Prentice Hall, 1965.

Maehrlaender, U. *Soziale Aspekte der Auslaenderbeschaeftigung.* Bonn: Verlag Neue Gesellschaft, 1974. Tables 12 and 13.

Magnarella, P.J. *The Peasant Venture, Tradition, Migration and Change among Georgian Peasants in Turkey.* Schenkman Publishing Company, 1979.

Melon, J., and Timsit, M. "Etudes statistique sur le psychopathologie des immigrés." *Acta Psychiat. Belg.* 1971, 71.

Meister, M. "Wie in einem Gefaengnis. Gastarbeitertöchter berichten von ihrem Leben in der BDR," *Korrespondenz: die Frau.* 1975, 5, 1-6.

Neumann, U. "Turkei." In U. Boos-Nünning and M. Hehmann (eds.), *Auslaendische Kinder, Schule und Gesellschaft im Herkunftsland.* Dusseldorf: Publikation Alfa, 1977, pp. 258-59.

Nikolinakos, M. *Politische Ökonomie der Gastarbeiter,* Rowohlt Verlag, 1973, pp. 142-43.

Nölkensmeier, I. "Spezifische Probleme der auslaendischen Frauen in der BDR." Paper presented in Geneva, 1976.

OECD. Continuous reporting system on migration. SOPEMI, 1979.

Özek, M. "Soziale Umstrukturierung als Provokationsfaktor depressiver Psychosen." In *Probleme der Provokation depressiver Psychosen.* Graz: Internationales Symposium, 1971.

Paine, S. *Exporting Workers: The Turkish Case.* Cambridge: Cambridge University Press, 1974, pp. 26-27, table 1.

Ronneberger, F. *Türkische Kinder in Deutschland."* Seminar der Südost-europa-Gesellschaft, November 15-17, 1976.

Seidel, H. "Auslaendische Arbeitnehmer in der BDR. Ein statischer Überblick," *Deutsch lernen,* 1979.

Suzuki, P.T. "A Themal Analysis of Turkish Films Viewed by Turkish Researchers in West Germany," *Document.*

Secrétariat d'etat aux travailleurs immigrés. *La nouvelle politique de l'Immigration,* Paris, 1975, p. 109.

Tadesse, Z. *Women and Technology in Agriculture: An Overview of the Problems in Developing Countries.* UN Institute for Training and Research, 1979.

Teber, S. *İşçi Göçü ve Davranış Bozuklukları.* Istanbul, 1980, p.99.

Thomlinson, R. *Population Dynamics, Causes and Consequences of World Demographic Change.* New York: 1976, p. 283.

UN Seminar on the Effects of Scientific and Technological Developments on the Status of Women. Isai, Roumania, August 1969. (St/TAO/HR/37.)

World Conference of the UN Decade for Women. *Technological Changes and Women Workers: The Development of Microelectronics.* Copenhagen, July 14–30, 1980. A/Conf. 94/26, p. 19.

_____ . *The Effects of Science and Technology on the Employment of Women.* A/Conf. 94/29, pp.8–9.

Weber, R. "Rotationsprinzip bei der Beschaeftigung von Auslaendern," *Auslandskurier.* 1970, 5, 10.

Wilpert, C. "Zukunftserwartungen der Kinder Türkischer Arbeitnehmer." In U. Boos-Nünning and M. Hehmann (eds.), *Auslaendische Kinder.* Düsseldorf: Publikation Alfa, 1977, pp. 258-59.

Yenisey, L. "The Social Effects of Migrant Labour in Boğazlıyan Villages." In N. Abadan-Unat, et al. (eds.), *Migration and Development.* Ankara, 1976, p. 358.

Youssef, N., M. Buvinic, and A. Kudat. *Women in Migration: A Third World Focus.* Washington, D.C.: International Center for Research on Women, 1979, pp. 43-46.

ECONOMIC CHANGE
AND THE GECEKONDU FAMILY

Tansı Şenyapılı

Introduction

Gecekondu families have been living in Turkish cities for the past 35-40 years. Through years of struggling against poverty, unemployment, hostility and periodic police persecution, they have finally become permanent elements of urban life. The rural impressions on attitudes and behavior have been abandoned in favor of urban norms, standards and values.

The demographic features of the gecekondu family have basically remained the same.[1] The family has always been nuclear in general; its size is between the urban (4.6) and rural (6.2) averages, but approaching the urban average in recent years. Marriages take place at early ages (18 or even below for women, 18-22 for men). Families with 2-3-4 children are in the majority. The average woman has her first child at the average age of 22. The intervals between births are 3-3.5 years, with the birth cycle being completed in about 10-15 years. Rates of divorce and separation are low and so is the rate of crime. The gecekondu neighborhood in general is a regular, orderly civic community. Compared to the first generation, the level of education is higher in the second generation, but still they can hardly reach college or university levels. In general the gecekondu families still constitute the lower income groups of the cities.

The main transformation that has taken place in the lives of the gecekondu families is in the field of employment. Within the past 35-40 years the function of the family in the urban economy has changed, and consequently the family has attained new standards of living, new consumption norms and new opportunities. Therefore, in this study the process of urbanization (mainly interpreted as adoption of urban consumption norms) and attainment of permanency in the urban environment will be analyzed as a function of the changes in the economic activities of the family. The changes that have taken place in the family structure, social and cultural relations, values and norms are treated as dependent variables.

The evolution of the economic function of the family will be analyzed in three consecutive decades. Although these periods do not indicate clear-cut changes in the economic function of the family, they are used to denote approximate thresholds of change.

Pre-1950 Period

In the 1940s a migration of unprecedented dimensions started from rural areas to the cities. The most important stimulant behind this movement was a transition in agricultural technology from labor intensive to capital intensive methods. This fact coupled with polarization of land in the hands of wealthier peasants caused dislocation of small farmers from land. This movement needs no elaboration, as it has already been widely discussed and documented in the Third World countries.

In the 1940s neither national transport nor communication systems were sufficiently developed. Therefore, the city was an unknown entity for the migrating farmer. No formal or informal organizations existed to take care of his employment and settlement problems, not did he have dependable social and economic contacts in the city. This migration was undertaken under near-compulsory conditions to an unknown and reputedly hostile environment with only enough money to last him a few days. His only guarantee was often the address of a coffeehouse attended by his countrymen. He was so unsure of his future that he even carried his mattress bundled up on his back along with his bag of food. Under these insecure conditions, migration was first undertaken by the household head and the rest of the family stayed to keep up the fight for subsistence until the household head could raise sufficient income to summon them.

The migrants were unwanted elements in the urban economy. There were no economic functions that could be performed by the quality of labor they provided; they were uneducated, unskilled, with no experience of urban economic and social life. Thus, the odd, periodic, unskilled, unorganized jobs they could find now and then were marginal in the economic sense of the word. They could be cut off from the economy with no important consequences. Yet even these marginal jobs were scarce. The migrants lingered in coffeehouses and informal "labor markets" on sidewalks and bus stops waiting for jobs.

The migrants, after a period of sleeping in coffeehouses, parks, construction or work places, finally could settle in the margins of urban land, concomitant to their marginal position in the economy. Thus, miles of tin-roofed, shabby huts with no infrastructure, built on public land or former agricultural fields, surrounded the urban peripheries. Only after building such a shack or earning enough to rent a room in the slums could the family be summoned from the village.

The family, living under extremely bare and unwholesome conditions in these shacks, usually with only one bread-earner in the household, kept up its rural way of life. Small-scale gardening and poultry raising were practiced around the shacks to support the insufficient income of the household head. It was a fight for life. This period of the Turkish gecekondus is documented in the newspapers of the time. The municipal news sections of the newspapers of the 1940s and early 1950s reflect increasing complaints of gecekondu dwellers demanding roads, electricity, water and sewage systems, schools and public baths, and protesting the indecisive policies of the officials, who alternated between tearing these neighborhoods down and supplying infrastructure to them.

1950-1960, The Liberal Period

In 1950 the liberal Democratic Party came to power and opened a new phase in the Turkish economy as well as in the lives of the gecekondu dwellers. Certain basic changes took place in the position of the gecekondu dwellers in urban economy.

With the liberal and inflationary economic policies of the Democratic Party, the private sector took the lead and a vast range of investments began, especially in the urban areas. The industrialization process started, based on import of expensive foreign technology and capital. Therefore, one other input, namely labor, had to be cheap. The adult male gecekondu dwellers provided this required cheap labor in the cities. The term "cheap" used here does not only refer to the remuneration for work, but it reflects a type of labor able to solve its problems without imposing extra financial burdens on the employers or the government. For example, such laborers solved their housing problems by their own means, occupying land without cost, using discarded, secondhand construction materials and contributing their own labor in the building process. Likewise, small-scale businesses were set up in deserted buildings with minimal infrastructure, using obsolete, secondhand tools and machinery.

Thus, for the first time the adult male gecekondu population moved up in general from marginal to small-scale, but not non-marginal, economic activities, in fact, to essential jobs of the economy. Essential, because due to the shortage of capital, all sectors of the economy could not be organized at the modern, contemporary level, so that most of the vital services, distribution and capital maintenance jobs had to be performed by "small-scale" work.

At this point we would like to emphasize the small scale of these jobs which ranged from marginal and unskilled construction work to unskilled factory work, small-scale clerical and service work and small, independent manufacturing and service work. The "small-ness" does not only reflect the dimensions of the work itself, but also denotes the scale of economic and social opportunities derived from it.

The acquisition of non-marginal status in the urban economy had its repercussions in settlement pattern and quality. Now at least one male member of the family was able to bring home steadier and better income although employment in small-scale jobs was still far from providing social security, job guarantee, permanence, and income adjustment to rising inflation; opportunities for extension and improvement were seriously limited. This income was supplemented by the irregular low income of younger children and women. Political backing and channeling of infrastructural investments to gecekondu areas, coupled with the increased family income, resulted in the improvement, crystallization and informal "legalization" of the gecekondu neighborhoods. Gecekondu building increased along with increasing migration, attracted to the cities by the extra pull of investments. The quality of the gecekondus improved, as by now the building process was informally organized, from confiscation of a lot, to supply of construction materials and labor. Former shacks in muddy fields started to become regular neighborhoods.

The conditions of migration changed as well. With increased transport, communication and density of rural populations in the cities, knowledge about city life and opportunities open to the potential migrant disseminated to the rural areas. Thus, the migrant no longer came to an unknown environment with his mattress on his back to gamble for his life; rather, most of the time, he had already secured a place to stay (in the home of a relative or a countryman) and he even was promised a job through the same connections. So more and more household heads started to bring their families along. They could enter their first jobs and build their own gecekondus in shorter periods of time, now that the arrangements for both were assisted by others.

Concomitant with passage to non-marginal jobs, the gecekondu population gained political importance as well. The Democratic Party soon discovered not only the economic, but also the political importance of the masses who had been pushed to the peripheries of the urban economy and space in the pre-1950 period. Infrastructural investments started flowing towards the gecekondu areas and deeds were distributed in exchange for enrollment to the party. This experience affected the gecekondu population. Although they could not get organized economically because of the highly competitive conditions under which they entered the urban economy, they always did get organized on a neighborhood basis (the most common form being a neighborhood improvement association), and they supported the prevailing political forces. This exchange at the political level provided an integration with the urban order in one dimension, whereas integration was carefully denied in the socio-cultural dimension by the urbanites.

Another change that took place in the family with the application of liberal and inflationary policies of the Democratic Party was the entrance of women (wives of the migrants) into the urban economy. With the development of industry, a concomitant private and especially public bureaucratic sector developed. This was a field very suitable for educated middle class women who used the opportunity. Homes of these women provided an area of employment for the gecekondu women who were totally unskilled and lacked the education needed to perform other types of marketable work. On the other hand, this field of housework was extremely open to exploitation due to imbalance of supply and demand. While the gecekondu women had no power to negotiate, the middle class women dictated all conditions of work and determined the fees. Although this field provided extra income for the family, it was earned in return for long hours of hard and undesirable work for inadequate remuneration performed under no work guarantee or security.

Thus, the years from 1950 to 1960 brought the following changes for the gecekondu family:

• Male adult members of the family entered small-scale jobs and, thus, became non-marginal, in fact essential, factors in the economy; younger male children along with newcomers took over the marginal jobs.

• Female adult members entered a single area of employment, housework.

Thus, the family became a multi-income earning unit. This economic change, coupled with political backing, resulted in transforming these families into a permanent feature of urban life. The gecekondu family became economically and politically established in the city.

1960-1970, The Planned Period

While in the former decade the main function of the gecekondu family was provision of "cheap labor" to the slowly industrializing economy, it assumed a second function with the planned phase of the economy after 1960. In this period investments continued, but emphasis on domestic consumption became more pronounced. The industrialists and merchants strengthened by the investments and inflation found out that they could not enter foreign world markets because of international competition, the pricing systems, their low bargaining power and because of the difficulties that arise from the type and quality of organization and industrialization in the country which did not always meet foreign standards. Therefore, the creation and expansion of an internal market became necessary in order to absorb the products of the national industrialization process. The main proponents of this enlarging internal consumption market were the gecekondu families along with the middle class. Most survey studies conducted in the gecekondu areas in Turkey reflect this stocking up on durable consumption goods such as household utensils despite low income levels. In the survey we observed, for example, several families had bought electrical appliances on installment, ranging from refrigerators and washing machines to tape recorders and record players when there was no electricity in the area. The families buy the largest TV sets on the market even though they live in very small rooms; they buy expensive printed bed sheets even though they sleep on mattresses on the floor, and lace table clothes even though they eat from trays on the floor. Young girls and boys from gecekondu areas are strict followers of the latest fashions although this costs them a large portion of their earnings. This propensity to consume is so pronounced that it is realized at the cost of inadequate feeding of the family.

The main reason for the family's exaggerated propensity to consume is the desire to integrate with the urban life. We have already underlined the fact that the main economic functions of the gecekondu family in the city are twofold: provision of "cheap" labor and support of the internal consumption market. This, however, is as far as the city is willing to accept and integrate into itself the gecekondu population. No integration beyond this point, i.e., along socio-cultural dimension, is allowed. This actually is the dimension where the real duality appears. The urbanites are not willing to share their homes and cultural institutions with the gecekondu population. Thus, for the gecekondu population the only way open to integrate with city life is to be able to consume like the urbanites.

In this decade we also observe the replacement of contentment with city life by disappointment. In the early years the migrant compared his life in the city with his pre-migration years, the only other environment he knew. Despite the hardships he suffered in the city he concluded that he was better off. Not only was his family now at least at subsistence level, but they had hopes for improvement of their condition in the near future. The source of these hopes lay in an aspect of their employment pattern.

Data collected from the field show that people engaged in small-scale jobs display high job mobility.[2] This mobility is due to unfavorable conditions of work, inadequate remuneration and job instability. On the other hand, further data from the field show that the gecekondu population evaluates these small-scale jobs in a priority range (Şenyapılı, 1978). The marginal and unskilled construction jobs occupy the lowest levels while small but independent service or manufacturing work has the highest rank. Factory and service work come in between. Yet the job mobility they experience does not enable them to move up in this priority list. Data show that they move back and forth among jobs at the same level.[3] During the early years of migration this job mobility was a source of hope because one who started his life in the city as a porter in the open market knew that he was not bound to remain in that job for long (Şenyapılı, 1977). He knew that soon, through his relatives and friends, a better job could be found and again through the same connections he could build a gecekondu and in time get the deed for it. If he was lucky enough, he could even save some capital to open a small grocery store in the gecekondu district and become an employer. He saw all around him people who had gone through the same cycle and now were "properly" settled. Thus, high job mobility encouraged the gecekondu family, even during the occasional period of unemployment of the household head.

Yet as years went by, it was realized that this job mobility did not provide vertical social and economic mobility and that the family was stuck in the small-job range. It could not move on to the desired levels of income and opportunity. Even the children could not get a sufficient education to rise up to white collar jobs. The male children in general entered small-scale jobs like their fathers and started to drift from job to job.[4] Thus, the high job mobility which was a source for stimulation and hope at the beginning caused disappointmnet especially for the second generation, as it failed to provide their passage to white collar jobs, to real urban standards of living, and to the opportunities that they observed around them. This, in our opinion, is also one of the reasons that has caused the drift of the many second- and third-generation youngsters to urban anarchy.

As more and more male members of the family passed to non-marginal small-scale jobs, as the family built a gecekondu and stocked it with the coveted durable consumption goods and as in time the children got married, the wives of the migrants withdrew from housework. As they had no education or further skills they remained at home. Today housework service is mostly supplied by janitors' wives in the apartment houses and wives of the newcomers to the city. The first generation gecekondu women enter this field only when their families are in temporary economic bottlenecks or when the family strives to make a new investment. Housework in general is considered temporary work and as soon as the family overcomes the economic bottleneck or fulfills its wish, the women withdraw into their homes. Thus, the relation between supply and demand is again upset, this time in favor of the gecekondu woman, enabling her to dictate many of the terms of work (Şenyapılı, 1979).

As to the second-generation girls, they have had better education compared to their mothers (yet not enough to enable them to acquire higher-level bureaucratic or professional jobs). They also have had more thorough experience with urban life than the migrant women.

They are willing to work, but would not consider going into housework. The main reason for this willingness to work is to be able to adopt urban consumption norms. They too mostly go into small-scale service jobs and work as typists, small clerks, manicurists, salesgirls in public and private organizations and as laborers if there are factories in the neighborhood. They are interested in these jobs for the consumption possibilities they offer. In general they tend to marry young, and in their engagement period they continue to work to save enough to establish a new household, but most of them leave work after marriage. If they continue to work, while their families grow, work becomes a source of most of their problems. It is performed at the cost of neglecting the family. The income the woman receives from her small-scale service or bureaucratic job is not enough to enable the family to live at the level she desires. Thus, work becomes a source of disappointment, an obligation to be suffered until the time of retirement or until the family is able to reach an income level where her income would not be needed.

Thus, in the 1960s the gecekondu family continued to supply the "cheap" small-scale labor required by increasing industrialization and the dependent investments, and it assumed a new and important role as the supporter of the internal market.

Conclusion

By the 1970s the gecekondu family had become an essential and permanent feature of the urban economy and of urban life. Because the nature of the industrialization process had not changed basically since the 1950s, the small-scale services, distribution and manufacturing still feed the organized sectors to a large extent, and the extension of the internal market is still important.[5]

Obtaining an essential position in the economy resulting from economic and social protection by the system, coupled with the multi-income nature of the gecekondu family, had certain consequences for urban space as well. The former shabby gecekondu neighborhoods are now proper, low density parts of the cities with clean, whitewashed single-story buildings, most of which are surrounded by small gardens. While in the 1950s the family provided "cheap" labor to the economy and through the 1960s its role as a consumption unit was emphasized, in the 1970s it has developed an economic guarantee against the system, namely, land speculation. With the rapid increase in the population of the cities, urban land values have soared. The former gecekondu rings at the peripheries, which are now connected to the city centers by regular bus or *dolmuş* service, have gained unexpected importance from the point of view of land values. Each gecekondu owner with a deed is almost a millionaire by today's inflationary standards. The value of the plot now surpasses several times the value of the construction on it. As value added is accumulated in the cities, gecekondu neighborhoods nearest to the city centers are torn down to be replaced by high rise buildings. Thus, the 1970s brought a new role to the gecekondu owners, that of land speculators. So the gecekondu dwellers are essential and permanent features of the urban scene, as they are also owners now of a great portion of valuable urban land. The owner now adds new stories to his house himself and becomes a *rentier*, or he gives the lot to a contractor in exchange for 2-3 flats, or he sells it at great profits. Thus, towards the end of the 1970s the general trend has been the transformation of the former gecekondu neighborhoods into high-rise, middle class cooperative housing. The rate of this transformation depends on the rate of accumulation of value added in the city. On the other hand, rapid inflation, especially in the late 1970s, slowed down new gecekondu building to a certain extent since the value of peripheral land is now very high and it is bid for by high and middle income groups who, due to increased car ownership, are moving away from the crowded city centers. The newcomers can now either rent houses in gecekondu neighborhoods or settle in the transition areas near the city centers. We can thus expect intensification of such transition areas in the near future.

Have these long years of life and experience in the urban environment enabled the gecekondu family to become a "real" urban family? Our answer will be only partially affirmative. The gecekondu family today consumes like the middle class urbanites, but it still cannot benefit from all the opportunities of living in an urban environment. Our field study shows that these families still do not use all urban facilities such as concerts, exhibitions, theaters, and such organizations offering financial and legal services. They even do not use all of the urban space except certain centers and sections. This segregation rises from the fact that they are still bound in the small-scale job range of the economy, the remuneration and opportunities derived from which are also at a small scale, as well as from their lower educational levels and cultural differences.

The aim of this study has been to analyze the acquisition of permanent status by the gecekondu family in the city as a function of the evolution of its economic role. Our conclusion is that the gecekondu families in the last 40 years have become permanent and essential factors in the urban economy; in return they have received economic and social support and protection from the economy which is only sufficient to enable them to maintain their positions. Their enclosure in small-scale economic work resulted in their constituting the lower income groups of the urban strata. No basic change in this pattern is to be expected unless the employment structure changes.

NOTES

[1]   "Gecekondu" is the name given to squatter areas and the households there. See also Introduction, pages 15-16 and 22. Data on demographic features are derived from two field studies. The first one was conducted by the author in five gecekondu neighborhoods in Istanbul in 1976 on a sample of 1,100 households. The second one was conducted in three gecekondu areas in Ankara on a sample of 700 households in 1977. This study was carried out by the students of the course CP.201, Planning Studio III, conducted by Dr. S. Aktüre and the author.

[2]   In Istanbul we found out that 58% of the 1,100 household heads changed jobs once, 22% twice and 10% four times. In Ankara of the 700 household heads 60% changed jobs once, 21% twice and 7% four times. The average period between jobs is 2.5-3 years.

[3]   A review of employment history of three typical subjects is given in the following list:

• *Case I* Unskilled factory work, marginal work, janitor at a public institution.

• *Case II* Marginal work, service work in a private organization, service work in public institution, vendor in an open market.

• *Case III* Construction work, owner of a grocery shop, janitor in an apartment house.

[4]   In the Istanbul sample we found out that of the working sons 96% had changed jobs twice. Another researcher working on the second generation in the gecekondu areas also noted the job mobility (Gökçe, 1971).

[5]   For example, Turkey has been manufacturing domestic cars for the last 20 years. This organized automotive industry is backed to a large extent by small-scale, even marginal, work. Since there are not adequate repair and maintenance stations which offer quick service at reasonable prices, hundreds of small repairers and manufacturers took over this kind of work. Instead of waiting in queues in service stations to have the car washed at expensive prices, young boys who walk around with brushes and pails of water, wash and polish the cars for half the price in parking places.

BIBLIOGRAPHY

Gökçe, B. *Gecekondu Gençliği* (Youth in Gecekondu). Ankara: Hacettepe Univ. Yayınları, 1971.

Şenyapılı, T. "Integration Through Mobility," *O.D.T.Ü. Mimarlik Fakültesi Dergisi*, 1977, 3, 2.

———. *Bütünleşmemiş Kentli Nüfus Sorunu* (The Problem of Unintegrated Urban Population). Ankara: O.D.T.Ü. Yayınları, 1978.

———. "Metropol Bölgelerin Yeni bir Ögesi: Gecekondu Kadını (A New Element in the Metropolises: The Gecekondu Woman). In N. Abadan-Unat (ed.), *Türk Toplumunda Kadın*. Ankara: Türk Sosyal Bilimler Yayınları, 1979.

THE PLIGHT OF URBAN MIGRANTS: DYNAMICS OF SERVICE PROCUREMENT IN A SQUATTER AREA

Metin Heper

Both liberal and neo-Marxist conceptions of political change have largely ignored the mechanisms and conditions under which the peasantry, urban migrants, and other marginal groups organize themselves to tap the resources of the state, and in so doing shape the course of change from below (Barkan, 1979). Thus, most studies give insufficient attention to the micro-level processes at the community or sub-community levels where much planned change must be implemented (Foster, 1978).

An important dimension of such dynamics is the relationship between the citizens and the public bureaucracy. Here, bureaucratic responsiveness and effectiveness emerge as two significant issues. Responsiveness of the street level bureaucracies particularly to underprivileged groups is a problem in developed countries, too. (Frederickson, 1976, p. 568). In developing countries the people are even more vulnerable before the public authorities (Goulet, 1968, pp. 295-312, and Milne, 1973, pp. 411-25). Feelings of unbridgeable distance and lurking distrust between the ordinary resident and the bureaucracy, gaps in communication, gulfs between promises and performance in amelioration of problems, and the inability of even the urban resident to find a "handle" by which he can alter his lot are frequently noted characteristics of these societies (Breese, 1966, pp. 96-97). Urban migrants are in a worse situation in this regard. The low capacity of the less privileged groups to organize in formal structures and to articulate their demands is a general phenomenon (Lamb, 1975).

Perhaps with this state of affairs in mind it has been noted that the prospects for stable modernization frequently require that efforts be made to grant legitimacy and provide status to essentially parochial elements in a transitional culture (Pye, 1969, p. 405). Bureaucratic structures, on the other hand, lead to the complete elimination of personalized relationships and non-rational considerations like hostility, anxiety, affective involvement, etc. Since functionaries minimize personal relations and resort to categorization, the peculiarities of individual cases are often ignored (Merton, 1968, pp. 250-56). Such arrangements are resented even in developed countries (Blau, 1960, pp. 59-60). They are often completely alien to traditional culture patterns. Middle Eastern culture, for instance, emphasizes personal contacts and relationships (Bill, 1973, pp. 131-51; Costelli, 1977, p. 57), probably an outcome of the fact that for centuries there was an absence of autonomous corporate structures in these societies.

In fact, as early as the nineteenth century, the Munro School in India, influenced by such Utilitarian philosophers as Jeremy Bentham and James Bill, revolted against what they considered to be the cold, lifeless, mechanical principles, the abstractions of the rule of law, and the blind automatic operation of an impersonal bureaucracy. They were of the opinion that the peasant was in effect deprived of justice because the sole administration of justice was confined to distant courts presided over by foreigners and employing a highly technical procedure. They held that administration in Asia should be simple, and that there should be few regulations (Abedin, 1973, pp. 16-17). Recently, it has been critically noted that "supralocal structures" confront any locality or its subdivisions with uniform and generalized norms (Leeds, 1973, p. 27).

It is patent that there is a need for different administrative structures, i.e., organizational blueprints and values and attitudes on the part of the officials in different environments. In devising an optimum arrangement for a given place and time one needs to take into account, among other things, the constraints under which the public agencies operate on one hand, and the attributes of the clients on the other, more specifically their capacity and their particular mode(s) of coping with the public bureaucratic structures.

Below, I examine some dimensions of the problem in a squatter area, Karlıdere,[1] in Istanbul. I reconstruct the ways by which the squatters have established the squatter area, striven to obtain services from the public agencies, and how in the process have come to tolerate, even if unwillingly, the takeover of the leadership of the community by a radical group. The study draws upon in-depth interviews that I personally carried out with various people in and out of the squatter area during the months of July through September, 1979, as well as upon a number of secondary sources.

Origins and Development of the Karlıdere Squatter Area

The Karlıdere squatter area is approximately six miles from the central business district of Istanbul.[2] The initial factors that led to the establishment of the squatter area were the availability of employment, the shortage of housing and high rents in the nearby urban districts. Initially a series of apartment houses had been built in the nearby choice residential areas. This was followed by the establishment of two factories and other plants not far from the settlement. Drug and electrical appliance plants in a nearby district, a quarter comprising hundreds of car repair shops again not far from the area, and a university situated next to the settlement, provided additional employment opportunities.

The Karlıdere land had originally belonged to the state, and was later transferred to the municipality.[3] At the time of invasion, it was occupied by a retired official. Inaccessibility, because of lack of roads, and undetectability from the nearby main thoroughfare provided the best security for the original usurper until a group of low paid employees at the university and their friends elsewhere pressed by the rising rents in a nearby district, decided to set up their own dwellings. All the people in this group were from the same Black Sea region. They had known each other for years. All of them had been living in the city for several years. These would-be invaders found out that the man who occupied the land had no legal title to it. They subsequently "persuaded" him to "sell" the land at a low price, as this sort of transaction is legally useful in claiming that the land was "bought."[4] A few days later the land was divided into several lots, and the first 20 to 30 dwellings were erected in two days. All this occurred in 1958.

After the initial settlement, the main problem was to assure the continued existence of the squatter area since the land belonged to the municipality. The squatters were aware of the fact that the survival of the settlement depended on their actual numerical strength and the resulting ability to defend it against the public authorities, since their action violated every building code and property law. Consequently, the founders sought to attract a large number of people to the site. The first settlers occupied larger lots.

They used them as building sites for their own dwellings, reserved some parts for their relatives, and/or divided and sold them to other persons, usually friends and acquaintances from the same region. The latter were more than willing to migrate as they could barely earn a livelihood in the countryside.

At a later date, about 1964, the settlement expanded again, this time onto privately owned land. The individual who had a valid legal title agreed to sell the land at a low price merely to avoid conflict with the squatters. The squatters, however, believed false rumors that the land could be obtained free, and broke the agreement with the owner. Consequently, the owner went to the court and the case was eventually settled as the occupants agreed to pay a rather insignificant sum for the land. Afterward, the population grew rapidly, chiefly with newcomers from villages. Soon, there was an official order for the dwellings to be removed. The squatters, however, organized a protest walk to the seat of the provincial government (vilâyet)[5] and managed to stop the action.

Obtaining Public Services

The initial improvements in the squatter area along with the main road and the secondary roads seem to have been the product of the ceaseless efforts of one man—Ahmet Alaylıoğlu, who later became headman from 1969 through 1973. (Alaylıoğlu is now 74 years old [1981].) He had been living in an old and adjacent urban area for about forty-five years. He is an engineer by profession. He worked for some years for the Ministry of Public Works, and after his retirement from public service was active in all kinds of social clubs and philanthropic organizations. While the first group of squatter houses was being built, he used to take walks in the area, and deplored the conditions of the dwellings hastily put up. He decided to help the squatters. He told them that they could not survive unless they got together to establish an association. He prepared the necessary documents himself.

In the early months of 1961, the Association for the Development and Improvement of the Karlıdere Squatter Area was formed. One of the initial activities of the association was to induce people to pool their resources, i.e., collect money, help them design their gardens, plant trees, and decide how the secondary roads should run in the area. Alaylıoğlu observed at this stage, however, that when it came to applying to the public agencies, the members of the association proved completely ineffective; the association was always being given short shrift. According to Alayhoğlu, this was due to the fact that the members had no status: "They were not members of a socially recognized profession like a doctor of medicine, engineer or civil servant."

Thus, Alayhoğlu thought that it was humane, if nothing else, to help them. He took over the administration of the association in 1962, and acted in that capacity until he himself became a headman in 1969. He handpicked as members of the executive board of the association a number of people "who would understand what they were told."

His first move as head of the association was to request from the Asian Club of Istanbul, a philanthropic organization, visitations by doctors of medicine two or three times a week in the area. At the time, the president of the club was Mehmet Hancıoğlu, a professor of medicine, who had earlier been the mayor of Istanbul. In the course of his philanthropic activities elsewhere Alayhoğlu had developed a close relationship with Hancıoğlu while the latter was mayor. The visitations in question began by a ceremony to which the newly appointed governor Ali Vefa, too, had been invited by Alayhoğlu. In this ceremony, Alayhoğlu gave a talk and said that the previous governor had always been true to his word and that he himself had no doubt that the new governor would act the same way; after all, he added, the new governor's name is Vefa—literally, "fidelity." Upon this, the new governor had no choice but to promise that he too would help the area with all the means at his disposal.

Alayhoğlu did not miss the opportunity. He submitted a request for a road that would link the settlement to the nearest urban area. The governor referred Alayhoğlu to the head of the Agency for Roads, Water, and Electricity. This agency is affiliated with the Ministry of Village Affairs, and is responsible for delivering services to areas outside the municipality boundaries. Although the squatter area was within the municipal boundaries, the governor had known the head of the agency for a long time. When he sent Alayhoğlu to him he also sent word that Alayhoğlu was an engineer. Before long teams came from the agency. The engineers in these teams turned out to be old friends of Alayhoğlu, a fact which speeded up the construction of the road, The road at this time was paved with ordinary stones in the most rudimentary manner.

In his contacts with the public agencies, Alayhoğlu often acted alone. He explained that if he took the members of the association along they turned out to be no more than "a crowd which was good for nothing."

His next such lonely expedition had to do with obtaining a bus service to the squatter area. He again went to the governor, who referred him to a director he personally knew in the municipality. It did not prove too difficult to obtain the bus service either, and the service soon started.

In the meantime, however, the main road had deteriorated. Alayhoğlu figured that the road should be paved with cobblestones. Upon his applying to the governor, the latter this time advised him that the director whom Alayhoğlu knew personally had been appointed to some other place, and therefore that he should apply alone to the municipality. This led Alayhoğlu to mobilize the support of councillors in the central Municipal Council.[6] He approached those whom he either personally knew or to whom he had been referred by mutual friends. It had been a standard practice in the area to resort to those councillors who belong to the same political party (or parties) which is (are) in office. When the construction began, Alayhoğlu realized at one point that the contractor was doing a poor job, and that if the whole neighborhood itself did not carry the cobblestones from one side of the road to the other so that the road could be widened by an extra couple of yards, the road would soon deteriorate. And one night they *did* carry the stones. Next morning, Alayhoğlu went to the municipality and persuaded them that the road should be constructed in a proper way.

Alayhoğlu was also active in the opening up of the secondary roads within the squatter area. This time, however, the Agency for Roads, Water, and Electricity did not help him; they told him that the area lay within the municipal boundaries. Alayhoğlu did not lose hope. In his opinion, he was "serving his motherland," and for this "lofty purpose" he would act as the circumstances required. It was necessary, in his opinion, "to carefully study the existing constraints, and find a loophole." Soon the municipal elections were to be held. Osman Yalçın, who became mayor after the elctions, was to visit the squatter area to campaign. Through the members of the association Alayhoğlu sent word to the dwellers that there was a candidate for mayor at hand, and better they be all present when he came. Alayhoğlu personally welcomed the candidate, and he himself made a long talk before the candidate could. He told the dwellers that before them they had a candidate for mayor, and that he could be very useful to the area as a mayor. This was followed by a talk by the candidate himself. Yalçın promised the dwellers that he would indeed help them. In fact, after he became mayor, he sent excavators to the area. The dwellers worked on the construction of the roads under Alaylıoğlu's direction.

Recently these secondary roads have deteriorated to a rather poor condition. Kadir Mert, a long-time member of the association, pointed out that the municipality did not pay attention to these roads at all. The municipality took the stance, "you built the roads, you take care of them."

Part of the time, while Alaylıoğlu was active having the main and secondary roads constructed and obtaining other services for the area, the headman was Taha Esmer, who stayed in that post from 1965 through 1968. For fifty years, he has been a resident in the same adjacent urban district in which Alaylıoğlu lives. He has been chairman of the local political party branch in the sub-province from 1946 until the present for the Democratic Party, the New Turkey Party, and for the Reliance Party, in that order.[7] At the time of the study, he was an employee at the nearby university.

In principle, he had always been against the manner in which the squatter dwellings were built, and the way these areas had grown. But once the squatter area was there he nevertheless helped the dwellers. This is because he did not approve "the state and municipal" action concerning the squatter houses. In his opinion, the public officials first tolerated the growth of the squatter houses, and then gave the impression that they were going to demolish them. He thought that, in fact, this is not what some members of the municipality had in mind; they only wanted to extort money from the dwellers. In one of his several efforts to prevent this sort of thing from happening, he had to go all the way to the vilâyet. His intercession on behalf of the dwellers, however, infuriated the officials there, and one of them was about to slap him in the face if it had not been for the sub-governor who just happened to be there. When the sub-governor revealed Esmer's identity the latter was asked why on earth he had not properly introduced himself in the first place. Kadir Mert, the long-time member of the association, pointed out that neither individually nor as a group had the squatter dwellers been welcome at the public agencies; they were always asked, "Where is your headman? Where is your association?" He added that the municipality people always had a condescending attitude toward the squatter dwellers.

Esmer always believed that obtaining services for the area from the subprovince to which the settlement is administratively affiliated was primarily the responsibility of the councillors in the municipality. In his opinion, it should never have been a preoccupation of the association. He never believed in receiving money from anybody in the area even for obtaining the official seal for his office or for paying for his transportation to the public agencies. He always met these and other such expenses out of his own pocket.

During his term in office he concluded that those at the very top did not follow up their orders lest they lose votes. Consequently, the police acquired *de facto* discretion. The police did not always use that discretion on the dwellers' behalf. It was, therefore, necessary to bribe the municipal police for what they were supposed to do or not do. According to Esmer, another reason why the squatter dwellers had recently had a hard time at the hands of the public officials and the police was that both of the latter two groups had become greatly politicized. He meant "radicalized."

If it had not been for the efforts of Hasan Kara, Karlıdere would not have had its sewer system and its primary school at the time these were obtained. Kara is an old man with a long white beard. He moved to the squatter area in 1969 from the nearby choice residential area. He had a shop at the time, and still has one. Earlier, he had been supplying building materials to the area, and figured that by moving there he would cut down on his transportation costs. After he moved, his primary concern was to have a mosque built. Thus, he and a few others set their eyes on a building which was earlier "owned" by a policeman, but was later "sold" to a university (other than the one adjacent to the settlement). This university still had title deed to almost one third of the area studied here. The university was not using the building at the time. Kara and his friends converted the building into a mini-mosque, but it was far from adequate. Besides, during the winter months it was frequently flooded. Thus, in 1970 they formed the Association for the Building of the Mosque. The primary goal of this association was collecting money from the dwellers and supervising the building of the mosque. Kara, however, met the initial as well as most of the later expenses out of his own pocket. Eventually, the mosque was completed.

Soon, however, its toilet facilities turned out to be a problem. Kara suggested that a sewer system be built from the mosque down the valley where it would be connected to a main system serving a nearby urban district. At this point, the people living in areas adjacent to the mosque asked Kara to build sewers for them too. They advised him that they were ready to meet the expenses. Kara went to Mayor Osman Yalçın, both of whom came from the same province. He also contacted their councillors in the Istanbul central municipality as well as a councillor from another subprovince. The latter was a close friend of Kara. Kara and his friends were promised 250 pipes, but the agency which was supposed to provide the pipes told them that it had none. Kara decided that under the circumstances the only thing to do was to buy them from the market. Thus he obtained the pipes on credit from someone he personally knew. Some of the dwellers did not pay what they promised. The seller of the pipes, however, did not press Kara for a long time. According to a member of the association "this was because he was a good Muslim." Eventually Kara paid the balance. In this way six roads in the southwestern tip of the squatter area, about one third of the settlement, was provided with sewers. Kara tried to collect money for this purpose not only from the dwellers, but also from people in other parts of the city as donations. He was accused, however, of corruption by people from other parts of the settlement as well as possibly by the headman himself. He became bitter at such accusations; he had "single-handedly developed the sewer, and his reward was accusation." He soon quit helping the dwellers to have their sewer system built.

Some dwellers thought at the time that at stake was the headmanship itself. According to some, Kara had his eyes on that job. At the time Alaylıoğlu was headman. Others tied the rift to the sectarian cleavage within the settlement. From the beginning, the Association for the Building of the Mosque was formed by the Sunnites, whereas the Association for the Development and Improvement of the Karlıdere Squatter Area was established by the Shiites (locally called *Alevis*).[8] The latter group were the first arrivals. They came mainly from two provinces, the population of which are mostly Shiites. They constituted the majority of the population. This group, too, built their sewers at a later date in their quarters as Kara did in his.

In each case, an effort was made to obtain pipes from the municipality, pay communally for the pipes not so obtained, lay the main pipes together, and make the house connections on an individual basis. The sewer system built in this fashion was linked to the main artery in an illegal fashion. The municipality chose to overlook the matter. On the contrary, the municipal officials, in this case the officials of the sub-province, were rather pleased with the fact that not much was asked of them. They later *praised* the dwellers concerning the sewer system.

Kara's efforts toward the building of the primary school started when one day he read in the newspaper that a famous actress was thinking of building a school in a squatter area, as a donation. Kara got very much interested in such a possibility. Through one of his acquaintances who was working at a construction for the actress, he managed to talk to the brother-in-law, a man who was close to the actress. This brother-in-law told Kara that the actress was indeed willing to build a school.

Learning this, Kara met with his friends in the association. They decided that a certain site at the southwestern edge of the settlement was convenient for this purpose. This area belonged to the municipality. Kara again went to Osman Yalçın, the mayor, who referred him to the Directorate of Housing in Squatter Areas (of the Municipality). He reminisced that his efforts to obtain services and facilities for the squatter areas met with utmost difficulty with the administrative units with the Central Municipality of Istanbul. He really could not understand why "things were so slow there." He remembered the officials reading their newspapers and drinking their tea while he waited. He commented: "It was as if you were having an audience with the President of the Republic. Perhaps they did not have funds. They might have been expecting money under the table, but perhaps because of my long white beard they could not suggest that to me. It was a good thing that both the mayor and I were from the same province. If it was not for him the officials would not even talk to me." During the construction of the school, the dwellers helped carry some building materials from another construction site where a house was being built for the actress.

In the case of water and electricity no one individual can be singled out as responsible for bringing these services to the settlement. At different times, different groups made efforts on these matters. It was only before the general elections of 1973, however, that the municipality largely of its volition decided to extend these services to the settlement. The bureaucratic hurdles, however, had still to be overcome by the headman and a few others themselves who carried the papers from one office to another.

The squatter dwellers have lately been most frustrated concerning the issue of title deed, which so far they have not been able to settle. The dwellers had beeen trying to obtain the deeds for a long time. They had been promised these titles since the early 1970s. Hüseyin Taş (headman, 1973-77) related that when technical work in the area started (mapping, zoning, etc.), for months the squatters even provided lunch to the people from the municipality. After a while, the municipality declared that everything was ready, and that the titles would soon be issued. However, nothing came out of this. When asked for explanation, the municipality more than once offered that there still remained certain steps to be taken. No one in the squatter area whom the author talked to knew what the real situation was.

Radicalization of the Organized Leadership of Karlıdere

The present administrators of the Association for the Development and Improvement of Karlıdere Squatter Area, however, did not have conciliatory attitudes toward the municipality in the particular and toward the state in general. For a long time the association stagnated. The explanations offered were various. Some claimed that the leaders after the original founder, Ahmet Alaylıoğlu, could not actively run the association, and in time it became a completely passive instrument. Those who had actually run the association during those years countered this argument by arguing that they had to bribe the officials from time to time, and that concerning such "transactions" they were often accused of corruption. They could not stand such accusation, and they therefore resigned. And the association, along with all such associations in Turkey, remained officially closed for three years after the indirect military intervention of 1971.

When the association was reestablished, it was taken over by younger people. These people could really be considered "second generation." The present head of the association, Ihsan Demirtaş, is thirty-six years old. He has been working in the association since 1964. During this period he has taken part in many efforts to bring services to the area. He often joined Ahmet Alaylıoğlu in the latter's several expeditions to the municipality. He related that the older people in the group told the younger ones to keep their mouths shut concerning the bribes they paid the officials, but the young did not always go along with this advice.

When the association was reactivated in 1973, because of personal conflicts it split into three factions. In recent years, however, under the leadership of the younger people already noted, the association presented a relatively homogeneous front. As earlier, it was under the control of the Shiites. But there was an additional element; the association was now very much politicized, or rather radicalized, in its attitudes toward, and in its relations with, the municipality and the state. According to Ihsan Demirtaş, why they had not been granted land titles to this day could only be explained in terms of class analysis, and not by bureaucratic ineffectiveness or corruption: "The municipality and the state in Turkey are controlled by the well-to-do groups." He pointed out that besides the issue of land titles,"the fact that the university across from the settlement recently attempted to have a wall erected between its land and the squatter area, and a major road is planned that would pass through the settlement, are further proof that in the eyes of the state the squatters are only a pariah group." He noted that the dwellers were fed up with the municipality which for years left them in a vulnerable position by not granting them land titles, extorted money from them by the threat that they would demolish their houses. He added that now it was too late for land titles. Their lands were divided into several lots. New squatter houses had been built within these lots. If land titles were granted, the squatters would have to bring down all those additional houses. Ihsan Demirtaş warned that the municipality had better leave them alone. If the police showed up again, he said, there would be trouble and nobody could prevent it.

His warning did not seem to be a mere bluff. Others in the squatter area related that when Ali Vefa, who had been very helpful to Ahmet Alaylıoğlu, particularly in the building of the main road while he was governor of Istanbul, came to the area years later as the Minister of Village Affairs, he was booed, stoned and otherwise not allowed to speak. Even Şeref Tolgaç who as a recent mayor used to have such high esteem among the dwellers because of his"integrity and honesty" could not talk when he visited the area in recent years. Some of the old-timers in the area despaired of getting any services from the municipality. They did not approve of the new strategy. Others were quite surprised, even confused. One said, "They must have a terrible article in their by-laws that they do all these things." But the majority must have had no serious reservations about the new leaders since they elected them.

The new leaders of the association were busy in trying to mobilize the whole squatter area behind themselves. Recently they established the Consumer's Cooperative in the squatter settlement and managed to include the well-known Sunnis of the settlement on the executive board of the cooperative.

Conclusion

The development in the Karlıdere squatter area has been based entirely upon chance factors. If it had not been for Hasan Kara, the old man with the white beard, deciding to move in because he wanted to cut his transportation costs, or Ahmet Alaylıoğlu, the engineer, getting interested in the area for humane or other personal reasons, or the actress, deciding to make a donation, perhaps for publicity reasons, or for the municipal elections in 1973, it is difficult to say when the settlement would have had its roads, sewer system, school, and its water and electricity. The settlement obtained those services neither as a consequence of organized and persistent interest group activity nor as a result of a well-planned and consistent policy of the public agencies.

Initially it was the tenacity of the dwellers themselves which helped them survive under the most adverse conditions. This tenacity and determination to survive were largely the consequence of the fact that they had no other options. The push factors from the countryside combined with the spiralling inflation which was also reflected in rents, left no alternative to the squatter dwellers but to hold on to their lands and squatter houses. Their initial survival may in part be explained by the fact that the local government in Turkey is under the democratic control of the citizens as well as by the overcentralization of the administration and its consequent branch-center frictions, ineffectiveness, and lack of control, all of which made it rather difficult for the public agencies consistently to pursue their policies. (See Heper, 1977, for a discussion of these and related characteristics of the Turkish public bureaucracy.)

Once survival was assured, success in obtaining public services was due to the ceaseless efforts of a few people, a point made earlier. These individuals utilized their status, their personal acquaintances and connections, and at the same time, resorted to ingenious political pressure. They also did not miss the opportunities that presented themselves. Their status at times was based on modern criteria like membership in a presently prestigious profession, e.g., engineering (Ahmet Alaylıoğlu) or being a local politician (Taha Esmer) and at times on traditional criteria like being an old man with a long white beard (Hasan Kara, shop owner). The personalized types of contacts, too, took many forms. It was either being from the same province (Hasan Kara and Osman Yalçın, mayor), or having encountered each other several times on other occasions (Ahmet Alaylıoğlu and Ali Vefa, governor) or both being an acquaintance of a third person (Ahmet Alaylıoğlu, Ali Vefa, and the Director of the Agency For Roads, Water, and Electricity). One example of political pressure was inviting the governor for some other purpose, and then cornering him there. The examples of not missing opportunities are numerous, but two are adequate here: capitalizing on the actress' intention of building a school, and making a speech and demanding concrete promises before a campaigning candidate himself could speak.

It must be noted that factors outside the control of the dwellers also helped them obtain public services. Upcoming municipal elctions were critical concerning water and electricity. The municipality's hands-off policy and its consequence of overlooking some illegal actions facilitated work on the sewer system.

How did the community otherwise carry out its contacts with the bureaucratic agencies and the local government? This question may be taken up at two levels: at the level of the individual entrepreneurs like Kara, Alaylıoğlu and others, or at the level of the community as a whole. Concerning the strategies of the individual entrepreneurs, the most favored mode of action was to approach the governor or the mayor through a personalized interaction pattern. If this was not possible, then the help of a councillor was sought. Here again, the fact that a councillor was from one's own ward was not as important as the fact that one could approach him on a personal basis. Kara's seeking the help of a councillor from another ward was a case in point. The squatter dwellers never thought of walking into an administrative office in the capacity of an ordinary citizen. In fact, they wished to avoid coming into contact with the administrators altogether if they could help it. While they directly approached those politicians with whom they had a personal relationship of some sort, they preferred to contact the higher level administrators through the mayor or governor; if that was not possible, they did go through the intermediation of the councillors. As far as contacts with the middle or lower level administrators were concerned, they drew upon their status and/or their ability to "please" them through "unorthodox" means.

At the level of the community, the only means of contact with the public agencies was through the associations. The associations had been formed on sectarian considerations, personal conflicts and/or ideological bases. The associations primarily collected money from the individual dwellers, mobilized self-help, and/or made *locally* significant decisions rather than pressuring the public agencies and local government through formal interest group activity.

The community as a whole has not been tightly knit. Sectarian and personal conflicts are the two types of conflict that immediately come to mind. The so-called "squatter area lords" create further rifts within the community.[9] Finally, the ideological approach of the present young leaders of the Association of Development and Improvement of the Karlıdere Squatter Area has not been accepted wholeheartedly by all the dwellers.

What were the attitudes of the administrators and the politicians toward the squatter area? What were the consequences of such attitudes? The administrative agencies and the local government have never come to accept the fact that the squatter areas posed a real challenge to their business-as-usual mode of operation. Besides, the bureaucratic and local political elite have always had a condescending attitude toward the periphery. For the members of the periphery who have attempted urbanization and urbanism, they have only had contempt. The upshot of this orientation was hands-off policy; where dealing with them was unavoidable, they adopted a mode of operation that did not make life easy for the squatter dwellers. They were unwilling to make a special effort to help the squatter dwellers to cope with the maze of rules and regulations, or to bend the rules on their behalf. And they had a cavalier attitude toward the petty corruption at the lower level which really hurt the squatter dwellers.[10]

The squatter dwellers, on the other hand, have always had a strong faith in the state. Despite the hardships and injustices they have suffered, they have consistently tended to attribute them to the malfeasance or incompetence of a few individual administrators, and not to the state as a whole. They have even accepted the aloof attitudes of the bureaucrats as becoming the agents of a state which they hold in very high esteem.

The fact that recently they did not openly oppose a radical group that challenged the very legitimacy of the state, however, is an ominous sign. The Turkish case indicates that one of the reasons why people may become ready customers for ideological goods is bureaucratic insensitivity to people's genuine needs and problems.[11]

Despite the fact that cushioning mechanisms are not absent and that the protestors are not necessarily second generation dwellers as far as their contacts with the administrative agencies and local governments are concerned, their recent implicit acceptance of, or passivity toward, radical solutions[12] seems to support this conclusion.

NOTES

[1] Except for the city and the country, the names of places and persons are fictitious.

[2] This section draws upon Heper (1978), Butler and Butler (1976), and Karpat (1976).

[3] Turkey has a unitary rather than a federal system of government. The central government has tutelary powers over the local government. There are three types of local government: the province, *il*, which is a unit of both central and local government; the municipal administration, *belediye*; and the village administration, *köy idaresi*.

[4] In 1926 Turkey adopted the Swiss civil code.

[5] The *vilâyet* is the seat of the provincial administration or the unit of the central govenment in the province. The country is administratively divided into provinces, run by a governor (*vali*), which are in turn divided into sub-provinces (*ilçes*), run by a subgovernor (*kaymakam*), which are further subdivided into districts (*bucaks*), run by a director (*müdür*). Sub-provinces and districts are divided into wards (*mahalles*), which are run by a headman (*muhtar*).

[6] Local government in Turkey is under the democratic control of the citizens. The municipality in each city consists of a central as well as branch municipalities. The citizens directly elect the head of each municipal unit as well as the members of the councils of each municipal unit. The latter are referred to as councillors.

[7] The Democratic Party (*Demokrat Parti*) was in office between 1950 and 1960. It was closed down after the military took over the government in 1960. When political democracy was restored in 1961, the New Turkey Party (*Yeni Türkiye Partisi*) emerged as one of the heirs to the votes of the defunct Democratic Party. The Reliance Party (*Güven Partisi*) was a splinter party from the Republican People's Party (*Cumhuriyet Halk Partisi*), the oldest political party of republican Turkey, until it merged with another political party in the late 1960s.

[8] The Sunni-Shiite split is the basic sectarian cleavage in Islam. This split came soon after the death of the Prophet, when claims on the Caliphate by his family (the line of Ali, the Prophet's cousin and son-in-law) were challenged by the Omayyad family of Mecca. Whereas Sunnism supplemented the *Koran* and the Traditions (of the Prophet) with "popular consensus," Shi'ism continued to insist on the ultimate authority of the Imam as the only justification for deviations from the strict letter of the *Koran* and the Traditions. These two sects are further subdivided among themselves. The Turkish Sunnis usually belong to the Hanefi School, while the Turkish Shiites constitute part of the Twelver Shia Shiite subject.

[9] The "squatter area lords" should be distinguished from the early settlers who also laid their hands on land in an illegal fashion. Whereas the latter came to the area earlier and for the purpose of settling there (and later subdivided and sold to others some of the land they so captured), the former

have commercial motives only. They are usually from outside the settlement. They do not refrain from using force or threat of force from time to time.

10 In several earlier papers I have taken up the problem of the rift between the bureaucratic center and the people that has continued from the Ottoman past up until today. See Heper (1976 a; 1976 b; 1979; 1980) and Heper, Kim and Pai (1980). See also Kazancı (1978).

11 Unresponsiveness and condescension by the bureaucracy toward urban migrants have been observed in other contexts, also. See, *inter alia,* Perlman (1976, p. 17); Peattie (1968, p. 81); Bonilla (1970, p. 74); and Mangin (1976, p. 25). It must be pointed out, however, that in the Turkish case this attitude is based upon a rather strong state tradition, whereas in Latin America state tradition has not been equally pervasive; e.g., compare Chalmers (1977) with Akarlı (1975). For the particular conception of a state tradition as referred to here, see Nettl (1968).

12 It has been pointed out that resort to violence by the squatter dwellers is often a consequence of lack of political-administrative responsiveness rather than psychological-social problems (Tilly, 1973).

BIBLIOGRAPHY

Abedin, N. *Local Administration and Politics in Modernizing Societies: Bangladesh and Pakistan.* Bengladesh: National Institute of Public Administration, 1973.

Akarlı, E. "The State as a Social-Cultural Phenomenon and Political Participation in Turkey." In Akarlı and G. Ben-Dor (eds.), *Political Participation in Turkey: Historical Background and Present Problems.* Istanbul: Boğaziçi Univ. Press, 1975.

Barkan, J.D. "The Development and Underdevelopment Theory: Why Political Science Has Failed in the Third World." Paper prepared for delivery at the XIth Congress of the International Political Science Association, Moscow, Aug. 12-18, 1979.

Bill, J.A. "The Plasticity of Informal Politics," *The Middle East Journal.* 1973, 27, 131-51.

Blau, P.M. *Bureaucracy in Modern Society.* New York: Random House, 1960.

Bonilla, F. "Rio's Favelas: the Rural Slum Within the City." In W. Mangin (ed.), *Peasants in Cities: Readings in Anthropology of Urbanization.* Boston: Houghton Mifflin Co., 1970.

Breese, G. *Urbanization in Newly Developing Countries.* Englewood Cliffs, N.J.: Prentice-Hall, Inc., 1966.

Butler, M.H. and N.T. *Urban Dwelling Environments: Istanbul, Turkey.* Cambridge: Mass. Inst. of Tech., 1976.

Chalmers, A.D. "The Politicized State in Latin America." In J.M. Malloy (ed.), *Authoritarianism and Corporatism in Latin America.* Pittsburgh: Univ. of Pittsburgh Press, 1977.

Costello, V.F. *Urbanization in the Middle East.* New York: Cambridge Univ. Press, 1977.

Foster, B. "Development, Modernization and Comparative Parochialism," *Comparative Studies in Society and History.* 1978, 20.

Frederickson, H.G. "Public Administration in the 1970s: Developments and Directions," *Public Administration Review.* 1976, 36.

Goulet, D.A. "Development For What?" *Comparative Political Studies.* 1968, 1, 295-312.

Heper, M. "Political Modernization as Reflected in Bureaucratic Change: the Turkish Bureaucracy and a 'Historical Bureaucratic Empire' Tradition." *International Journal of Middle East Studies.* Oct. 1976a.

————. "Recalcitrance of the Turkish Public Bureaucracy to 'Bourgeois Politics': Multi Factor Political Stratification Analysis," *The Middle East Journal.* Fall, 1976b.

————. *Türk Kamu Bürokrasisinde Gelenekçilik ve Modernleşme: Siyaset Sosyolojisi Açısından Bir İnceleme* (Traditionalism and Modernization in Turkish Public Bureaucracy: An Analysis in the Light of Political Sociology). Istanbul: Boğaziçi Univ. Publications, 1977.

————. *Gecekondu Policy in Turkey: An Evaluation With a Case Study of Rumelihisarüstü Squatter Area in Istanbul.* Boğaziçi Univ. Publications, 1978.

————. "Patrimonialism in the Ottoman-Turkish Public Bureaucracy," *Asian and African Studies.* March, 1979.

————. "Center and Periphery in the Ottoman Empire With Special Reference to the Nineteenth Century," *International Political Science Review.* Jan. 1980.

————, C.L. Kim, and S.T. Pai. "The Role of Bureaucracy and Regime Types: a Comparative Study of Turkish and Korean Higher Civil Servants," *Administration and Society.* Aug. 1980.

Karpat, K.H. *The Gecekondu: Rural Migration and Urbanization.* London: Cambridge Univ. Press, 1976.

Kazancı, M. *Halkla İlişkiler Açısından Yönetim ve Yönetilenler* (Ruling and the Rulers in Terms of Public Relations). Ankara: Ankara Univ. Faculty of Political Science Publications, 1978.

Lamb. C. *Political Power in Poor Neighborhoods.* New York: John Wiley and Sons, 1975.

Leeds, A. "Locality Power in Relation to Supralocal Power Institutions." In A. Southall (ed.), *Urban Anthropology: Cross-Cultural Studies of Urbanization.* New York: Oxford Univ. Press, 1973.

Mangin, N. "Squatter Settlements," *Scientific American.* 1967, 217.

Merton, R.K. *Social Theory and Social Structure.* New York: The Free Press, 1968.

Milne, R.S. "Bureaucracy and Development Administration," *Public Administration.* 1973, 51.

Nettl, J.P. "The State as a Conceptual Variable," *World Politics,* 1968, 31.

Peattie, L.R. *The View from the Barrio.* Ann Arbor: Univ. of Michigan Press, 1968.

Perlman, E. *The Myth of Marginality: Urban Poverty and Politics in Rio de Janeiro.* Berkeley: Univ. of California Press, 1976.

Tilly, C. "Does Modernization Breed Revolution?" *Comparative Politics,* 1973, 5, 425-47.

CHANGING PATTERNS OF PATRONAGE:
A STUDY IN STRUCTURAL CHANGE

Mübeccel B. Kıray

Introduction

Taşköprü is a settlement in the Western Marmara region on the Bay of Izmit near Yalova, a part of the urban sprawl around Istanbul. Today it can no longer be called a village. But up to 1950 that is exactly what it was. There has taken place a succession of changes that have led the community from being a self-sufficient, isolated agricultural village to one involved in cash cropping, heavy industry, and urbanization. As a case of truly basic structural transformation, I found that it provides a rare opportunity to observe social change with external dynamics.[1] Here, in the 1950s the old pre-modern rural social structure came into direct collision with an almost pure form of modern capitalist agriculture and its related human relations and values. The outcome is interesting, since it reveals the relative position of each structure in change and the intermediary processes and forms that structure, as a system, undergoes while it transforms and rearranges itself.

Taşköprü today is not a community representing the "usual" or "typical," even in Turkey. But the peculiarities it presents provide a special environment in which change as it actually takes place in a microsphere, when relatively "pure" or "typical" structures collide, may be studied. The types of intermediary processes and forms, either interaction patterns or values and mental categories, that come about and the reasons they evolve may be observed.[2] In this general frame patronage is also a particularly good area of observation, both because of its larger importance, as it envelopes the largest political, economic, social, and moral bearings of the society, and also as it is directly relevant to structural changes. Patronage had always formed a basic part of the pre-modern system. It constituted a reciprocal but unequal relationship in which the welfare and particularly the security of the peasants were the personal responsibility of the patron, in return for many economic services, political obedience, honors and prestige. It was a well-structured face-to-face relationship which, before change, neither party questioned; nor were they articulate about it.[3]

In 1950 the traditional "patron" unexpectedly opted to move out of the village and left his clientele without his side of the relationship; concurrently an agricultural entrepreneur moved into the village. He demanded only wage labor and anonymous relations, while refusing to take over the role and functions of the old patron. In a sense the old structure suddenly lost its cornerstone and a most important element of a new structure entered to replace it without losing its main characteristics.

In this rather unique situation Taşköprü indeed provides as good a chance for a controlled observation as any social scientist could hope for. As may easily be perceived, the data collected are not a simple description of Taşköprü society or patronage in general, but observations of newly emerging relationships and the processes that bring them about.

Thus, in this paper I shall try to trace, selectively, what happened to clientelism after the old traditional patron moved out and a "modern" entrepreneur who refused patronage moved into Taşköprü. I hope such observations will further lead us to some understanding of the attributes of social structures and changes at large.

Basic Structure of the Village Before Change

In 1950 when Turkey's rural areas and agriculture were opening up to cash cropping for the first time, the small village of Taşköprü on the narrow coastal plain on the Marmara Sea near Yalova had 50 households with a population of around 200. It was 11 kilometers to Yalova, then a small unimportant settlement since it was only a small market town. A narrow macadam road connected the village with the town. It was an immigrant–peasant village of the type which used to be numerous in Anatolia (Hutteroth, 1974). It was a closed, cereal growing, self-sufficient community with a very low standard of living. Its contact with the outside consisted mainly of the military service of its young men, the payment of tax (which was extremely limited after the establishment of the Republic), and the sale of their women's tiny surplus of eggs and butter in the weekly open market of Yalova when the road was open.

Taşköprü was a concrete example of the recent history of the country in the rural context as well, in that one influential man dominated the community. This also was a rather widespread characteristic of social organization in Anatolian marginal settlements. Here, domination meant protection at the same time: protection, for instance, from other immigrants who wished to settle in the same area and use the same land; from tax authorities or simply from hunger. The protection of the people's rights and solution of their problems with the outside world and their survival during harsh winters, crop failures or epidemics was possible with the help of Davut Bey, as we shall call him. Although he had only 500 dönüm of land and used extra family labor only as farmhands (not wage work), still because of his "protection" (which was much required in the late 1920s and '30s after long wars) he had become the sole patron of the community. He acted as arbitrator in disputes, he decided when and where a new field should be ploughed by the peasants, or when and where a house could be built. As the peasants were extremely poor and could not accomplish such undertakings without his help, and more importantly without his arbitration vis-a-vis other peasants, such domination in decision making became his right.

In this undifferentiated village he was also appointed headman. Thus he had become the official representative of the village. His duties were not trivial. He used to receive all visitors, especially all officials. He passed on orders and regulations, prepared statistical returns, reported those crimes and conflicts he could not settle himself, conveyed special requests, was responsible for seeing that military conscripts answered the call, and assisted tax collectors. He was also responsible for collecting the village local tax and administering village funds. This status, particularly in the pre-1950 set up, further intensified his dominance and protection or, in short, his patronage.[4]

In Turkish he was an *Ağa,* a lord in the widest meaning of the word. Had social scientists begun their observations with rural Turkey instead of Spain or Italy, from which they borrowed the term *patron,* they might have used the term *ağa* to signify a person of power and status who gives protection to the peasants in a nonsymmetrical relationship and receives various services. Taş-

köprü's Davut Bey and peasants were thus typical in their enact-
ment of the patron–client relationship of an earlier era. What should
be underscored here is the undifferentiated social structure of the
community and the total patronage that is protection and dominance
of the relationship.

The other well-defined aspect of the structure consisted of
kinship groups in which the elderly played an important role with
their authority. The source of their power was their role in organizing almost every aspect of life, from work to marriage, from routine
everyday chores to ceremonies in the family. In this organization,
the elder male members of the families were the decision makers in
everyday activities as well as in extraordinary times such as in
disputes. A role parallel to the one played by the total patron in the
community was played by the elderly male in the family and the
kinship group. Thus the community perpetuated its existence.

In 1950, changes brewing outside of Taşköprü collided with the
community in an unexpected way. After the Second World War, as
rural areas were moving out of their ages-old stagnation, new
economic possibilities were arising and concurrently the political
structure was assuming a multi-party form. Sensitive to the changes
in the larger society, Davut Bey, who had no relatives in Taşköprü,
opted to sell his land in the village and move out, leaving his
clientele without a patron.

Right at the same time modern cash cropping was introduced to
the village by an outsider. This new man, with his enterprise as well
as his values and behavior, was a member of upper class urban
Turkey. As is well known, the urban elite of Turkey, for that matter,
of all developing countries, presents a dualism vis-a-vis the peasants.
But as they keep their distance from each other these dual cultures
do not signify much to each other. But now a member of the first was
buying Davut Bey's land and moving into his house in the village,
but refusing to play Davut Bey's role, namely to be a patron.

The reaction of Taşköprü has been slow and hesitant.

Portrait from the Village: Ali Bey

The painfully slow change from self-sufficiency farming to
intensive vegetable growing took place in the early 1950s in
Taşköprü with an external factor, that is, after Davut Bey moved
out, with the settlement of a very young man with sophisticated
training in agriculture—a "gentleman farmer." This son of an upper
class Istanbul family, with graduate degrees in fruit growing from

the United States, decided to invest capital given by the family in land and to grow an orchard. He shopped for suitable land all around the Marmara region and found the Taşköprü Ağa Davut Bey, now an old man, selling his land basically because of political changes in the country. He bought the land and, equally important perhaps for the village, he moved first to Davut Bey's house, then built his own and settled in the village with his wife Reyhan Hanım. He was very much involved in successful farming, but his interest in the village had nothing to do with the patron–client relationship of the old ağa. He needed labor with differing skills from the villagers and paid them the wages prevailing then. But it had to be an anonymous relationship, since he did not want to be concerned with their lives, either as fellow villagers or as people whose problems were his responsibility. He never participated in the activities of the villagers, but he provided both wage work, and, to those working for him, information and necessary knowledge about fruit growing. The villagers felt ambivalent at the time, as some of the middle-aged villagers report. They wanted him to be a patron. They were ready to supply their share of "service" and they asked his "protection." They offered him free labor and they wanted him to act as arbiter in disputes. They even wanted to force him into such relations. But he refused all. They were accustomed for instance to borrow wheat in time of need in winter and return it with some extra after the harvest. Most significant to the villagers was his refusal to accept the return of the borrowed wheat with its extra. That took them out of the prescribed interaction pattern of the patron–client relationship. For them it was "alms," which had other connotations. A client was never ashamed of the protection since the group knew the reciprocity it implied. But help in the form of alms was degrading. This, they say, made them realize that his work and relationship in the village were different. Accordingly they did not borrow wheat ever again, but worked for wages in his orchard.

Ali Bey's practices of sheep and chicken raising and particularly his apple growing became a model for the village. Men not only worked for wages in Ali Bey's orchard but also learned how to water, to fight pests, to prune and pick, and other activities related to fruit growing. His installations and establishment formed a model. It seems he was always patient enough to show and teach whenever anybody asked questions about agriculture, but never accepted any role in patron–client relationships which would have led to dependency. The significant form of association between Ali Bey and villagers always remained the anonymous relations of employer and employed, albeit some sort of informal training on the job was also involved. But this was much too short of villagers' expectations. Thus he was never accepted as a villager, and he was simply ignored in daily life and left outside in village activities. He never became a "member" of the "in group" of the village.

The role his wife played in the community, however, was very different. She was also trained as an agriculturist with the best elite education the country could give. With a very inquisitive mind, she became involved with the women and children of the village. Many of the changes in the style of life in the houses have been due to her. She took over the role of patron to help the villagers with hospitals, schools and certain government circles, and it seems that only her contacts and behavior really made the family an integrated part of the community. Reyhan Hanım, as she took an active interest in the village, also tried to bring larger organized changes to the lives of women and girls. With the cooperation of an international women's association she organized the women into a club for mutual help in home economics and various other activities.

At first, learning how to can fruits and vegetables was very attractive to the members. Many learned it and they are still practicing it. But as village grocery stores are now full of commercially tinned fruits and vegetables one may assume that the practice will die off. Another action was a literacy course for adult women. Government school teachers participated, and the school facilities were also used. It was successfully completed. But Reyhan Hanım admits that, in the elections the following year, none of the women signed their names but still used their fingerprints. However, the daughters of today are all graduates of primary school, and if they are not going to secondary school it is because there is not one in the vicinity.

Despite this involvement with the village, the social life of the family of Ali Bey and the informal network in which they circulated was outside the village. They kept all their relations with the city; they entertained many guests from both Istanbul and the national elite, as well as international groups. So the villagers accepted them both as one of them, but surely very "different."

In fact, the villagers explicitly indicated, for instance, that Reyhan Hanım could go around with short sleeved dresses and without covering her head because she was "different." Still, there is no doubt that they constituted a model: first of all in their agricultural practices, and secondly, at least for some of the families, in the way they educated their children.

Ali Bey's family which was involved with the political life of the country from the beginning took an active part in 1973 and left the village in 1974 for national political activities.

Changes in the Basic Structure of the Village

Although Davut Bey, the total patron, moved out, and although a modern farm was established exactly on the same land, house and place in the village, and its owner demanded new types of relations, things did not change overnight for the villagers. The agricultural practice of several millenia with simple technology of ox and plough only slowly started to give way first into intensive vegetable cultivation and then to fruit growing. Orchards that were started in the late 1950s matured by the 1960s, and the village started to enjoy an increase of income.

In 1960 the narrow road was enlarged into a hard surfaced highway which connected various nearby towns to each other and to Bursa, a larger center. At the same time Istanbul's contact with Bursa, where the industry of the metropolitan area was located, increased the importance of the nearest town, Yalova. Thus Taşköprü gained better accessibility not merely to a town but to a town which was becoming an important center at the same time. Fruit growing was gaining importance and the sale of apples and peaches was expanding its market to international areas. At this time not only the orchards but cold storage establishments, transportation facilities and organizational aspects were also expanding in the area.

Meanwhile, for those who did not have land in the village, the chance to earn more money opened up. Western European countries were demanding unskilled labor (Abadan-Unat, 1964, 1977). Between 1965 and 1971, three families—men, women and children—went to Germany to work. One came back in 1968, the other two in 1975. Also, since the village is situated in the metropolitan growth area of Istanbul, two large artificial fiber factories and one cellulose factory were established in the area. They suddenly opened up chances for wage-labor in industry for the villagers. They also opened up the village for the settlement of outsiders.

As if all those changes were not enough, Yalova, the nearby town, found itself the breaking point of routes that developed in the metropolitan area of Istanbul. From Yalova the highway which bounds the Bay of Izmit and encircles one of the important industrial growth areas of the Istanbul metropolis joins the Bursa area of industrial development. The highway is complemented by the ferryboat service from Istanbul which carries half of the transportation to the coast of the Aegean Sea and Western Central Anatolian. Indeed Yalova today, with its daily contact with Istanbul, is just an adjoining subcenter for all of Istanbul's metropolitan services, so much so that the whole subregion uses Yalova for its banking, transportation and communication services.

The growth of Yalova meant expansion towards Taşköprü as the coastal strip became a desirable residential area for Yalova and environs. All of this meant unheard-of increases in land prices, and agricultural fields became urban, in fact, metropolitan land as lots. Today, intensive farming constitutes the second largest field of activity. The leading one is skilled labor which includes drivers of various vehicles and workers in the factories and workshops. Unskilled work, particularly as agricultural wage work, is the third most frequent. One has to notice that trade and white collar salaried people, who had no place in the self-sufficient peasant village, are here as well. In fact, those who say that they earn their living through cereal growing or sheep raising are a few old people who are helped by the younger generation for their main expenses. When the activities of today's generation are compared with those of their fathers, the contrast is striking. While only a tiny fraction (4%) today are dealing with grain growing, more than half of the fathers made their living by it. If one thinks that another 12% were landless peasants employed on a yearly basis—not wage workers—the self-sufficient basis of the village of 30 years ago can easily be pictured.

The small orchard garden owners all have their wives, sons and daughters working on family property. Furthermore, if the property is very small it is very common for the men to work for wages in larger orchards, and for the women to work in the cold storage establishments that have appeared like mushrooms all around the area. Continuous or temporary wage work in agriculture and in factories in the vicinity is so widespread that except for the oldest and youngest, everybody is gainfully employed. Households with more than one wage earner constitute 80% of all households in Taşköprü. There has been a succession from self sufficiency with basically cereal growing, to orchard and garden farming, and from there on to wage work either in agricultural processing or in industry proper. Industrial wage work certainly does not pay as high an income as a small- to medium-sized orchard. But it is definitely considered better than agricultural wage work because of its social security plans and still open ladder to higher skill acquisition on the job. The metropolitan influence in terms of jobs and ways of earning a living shows itself also in trade and salaried jobs, which are limited but do exist.

The change in crops is very clear, too. Only 10 years ago, among those who had land, almost 60% were cultivating cereal. But already the other 27% had turned to vegetable gardening and 10% to fruit. Cereal was rarely sold as a cash crop. Today it is still the same, except that now only one-fifth of the villagers grow cereals as a partial crop. But the ratio of fruit growers has increased to 62.3% while vegetable gardening has gone down to 14.7%.

The demonstration effect of the larger producers definitely constituted the main source of knowledge in agriculture (89%). The other sources for the younger generation are fathers and friends. Thus, some claim that there is no need for special skill in gardening (11%). Obviously, whether intended or not, those who came from outside with knowledge and practiced successful agriculture were influential, even though Ali Bey did not allow dependency to develop.

In turning from self-sufficiency to cash cropping, marketing is the most devastating problem, both in terms of technology and human relations, and creates new dependency relations for the peasants. In Taşköprü, because it is close to large cities, it was easy to start marketing in a small way. Ten years ago the vegetables which constituted the main crop were basically sold in the weekly open market of Yalova, the most primitive way of marketing. Today only one gardener is doing it. Even 10 years ago the larger producers were selling wholesale to exporters. The next most important outlet is the wholesalers in Istanbul. Such a way of marketing, while constituting only 17% 10 years ago, accounts for 40% today. As the country as a whole demands more agricultural products both for local consumption as well as for export, the organizations developing in metropolitan areas also make efforts to find the crop in the orchards and to make arrangements to buy on large scale. Now 14% of the growers sell their product to the representatives of the metropolitan firms directly from their gardens. Here has arisen again a sphere of activity that has brought the large scale buyer into contact with the small producer. The person or persons who are in contact with both parties have become important people. Ali Bey was never interested in such deals. But anybody who takes over such a role obviously could become a new "patron" and—as we shall see—it did come about.

Next to marketing, financing the enterprise in different stages is a bottleneck for the ex-peasant villager who has now ventured into gardening and fruit growing. First of all, the size of the enterprise determines whether anonymous complex organizations, such as banks, will be used or not. The small ones insist that they do not borrow money (34%) or that the only party they can ask for money is their close relatives (17%). However, the larger the enterprise, the more dominant become the banks. Credit given by banks is rarely enough to keep the business going. Thus a lot of borrowing is done from wealthier members of the community, although it is not readily admitted.

Such borrowing is done with signed papers and counter provisions by specific times in specific ways. Thus it is relatively formal. But the transaction takes place, for instance, in coffeeshops. Thus another type of dependency and patron–client relationship has arisen in the village. Establishing new relations for marketing, for cold storage, for transportation and in general for the financing of the orchards and vegetable gardens of small- to medium-scale producers in the village constitutes the source of new relations of dependency as it requires protection from many outside hazards that villagers do not have clear knowledge of.

Two other lively aspects of activity in Taşköprü have to be analyzed, as they also require close interaction with outside agencies. One of these is the sale of land to buyers in Yalova and Istanbul. Land speculation in metropolitan areas is one of the most ruthless transactions; and how an isolated villager will enter this transaction to sell his land and use the money in another enterprise is a very serious question. If there are no intermediary organizations that he can "trust," he may well decline from any transaction and keep his land to himself. The other aspect is the process of finding wage work. As mentioned above, for the majority the main means of earning a living is wage work in factories and cold storage establishments. If one keeps in mind that the Istanbul metropolitan area attracts migrants set free from land from all over Turkey, and that there is not one employment bureau in the whole area, the question becomes more significant.

Here again the old isolated village is in collision with a new, much more differentiated structure. Understanding how the two merge with one another, when even the more demanding structure has no new organizations or planned institutions to arrange such transactions, is critical to understanding structural change. Closer investigation shows that newly rising dependency relations and patronage, leading to party politics, were the mechanisms provided by the villagers.

However, before this solution was attempted, the family was the institution manipulated for an early adjustment to the crisis.

Family as an Adjustment Mechanism

The first decade or 15 years after Davut Bey left the village was a period of great difficulties for the villagers. They struggled with their own resources. The main resource was the kinship group. Among the relatives, various mechanisms evolved for the provision of mutual aid and protection. Such relations are assumed to be horizontal between equals on a more or less equal plane. Although hypothetically mutual help is one of the prerequisites of kinship relations, from blood feud to old age security, it has taken other forms under new types of pressure on the community. The first reaction to the tensions created by the difficulties of change was to split the extended family and continue to have not only simple neighborly relations but close mutual help contacts. The family thus, at least at the beginning, is an important institution which adjusts itself to enable other changes to take place. It constitutes a major buffer institution in the social structure.

Taşköprü today consists of 260 households. Among them, traditional patrilineal extended families are as few as 4.8% (Turkey's average for rural areas is 25.4%; Timur, 1972, p. 34). The ratio of nuclear families, on the other hand, is as high as 75% (Turkey's average for rural areas is 55%; Timur, 1972, p. 34). Families with one or the other parents of the husband living with the family is 15.3% as in Timur (1972). These transient families are partly those in the process of change from an extended to a nuclear structure, and partly a result of the changes taking place in domestic cycles. Whatever is the composition of the household, when family affairs are in question, authority is in the hands of the male household heads, who are in the active age groups between 20 and 45.

In fact, today, 30% of the heads of the families seem to be less than 30 years of age and more than 50% below 40 years of age. The average size of the households is 4.56. (The average for Turkey's rural areas is 6.1, while for Turkey as a whole it is 5.4, and for metropolises 4.1; Timur, 1972, p. 38.) It seems that gradually the elder male member's authority and dominance has declined. The importance of the elders in the community now does not call for anything beyond simple respect. But authority and power are different from respect and prestige, which do not command obedience or compliance. Our various approaches to check the influence of the elder males on the younger generation has always given the same result: it has disappeared.

When we asked the heads of the households who could be influential on the younger members of the community, about 10% agreed that the elders of their families could be influential; but approximately another fifth claimed that nobody could tell them what to do. The rest of the answers indicated extra-family relations, particularly new relations of patronage. When the question was asked in a more specific way, such as from whom they would seek help or advice when things went wrong, the answers did not change either. Closer examination of the dependency revealed, however, that no matter how dependent they have become on one or the other patron, the most striking characteristic of their general state of feeling is the extreme self-reliance of the respondents. They always answer that they rely only on themselves.

It is quite understandable that, as the village opened up to cash cropping and industrial wage work, the knowledge and experience of the elder generation became obsolete; and those who are 30 to 40 years old now, the most active age group, were only teenagers in the 1960s. They know nothing about agricultural self sufficiency or total patronage. Even to be the client of a newly emerging patron is an effort on their part. On the other hand, they were around the new patrons before the latter became important, and they observed their ascent from close proximity. So they feel that the new patrons are still "one of themselves." The talks in the coffeeshops, the orchards, or the town are informal and "between friends." Any answer to the questions on whom they go to for help and advice, whether it is "nobody; I rely on myself," or "to my friends," or "to the headman," or "to a rich villager," is basically the same thing. Taşköprü is gradually creating its channel of interaction with the colliding social system in its limited ways. Consequently its members are being exposed on the one hand to self-reliance, as there is no other recourse, or on the other hand to openly becoming engaged in clientelism with newly emerging patrons as a path to full integration with the coming society.

Other Portraits from the Village: Bekir Bey

As the community lived through the transition from one state to the other, each member had his share of change. Some stayed in cereal growing; some passed from self-sufficiency to factory wage work or to small trade. Bekir Bey and his family provide a dramatic picture of what change at its maximum brought to the people of Taşköprü.

In 1955 Bekir Bey was a young man of 19 without land and without family. All he could do was work for wages in agriculture. By 1955 the old-fashioned *ırgatlık* (yearly work on farms) had disappeared and he was employed as a wage worker in the orchard of Ali Bey, a strictly modern cash cropping large land owner as we saw above. When in 1961 it became possible to go to Germany as an industrial worker, he applied immediately, and married one of the poorer girls who worked as a maid in the house of Ali Bey. They went to Germany together and worked there until 1968. In an industrialized country this could have been the last stage of his career. Or even if he migrated to Istanbul the result could have been the same. But they came back to the village with some cash they had saved. First he bought land to raise vegetables. He also attempted cattle raising for milk. The gardens succeeded. But cattle raising, for which he collaborated closely with a government extension service, failed, and as metropolitan growth and land speculation had reached new heights, he sold some of his garden and bought new land on the coast. He sold it again immediately at very high prices—the well known land speculation. From then on, although he continued to live in the village, he shifted his sphere of activity to Yalova, opened up an office as a real estate broker, and entered party politics. In Yalova and in the village he "helps" the villagers sell their land, advises them about whom they should go to to start new gardens, lends them money and asks their backing in elections. However, he also kept his garden with an overseer and built a cold storage establishment to rent out. Now he is one of the richest men in the area.

His first attempt was to build a large new concrete house in the village. He installed electricity and brought running water to the house. He furnished the house with modern living, dining and bedroom furniture, curtains and other household appliances such as a refrigerator and washing machine. He owns a Mercedes car. He no longer goes regularly to the coffeeshops in the village. In addition to his village contacts he has also entered into a new network of relations in the town with its elite. He is becoming a Yalova and Istanbul man. He entertains—in his home—the district officer (*kaymakam*) and the judge with their wives.

What really symbolizes the processes of change for the family and is a model for the village is the education of the daughter. She was born in 1961, and completed the village primary school in 1971.

As is usual for rural Turkey, they decided that this much education was sufficient for a daughter. But three years later, in 1974, when the family started to change its status and to circulate in circles outside Taşköprü, they changed their minds and decided that their daughter deserved better education. After a period of intensive private tutoring the daughter took examinations from outside and graduated from the junior high school. Then she attended the high school (lycee) proper. She graduated from there as well and took university entrance examinations. Obviously she is a talented individual, but no capacity on her part could have made her parents decide to educate her, particularly after they had made her stop going to school, if they had not changed their socio-economic status, their reference groups in town, and their role as a new source of power and influence in the village.

The wife of Bekir Bey was the daughter of a poor peasant. She started to work as a maid in Ali Bey's house and was illiterate. She learned how to read and write in an adult literacy course for women, conducted by a voluntary association. An able person herself, she also learned the lifestyle of an elite family with different, finer ways of cooking, dressing, and cleaning—in short, a higher level of living. Such an intimate knowledge of upper middle class urban life, together with the experience of Germany, also gave her the best chance to carry her family to a higher status lifestyle. She further showed great flexibility in switching her role from the expectations of the villagers to the expectations of her husband's urban contacts. She has no difficulty in entertaining them with teas and cakes and dinners at home.

Her clothing, however, is something controversial. The village women of her age group still cover their heads with scarves and many of them wear baggy pantaloons. She usually wears city-style dresses, but when with the village women she changes into long, large skirts. As for covering her head, she says she does as her husband asks: if he says she should not cover it today with such and such people she keeps it bare, but if she is asked to cover it another time, she puts on her scarf. In the village when alone she goes around with a scarf. Her daughter dresses totally like her urban age group, including blue jeans and T-shirts. The son is still young; he goes to junior high school in Yalova. The father does not worry much about him, saying that he has earned enough money to last his son up to his death. It is intriguing to see how the need for education has changed. For the girl it has become a necessity, while for the boy it is not so urgent.

Bekir Bey is very important as a real estate broker for a large number of the villagers. In addition he is an employer in his cold storage establishment and also lends money. Furthermore, his contacts in the town with lawyers, bank managers, doctors, and even shopkeepers are valuable for villagers. The villagers are important for him too, as customers, workers and to demonstrate his clientele in the town in the eyes of lawyers, judges and others. Now he aspires to extend his influence in active politics. To be an ordinary member of a party is not enough. He cannot yet compete in Yalova, thus he ran in Taşköprü for the position of headman and won. This was also very useful for real estate transactions, but he lost the position in the last elections. Since Yalova is growing, and some time in the future Taşköprü will be adjoining it, he is perpetuating his political activities and close contacts with both settlements.

Halil and Murat Beys

Two other men are interesting for us. They had similar backgrounds as small landowners who tried to switch from cereal cultivation to vegetable gardening, but they ultimately followed different paths. Up until the 1960s nothing spectacular happened in their lives. In 1957 as a young man Halil Bey started to work for Ali Bey, first as an ordinary wage worker, and later, since he proved himself as an able and reliable element in the management of the establishment, as overseer and junior manager. Since for Ali Bey it was difficult to find people with such qualifications, he agreed to allow him to work for him and at the same time to look after his own land.

For long years Halil Bey worked closely with Ali Bey, assisting him in every aspect of fruit growing and managing a large orchard. Ali Bey not only let him work on his land, but allowed him to use his machinery, his cold storage, his trucks and even sold his crop with his own with the best market possibilities, without any return except Halil Bey's hard work and loyalty. Their close association extended beyond business so much so that the same car took Ali Bey's and Halil Bey's children to school together. When Ali Bey found a spring in the hills behind their house and piped the water down, a pipe was extended to Halil Bey's house as well.

By the time Ali Bey moved to Istanbul in 1973, playing a rather important role in national politics, Halil Bey was ready to take over fully the management of Ali Bey's establishment. He also had an almost equally large orchard himself. In 1979 he was, next to Ali Bey and Bekir Bey, the richest and most sophisticated member of the community, and was a part of the political life of Yalova opposing Bekir Bey. He is rather dominant in every interaction pertaining to orchard activities, such as labor and wages in the orchards, "helping" and advising the villagers in finding credit, marketing, buying equipment, and the like, and in their welfare in general. But he is not interested in village level politics. There he follows Ali Bey but remains on the Yalova level. However, he goes to the coffeeshop rather regularly, follows closely what goes on in the village, and maintains contact with his clients there.

Halil Bey's wife has remained quite traditional in the shadow of his ascendency. But he has made great efforts to educate his daughters in the same way that Ali Bey had done. His elder daughter has become a pharmacist for whom he has provided a shop in Yalova. The second daughter has become a primary school teacher. She has always been close to Ali Bey's wife in her activities in voluntary associations. Ultimately she spent a year in England with a scholarship from the World Association of Rural Women. She is teaching now in a nearby town.[5] Their father is very proud of their professions, and sees it as his own accomplishment. He thinks that they have surpassed Taşköprü just as he did. The way he surpassed Taşköprü is rather different from Bekir Bey. He has remained a farmer after Ali Bey's model. Like Ali Bey he has acquired the values of the urban elite in terms of professional education for daughters, tolerance in world view, higher quality of life for his family, and also remaining aloof from village political life. But unlike Ali Bey, he has become a patron for villagers who are still orchard growers. He gladly acts as intermediary in all types of transactions of the villagers.

Murat Bey also had some land on which he tried to cultivate vegetables until the 1960s. In 1965 he managed to go to Germany as a guest worker. He took his wife and two children with him and left his garden to his relatives to be cultivated in a half-tenant/half-sharecropper arrangement. Every year during his vacation they came to visit the village and see their garden converted to an orchard. His wife was also employed abroad. In 1976 they returned, invested their savings into their land and enlarged the orchard. They not only rebuilt and refurnished their home, but they also opened a well-equipped grocery store. In Turkish villages such a store, although called a grocery store, is really a general store. His wife manages the store and acts also as a saleswoman, while he is busy with the orchard and his contacts in and out of the village.

He is not one of the richest men in the community. But through his sales with credit in the store, his close association with the wage workers, and his opposition to the other "patrons" in the village, he has become a well-accepted member. Instead of seeking the assistance of the government circles and highly influential men of Yalova, like Bekir Bey, he established intimacy with the average traders of the town. And because a vacuum was left by Ali Bey and Halil Bey in representing the opposition to Bekir Bey and his party, at the village level, he also turned to political leadership. He channelized the dissatisfaction with Bekir Bey's headmanship and his indifference to the wage workers, particularly newcomers and young villagers, towards himself. He campaigned successfully during the last elections against Bekir Bey and won the headmanship of the village. His good relationship with Halil Bey opens his way to the opposing party in the town. But his main strength is his shop, and more important, his role in finding jobs in factories and storages. Increasingly he is enlarging his activities as a labor broker. He has succeeded in establishing good relations with the managements of the nearby factories. His recommendations there are valued, and he has become important to the young men of the village as somebody who can find good jobs and who sells goods on credit in his shop.

In the last election, when he was elected headman, the issue on which he had campaigned was to supply a clean water system to the whole village, and distribute it to every villager. Up until then, individual houses, such as Ali Bey's and Bekir Bey's, had managed to find springs and to have their own small reservoirs for their private consumption. Murat Bey claimed a right to water for the whole village. It was a difficult undertaking, particularly when one remembers that Bekir Bey's contacts with the town power circles had been much stronger and more extensive. Ingeniously Murat Bey directed his efforts to the circles with which he had influence, namely the large plants. With the financial and technical aid of the plant manager there is now clean water in the village. Murat Bey is a rich grocer, labor broker and headman. His children attend secondary school in Yalova, together with 14 others from Taşköprü. He has arranged a minibus to take them every morning to Yalova and bring them back in the afternoon. Murat Bey is a patron today very close to the hearts of the average young household heads in Taşköprü.[6]

Davut Bey with all his absolute dominance was an *ağa* (lord). He is still mentioned as *ağa*. Nobody yet mentions either Ali Bey or the headman or the two other patrons as *ağa*. Conceptualization is an important stage in the development of new relations as it brings full cognition of the situation to the perceivers. There may be two reasons for it, which are complementary to each other. On the one hand, as mentioned above, the villagers know the origins of these men and how they reached their present status. They may even hope that they themselves may occupy a similar status some time in the future. On the other hand their clientelism to any one of the three patrons is still fluid; once this gets settled, the term *ağa* may be used for them, as well. Although the term *ağa* is not used, the title of "bey" is being used for Halil Bey and Bekir Bey, and partially for Murat Bey, indicating their differentiated status as rich and influential, and capable of patronage.

Patronage, Informal Networks and Coffeehouses

Traditionally interaction among the male population of rural communities does not take place in houses. No man, even today, can easily visit another one for business or companionship in his house, even if the one visited is ill in bed. The house is the woman's domain. The place to see one another and interact for men is the coffeehouse. Previously it was a guest room, *oda,* provided by the total patron, Davut Bey, to be used for this purpose. He furnished the room and supplied it with heat and light. The village men used to come, sit and talk according to a well-defined protocol. It is easy to see the significance of the traditional *oda,* which is provided by the *ağa.* It showed his dominance to the outsiders and made his clients aware of their relationship to him.

When Davut Bey moved out, as one could imagine, it never occured to Ali Bey to have an *oda.* Instead, in the late 1950s the first commercial coffeehouse opened. Today there are three coffeehouses in the village. In slack season, on Sundays and holidays and in the evenings they are full. During business hours or weekdays there are only old men or those who have come to see each other by arrangement. Coffeehouses today represent the transitional character of the network of relationships. They have become differentiated from kinship contacts at home or from the old *ağa's* guest room interaction. The coffeehouse is a commercialized space for many activities which have not yet obtained specialized space for themselves. It is a place for purposes ranging from leisure to communication of various types, from serious business transactions to political party campaign meetings. Most significant for us is that coffeehouses are the *locale* of the newly developing patron–client relations. The parties involved see each other and arrange the necessary papers or appointments there.

Time spent in a coffeehouse is not a continuous discussion of "serious" affairs. There is no specialized differentiated time or section reserved for structured "meetings" in these shops. The pattern is that people trickle in according to their own time schedules, go and sit next to their buddies or to a group playing cards or backgammon. Or they may just sit alone. As time goes by they shift around. Usually nothing much happens. But at one point someone starts to talk about some subject that interests some other people; then more join the discussion, and if it is an issue that concerns a large group it becomes a regular meeting. However, it has no chairman, secretary or any such structured organization. The meeting is perpetuated by those who talk louder or who have made a point. If someone keeps talking "nonsense," either the group shuts him up or they leave him and turn to their games or small group chatting.

The largest coffeehouse is located at the main nucleus of the business place in the village where a grocery store, a repair shop, and a school are located. Since the village has been growing two more coffeeshops have been opened. Interestingly these coffeehouses have no differentiated customers yet. Many men go to all of them and talk could turn to a serious discussion in any one of them. Still the important one seems to be the large one at the center. If one would like to see someone away from the eyes of others, it has to be a quiet period during the day, or in one of the off-center coffeehouses, or even better, coffeehouses in Yalova.

This suggests that patronage in the village is still flexible. The clientele has not been frozen. Further, each patron seems to provide protection to a different group and receives different services. Halil Bey's group has more to do with improving the orchards. The banks and larger traders that he is in contact with are different from Bekir Bey's bank and circles. Bekir Bey, on the other hand, is interested in land and those who sell and invest in other areas. For Murat Bey it is altogether different. His clientele consists of wage workers. Thus as people pass from orchard growing to selling their land, or as young men leave their families and look for jobs, the reference group in patronage also changes from one patron to the other. So it is not surprising that coffeehouses as the locale of patron-client inter-action are not specialized.

That informal networks in general are not structured in the village can also be seen in the coffeehouses, where, although teachers or *imam* (religious leaders) or patrons can talk, their influence would not be easy to observe at once. As indicated above, whatever informal patronage takes place—such as borrowing money, signing papers for formal transactions, taking advice for enterpris-ing, asking for company to go and buy large items such as tractors, refrigerators, or spare parts from town, or seeking a job in one of the establishments—is done here. No offices have evolved for the men who act as patrons. There seems to be a differential grouping in the same coffeehouse only according to age, occupation, the way of earning the living and patronage at a given *time*. Those who are "helped" and "protected" by the same patron *at that moment* stick together. As the reference groups now are several, industrial wage workers' interests are very different from those of the small orchard growers', so shift the patronage and groupings in the coffeehouses. Thus the coffeehouse is nowadays a most important institution in this village where there is little organizational development, and the villagers' access to outside circles is very narrow.

Those who have any claim to influence in the village can not help but come to the coffeehouse to see their clients and vice-versa. Murat Bey, the headman, and Halil Bey are regular customers. Bekir Bey, although he spends considerable time in Yalova, never allows too much time to pass without coming to the Taşköprü coffeeshops. That the place for patronage is the coffeehouse becomes more conspicuous when the behavior of Ali Bey is observed. As he never sought influence in the village and as he has always remained outside of the village network of relations, he never went to coffeehouses to join in the talks. Such a behavior makes the others stand out more. Furthermore, the villagers' rejection of him and the emergence of the new patrons and the significance of the coffee-houses illustrate the structure and its change.

Conclusions

The most conspicuous aspect of newly developing patron-client relations in Taşköprü is that they are not residues of an old system of relations. The disruption of the old patterns brought about by Davut Bey's departure and Ali Bey's refusal of patronage and offer of "modern" relations, and the subsequent decade of struggle without an *ağa* makes this clear. Furthermore, the new patrons are all "self-made" ones. They are relatively young and their families are all ordinary members of the community. The main sphere of their activities, the basic subjects where their "help" is asked, are all economic activities which are new to the settlement. But one function they share with the old classic patron is that they all supply a channel of access to the larger society and provide protection to their clientele. In fact it was precisely on this aspect of protection in relating to the larger society that Ali Bey fell short of the expectations of the villagers.

Looking from another angle, one may assert that the external system as a whole does not supply mechanisms or institutions for security and channels for contact which readily serve the ex-peasants. With the disappearance of the self-sufficient agricultural economy and the old *ağa's* protection, it was critically important to provide institutions and relations from the external structure to ease the strain. When this was not provided, the community channeled its social change into the type of relationships which lead to more security.

Every social structure, with its integrated sets of institutions, interaction patterns and values, provides its members with mechanisms of security. The pre-industrial social structure with its small communities, family–centered activities, and face-to-face relations with its patrons, was well-equipped to provide the security. Rights, responsibilities and assets of the lords (*ağas*) and peasants were organized in such a fashion that everybody knew what to do in ordinary as well as in extraordinary times and situations. The system was so well integrated that its members usually were not aware that the group and its interaction patterns were providing them with security. In fact, it is only after some changes take place and new interaction patterns emerge in the lives of the members of the group that they become aware that something important is missing in the new situation. As the incoming systems fail to provide any security mechanism or channels of contact with the outside, the receiving system creates intermediary forms as buffer mechanisms very much in accord with its own structure and experience that is based on face-to-face service/protection relations of clientelism.

The new patrons have no belief in social welfare as such. They freely admit that they give assistance and maintain face-to-face relationships with villagers because these are profitable for their business. They are "modern" enterprisers. But they have learned quickly that they cannot establish and promote themselves fully if they do not function as an agency to meet individual emergencies or provide relief in difficult times. Here a particular aspect of the old system has changed totally: the relationship of the *ağa* and the peasant on the level of self-sufficiency. On the other hand certain needs and functions have remained unfulfilled. Thus there appear *intermediary forms* that are directed towards new functions but *also* take over unfulfilled ones. In a way what makes patronage an intermediary form in the structure is precisely this. Although new patrons are orchard growers or real estate agents or large store owners, they have to act also as protector, security agent or labor broker, in short, serving whatever function is left unfilled by the external system. With their performance, the community becomes integrated both with external structure and in itself.

In the process of late and intermittent development of "industrial" societies such as Turkey, the class structure and class base of political parties also become confused as their members, in accord with periods of fast industrial growth following periods of slow change, oscillate between large organizations with anonymous relations and definite class affiliations and small- or medium-scale self-employed free enterprising with obscure class status. Surely the definitive relationship of the preindustrial era, namely that of lord and peasant, is dissolved forever. But in countries like Turkey, the class structure of an industrial society has not yet fully established itself, not only because profit-oriented enterprises employing wage labor are not dominant, but also because there is no stable well-defined working class. Great numbers of peasants have been set free from the land, and are absorbed only into marginal sectors which have no class characteristics. Also even the biggest industrial enterprises show extremely high labor turnover, and large numbers of workers cannot decide whether to remain workers or leave and start one of the millions of small- to medium-sized individual to ten-man enterprises in agriculture, service or manufacture (Kıray, 1971, 1973; Şenyapılı, 1978). Such activities are particularly fertile for the intermediary forms of adjustment such as patronage. If these small entrepreneurs fail, they may go back to wage labor; but then the relatively limited number of wage-paying jobs still calls for great competition, and again favoritism and patronage become functional. The ex-peasants of Taşköprü who are enterprising or looking for wage work are not exceptions; hence, the floating clientele of Taşköprü patrons.

Thus, patron-client relations emerge as intermediary forms in social structures that change with external dynamics. They are buffer mechanisms and provide adjustment when the external system's impact lacks channels of contact and protection for the receiving one, and old ones are lost during change. Hence, two structures come together and go on functioning.

Knowledge of the attributes of the evolutionary stages of societies has been extensive in the literature of social sciences, both in the Weberian-Parsonian and the Marxist frames of reference. Equally rich is the literature in both frames on change with internal dynamics. Studies that deal with change where insight and sensitivity are directed to the speed of change and the partial, selective intrusion of external structures into less differentiated ones, and the resultant intermediary forms and mechanisms that actually accomplish the change are not yet many. Patronage in Taşköprü has given a chance to observe on the micro level one of these intermediary mechanisms that have made the old local structure able to rearrange itself and function again.

The implications for macro analysis could be seen as those structures are not only functional wholes, a truism nowadays, but are transformable and able to rearrange themselves under the changing conditions of external dynamics particularly in accord with their own attributes. This they achieve by providing intermediary forms and mechanisms that establish the balance again, but which divert the general direction of change.

NOTES

[1]   The fieldwork for this study was carried out in 1978 through monthly visits to Taşköprü by the author. The author is grateful to the World Association of Rural Women for its grant which made the study possible.

[2]   In social sciences, fundamental concepts are particularly rich in ambiguity. Social structure and change are two such concepts. One way to clarify is certainly by systematic thinking. Another one, in line with the genesis of concepts and terms concerning "reality," is "observation." Thus summarizing the experience provides the concepts and "terms." In turn, these terms provide tools for further grasp of the social reality. Among many different ways of acquiring knowledge, the empirical and heuristic approach to changing structures still carries potency for understanding "reality."

At this stage, not only in social sciences but in general in our knowledge of "reality," recognition of the structure as a whole consisting of inter-dependent parts has been a very important step. Now we can proceed perhaps with a further characteristic which will make a structure some-thing rather different from the previous one. It can be asserted that the structure formed by the interdependent parts is always ready to change. In other words, the structure in equilibrium is in a delicate balance, ready to transform its parts and their interdependence. It is a dynamic (not static) whole, ready to change particularly when it is in contact with another structure. The processes and mechanisms each one provides are more for change than for maintenance. The other attribute is that the structure is self-regulatory which is complementary to its being transformable. Thus in a given time, a structure is in equilibrium but ready to change and rearrange itself. The crucial point here, as far as the "knowledge" of change is concerned, is information on the mechanisms of interchange of parts between two structures in contact, which makes them absorb change and keep themselves in a given time as structures in equilibrium *and* change.

3   Patronage as an important interdependence has attracted the attention of first anthropologists and later political scientists since the early 1960s. Since then the literature has continuously grown, bringing new information and analyses to this important institution. As examples of such studies, see the following: Boissevain (1962); Campbell (1964); Silverman, Gellner and Waterburg (1977). As for patronage in Turkey, see the following: Kıray (1966, ch. 4; 1969; 1974); Kudat (1974); Meeker (1972); Sayarı (1977); Yalman (1971).

4   It must be clarified that for patronage in rural areas large ownership or sharecropping is not a determining factor. Davut Bey did not have sharecroppers since his land was not large. But with the protection and security he provided and authority he carried he was a patron, in fact, a single patron for the whole village, like a lord. Large land owners and their patronage on their sharecroppers resembles more the classic feudal lord--peasant dependence. Various forms of lord–peasant dependencies either as lord-bureaucrats of the Ottoman palace, or ordinary local notables or ayans were cases of patrons in historic rural Turkey as well. Throughout history, a variety of such dependencies have appeared. See for instance: İnalcık (1974); Mardin (1963); Meeker (1972); Kıray (1964).

5   For her wedding she herself sent printed invitations indicating that "they had met, loved each other and decided to marry each other." This is unorthodox to the highest degree for a village family. It should be added that the wedding was taking place in her father's house.

6   Turkey does not have a well-established political party that serves the interests of workers. Should there be one, whether Murat Bey will be a part of it and act through it is an intriguing question. What has been observed in Italy with communist party members acting as patrons to workers and peasants should not be forgotten. See Tarrow (1967).

BIBLIOGRAPHY

Abadan-Unat, N. *Almanya'da Türk İşçileri.* Ankara: Devlet Planlama Teşkilatı, 1964.

Boissevain, J. "Patronage in Sicily," *Man,* l, pp. 18-33.

————. *Saints and Fire Works: Religion and Politics in Rural Malta.* London: Atholene Press, 1962.

Campbell, J.K. *Honour, Family and Patronage.* Oxford: Clarendon Press, 1964.

Gellner, E., and J. Waterbury (eds.). *Patron and Clients in Mediterrenean Societies.* Liverpool: Duckworth, 1977.

Hutteroth, W.D. "The Influence of Social Structure in Anatolia." In P. Benedict, E. Tümertekin, and F. Mansur (eds.), *Turkey: Geographic and Social Perspectives.* Leiden: E.J. Brill, 1974.

İnalcık, H. *The Ottoman Empire.* London: Cambridge University Press, 1974.

Kıray, M. *Ereğli: Ağır Sanayiden Önce Bir Sahil Kasabası.* Ankara: Devlet Planlama Teşkilati, 1964.

————. "Values, Social Stratification and Development," *Journal of Social Issues,* 26:2 (1968), 87-102.

————. "Social Change in Çukurova. A Comparison of Four Villages." In P. Benedict, E. Tümertekin, and F. Mansur (eds.), *Turkey: Geographical and Social Perspectives.* Leiden: E.J. Brill, 1974.

Kudat, A. "Patron–Client Relations: The State of the Art and Research in Eastern Turkey." In E.D. Akarlı and G. Ben-Dor (eds.), *Political Participation in Turkey.* Istanbul, 1974, pp. 61-87.

Mardin, S. "Power, Civil Society and Culture in the Ottoman Empire," *Comparative Studies in History and Society,* 1963, 11

Meeker, M.E. "The Great Family Aghas of Turkey: A Study of Changing Political Culture." In R. Antoin and I. Harik (eds.), *Rural Politics and Social Change in the Middle East.* Bloomington, Indiana: Indiana Univ. Press, 1972, pp. 237-66.

Sayarı, S. "Political Patronage in Turkey." In E. Gellner and J. Waterbury (eds.), *Patrons and Clients in Mediterranean Societies.* London: Duckworth, 1977.

Silverman, S. "Patronage and Community Nation Relationships in Central Italy," *Ethnology,* 4, 172-89.

Şenyapılı, T. *Kentle Bütünleşemeyen Nufus Sorunu.* Ankara: ODTÜ Yayınları, 1978.

Tarrow, S. *Peasant Communism in Southern Italy.* New Haven, 1967.

Timur, S. *Türkiye'de aile yapısı.* Ankara: Hacettepe Univ. Publications, 1972.

Yalman, N. "On Land Disputes in Eastern Turkey." In G. Tikku (ed.), *Islam and Its Cultural Diversions: Studies in Honour of G.E. von Grunebaum.* Urbana, Illinois, 1971.

PSYCHOPATHOLOGY AND THE TURKISH FAMILY: A FAMILY SYSTEMS THEORY ANALYSIS

Güler Okman Fişek

The aim of this paper is to attempt an analysis of the Turkish family within a Family Systems Theory framework and to investigate the implications of this analysis for the kinds of pathology we might expect to occur in Turkish families. To achieve this aim, first, a summary of the literature on family functioning in Turkish culture will be presented, followed by a description of the basic premises of Family Systems Theory. Against the background provided by these summaries, the "typical" Turkish family will be analyzed from the systems theory perspective. Finally, some speculations will be made regarding the weak points in the family system, which could be potentially vulnerable to stress and therefore pathology. These speculations will be followed by illustrative clinical case material.

A word about the "typical" Turkish family. While Turkish culture in general and Turkish families in particular are undergoing far too rapid a process of social change and are far too complex for there to be a truly typical Turkish family, it is felt that enough common patterns exist among most families to make some amount of generalization viable. Further, there is such a dearth of clinically oriented literature on the Turkish family that, at least, these generalizations could be considered as a starting point for empirically oriented investigation.

The Family and the Individual in Turkish Culture

The Social Context
It is a well known fact that Turkish society is undergoing rapid social change from being a traditional, agricultural, rural, patriarchal

society into an increasingly urbanized, industrial, modern, egalitarian society (Kâğıtçıbaşı, 1978). However, this change is not equally rapid in all areas of social functioning. As would be expected, values and attitudes tend to lag behind changing social structures and functions.

Thus, the culture can still be described as somewhat traditional, authoritarian and patriarchal. Close blood and kinship ties still form the basis of most social relationships, especially in rural areas (Stirling, 1965). Where the nuclear family is unable to fulfill its tasks, the extended family provides support and security, as in the cases where the man of the family is working abroad (Abadan-Unat, 1976). In urban areas neighbors fulfill this supportive role (Kandiyoti, 1977). Social relationships are based on mutual responsibilities and loyalties among members of hierarchically ordered groups. This is especially true in rural communities where face-to-face interaction is predominant and individuals cannot disregard each other's opinion. Thus, the individual is embedded in an ever-widening network of close ties, beginning with the nuclear family and extending out to the relatives and close neighbors (Kâğıtçıbaşı, 1981).

Marriage

While customs and practices surrounding marriage differ across communities, there are many common features. Most marriages are monogamous. There is much intermarrying among relatives as a means both of mutual support and enhancing economic power. While young couples are increasingly in favor of choosing their own partners, arranged marriages of some sort are quite common. In many ways, marriage is still viewed as a financial and social transaction between two families, more than an individual decision by two partners (Kâğıtçıbaşı, 1981; Stirling, 1965). While customs such as the bride price may not be relevent in urban areas, middle class families are especially concerned with the status compatibility of the two families involved in a marriage (Olson-Prather, 1976).

Family Structure

While the extended family is preferred as an indicator of wealth, the predominant structure is the nuclear family in urban, rural and gecekondu areas (Gökçe, 1976; Kâğıtçıbaşı, 1981; Kandiyoti, 1974; Timur, 1972; Yasa, 1970).

However, it would appear that the functionally extended family is very much a psychological presence for most people. Patterns such as transitional extended families (Kandiyoti, 1974; Timur, 1972) and findings that relatives tend to live in the same neighborhood even in urban areas (Kongar, 1972) support this notion. In fact, the extended family is still a source of support and security in a society which does not provide institutional support structures.

Within the nuclear family, just as within the wider social network, there is a hierarchical ordering of members, with clear delineation of status and roles, especially with regards to the factors of gender and generation. While modernization and increasing egalitarianism are making some inroads into the family system, it is not too long since the women of the household waited for the men to finish eating before they could eat their meals. The status differentiation by sex and generation deserves a closer look.

On the subject of status differentiation and gender, we can make one single generalization regarding Turkey: despite all changes, women's status is still clearly lower than that of men (Kâğıtçıbaşı, 1981; Kandiyoti, 1974, 1978; Kıray, 1976; Köknel, 1970). This generalization holds to varying degrees for all subgroups within the larger society, from migrant communities, to villages, to cities. Whether the woman has a large share in the productivity of the household makes little difference regarding her status (Kandiyoti, 1974; Kuyaş, 1980). In traditional areas a woman's status starts improving only after she gives birth, especially to a boy, and this climb in status culminates when she becomes a mother-in-law (Kâğıtçıbaşı, 1981; Kandiyoti, 1974).

This status difference is reflected in a stereotypic definition of sex roles as well as the custom of physical and social segregation. The women's arena is the home, domestic labor and child care, while the man deals with the external world and there is little opportunity for role-sharing (Kâğıtçıbaşı, 1981; Kandiyoti, 1977; Köknel, 1970).

Social change has led to some attitudinal change so that younger people tend to favor a more individualistic, independent and egalitarian approach to family life. However, all this has not yet made a clear impact on women's roles (Kandiyoti, 1974; Timur, 1972). For example, while it would be acceptable for a woman to work while she is single, to continue to do so would reflect on the husband's ability to take care of his family. Thus, while economic necessities and women's demands may lead to more role-sharing, they also may lead to more stress on the husband and, therefore, family conflict.

The second area of status differentiation involves the generations, namely, the children and the in-laws. Children are an important and valued part of the Turkish family. However, by and large, children are still valued more as sources of future economic support and security and as promoters of the family name than as sources of psychological and emotional fulfillment (Kâğıtçıbaşı, 1981).

While the status of children is low in the family, boys definitely have higher status than girls. In some cases, the oldest boy may have higher status than the mother, especially as he grows older and becomes initiated into the world of men. This situation seems to imply that sex as a determinant of status can be more important than generation. Indeed, sex role training starts early and definitively (Öztürk, 1969a).

As far as the in-laws go, in traditional households, the paternal grandparents used to have the highest status. But as economic power moves from the patriarch to the son, usually the oldest son, he becomes the dominant figure (Timur, 1972). However, the grandparents continue to exert influence, especially on the bride. An extreme example is from the environs of Sivas in central Anatolia, where a bride cannot even talk to her parents-in-law before she gives birth. Neither she nor her husband can express affection for their own children in front of the grandparents (Sümer, 1969). Grandparents may be more lenient towards the children since they do not have to be primarily responsible for discipline. But this lack of responsibility does not necessarily mean a lack of authority and they feel free to interfere with the parents' child-rearing practices (Gökçe, 1976).

The parental in-laws are expected to have more say-so in the life of the nuclear family in traditional sectors, especially since they are physically within closer range (Timur, 1972). Where the maternal side becomes dominant, it is usually because that side is more wealthy and offers more economic support. However, it is always the son's duty to economically support his elderly parents when they need it, rather than the son-in-law's (Kâğıtçıbaşı, 1981; Timur, 1972).

Family Dynamics

In this section we will review intra-family relationships, as seen between husband and wife and between parents and children. As would be expected from reading the previous sections, intra-family relationships are based on clear role differentiation and revolve more around the economic survival and propagation aspects of family life than around mutual emotional support and fulfillment (Olson-Prather, 1976). It is no surprise then that in one study couples cite the most common sources of dispute as being economic and child-rearing concerns (Gökçe, 1976). There actually is not much emotional expression between spouses in the traditional marriage, nor is there much communication on general topics (Kandiyoti, 1977; Olson-Prather, 1976; Stirling, 1965). This is to be expected since the spouses live largely in separate worlds and probably have not had much say in choosing each other to begin with. It is interesting that even relevant topics such as how many children to have do not receive much discussion (Kâğıtçıbaşı, 1981).

If we consider that much of the communication between spouses revolves around negotiations of role sharing and allocation of responsibilities, i.e., defining the relationship and the position of the spouses in that relationship, we should not be very surprised at the relative lack of communication in a traditional Turkish family. The social and cultural norms regulating role allocation and spheres of functioning for the spouses are usually so delineated by clear enough boundaries, which are consensually accepted, that there isn't much need for negotiation.

The area of decision-making power is a clear illustration. Decisions on major issues involving the household are the husband's responsibility. For example, in one survey, only 1% of the male respondents acknowledged that their wives could make important decisions, while only 3% of the women made such an acknowledgement (Timur, 1972). This pattern does not seem to differ too much between rural and urban couples (Gökçe, 1976). The husband's decision-making prerogative may even extend to areas such as whom the wife may visit, what she can buy and how much she can spend on purchases.

More modern, urban families show a trend toward status equalization (Kongar, 1972; Timur, 1972). In many cases where a weakening of the traditional norms occurs, the tendency towards increased egalitarianism and role sharing is not without its price in conflict. For example, recently migrated gecekondu families suffer from the lack of traditional controls, such as powerful older authority figures and consensually supported role expectations. The result is usually direct conflict between husband and wife (Sümer, 1969). The fact that most divorces occur in this segment undergoing most stress from social change also supports this statement (see Levine's article in this volume). Sencer also (1976) ties intra-family conflict to differing role expectations, reduced family size and differing functional and relationship demands among gecekondu families.

Going further on the scale of stress, a study of suicide attempters found that the largest subgroup (31%) reported family conflict as their reason (Gürgen, 1969). Within this group, husband/wife conflict came first (38%), with mother/daughter and mother-in-law/bride conflict following at 12 and 9%, respectively.

Middle and upper class families are not settled enough into their egalitarian attitudes to be immune from conflict over differing role expectations. One study found that higher SES women reject the homemaker role more strenuously than middle class women (Le Compte, et. al., 1978). Another survey of middle class couples applying to a medical school clinic for psychological assistance showed that the so-called "neurotic couples" differed from normal control couples on a number of dimensions. Some of these were: neurotic couples had more problems with joint decision-making, with less agreement on child rearing, how to spend money, entertainment priorities. Mutual caring and praise was not a feature of the neurotic marriage, whereas the control couples could express affection and agree on jointly-decided role sharing (Büyükberker and Kerimoğlu, 1972).

With respect to relations between parents and children, the general atmosphere surrounding children is one of love and control, in contrast to Western families in which love goes with permissiveness, and a preponderance of control usually implies an insufficiency of love (Kâğıtçıbaşı, 1972).

It was stated earlier that while there was a clear status distinction and separation between the sexes and generations, these distinctions are sometimes blurred. This is especially true in the case of the mother/son relationship. While some authors find a relationship of affection and tolerance between father and daughter (Kandiyoti, 1977; Stirling, 1965), most authors agree in emphasizing the close mother/son relationship (Kâğıtçıbaşı, 1981; Kandiyoti, 1977; Kıray, 1976; Öztürk, 1969b; Stirling, 1965).

This close relationship is to be expected to some degree in a traditional society since the son starts conferring status on his mother beginning with his birth. Add to this the fact that husband and wife are not allowed much open expression of emotional closeness, and it is then natural for the house-bound wife to seek closeness with her children, and mainly her more valuable son. In most traditional areas, this closeness endures into adulthood. As an extreme symbolic example, in some villages of Balikesir, the son crawls between his mother's legs on his way to the bride's room on his wedding night (Sümer, 1969).

In contrast to the closeness between mother and son, the father/son relationship is formal, authoritarian and somewhat distant. This combination, along with early sex role training and circumcision between the ages of 3-6, is seen by some authors as conducive to Oedipal conflicts (Cansever, 1965; Öztürk, 1969b). However, the fact that the circumcision ritual is seen as an initiation into manhood and as increasing the value of the boy would seem to mitigate such possibilities (Kâğıtçıbaşı, 1981). This process also serves to initiate the gradual separation between mother and son (Sümer, 1969).

In the area of discipline, while infants and toddlers are indulged, the general attitude is still controlling and protective. Harshness is not implied here so much as a restriction of autonomous action, as seen in toilet training practices, for example (Öztürk, 1969a). The expectation of obedience to authority transcends differential sex role expectations (Kâğıtçıbaşı, 1981; Köknel, 1970; Stirling, 1965). Compliance, meekness, respect and quietness are rewarded, while activity, liveliness, curiosity, talk and initiative are punished (Öztürk, 1969a).

Common means of discipline are shaming, scaring through threats of castration or calling upon supernatural beings, and beating (Le Compte, 1979; Öztürk, 1969a; Sümer, 1969; Yörükoğlu, 1978). Helling found rural discipline to be inconsistent, not based on verbal reasoning, dependent on adult moods, and generally warm but controlling (1966).

As in many areas, social change is also making inroads into the issue of discipline. Kongar's subjects reported that their children had more freedom and autonomy than they did as children (1972). Other studies found an increased tendency to favor a democratic, egalitarian approach to discipline and avoidance of corporal punishment among urban middle and upper classes (Le Compte et. al., 1978; Okman, 1980).

Another aspect of parent/child relationships which deserves mention has to do with training for autonomous coping skills, specifically cognitive skills. The traditional rural approach to teaching cognitive skills has been by example, emphasizing motor rather than symbolic learning, imitation, and limiting the use of problem solving, all of which lead to the formation of a constricted cognitive framework (Helling, 1966; Öztürk and Volkan, 1977). Urban lower SES families tend to repeat this pattern (Ataman and Epir, 1972; Kâğıtçıbaşı, 1979; Uçman, 1972).

While middle class urban parents are more attentive to the development of conceptual skills in their children, they still tend to reinforce reliance on parental authority rather than on the child's own resources, which results in a field dependent cognitive style among the children (Okman, 1980). In fact, in this last study it was found that increased democratization in discipline among middle class parents was not accompanied by increased training for autonomy, in contrast to Western studies in which the two child-rearing attitudes have been generally found to co-vary.

Regarding the implication for personality development of the above, most authors agree that the traditional Turkish family dynamics would foster the development of a passive, dependent, constricted and somewhat frustrated person without a sense of autonomy and with a reliance on external sources of control and reinforcement (Cansever, 1965; Geçtan, 1973; Helling, 1966; Kâğıtçı-başı, 1981; Köknel, 1970; Öztürk, 1969).

The restrictive and suppressive practices of early training are expected to lead to frustration and concomitant anger, but since the overt expression of hostility to adults is forbidden, these feelings would have to be repressed or suppressed. Öztürk and Volkan (1977), interpreting this state of affairs from a psychodynamic point of view, conclude that an identification with the aggressor (in this case, the authority figure) would have to occur. Thus, the individual's use of initiative and autonomy would be constricted, and only expressed through normatively approved outlets, such as militarism, heroism, and overvaluation of maleness. Similarly, they reason that early sex role training leads to an early and intense identification with the parent of the same sex and an early adoption of adult roles and attitudes, which further serve to inhibit curiosity and initiative and to foreclose on the experimentation of childhood and youth.

Consistent with the above speculations, the Turkish adolescent has been found to be patriotic, politically aware, attached to and dependent on his parents, and respectful of his elders (Kâğıtçıbaşı, 1972; Öztürk and Volkan, 1977). Many express problems with their self-concept and with family relationships (Baymur, 1961). Those who report coming from more restrictive families report lower self-actualization levels (Kuzgun, 1973).

Needless to say, the above generalizations refer mainly to the urban male adolescent. The girl would be expected to become aware of her lower status early on. Since identification with a powerful parent is not available to her, she would be expected to suffer feelings of low self-esteem with regards to her female identity. In fact, there are a number of studies in which girls report less ego strength and more anxiety, anomie and pessimism than boys in childhood and adolescent years (Demiröz, 1976; Kâğıtçıbaşı, 1972; Okman, 1980; Zülemyan, 1979).

This sex difference in what we may call overall self-esteem seems not to be so apparent in adulthood. Contrary to the childhood and adolescence data, male and female adults do not differ in the amount of anxiety they report (Öner, 1977). This leads one to wonder what happens to the Turkish male as he enters adulthood; whether, in fact, he undergoes a crisis of self-esteem. Findings from the tangentially related research area of need achievement may have a bearing on this question, in so far as the high need achievement reported for young Turkish boys reverses to low need achievement in late adolescence and adulthood (Kâğıtçıbaşı, 1976). In contrast, one may speculate that the girl child who starts out with low self-esteem would not suffer a crisis of self-esteem, but would feel strengthened as she gets older and her status improves through marriage and childbirth.

A Family Systems Theory Model

In this section a Family Systems Theory model of the nuclear family will be presented to provide a theoretical framework within which to place the empirical and observational findings reported in the previous section.

The fact that there is a dearth of clinical literature on the Turkish family should come as no surprise, since the family as a focus of study for applied social science is a recent phenomenon in the world at large. It was only when the individual, intra-psychic emphasis of traditional models of psychopathology proved inadequate, that a search for a new conceptual paradigm got underway in the late 1940s and early 1950s (Guerin, 1976). At this point the family emerged as an agent and matrix of psychopathology as well as of therapeutic change (Erikson and Hogan, 1972). This approach to psychopathology originated in the United States and over the past thirty years has spread to Europe, but its practice remains very limited in Turkey.

The conceptual paradigms underlying Family Systems Theory are based on general systems theory and communications theory. With the help of systems thinking, the family can be seen as an operating unit which can take in information from the environment, process it and act upon it; in which any change in one member influences other members and the functioning of which can be understood apart from that of any individual member (Erikson and Hogan, 1972).

As new as it is, Family Systems Theory is not so much a unified theory as a general way of conceptualizing the family, within which there are may diversities of outlook. The model presented below is a distillation of the common points to be found among the most important representatives of the approach.

At this point it may be useful to define the word "system," as it is used here. Bowen defines a system as "any relationship with balancing forces and counterforces in constant operation" (1976, p.62). That is, the family system is a unit which is always in the process of maintaining some kind of homeostatic balance in reaction to changes either in one member or in the external situation, and which also acts upon its surroundings. The unit of study in the systems model is the nuclear family which is seen as the "typical unit in Western society" (Fleck, 1972). However, it will be seen later that the extended families or the families of origin of the spouses play a rather important role in the functioning of the nuclear family. Thus, in considering the family model, we will review the following features of the family system: family structure, family dynamics, the extended family and family pathology.

Family Structure

Family structure refers to the "invisible set of functional demands that organize the ways in which family members interact" (Minuchin, 1974, p. 51). These ways of interacting develop into transactional patterns indicating when, how and to whom a member is to relate to in the family, that is, these transactional patterns define the relationship of the family members to each other. These transactional patterns function within the constraints imposed by certain universal rules of family organization (such as a need for complementarity of functions among members in each family), as well as by idiosyncratic mutual expectations developed over time. Family structure is made up of subsystems and their boundaries, and the individuals in the subsystems.

Subsystems are made up of groups of family members, with each individual belonging to a number of subsystems (Minuchin, 1974). For example, the wife belongs to the spouse subsystem, the parental subsystem, as well as the female subsystem. The number of separately functioning subsystems in the family reflects that family system's level of differentiation. This division into subsystems aids the family in carrying out its functions.

Subsystems are separated from each other by boundaries, which are the rules that define who participates in a subsystem and how (Minuchin, 1974). For example, ordinarily children do not participate in the parental subsystem, but when the father is unavailable for some reason, the oldest son may take on parts of the father role, thereby becoming a member of the parental subsystem. The function of boundaries is to protect the differentiation of the system and allow the functioning of one subsystem without undue interference from other subsystems. For example, a well-differentiated spouse subsystem with clear boundaries would be more free of the influence of inlaws, than a spouse subsystem with diffuse boundaries, i.e., unclear rules as to the lines of responsibility and authority.

The individual family member is a special subsystem. The sense of self or identity is conferred by the family to the individual in his or her early socialization, and consists of a sense of belonging and a sense of separateness (Minuchin, 1974). The sense of belonging develops through the child's accomodation to the family's patterns of functioning, and the sense of separateness develops through the child's participation in different subsystems in different contexts. Through the interplay of these two forces, the child's self is differentiated as an autonomous subsystem which is nevertheless rooted in the family system. The child's self also undergoes differentiation into the emotional and intellectual systems of psychic functioning (Bowen, 1976).

Thus, the model conceptualizes the self as a part of the total system and subject to the same laws. The self also has a boundary, which consists of "how people define themselves and their personal space in relation to the others" (Guerin and Guerin, 1976, p. 95).

In summary, the structural components of the family system consist of various subsystems. Family members fall within a given subsystem based on the rules of participation within that subsystem, rules which define the boundaries of that subsystem. The individual self is also a subsystem with its own boundary conceptualized as the person's self definition vis-a-vis others.

The next question deals with the movements, interactions and shifts in the dynamic patterning which occurs within and between these subsystems in reaction to each other and the external world. This, in short, is the area of family dynamics.

Family Dynamics

Let us begin with the basic components of the nuclear family system, the selves of the two spouses coming together in marriage. What occurs at the interface of these two selves? All couples seek a certain amount of closeness while at the same time needing to maintain a sense of separateness and emotional space around themselves (Fogarty, 1976). Thus, the sense of belonging and separateness in the families of origin seek replication in the new family.

As the spouses form their own family system, they need to relate to each other in certain ways in order for the system to fulfill these needs for belonging and separateness optimally. The main skills couples need to develop are those of "mutuality, accomodation and complementarity" (Minuchin, 1974, p. 52). That is, they need to develop transactional patterns in which each spouse supports the other's functioning in many areas. Each spouse has to yield part of his or her separateness in order to belong and become mutually interdependent in a symmetrical relationship. Yet at the same time, each spouse has to allow enough emotional space within which the other can feel his or her individuality.

As the spouses move toward each other in emotional intimacy, a certain amount of "blurring of the self boundaries" and joining of the two selves occurs, which is termed "fusion" in the systems language (Guerin and Guerin, 1976, p. 94). The force behind this fusion is the hope of filling the emptiness in one's self which one may bring to the marriage (Fogarty, 1976). As the spouses move toward fusion, the level of emotionality and mutual expectations within the subsystem rises. When the increase is beyond a certain level of tolerance for one or both spouses, anxiety occurs. The reaction to anxiety is usually an awakening of the need for separateness or "emotional distance" (Bowen, 1976; Fogarty, 1976). This emotional distancing is accomplished through a variety of mechanisms, one of which is marital conflict. Over time, the spouses develop predictable sensitivities and do not want these areas encroached upon. When this encroachment occurs, a distancing maneuver developed as a transactional pattern in that family takes place.

"The two spouses begin a marriage with life style patterns and levels of differentiation developed in their families of origin" (Bowen, 1976, p. 79). The more highly differentiated the individuals were previous to the marriage, the less marital fusion there will be; rather there will be a more functional integration of selves without the loss of one's own self, which would result from a state of low differentiation and high fusion among spouses.

However, we should not see differentiation and fusion as absolute and unchangeable states, but as "transactional styles" (Minuchin, 1974, p. 55). Most families have different subsystems which tend to be at one or the other end of this continuum and which change depending on the developmental phase of the family. For example, a state of fusion between mother and infant is functional, as is increasing differentiation as the child grows older.

When a couple has gone too far in the direction of marital fusion and anxiety is aroused in one or both spouses, triangulation is often the mechanism used to achieve the needed emotional distance. In the systems framework, a triangle is a three-person emotional configuration which is the "the smallest stable relationship system that can allow differentiation of the self from the other" and displacement of intense emotionality onto a third party (Bowen, 1976, p. 76). The third party can occasionally be something other than a person. Typical foci of triangulation in couple subsystems are the in-laws, the husband's overwork or drinking, the wife's ailments, etc. The birth of a child forces a significant change in the balance of the family system, providing increased opportunities for triangulation. When the number of family members goes beyond two, coalition of two members against a third also becomes a common mechanism for avoiding fusion.

The Extended Family

While the systems approach emphasizes current family functioning, it recognizes the fact that the families of origin of the spouse were the matrix within which each spouse learned to develop a preference for a particular transactional style (Minuchin, 1974). In fact, Bowen (1976) states that the basic patterns of emotional functioning in the family system are replications of the patterns of previous generations. In addition to their learned transactional style, the spouses also bring their unfinished business from their families of origin. Thus, as the process of marital fusion unfolds, there is an inevitable tie in to the extended family (Guerin and Guerin, 1976, p. 93). Needless to say, this process involves quite a bit of compromise and conflict (Haley, 1972).

Given the above statement, it can be expected that much marital conflict will revolve around triangulation to the extended families and/or a blurring of the boundary between the spouse subsystem and in-law subsystems. The resolution of such conflicts should be neither through fusion with the extended families, not emotional cut off from them (Bowen, 1976). The ideal state would be a meaningful coexistence as separate but interacting subsystems within the larger extended family system.

The problems which can occur in relation to the extended family can range from fusion and triangulation on both sides, where the spouse subsystem can project conflict on to the extended family, or the in-law subsystem can stimulate conflict and compete for support and indulgence (Bell, 1962).

Family Pathology

Stress is an inevitable concomitant of family life, whether the source lies in internal changes on the part of family members or in changes in external situations and institutions. A family has to try to maintain continuity while constantly restructuring in adaptation to stress. Thus, a family is always "a social system in transformation" (Minuchin, 1974, p. 60), and the anxiety and conflict which accompanies such transformation is not necessarily pathological. Pathology occurs when the response to stress is an increase in the rigidity of the transactional patterns of the family and an avoidance of seeking for alternative coping mechanisms.

Such rigidity is seen in the extremes of emotional fusion or cut off (Bowen, 1976). While extreme fusion provides a heightened sense of belonging, it also involves a yielding of autonomy within undifferentiated subsystems, resulting in an inhibition of affective and cognitive skills. Extreme emotional cut off allows autonomy but provides no sense of belonging, loyalty, support or interdependence. These families are isolated, uninvolved and unable to provide basic warmth and comfort. The extremely fused families, on the other hand, show high emotionality, unfulfilled expectations, blurred boundaries and a lack of a sense of self on the part of the members. In such families, no one member feels free to be autonomous and independent, for fear of disturbing family unity (Napier and Whitaker, 1978).

Symptoms are ways of handling rigidity in transactional styles. Symptoms can be used as aids to distancing in cases of too much marital fusion (e.g., wife's headaches), forming part of a fusion-distancing/making up cycle.

Dysfunction in one spouse is usually due to the rigidity in the dominance hierarchy of the family system. The spouse who adapts to the dominant one begins to lose his or her sense of self, cannot act independently and becomes symptomatic under stress (Bowen, 1976; Minuchin, 1974).

Dysfunction in the child is often the result of a triangulation in which the intensity of the emotional fusion between the spouses is projected onto the child. In fact, triangulation is one of the most basic mechanisms underlying symptoms. Haley sees family pathology as a network of perverse triangles "in which people of different generations violate boundaries, deny power hierarchies and two people form a coalition of two generations against a third" (1967, p. 17). An example would be a couple who cannot resolve their unmet needs in the spouse subsystem and triangulate onto an adolescent son, with whom the mother forms a coalition, violating sex and generation boundaries and distancing the father, who then has to contend with a rebellious son.

A further complication is that usually these breaches of boundaries and triangulations are not articulated and may even be denied (Haley, 1967). This kind of communication blockage which underlies the theory of the "double bind" serves to strengthen fusion and impede conflict resolution.

The systems approach would hold that the above formulation of family pathology is applicable to couples and families in all cultures (Haley, 1972). Haley states that increased family conflict should be expected in the context of changing cultures.

In a static, stable culture, the rules regarding the definition of relationships within systems, this is, the rules governing the formation and maintenance of boundaries, are usually clear and normatively agreed upon. In a changing culture in flux, however, those very rules are open to disagreement and negotiation. Thus, couples whose learned transactional styles meet neither the changing constraints of their cultural context nor each other's expectations are faced with having to negotiate and differentiate along new dimensions. Stress and conflict are all too natural a consequence. The most typical current example of such a situation in most countries is the stress engendered by the changed role of women in society and in the family.

The Turkish Family from the Family Systems Theory Perspective

This section will attempt to integrate the two previous sections and present an analysis of the Turkish family from a Family Systems Theory perspective. This analysis will be followed by a discussion of the implication of this analysis for the kinds of pathology to be expected in the Turkish family, and by illustrative case material.

The Social Context

The social context of the Turkish family, in so far as it is based on close group ties, accountability, loyalty and interdependence rather than autonomy and individualism, would translate into a somewhat fused, undifferentiated system of relationships within the systems theory framework. This is not entirely the case, however, in that the hierarchical authoritarian structure of the society provides for differentiation on a normative level. That is, the system is differentiated and clear as to the roles and functions normatively expected from any given individual of a given status. However, as far as individual, idiosyncratic psychological functioning, decision making and action go, one would expect relatively low differentiation and lack of autonomy. Individuals in such a system would be only too quick in tending to fuse with others when normative expectations do not guide their emotional expression and behavior.

Family Structure

The same situation would seem to exist in the family context, so that the Turkish nuclear family structure could be seen as a mixture of high role differentiation and low personal differentiation. The status distinction between husband and wife and the separation of their spheres of activity would result in a spouse subsystem which is differentiated along the sex roles dimension, with clear boundaries between the selves of the two spouses. The relative lack of emotional expression and communication between the spouses is an indication of these boundaries.

Given a state of differentiation between husband and wife, one would expect the spouses to experience a sense of clarity and comfort with regards to their role expectations. In so far as the family remains traditional in its values concerning sex roles, this would seem to be the case. However, this does not mean that the spouses also experience a sense of autonomy and comfort with regards to their personal experience. The reason for this may be sought in the lack of differentiation from the extended family, as presented below.

The nuclear family sytem, instead of being a complete unit with clear boundaries, appears to be more or less enmeshed in a visible functionally-extended family network, so much so that we may even conceptualize the Turkish nuclear family as a subsystem within a larger extended family system, from which it is imperfectly differentiated. The lack of clear boundaries is especially evident with regard to the rules governing economic support and decision making. This state of fusion between the nuclear and the extended families is also reflected in the idea that often it is not the spouses who join together in marriage, but the two extended families, with the spouses providing the joining interface.

Family Dynamics

Given this blurring of boundaries between the nuclear and extended family, the spouses would be expected to experience difficulty transferring their loyalties (i.e., differentiating) from their families of origin to their own nuclear family. The Family Systems Theory model depicted the new couple coming together (fusing) in order to reach closeness and fill the areas of emptiness within their self systems. It would appear that such fusion would be difficult to achieve in the Turkish nuclear family system, especially in the cases where the spouses have not even chosen each other.

Thus we end up with two individuals who co-exist in a spouse subsystem which is not so much a subsystem as an interface for the interaction of two selves who continue to be somewhat fused with their families of origin.

In the traditional family, the husband and the wife would be expected to experience this situation somewhat differently. The husband who maintains frequent interaction with his family of origin or even shares its household and/or work setting can maintain his balance pretty much as before. The wife, however, is somewhat cut off from her family of origin and, thus, has to look elsewhere to fulfill her needs for closeness and fusion. The status hierarchy (i.e., the subsystem boundaries) does not allow for much fusion with her husband or in-laws who persist in seeing her as an outsider. Her natural recourse is to turn to her children to fill the areas of emptiness in her self system.

The mother's turning to her children is facilitated by the fact that the sex and generation boundaries are not very clear in separating her from her children. This may be due to the above-stated factors of her own lack of differentiation from her family of origin and her inability to achieve fusion with her husband. Add to these the frequently existing closeness of status between the low status mother and the relatively high status eldest son, and it is clear that the outcome would be a blurring of the generational boundary and fusion between mother and son. Such fusion could take the form of a diffusion of responsibility and authority as well as, and mainly, heightened emotionality and expectations between mother and son. The mother/daughter relationship, while close due to a shared same sex subsystem which fosters identification, would not have as many forces converging on it to create a high emotional charge.

The father who is still fused with his family of origin would be expected to be cut off from his children as well as his wife. The father/son relationship especially would have to show enough distance to maintain the family status hierarchy intact and compensate for the boundary crossover between mother and son. Since status considerations are not so crucial between father and daughter, that relationship can potentially be somewhat closer within the limits imposed by the gender boundary.

Child-rearing practices would seem to be the mechanism through which the combination of differentiated role expectations and fused emotional relationships, characteristic of the total system, get transmitted to each new generation. The product of these practices is an individual who is dependent, somewhat constricted, externally controlled and lacking autonomy. Within the systems framework, this translates into an undifferentiated individual who is likely to have a high need for a sense of belonging but will not be as aware of a need for separateness. This individual would be quite clear as to his roles and status in his group but would not be expected to have equal clarity in his emotional experience.

Family Pathology

Within this context, the well-functioning individual would be the one who perceives little or no disjunction between his role demands and actual experience. As long as cultural norms regulate subsystem boundaries and the individual stays within these boundaries he should feel no serious discomfort. For example, the wife who accepts her low status and segregation from her husband or the son who accepts his father's distance as a sign of proper authority will not feel rejected or unloved. Similarly, acceptance of norm-based boundaries would reduce the need for interpersonal negotiation, thereby reducing the potential for conflict.

However, as norm-based boundaries especially those regarding sex roles and inter-generational transactions weaken a state of disequilibrium would emerge, eventuating in a disjuction between the individual's role expectations and personal experience. The inevitable result is conflict.

When would such a situation lead to pathology? First of all, we have to keep in mind that the structural and dynamic properties under discussion are transactional styles and that most families are quite flexible in modifying their styles to fit the demand of their situations. The families who cannot flexibly adapt to their situation might fall into two abroad groups. One would be those whose pathology is due to idiosyncratic deviance from the norm and accompanying rigidity in transactional styles. Another group of families would be those who are subject to rapid and wide-reaching changes in their cultural context which undermine the norm-based structures that used to maintain their functioning.

The second kind of pathology is, in some respects, more interesting in reflecting the stresses impinging on the larger societal system, as well as being ultimately more amenable to psychotherapeutic and psychoeducational intervention. The families who have lost the support provided by clear and consensually accepted boundaries have in fact lost the main source of differentiation within their system and are, thus, hampered in fulfilling their tasks. In the extreme case, we would have a system consisting of undifferentiated individuals adrift in a game, the rules of which are suddenly open to negotiation. And these individuals would have neither learned the skill of negotiating as a transactional style, nor would they be sure about the new rules needed in their system. With the relative unavailability of extended family supports, and under pressure from modern expectations of emotional intimacy, husband and wife would bring their needs for closeness to each other and be faced with a situation of highly charged fusion with which they would be unprepared to cope.

For example, a husband faced with an educated wife demanding acknowledgement of her emotional needs might very well feel that his authority would be undermined if he moved towards her in fusion, while at the same time feeling inadequate to meet her needs. The wife may have learned that a modern couple should share their feelings, but being unprepared to communicate her wishes clearly, might in fact act in a challenging and intrusive manner. The net result might be a distancing and triangulation maneuver on the part of the husband and a fruitless pursuit on the part of the wife. Feelings of low self-esteem, distrust, anomie, depression and anger would be natural concomitants of such a state and could easily escalate to symptomatic levels.

Such a situation should be all too common in today's Turkey, where socio-economic changes are disturbing the normative role expectations of individuals as well as intra-group relationships. Indeed, studies reflecting increased egalitarian and individualistic values in sectors undergoing social change would seem to indicate that, while these people are moving towards increased differentiation, they are paying a price in conflicted intra- and interpersonal experience.

Illustrative Case Material

The case presented below is a clear example of the above-mentioned sources of conflict. As would be expected in a country where psychologically oriented interventions are mainly sought by the relatively modernized upper middle classes, Mr. and Mrs T. are both university-educated and well-to-do; they live in a metropolitan center and come from established families. As such, their conflict reflects the difficulties experienced by the relatively modernized younger generation, who come from a traditional extended family background and have to establish a new transactional style which allows them autonomy without cutting them off from their roots.

Mr. and Mrs. T., who are in their late thirties, sought help for recurrent and escalating fights which were bringing them to the brink of divorce. Both came from large extended families with which their lives continued to be interlinked. The husband was the oldest of three children, with a younger brother and sister, and the wife was the youngest of three daughters. The couple lived in an apartment building owned by Mrs. T.'s father, which also housed her parents and one older sister's family. The T.s had been married for eight years and had two daughters, aged six and three.

This couple had been introduced to each other by Mr. T.'s mother and had gotten married after a short courtship. While they had a lot in common and enjoyed each other's company, they had had recurrent fights, focused mainly around Mrs. T.'s complaints that Mr. T. was too close to his family of origin and left her out. The fact that Mr. T. had recently started a new business with his father and brother made her feel more isolated and suspicious. The fighting escalated to such a point that the husband left home for a week. An attempt at reconciliation did not work out and Mrs. T. sought help, later bringing her husband. During the first session, after a period of heated name calling and vituperation, the following picture emerged.

Mrs. T.'s main complaint centered on Mr. T.'s closeness to his family, especially his mother. Mrs. T. had never gotten along with her mother-in-law, who, she said, intruded into their marriage, wanted to know everything that was going on and constantly claimed Mr. T.'s help and attention for trivial reasons, while ignoring Mrs. T., even in childbirth. Allegedly, the claims on Mr. T. could occur at any time, even disrupt the couple's vacations. The recent joint business venture made Mrs. T. feel all the more threatened and left out. She said his family drained him so much that he came home as an empty husk and paid no attention to her needs. She reported feeling victimized, neglected, resentful, angry and unable to cope with the situation anymore.

Mr. T. countered with exactly the same feelings of victimization and resentment and reported that she was hounding him with her complaints, showing no sympathy for his business pressures and giving him no peace when he came home exhausted at night. All he asked for, he said, was that she perform her wifely duties, have supper on the table and leave him alone for a while until his business established a routine. Mrs. T. was plainly unable to do so and voiced her fear that if she let go, her mother-in-law would succeed in pulling him away completely. Mr. T. refused to give in to his wife's demands that he cut off relations with his parents, saying he was responsible for them as the oldest, despite his wife's claims that they were using him. Besides, he voiced a fear that if he gave in to all of Mrs. T.'s demands, she might get so cocky as to "kick him out" of her father's apartment after some future fight.

In short, the T.s were faced with a situation in which their ongoing functional fusion with their families of origin was making it very difficult for them to form an adequate marital fusion, despite years of marriage, a Westernized education and a notion of openness and intimacy between couples. Mrs. T. felt so threatened by the blurring of the boundaries separating her from the paternal in-laws that she experienced the spouse subsystem as being invaded and her selfhood as being denied.

Similarly, Mr. T. felt his selfhood and masculinity being threatened by the fact that the T.s' family system was physically enmeshed within the maternal extended family system and that letting go of his own family of origin might mean letting go of all his autonomy vis-a-vis his in-laws. Besides, Mrs. T. was challenging some of his basic role assumptions regarding his responsibilities and status. He responded to these fears and to Mrs. T.'s demands with distancing, to the point of leaving the house one night, while Mrs. T's reaction was to pursue him fruitlessly in her attempts to achieve fusion and fill her areas of emptiness.

The children were not drawn into this fight for two reasons. Both spouses acknowledged each other's genuine care for the children; more importantly, they themselves were acting from such a position of weakness and "childishness" vis-a-vis each other and each other's families of origin that the children were not useful foci of triangulation.

In short, the main problem with this couple was the fact that they had not differentiated enough from their families of origin to achieve autonomy as adults and to form a spouse subsystem with clear boundaries. Nor had they acknowledged their functionally extended family way of life as a style which to some degree they had chosen and which they agreed to maintain. Thus, they were left vacillating between conflicting needs and values and experiencing pain, but too enmeshed in the system to identify its source.

As a result, their attempts at marial fusion were frustrated by mutual fears of engulfment within each other's extended family system. The T.s' own needs for and fears of marital closeness led to a distancing and triangulation around the in-laws, especially the paternal mother-in-law, whose own demanding style apparently colluded with the T.s' triangulation attempts. The resulting symptomatic conflict was open fighting, which escalated to unbearable proportions under the stress of Mr. T.'s new working situation, which served to intensify Mr. T's preoccupation with his family and Mrs. T.'s suspicions.

Despite their lack of adequate differentiation, this couple had many strengths, such as mutuality in other areas of their joint life, their brightness and articulateness and their freedom from idiosyncratic sources of pathology. They basically cared for each other and wanted to remain together. In many ways they were victims of a system in which the in-laws and they themselves were operating with conflicting values, demands and role expectations and being unable to reach a viable synthesis.

Their strengths enabled the T.s to benefit from only three, albeit long and intensive, sessions, in which the main intervention was to get them to articulate their ownership of their nuclear family system. This attempt at differentiation and boundary clarification vis-a-vis the extended family was supported by reinforcing their attempts at maintaining their spouse subsystem. At the same time, they were encouraged to explore and acknowledge their choice in maintaining a functionally extended family way of life. The T.s were able to make use of what they termed "the idea of primary loyalty to *our* own family" and have reported increased mutuality and a significant reduction in stress a year later.

Conclusion

This paper represents an attempt to apply the conceptual framework offered by Family Systems Theory to empirical data on the Turkish family, gathered from a variety of diverse sources. This analysis provides us with a fairly consistent picture which seems to fit the empirical data as well as clinical experience. Of course, as with all discussions of the typical, we have to keep in mind that the picture is limited in involving a certain amount of generalization and stereotyping.

In summary, both the structural and the dynamic properties of the Turkish family system serve to make it highly differentiated with regards to normative role expectations; but its emphasis on belonging and interdependency makes the system undifferentiated with regard to the psychological and emotional experiences and relationships of the individuals within it. The couple forming a new family would not expect to meet their needs for closeness and fulfillment through marital fusion. Instead they would rely on their families of origin and other kinship and friendship subsystems. The wife who may be at a disadvantage by virtue of her restricted mobility has her children available as alternate sources of emotional fusion. The children would grow up with a clear idea of their place in their family and the world. In all individuals, belongingness would take precedence over individuality.

As long as the social context is compatible with this family system, it would be functional and healthy. However, with the dislocation engendered by social change, both the system and the individuals within it would be subject to conflict and potential pathology, as illustrated in the case example.

The institution of the family has clearly faced numerous challenges in its history in all cultures, and has had the resiliency to adapt to those challenges successfully enough to endure so far. One would expect that in most cultures it will continue to succeed in modifying itself to meet newly emerging demands. The Turkish nuclear family system is surely in the midst of such an evolutionary process right now. It would appear that the Family Systems Theory approach might be a useful tool with which to study this process in further depth.

BIBLIOGRAPHY

Abadan-Unat, N. "Implications of Migrations on Emancipation and Pseudo-Emancipation of Turkish Women." Paper given at the Wellesley College Conference on Women and Development, 1976.

Ataman, I. and S. Epir. "Age, Socioeconomic Status and Classificatory Behavior Among Turkish Children." In L.J. Cronback and P.J.D. Drenth (eds.), *Mental Tests and Cultural Adaptation*. The Hague: Mouton, 1972, pp. 329-37.

Baymur, F. *Lise ve Dengi Okullara Devam Eden Öğrencilerin Problemleri* (The problems of students attending Lycees and equivalent schools). M.E.B. Test ve Araştırma Bürosu Eğitim Araştırmaları Serisi, 15, 1961.

Bell, N.W. "Extended Family Relations of Disturbed and Well Families," *Family Process* , 1962, 1, 2, 175-93.

Bowen, M. "Theory in the Practice of Psychotherapy." In P.J. Guerin (ed.), *Family Therapy: Theory and Practice*. New York: Gardner Press, 1976, pp. 42-90.

Büyükberker, C. and E. Kerimoğlu. "Patolojik karı-koca etkileşimi üzerine bir araştırma" (A study on pathological husband-wife interaction). Sekizinci Milli Nöro-Psikiyatri Kongresi, 1972.

Cansever, G. "Psychological Effects of Circumcision," *British Journal of Medical Psychology*, 1965, 38, 321-31.

Demiröz, I. *Çocukların Diş Hekimlerine Karşı Duydukları Kaygının Çeşitli Psikolojik Testlerle İncelenmesi* (An investigation of the anxiety children feel towards dentists, using selected psychological tests). Unpublished Ph.D. dissertation, Hacettepe Univ., 1976.

Erickson, G.D. and T.P. Hogan (eds.), "Historical Perspectives." In *Family Therapy*. Monterey, Calif.: Brooks/Cole Publishers, 1972, pp. 1-3.

Fleck, S. "An Approach to Family Pathology." In G.D. Erickson and T.P. Hogan (eds.), *Family Therapy*. Monterey, Calif.: Brooks/Cole Publishers, 1972, pp. 103-19.

Fogarty, T.F. "Systems Concepts and the Dimensions of Self." In P.J. Guerin (ed.), *Family Therapy: Theory and Practice*. New York: Gardner Press, 1976, pp. 144-53.

Geçtan, E. "Toplumumuz bireylerinde kimlik kavramları ile ilgili sorunlar üzerinde bir tartışma" (A debate on problems concerning identity concepts in the individuals of our society), *50. Yıla Armağan*. Ankara: Eğitim Fakultesi Yayınları, 1973, 63-77.

Gökçe, B. *Gecekondu Gençliği* (Gecekondu Youth). Ankara: Hacettepe Universitesi Yayınları, C-15, 1976.

Guerin, P.J. (ed.), "Family Therapy: The First Twenty-Five Years." In *Family Therapy: Theory and Practice*. New York: Gardner Press, 1976, pp. 2-22.

_____ and K.B. Guerin. "Theoretical Aspects and Clinical Relevance of the Multi-Generational Model of Family Therapy." In *Family Therapy: Theory and Practice*. New York: Gardner Press, pp. 91-110.

Gürgen, T.Y. "Sosyal ve Kültürel özelliklerin Türkiyede intiharlar üzerine etkisi" (The influence of social and cultural characteristics on suicides in Turkey), *Nöro-Psikiyatri Arşivi*, 1969, 6, 1.

Haley, T. "Toward a Theory of Pathological Systems." In G.H. Zuk and I. Borzormenyi-Nagy (eds.), *Family Therapy and Disturbed Families*. Palo Alto, Calif.: Science and Behavior Books, 1967, pp. 11-27.

Haley, J. "Marriage Therapy." In G.D. Erickson and T.P. Hogan (eds.), *Family Therapy*. Monterey, Calif.: Brook/Cole Publishers, 1972, pp. 180-210.

Helling, G.A. *The Turkish Village as a Social System*. Unpublished monograph. Los Angeles: Occidental College, 1966.

Kâğıtçıbaşı, Ç. "Social Norms and Authoritarianism: A Comparison of Turkish and American Adolescents." *Journal of Personality and Social Psychology*, 1970, 17, 3, 444-51.

_____. *Sosyal Değişmenin Psikolojik Boyutları* (The psychological dimensions of social change). Ankara: Türk Sosyal Bilimler Derneği Yayınları, 1972.

_____. *İnsan ve İnsanlar: Sosyal Psikolojiye Giriş* (The person and people: an introduction to social psychology). Duran offset Matbaacılik San. A.Ş., 1976.

_____. "The Effects of Socioeconomic Development on Draw-A-Man Scores in Turkey."*Journal of Social Psychology*. 1979, 108, 3-8.

_____. *Çocuğun Değeri: Türkiye'de Değerler ve Doğurganlık* (The value of children: values and fertility in Turkey). Istanbul: Boğaziçi Univ. Publication, 1981.

Kandiyoti, D. "Some Social-Psychological Dimensions of Social Change in a Turkish Village," *The British Journal of Sociology*. 1974, 15, 1, 47-62.

_____. "Sex Roles and Social Change: a Comparative Appraisal of Turkey's Women. *Signs: Journal of Women in Culture and Society*. 1977, 3, 57-73.

_____. *Kadınlarda Psikososyal Değişimin Boyutları: Cinsiyetler ve Kuşaklar arasında bir karşılaştırma* (The dimensions of psychosocial change in women: a comparison of the sexes and generations). Unpublished monograph. Boğaziçi Univ., 1978.

Kıray, M. "Changing Roles of Mothers: Changing Intra-Family Relations in a Turkish Town." In J.G. Peristiany (ed.), *Mediterranean Family Structures*. London: Cambridge Univ. Press, 1976, pp. 261-71.

Kongar, E. *Izmirde Kentsel Aile* (The urban family in Izmir). Ankara: Türk Sosyal Bilimler Derneği Yayınları, 1972.

Köknel, Ö. *Türk toplumunda Bugünün Gençliği* (Today's youth in Turkish society). Istanbul: Bozak Matbaası, 1970.

Kuyaş, N. *The Family as Power Relation: A Comparison Between Two Social Classes.* Unpublished Masters thesis. Boğaziçi Univ., 1980.

Kuzgun, Y. "Ana-baba tutumlarının bireyin kendini gerçekleştirme düzeyine etkisi (The influence of parental attitudes on the self-actualization levels of individuals). *Hacettepe Univ. Bulletin of Social Sciences and Humanities,* 1973, 5, 1.

Le Compte, G. and A., and S. Özer. "Üç sosyo-ekonomik düzeyde Ankaralı annelerin çocuk yetiştirme tutumları: bir ölçek uyarlaması (The child-rearing attitudes of mothers from three socio-economic levels in Ankara: adaptation of an instrument). *Psikoloji Dergisi,* 1978, 1, 5-8.

Le Compte, G. "Türkiyede Aile içi çocuk gelişimi ve eğitimi sistemi (The system of intra-family child development and education in Turkey). In S. Özgediz (ed.), *Türkiyede Okul öncesi Çocuk Gelişimi ve Eğitimi Sistemi: Bugünkü Durum, Sorumlar, Öneriler* (The system of pre-school child development and education in Turkey: the situation today, problems and suggestions). Unpublished project report. Boğaziçi Univ., 1979.

Minuchin, S. *Families and Family Therapy.* Cambridge, Mass.: Harvard Univ. Press, 1974.

Napier, A.Y. and C.A. Whitaker. *The Family Crucible.* New York: Harper and Row, 1978.

Okman, G. *Bilişsel Stilin Etkenleri: Ergenler Üzerinde Bir Çalişma* (The factors influencing cognitive style: a study of adolescents). Unpublished monograph. Boğaziçi Univ., 1980.

Olson-Prather, E. *Family Planning and Husband-Wife Relationships in Modern Turkey.* Unpublished Ph.D. disseration. Univ. of California, Los Angeles, 1976.

Öner, N. *Durumluk-Sürekli Kaygı Envanterinin Türk Toplumunda Geçerliliği* (The validity of the state-trait anxiety inventory in Turkey). Unpublished monograph. Hacettepe Univ., 1977.

Öztürk, M.O. "Anadolu kişiliğinde özerklik ve girişme duygularının kısıtlanması" (Inhibition of autonomy and initiative in the Anatolian personality). Beşinci Milli Nöro-Psikiyatri Kongresi, 1969a.

_____. "Anadolu Toplumunda Oedipus Kompleksi Teorisinin Geçerliliği" (The validity of the theory of the Oedipus Complex in Anatolian society). Beşinci Milli Nöro-Psikiyatri Kongresi, 1969b.

_____ and V. Volkan. "The Theory and Practice of Psychiatry in Turkey." In C.L. Brown and N. Itzkowitc (eds.), *Psychological Dimensions of Near Eastern Studies.* Princeton, N.J.: The Darwin Press, 1977, pp. 330-61.

Sencer, Y.I. Toplumsal değişme ve uyumsuzluk (Social change and maladjustment). Onikinci Milli Nöro-Psikiyatri Kongresi, 1976.

Stirling, P. *Turkish Village.* London: Weidengeld and Nicholson, 1965.

Sümer, E.A. "Değişen Türk kültürünün dinamik yönden analizi" (The analysis of the changing Turkish culture from a dynamic viewpoint). Beşinci Milli Nöro-Psikiyatri Kongresi, 1969.

Timur, S. *Türkiyede Aile Yapısı* (The structure of the family in Turkey). Hacettepe Univ. Yayınları, 1972.

Uçman, P. "A Normative Study of the Goodenough Harris Drawing Test on a Turkish Sample." In L.J. Cronback and P.J.D. Drenth (eds.), *Mental Tests and Cultural Adaptation.*The Hague: Mouton, 1972, pp. 365-70.

Yasa, I. "Gecekondu Ailesi"(The gecekondu family),*A.Ü.S.B.F. Dergisi*, 1970, 25, 4.

Yörükoğlu, A. *Çocuk Ruh Sağlığı* (Child mental health). Ankara: Türkiye İş Bankası Kültür Yayınları, 1978.

Zülemyan, A. *A Comparison of Cognitive Therapy, Modified Desensitization, Cognitive Behavior Modification and Control Groups for Reducing Test Anxiety.* Unpublished Masters thesis. Boğaziçi Univ., 1979.

SOCIAL CHANGE AND FAMILY CRISIS—
THE NATURE OF TURKISH DIVORCE

Ned Levine

The facts of contemporary history are also facts about the success and the failure of individual men and women. When a society is industrialized, a peasant becomes a worker; a feudal lord is liquidated or becomes a businessman. When classes rise or fall, a man is employed or unemployed; when the rate of investment goes up or down, a man takes new heart or goes broke. When wars happen, an insurance salesman becomes a rocket launcher; a store clerk, a radar man; a wife lives alone; a child grows up without a father. Neither the life of an individual nor the history of a society can be understood without understanding both (C. Wright Mills, *The Sociological Imagination*, 1959, p.3).

Why do people get divorced? The question is not as naive as it seems, nor is the answer as obvious. On the one hand, divorce, like marriage, is a unique event affecting only the individuals involved. But, on the other hand, it is also a social event, related to the workings of the surrounding society. When a particular man and a particular woman decide to get married and live together, their decision is highly affected by the society in which they live. Their marriage is recognized by official registration or through community assent. The housing of the couple is affected by the stock of housing available. The work that they do, the money that they earn, the food that they eat, the number of children they have, their ability to bring up their children are affected by the society in which they live. Similarly, when a couple decides to divorce, they are also affected by (and affect in turn) the society.

It is perhaps a truism to say that rapid social change, as is occuring in Turkey, subjects families to various environmental stresses. Divorce is an index of the process of social change. Though it occurs to only a minority of couples, and is rare in many societies, it acts as a barometer, registering changes in social conditions. Divorce reveals something about the nature of families and how they are adapting to change, about the kinds of people who experience stress the most, about the nature of changing sex roles, and, even more fundamentally, something about how a society as a whole adapts to change.

Divorce reflects changing economic structure and alternative social values. A brief overview of this process is in order. In Turkey, divorce is encouraged by the interaction of four social conditions: 1) changes in fertility and mortality; 2) alternative social roles for women; 3) economic vulnerability; and 4) opportunities for separating households. The first two derive from changes brought about directly by modernization. The spread of public health, education, family planning and other services has significantly reduced infant mortality and fertility in Turkey. Women's traditional child-bearing role has substantially changed and alternative sex role expectations have emerged, emphasizing equality and increasing public participation. In Turkey, this has been reinforced by official state policy affirming the rights of women and advocating social and economic equality. The third condition is an indirect effect of modernization. Turkey has been committed to an industrialization process since early in the twentieth century. The relatively effective implementation of this policy and the increasing elaboration of this in a national and international economy has brought major economic changes to communities throughout the country, both positive and negative. New opportunities have been created for many by these changes, but loss of economic independence has come to others. Large proportions of the rural population have severed their rights to rural production and have sought employment in the urban areas. For many people, economic success has not been forthcoming and it is those persons who are economically most vulnerable who are most likely to experience marital stress. Conflicting role expectations for women become re-produced within the family and stress increases.

The fourth condition involves the "cost" of divorce. Divorce depends on the alternative possibilities for separating households. It is argued that in Turkey marital stress has been heightened by increasing economic and value conflicts brought on by modernization, but the cost of separating households has also increased. The result is that many families now have to absorb enormous increases in marital tensions with limited alternatives for satisfying individual needs.

I will examine some facts about Turkish divorce which illustrate this process and will speculate on what this tells us about changing sex roles and family structure in Turkey. But it is important to emphasize that divorce is also a result of individual choice and consequence. Changes at a societal level are experienced at an individual level in terms of different economic possibilities and alternative decisions that must be considered. People shape their own fate and are not merely the passive receptacles for impersonal social forces. They can collude with these forces or they can resist them. They can channel their behavior into individual actions or collective ones. They can defend the past, emulate the present or strive for the future. It is the manner in which these changes are understood and reacted to which determines the extent to which individuals become vulnerable to social conflict.

Divorce in Turkey

Turkish divorce law dervies from the 1926 Civil Code instituted by the new Republic of Turkey (Timur, 1975). It was and still is one of the most permissive divorce laws in the world. The law grants complete equality to women and allows divorce on the grounds of incompatibility (geçimsizlik) if both partners agree or on other grounds if they don't. Further, the administrative procedures designed to implement this law were considerably simplified. A brief time period intervenes between the filing of a petition and the granting of a writ of divorce. In theory, this requires a month, though in practice it t akes a few months. Further, divorce procedures are completely standardized throughout the country, so that granted decrees are immediately recorded and published yearly in volumes of divorce statistics. Consequently, divorce data are uniform and current. Some religious divorces are not reported, but the effect is very small. (In 1976, 86% of all divorce decrees were granted on grounds of incompatibility. *TSIS*, 1976). In spite of ease of divorce, however, Turkey has a very low divorce rate, even by developing country standards. In 1976, Turkey had Crude Divorce Rate of 0.35 per 1000 population, the lowest of any country in the Mediterranean basin. It has sometimes been suggested that divorce is high in

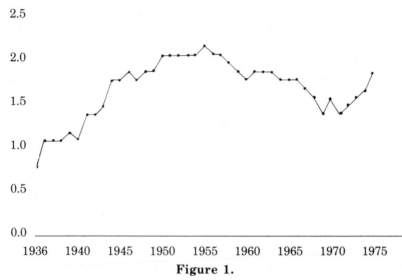

Figure 1.

Turkey—Refined Divorce Rates: 1936–76 (Per 1000 Married Females)

Source: TSIS, 1975, table II; TSIS, 1978, table 2.

Islamic countries (Goode, 1964; Bogue, 1969). Yet, among Mediterranean Islamic countries, divorce rates vary from very low, such as Turkey, Iraq (0.55 per 1000 population), and Iran (0.64) to very high, such as Libya (1.98) and Egypt (2.02)(all data from United Nations, 1976).

Divorce and Economic Growth

Even more interesting is that the divorce rate in Turkey is generally decreasing, not increasing, a trend in other Mediterranean countries as well. Figure 1 shows the Refined Divorce Rate from 1936 to 1976. Since early in the Republic's history, the divorce rate has risen steadily, reaching a peak in 1956. Since then it has dropped fairly consistently until 1973, when it then rose slightly over the next three years.

There is a rough relationship between the divorce rate and changes in the economy, especially the "modern" sector. Starting in the 1930s, Turkey underwent a fairly rapid industrialization effort, which slowed somewhat during World War II, then continued until the mid-1950s. The divorce rate rose fairly steadily during this period. From the mid-1950s to the beginning of the 1960s, on the other hand, the economy experienced a major recession and the divorce rate dropped accordingly. The early 1960s to the mid-1960s was another expansion period and the divorce rate also rose somewhat. From the mid-1960s to the beginning of the 1970s, there was another slowdown, reflected in the divorce rate, and from the beginning of the 1970s to the mid-1970s another period of expansion was accompanied by a rising divorce rate. The fit between changes in the economy and the divorce rate is loose and no one index predicts it with great precision. But three indices give partial predictions. First, a weighted average of modern economic sectors shows that when the economy expands, the divorce rate rises. Second, there is a negative relationship for a consumer price index so that when inflation increases rapidly, the divorce rate decreases. Third, there is a positive relationship for an index of the housing stock so that when housing is more available, the divorce rate rises. In other words, the divorce rate is facilitated by economic expansion and the availability of housing, and is inhibited by inflation.

The most interesting part of these relationships is that there is a two- to three-year time period between an economic change and a change in the divorce rate. Part of this delay is administrative. The time necessary to file for a divorce before receiving it is about six months on average. However, the two- to three-year time period following change in the economy strongly suggests that couples decide to divorce some time before they actually separate households. Divorce, therefore, registers economic change.

Divorce is affected by individuals' ability to maintain separate households, but since the 1950s, an extremely rapid rate of rural-to--urban migration has led to tremendous pressures on urban job markets, housing and urban services. For example, in 1935 only 17% of the population lived in urban areas (defined as places of 10,000 population or more), and in 1950, the percentage was still only 19%. In 1960, 25% of the population lived in urban areas and by 1970, 36% did. At present, the percent urban is around 45% and should be 50% within five years (TSIS, 1935; 1950; 1960; 1970; 1975). Reasons for the rapid urbanization are complex but reflect the economic advantages of urban areas; higher incomes, better educational possibilities, available health facilities and other services, and cheaper consumer goods (Keleş, 1972; Levine, 1973a; 1980; Karpat, 1976).

Nonetheless, rapid migration has placed tremendous pressure on employment, housing, and services, and has severely restricted the growth of personal income. Productive employment has grown only slowly while the majority of migrants are forced into low productivity jobs, usually involving small or petty services (e.g. street salesmen, porters, unskilled construction workers, janitors, household services). Growth of per capita income has also been very uneven over the period, which has seen several major recessions. Impressionistically, it appears that the means for realization of individual aspirations have been significantly curtailed, and frustration has been expressed through political and collective means rather than through divorce. There has been since the late 1960s a period of enormous political instability and violence and the society has become extremely politicized.

In addition to limited growth of personal income have been restrictions in housing. Turkey, like many developing countries, has seen the rapid growth of so-called "squatter housing," *gecekondu* (Keleş, 1972; Suzuki, 1964; Levine, 1973b; Karpat, 1976). Most of the poor migrants from the rural areas settle in this type of housing, and the proportion of the urban population living in these areas varies from around 25% for the smaller cities to 65% in the case of Ankara (Keleş, 1972). Further, not only the poor, but also the middle classes have experienced an acute housing shortage. In the last 15 years, the cost of housing has jumped dramatically for the middle and higher income groups, with corresponding increased density, land speculation, weakening of building standards, and breakdown in control over the planned urban areas (Clark, 1971; Levine, 1974). Again, the effect on individuals has been to lower realization of personal aspirations. Few single persons can afford to set up a separate household (even in the upper classes) and the pressure on a married couple to maintain a house, in spite of marital stress, becomes very strong. Inflation, now at 100%, has also become a major problem and disproportionately affects the urban population.

In short, a number of different economic mechanisms have combined to severely restrict the growth of income, housing and services in urban areas; and life has become very difficult for most people. This appears to have strengthened group ties, especially family and kin structures, and resolution of marital and family stress appears to have been shifted to collective and political struggles, rather than through divorce or other individual solutions. "Traditional" family structure has been reinforced and the divorce rate has declined since the 1950s. The authoritarian, patriarchal family has survived, but more through economic necessity than design.

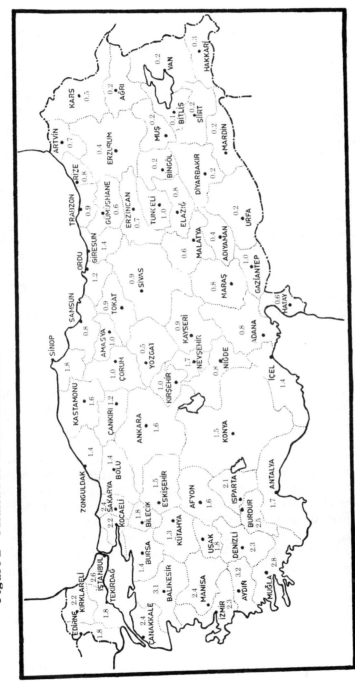

Figure 2 Turkish Provincial Refined Divorce Rates: 1968–1972 (Per 1000 Married Females)

Source: Provincial divorce data from TSIS, 1968, table 2; TSIS, 1969–70, table 4; TSIS, 1971, table 1; TSIS, 1972, table 1. Rates were calculated in relation to the number of married females, age 15 +, from 1970 Provincial census (TSIS, 1970, table 9).

Geographical Distribution of Divorce

In general, divorce is much higher in the urban population of Turkey than in rural areas. In 1976, for example, 67% of all divorces occurred in urban areas of Turkey (TSIS, 1976). Since slightly over 40% of the population lived in urban areas at the time, this represents an urban divorce rate about three times higher than that for rural areas. Part of this is overstated, since more divorces are unreported in rural areas than in urban areas. Nonetheless, urban--rural differentials remain.

The geographical distribution of divorce presents an interesting pattern. Figure 2 gives the Refined Divorce Rates for each of Turkey's 67 provinces from 1968 to 1972. There is a clear east–west gradient in divorce rates, with rates rising consistently from east to west. Some western provinces, in fact, have divorce rates 10 to 13 times those of provinces in the east. This pattern is congruent with the dual economic structure of Turkey. The western part of the country is more developed, whereas the east is less developed. Clearly, there is a relationship between the level of economic development and the divorce rate.

Briefly, certain characteristics associated with the distribution of divorce deserve comment. First, divorce is associated with the level of development of an area. Across the country, provinces with higher divorce rates have higher income levels and generally higher standards of living. Second, divorce seems to be associated with changes in women's roles. Virtually all provinces with higher divorce rates have gone some way toward a demographic "transition." These provinces generally have lower fertility and mortality rates, smaller household sizes, and lower infant mortality rates. These provinces also have higher literacy and education levels, especially for women. The social and economic base underlying the "traditional" female role has changed considerably, and is widespread throughout the western part of the country, the non-industrial areas as well as the urbanized, industrial areas.

Third, divorce is more associated with developed agriculture than with industrialization. The southwestern and Aegean regions of the country in particular have generally higher divorce rates than the more industrialized and urbanized areas (Istanbul, Izmir, Ankara, Kocaeli, Bursa, Adana). The southwest has experienced the development of agriculture, but industry and urbanization have lagged behind. There are certain aspects of this development which are critical for understanding divorce. Economically, agriculture in this region has developed through mechanization and expansion of agricultural lands, rather than through increasing efficiency (Tekeli, 1976). There has been an increasing tendency to depend on single cash crops, such as tobacco, cotton, and citrus fruits, with limited crop diversification. While production has increased enormously over the last 30 years, access to financing and markets and differential productivity has tended to favor the richer farmers disproportionately more than the poorer farmers (Benedict, 1974). This, combined with the increasing mechanization, has displaced large numbers of people from the land who have been forced to seek employment in the urban areas. Robinson (1958), for example, estimated that around three million persons moved from the rural to the urban areas in the 1950s alone, mostly from this region. For those going to the provincial centers, there have been few opportunities as limited industrialization has occurred in these cities. Producers tend to ship directly abroad or to the large cities of Istanbul, Izmir and Ankara and, to a large extent, avoid the provincial centers (Benedict, 1974). A kind of structural dependency has developed between this region and the large metropolitan centers. At the same time, there have been a number of important social changes which have altered the demographic balance of the area: health and educational services are good; roads and communication are better than in most areas of the country; and more recently the growth of services has been associated with tourism (Mansur, 1972). Fertility and mortality are generally low in this region and educational levels are higher than most other agricultural areas of the country, but income is distributed somewhat unequally (HIPS, 1975). The region has experienced social and economic change, but not industrial development.

This suggests that divorce is related to a conflict between the two types of economy existing here, between a developed agricultural society and the dominance of an outside market. Stable provincial communities become disrupted by external economic influences, making them dependent on the outside world. Yet, insufficient capital accumulates locally to allow the community to maintain economic autonomy; the society loses its independence. At the same time, external societal values intrude and conflict with those already existing. Clearly, a high emphasis on education and achievement, especially for women, is an urban, industrial value. It appears that this value also has greater consequences for women than for men. The result is a kind of value conflict which reflects an underlying material conflict. Divorce, therefore, becomes a product of a structural dependency. It is the loss of economic independence for an area which provides the necessary material conditions for divorce (Kıray and Hinderink, 1968). But it is the alternatives available which create the conflict within the family.

Divorce and Socioeconomic Status

Divorce occurs because people are caught in the middle of this material conflict. If aspirations are increased, but not allowed to be fulfilled, frustrations and stress are increased. The problem in understanding this mechanism in Turkey, or in other developing countries, is not so much in seeing the conflict occurring between a "modern" and a "traditional" society, but rather in seeing where the conflict occurs in the social structure. It is those people "caught in the middle" who are most vulnerable, who have either been forced to change against their desires or who have tried to change, without success. These are not the most "modern" nor the most "traditional" people, but those at the juncture of social conflict.

What are some of the characteristics of those persons who get divorced in Turkey? Table 1 presents Crude Divorce Rates by completed educational levels for females and males for the years 1969–1971. Those men and women who have the lowest divorce rates are those who are completely illiterate, while those who have the highest divorce rates are those who are *just* literate. However, for the literate, the divorce rate decreases with level of education. In other words, people who have only enough education to read are those most likely to get divorced, while those who can't read are least likely to get divorced. What is even more significant is that the difference in divorce rates for just-literate versus illiterate is much greater for women than for men. The likelihood that a just-literate woman will get a divorce is almost ten times that for an illiterate woman, while the ratio for men is slightly over three.

Turkey's level of education is quite low. In 1975, male literacy was 75% and female literacy was only 48% (TSIS, 1975). After elementary school, educational attendance drops off quickly. In 1975, only 13% of males and 6% of females had gone beyond elementary school (TSIS, 1975). Thus, most small communities have large proportions of women and men who are either illiterate or just-literate, or who have only an elementary education. One could argue that the impact of this on many small communities must be enormous. The great gap in the divorce rate between the two adjacent educational groups must result from great strain and

Table 1

Crude Divorce Rate by Completed Educational Levels,
Both Sexes: 1969-71   (Per 1000 Population)

FEMALES

Age Group	Illiterate	Literate, Non-Primary Graduate	Primary School	All Secondary Schools	Higher Education
15-19	0.46	2.27	0.73	0.15	—
20-29	1.00	6.99	2.50	1.44	1.14
30-39	0.55	4.18	1.92	1.71	1.47
40-49	0.45	4.47	1.56	1.29	0.82
50-59	0.39	4.34	1.07	0.73	0.88
60+	0.24	3.76	0.69	0.30	0.00
All Ages	0.55	5.20	2.08	1.37	1.12

MALES

Age Group	Illiterate	Literate, Non-Primary Graduate	Primary School	All Secondary Schools	Higher Education
15-19	0.16	0.55	0.13	0.03	—
20-29	1.23	3.00	1.45	0.89	0.69
30-39	0.83	2.41	1.82	1.52	1.24
40-49	0.53	1.59	1.19	1.31	0.78
50-59	0.49	1.23	0.87	0.89	0.60
60+	0.39	1.47	0.78	0.31	0.28
All Ages	0.64	2.07	1.44	1.03	0.83

Source: Divorces by Educational Level from TSIS, 1969-70, table 21; TSIS, 1971, table 20. Population base rates are from 1970 census, TSIS, 1970, table 1.

conflict in role expectations associated with just a little education. If some women in a community start to assert their independence, this must psychologically affect other women and men in the community. The changes occurring appear to have much greater impact on women than men.

Further, since the highest divorce rates are in the more developed provinces, especially those associated with agricultural development, and as the population most likely to get divorced are those with only a little education, then it is the poorer people in the richer areas who are more likely to divorce, not those who are wealthier. It is, in short, the urban poor. This result is similar to those found in the United States, with the major difference being that illiteracy is

Table 2
Crude Divorce Rates by Last Week's Occupation,
Males: 1969-71 (Per 1000 Population)

| | Occupational Group | | | |
| | I | II | III | IV |
Age Group	Technical, Professional	Managerial, Administrative, Clerical	Trade, Salesmen	Farmers, Lumberman, Fisherman, Hunters
15-19	0.18	0.40	0.30	0.19
20-29	0.77	2.11	2.31	2.09
30-39	1.16	2.20	1.89	1.30
40-49	0.92	1.30	1.45	0.72
50-59	0.72	0.92	1.10	0.58
60+	0.62	0.90	0.88	0.49
All Ages	0.87	1.69	1.53	0.94

| | Occupational Group | | | |
| | V | VI | VII | VIII |
Age Group	Miners, Quarrymen	Transport, Storage, Communication	Craftsmen, Production Workers, Repairmen, Manual Work	Services
15-19	0.20	0.06	0.16	0.11
20-29	0.58	0.83	2.05	0.99
30-39	0.39	0.94	2.43	1.36
40-49	0.19	0.59	1.88	0.86
50-59	0.35	0.52	1.41	0.61
60+	base too low	0.47	1.54	0.70
All Ages	0.40	0.72	1.70	0.91

Source: Divorces by Last Week's Occupation from TSIS, 1969-70, table 22;
TSIS, 1971, table 21. Occupational base rates are from 1970 census,
TSIS, 1970, tables 7-8.

almost non-existent in the U.S. (Glick and Norton, 1971; Udry, 1966; Bumpass and Sweet, 1972; Rosow and Rose, 1972; Glick, 1975).

Further insights into the process can be gained by examining the occupations of divorced males (Table 2); unfortunately, too few urban women work to calculate meaningful rates. The data are Crude Divorce Rates whose bases are the number of men in each occupational category. Occupational groups II (managerial, administrative and clerical), III (trade, salesmen), and VII (craftsmen, production workers, repairmen, manual workers) have the highest divorce rates. These occupations are associated with urban areas and with the non-agricultural economy. At the other end of the spectrum, occupation group V (miners, quarrymen) have by far the lowest divorce rates. Intermediate levels are found for group IV, agricultural occupations, and groups I, VI, and VIII, a number of service occupations.

Occupation interacts with age. Occupational groups III (salesmen), IV (farmers, lumbermen, fishermen, hunters) and V (miners) show their highest rate in the 20-29 age group, while all other occupations have their highest rate in the 30-39 age group. In part, this reflects a slight difference in age at marriage. Agricultural workers and miners tend to marry early in Turkey, while men in the more urban occupations tend to marry later (Timur, 1972). But this also suggests that stress in urban marriages occurs later in the marriage than in rural areas. Rates for occupational group VII, the industrial workers, rise relatively with age so that these occupations are more at risk after age 30 compared to other occupations. In Europe and America generally, working class families show a relative decrease in income after 40 compared to the middle classes, where income rises consistently almost until retirement age (Rainwater, Coleman and Handel, 1959). This might point to increasing family stress on working class families compared to more middle class families. If the divorce rates for occupational group VII, the industrial workers, are compared with those of group II, the white collar workers, then the ratio of divorce increases with age: at 15-19, it is *0.40;* at 20-29, *0.97;* at 30-39, *1.10;* at 40-49, *1.45;* at 50-59, *1.53;* at 60+, *1.71.* In other words, industrial workers become relatively more vulnerable as they get older compared to white collar workers.

The data indicate that economic strains underlie divorce, a point made often enough (Terman, 1938; Schroeder, 1939; Burgess and Cottrell, 1939; Goode, 1956). But it also shows that the degree of integration in the community can mediate these strains. In Turkey, the "tightest" communities are rural and small town, affecting agricultural workers and most miners. We find that miners have the lowest divorce rate and farmers have relatively low ones. Most of the occupations associated with the larger urban areas, on the other hand, have much higher divorce rates. In short, it is in the "modern" economy where marital stress is more likely to occur, but for people who have low educational and skill levels and who are poorer. As usual, the urban poor bear the brunt of social change.

Social Change and Family Crisis: Some Thoughts

People who are economically vulnerable are more likely to get divorced, partly because they have little economic security, but also because they fail to adapt to changing conditions. Society imposes strains on a couple, but the couple makes the situations worse by blaming each other for their frustrations. The changing society is creating new roles for men and women to play and people who do not learn these expose themselves to stress. We must, therefore, try to understand divorce in terms of changes in social roles for men and women.

Divorce and Sex Roles

Provinces with the highest divorce rates are those experiencing the greatest changes in women's roles: lower fertility, lower infant mortality, smaller household sizes, higher female literacy. Economic development frees women of the burden of large families and encourages them to play more active social roles. Thus, the change in women's roles is a move toward women's liberation. At the same time, though, it poses more conflicts within their families.

What social roles that men and women are expected to play are changing with economic development? It is always easy to over-generalize a complex set of behaviors; but perhaps we can typify a set of social ideals, desired by most people but rarely achieved in practice. Rural, agricultural communities in Turkey have well-distinguished but conservative roles for men and women. When people leave these communities and migrate to the urban areas, roles change only very slowly. Even the urban middle classes have many of these elements. Men are expected to be the major economic procurer in the family (though, in fact, women do a large proportion of the agricultural work). Land is patrilineal and men are expected to make major economic decisions for the family and handle any exchanges with the outside world. Women, on the other hand, are expected to raise children and manage the household, and their social contact is restricted to their family and other wives in the community.

Both men and women are also expected to exhibit certain behaviors which symbolize adulthood and integration into the community. Success is defined partly by the type of community. In the rural areas, "success" is defined by the amount of land that the family owns, and men must show that they can manage such a holding, with women combining unquestioned loyalty, subservience and hard work. There is great importance placed on having a large family, especially in having several sons. In the small, provincial towns, the high fertility value remains, but the working role for women does not. Men are supposed to show that they can take care of their wives and children by exhibiting their wealth. Thus, jewelry takes on an important symbolic role in demonstrating a man is successful. In the cities, such behavior continues among the urban population, though it is expressed in terms of consumer goods. The middle classes, for example, exhibit their wealth in terms of such visible luxuries as fur coats, expensive automobiles, chic clothing, various household appliances, and jewelry. Women are expected to acknowledge wealth by showing it on certain symbolic occasions (e.g. weddings, afternoon tea and cake gatherings, card parties [*konken*], and occasionally at fancy parties). Also, city women are expected to demonstrate success in marriage by remaining beautiful and feminine at all moments.

Out of these behaviors follow a number of psychological states. Men are expected to be masculine and virile (*erkeklik*). They are expected to be strong and powerful, unafraid of anything, active, independent, unemotional, intelligent and interested in things, not people. They are also expected to be unlimited in their sexual appetites. Women, on the other hand, are expected to demonstrate the opposite of these states: weakness, passivity, helplessness, submissiveness, dependency, emotional expressiveness, nurturing, clever but not *too* intelligent, and interested in people, not things. Women are also expected to be undersexed.

Now, such ideal roles for men and women are never realized in practice. Nonetheless, most people believe there are inherent sex differences, and these ideas have very powerful effects. Men and women grow up believing that they must live up to idealized roles. It is not surprising, therefore, that many people develop deep, unconscious feelings of inadequacy because they cannot act as they think they should. As the society changes, however, the expectations of men and women change quite radically. In an urban, industrial society, men and women are expected to play interchangeable roles. There is limited land ownership and inheritance in the urban areas so that the economic base of sex role differentiation is strongly mitigated. Both men and women sell their labor on the market and use their capital for production. Equality becomes emphasized, rather than complementarity. This process, however, emerges only slowly. In such a transition period, conservative ideals stand side-by-side with new egalitarian ideals. Many people are quite confused in their behavior, acting one moment as an egalitarian liberal and the next like a chauvinistic conservative. Such confusion forms the basis of many conflicts in marriage and becomes the genesis of later divorce.

Conflicting values between the differentiated roles of rural society and the egalitarian roles of urban society lead to many contradictory behaviors on the part of couples. In Turkey, men often act more egalitarian during courtship than after marriage. Similarly, women often act more independent during this period than later. In marriage, men and women fall back on traditional roles quite easily, roles that they learned as children and which form part of their expectations.

Parents often discourage their daughters from acquiring higher education, lest they become unmarriageable. Degree of permissible education, of course, varies with social class. The middle classes want their daughters to finish secondary education (*lise*) but hesitate about university. If they do attend university, they are not encouraged to undertake graduate study. In the squatter areas of the cities, *gecekondu,* parents encourage their daughters to complete only primary school. In rural areas, girls are even discouraged from going to primary school, though increasingly less so. Such limitations are not placed on sons, who are encouraged to get as much education as possible. Thus, women are subjected to severe prejudice and discrimination even by their parents, who prevent them from developing their skills and intelligence. Nevertheless, many women are able to surmount this prejudice and obtain higher levels of education. Turkey has one of the highest rates of women in the professions in the world (Blitz, 1975). Thus, we have the anomaly of the top seven percent of the female population breaking through discriminatory barriers to a professional career, while 93% remain behind these barriers. In addition, employers take advantage of the low educational levels of urban women by paying very low wages, especially in textiles, garment, and food processing industries. What appears as no discrimination (women being paid according to their educational level), in actual fact is. Few men work at the wage levels that many women receive.

Social discrimination is imported into the household and further acts to the detriment of women. Most women are less educated than their husbands, and their lower income than their husbands' places them in a disadvantageous bargaining position with respect to household decisions. Those women who don't work, a majority of women in the urban areas, are at an even greater disadvantage.

Because this situation is changing, conflict inside the home inevitably emerges. Women in Turkey will demand their freedom and independence in greater degrees because their society will also demand their independence. Up to now, the tight structure of the Turkish family has kept such demands under control. Most women have been unable to express their feelings openly because the community has also been tight, suffocating and anti-individualistic. Consequently, women appear to have developed all kinds of indirect acts, such as overeating and psychosomatic illness, as conscious or unconscious expressions of their resentment toward a submissive role in the family. It is, of course, difficult to document such behavior in Turkey, but it appears to be common. Probably, most husbands do not correctly interpret such communications, or do not want to. They continue to act in traditional ways, throwing the burden of household chores onto their wives, encumbering them with excessive cooking obligations (all visitors to a household *must* be fed), and holding them responsible for the children. In the urban areas, men often drink heavily and are irresponsible about family finances. Yet, any expression of increased personal freedom by their wives is blocked by the claim that they "can't afford it." But indirect acts can surface into direct acts, if given social legitimation. As Turkey changes, consciousness develops among women about their roles and about the inequalities inherent in them. With this comes increased assertiveness and a demand that men change along with women in their behavior and attitudes. For men who can adapt, social change poses no source of marital stress, but for those who insist on traditional roles for their wives, a societal striving for women's equality becomes a personal struggle for freedom in the home.

Divorce and the Turkish Family

Most people in Turkey react uncomfortably to the idea of divorce. Because divorce is an unpleasant experience, family and friends often feel that it shouldn't have happened and may condemn it. Some parents, in fact, feel so ashamed that their son or daughter has become divorced that they try to hide the fact from others. At the root of such feelings is a belief about the sanctity of the family as an institution to which people must express loyalty. Divorce is, therefore, seen as evidence that the family has somehow failed to work.

These beliefs are bound to change. Just as divorce becomes a product of social change, so then must the family as an institution change. Examples of it can already be seen in Turkey. The average number of children in a family has decreased consistently since the mid-1930s, and is currently about four children per married woman over a reproductive cycle (Özbay and Shorter, 1970; Timur, 1974; Shorter and Tekçe, 1973; Özbay, 1975). In the larger cities and in the more developed provinces, couples have still fewer children than in the less developed areas, the small towns and rural areas. There are fewer relatives living with a couple and children leave home earlier. The Turkish family type is changing and as this process continues, so will the values of this family type.

A traditional type of family in Turkey, as in most peasant societies around the world, is the authoritarian, patriarchal family (Reich, 1933; Murdock, 1949; Nimkoff, 1966; Goode, 1964; Wolf, 1966). In this kind of family, roles are very differentiated and authority is well-established. Adults dominate children in all aspects of life and children do not have any rights until they are grown. The authority structure is maintained when more than one generation live together. Parents obey their parents and their children obey them. Men dominate women at all levels. The most dominant member of the family, therefore, is the father and the most submissive is the daughter.

The authoritarian, patriarchal family type has a particular set of norms associated with it. The most important is that loyalty to the family is absolutely essential. The family comes first and only then are individual needs satisfied. Thus, if there is a conflict between the family and the individual, the family must take priority. There is an economic basis to this dominant norm, for this family type is an economic unit in which members pool their resources. The family guarantees security for all members and protection in sickness and old age. In giving up one's individuality to such a structure, one reaps many advantages in return.

In the rural areas of Turkey, such a family type is a necessity, for it forms the basis of survival. But in urban areas, this family type proves to be an impediment to economic and social development. It is significant that in both capitalist and socialist thought, the authoritarian, patriarchal family is seen as a barrier to economic and social change. In capitalist thought, this family type is a barrier because it interferes with the free interaction of supply and demand in the market (Zaretsky, 1976; Lasch, 1977). In early capitalist thought, only the production side of the patriarchal family was criticized as being inefficient (the factory being much more rational for production), while the family was seen as a necessary haven for emotional succor, independent of the competitiveness and "rationality" of society. But even in later capitalist thought, this emotional independence was questioned both from the viewpoint of consumption and from socialization. Because the family pools its consumption, more people can be maintained on a given income than if such persons or each couple were their own consumption unit; hence, it is not the most "rational" consumption unit for maximizing production. In addition, the family's socialization and emotional role has slowly been invaded by an "army" of social workers, psychologists, psychiatrists, nutritionists, child development specialists, sex therapists and others who have provided education and instruction on the "best" ways for socializing children and satisfying emotional needs (Lasch, 1977). In socialist thought, the authoritarian, patriarchal family is also condemned, often in ways overlapping with capitalist critiques (Zaretsky, 1976). Most fundamentally, it is seen as an inegalitarian institution in which women and children play subordinate roles to the property relationships in society (Marx and Engels, 1848; Engels, 1891). Also, it is socially irrational in that it maintains unemployed persons—the "reserve army of labor," and thereby lowers the wage level of those who are employed. Even in socialist economies, the patriarchal family has been attacked because it places a heavy strain on the rational use of social resources while supporting unemployed persons. For example, in Albania a few years ago, a campaign was started to "live on your own income" because so many migrants had come to the urban areas without jobs that the government had tremendous difficulty in employing them, being required to do so by law (Mihailovic, 1973). Lastly, the authoritarian, patriarchal family is seen as perpetuating a conservative ideology. Socially, it overprotects people and limits their participation in society. It prevents them from developing their individual personalities and requires them to repress their sexual and creative impulses (Reich, 1933). It makes them less adaptable to new situations.

It is also significant that those political parties who have most defended the authoritarian, patriarchal family are those groups most resistant to social change. In Nazi Germany, for example, the authoritarian, patriarchal family was defended as a social ideal and the moral basis of society (Reich, 1933). "Loyalty to the family" was equated with "loyalty to the state"; "loyalty to the father" was transformed into "loyalty to the Führer." It is perhaps ironic that currently in Turkey the two most conservative parties, the religious-based *National Salvation Party (Milli Selâmet Partisi)* and the neo-fascist *National Action Party (Milli Haraket Partisi)* also staunchly defend the inviolability of the authoritarian, patriarchal family.

As the family in Turkey is in transition, most people do not fully understand the contradictions between their publicly expressed attitudes and their private behavior. They advocate modernity and then act to undermine it. The immediate family, as well as relatives and friends, is supported at all costs and society suffers as a result. For example, rural migrants continue to come to the cities even though there are insufficient jobs in the belief that "My relatives will take care of me until I find a job." While some actually do find jobs, unemployment is very high and possibly growing. One job will become subdivided into two, three or even more in order to spread income, and the work process becomes inefficient. This places a great strain on employment, limits investment, and puts heavy strain on urban services. Gas, electricity, water reserves, and transportation cannot be augmented fast enough to match the inflow of migrants. Individually, migrants are acting rationally. After all, why should they remain where their income is very low, when in the city there is at least a possibility for improvement? Nonetheless, individual "rationality" becomes translated at a social level into "irrationality."

As another example, middle class parents are the most vocal advocates of education as a means for solving Turkey's development problems. They are the major force behind the creation and expansion of new universities and higher education institutions. They reason that training people will provide Turkey with skills useful for development and provide their children with specific skills so that they can easily obtain jobs. Yet these same parents, when their children graduate, are the first to rely upon their relatives and friends to get their children placed in secure jobs. Their behavior undermines the whole value of having established a system of higher education based on entry through merit in the first place. For if people are placed in jobs through their connections with relatives and friends, this means placing people in jobs who are untrained for the particular requirements. Again, families are "rational" from their viewpoint in wanting to get their children into secure jobs, but from a social viewpoint they are "irrational."

As a third example, parents, especially middle class ones, encourage their children to be "modern" and independent by giving them the latest fashions in clothes, the most "Western" books and records, trips to Europe and other advantages. Yet, these same parents then undermine these values by continually interfering in their children's lives. They choose their children's schooling, try to determine their careers, push them into early marriage and try to decide who they will or will not marry. They then push their children to have their own children before they are ready and insist that their children live near them. In short, children are simultaneously encouraged to be independent and dependent. That Turkish middle class children grow up confused is all too understandable.

These contradictory behaviors, however, are also understandable. If there are limited job opportunities, if there are few institutions to give people life insurance and health security, if the schools and the mass media do not properly discuss the problems of change, then one can't blame people for falling back on their families. Who else do they have? Yet, by relying on this kind of social solution, Turkey's development problems are not being solved but are instead being confounded and made worse. The conservative ideology and behavior of the authoritarian, patriarchal family perpetuate under-development.

Conclusion

It is this aspect of Turkish family structure which makes divorce currently a progressive action. As we have seen, divorce represents a struggle against conservatism, an act of female emancipation. It is women who presently gain most from divorce, which is a necessary step in breaking down the barriers of exploitation and increasing social equality. Poor people experience the contradictions of the development process most intensely because they are subject to economic forces outside their control. However, the existence of inequalities in society become retooled inside the family and women suffer more from it than men. Therefore, divorce represents a step towards female emancipation. The solution to economic inequalities and regional lack of autonomy lies in distributing production and income more equitably, not in asking women to back away from emancipation as the National Salvation Party, the Islamic revolution in Iran and other neo-traditionalist movements suggest. Preserving the authority within the patriarchal family is not a solution to economic and social inequality.

The development process produces regional inequalities, making peripheral regions economically dependent on the big metropolises and polarizing economic opportunities. Change is, therefore, forced on some people, especially poor ones, by processes outside of their control. A solution to the problem will require acceptance of the change process, not rejection. Families must change in order to adapt to forces more powerful than themselves, but in doing so must also help fight the inequalities produced by the process in the first place. By liberating women within the family, by teaching one's children to be independent and self-reliant, by demanding of the society collective solutions to problems now solely the province of the family, pressure becomes exerted on the State apparatus to rectify the sources of inequality.

Unfortunately, this process takes a very long time to complete. Furthermore, without people understanding the necessity for change, it takes even longer. People are responsible for their own actions and are not merely the products of impersonal social forces. In Turkey, however, consciousness of the means for change lags and people fall back on familiar models. The problem is basically an issue of social equality, rather than family morality. Until such fundamental changes are instituted in Turkey, until there are sufficient jobs, until people are better off, until there are public institutions that provide services that the family now provides, the authoritarian, patriarchal family is going to remain a major institution, archaic as it is. Only then will this family type disappear and be replaced by a "new" family type based on equality and mutual relations. Only then will the repressive, stifling atmosphere of the authoritarian, patriarchal family be replaced by a more liberal, constructive, freer family atmosphere which helps people satisfy their indiviual needs more easily.

In this sense, to go back to the original idea, divorce must be seen as a barometer of social change. For as divorce increases, one can read this as an intensification of the social struggles for economic development and increasing social equality.

NOTES

[1]   A brief methodological note is in order. The two most common indices

of divorce are the Crude Divorce Rate (number of divorces in a year per 1000 population) and the Refined Divorce Rate (number of divorces in a year per 1000 married females). The latter is, obviously, preferable to the former, as it considers the rate in relation to the population at risk. The Refined Divorce Rate has limitations, however, as it does not accurately reflect differences in the proportion married at different ages (Bogue, 1969; Carter and Glick, 1970; England and Kunz, 1975). Divorce rates are almost always higher in younger age groups, decreasing consistently with age. For example, Weed (1974) found that the proportion married, ages 15-19, was the best predictor of state Age-Controlled Refined Divorce Rates in the United States. The best index would be an Age-at-Decree-Specific Refined Divorce Rate, which would take cognizance of both the age structure as well as the population at risk. Unfortunately, rarely are numbers of age-specific divorces published (in Turkey, only at national level), so that the Refined Divorce Rate is more commonly used. For some indices, the proportion married is not known so that Crude Divorce Rates have to be used.

BIBLIOGRAPHY

Benedict, Peter. *Ula: An Anatolian Town.* Leiden: E.J. Brill, 1974.

Blitz, Rudolph C. "An International Comparison of Women's Participation in the Professions," *Journal of Developing Areas.* 1975, 9, 499-510.

Bogue, Donald J. *Principles of Demography.* New York: J. Wiley, 1969.

Bumpass, Larry L. and James A. Sweet. "Differentials in Marital Instability: 1970," *American Sociological Review,* 1972, 37, 754-66.

Burgess, Ernest W. and Leonard S. Cottrell, Jr. *Predicting Success or Failure in Marriage.* New York: Prentice-Hall, 1939.

Carter, Hugh and Paul C. Glick. *Marriage and Divorce: A Social and Economic Study.* Cambridge, Mass.: Harvard Univ. Press, 1970.

Clark, John. "The Growth of Ankara, 1961-1969," *Review of the Geographical Institute of the University of Istanbul.* 1971, 13, 119-39.

Engels, Frederick. *The Origin of the Family, Private Property and the State* (4th edition). London: Lawrence and Wishart, 1962. Originally published 1891.

England, J. Lynn and Philip R. Kunz. "The Application of Age-Specific Rates to Divorce," *Journal of Marriage and the Family.* 1975, 37, 40-46.

Glick, Paul C. and Arthur J. Norton. "Frequency, Duration and Probability of Marriage and Divorce," *Journal of Marriage and the Family.* 1971, 33, 307-17.

Glick, Paul C. "A Demographer Looks at American Families," *Journal of Marriage and the Family.* 1975, 37, 40-46.

Goode, William J. *After Divorce.* New York: Free Press of Glencoe, 1956.

_____. *The Family.* Englewood Cliffs: Prentice-Hall, 1964.

HIPS. *Population in Turkey: A Factbook.* Ankara: Hacettepe University Institute of Population Studies, 1975.

Karpat, Kemal. *The Gecekondu: Rural Migration and Urbanization.* London: Cambridge Univ. Press, 1976.

Keleş, Ruşen. *Urbanization in Turkey.* New York: Ford Foundation, 1972.

Kıray, Mübeccel and Jan Hinderink. "Interdependence Between Agro-Economic Development and Social Change: A Comparative Study Conducted in the Çukurova Region of Southern Turkey," *Journal of Development Studies.* 1968, 4, 499-507.

Lasch, Christopher. *Haven in a Heartless World.* New York: Basic Books, 1977.

Levine, Ned. "Old Culture–New Culture: A Study of Migrants in Ankara, Turkey," *Social Forces,* 1973a, 51, 355-68.

———. "Value Orientation Among Migrants in Ankara, Turkey: A Case Study," *Journal of Asian and African Studies.* 1973b, 8, 50-68.

———. "Rural–Urban Migration and Its Effects on Urbanization over the Next Fifty Years." Paper presented at the Conference on Development Trends in Turkey: 1974-2024. Ankara: Hacettepe University, 1974.

———. "Anti-Urbanization: An Implicit Development Policy in Turkey," *Journal of Developing Areas,* 1980.

Marx, Karl and Frederick Engels. *The Manifesto of the Communist Party* (English edition, 1888). In David Fernbach (ed.), *Karl Marx, The Revolutions of 1848: Political Writings, Vol. 1.* Harmondsworth, Middlesex: Penguin, 1973, pp. 62-98. Originally published 1848.

Mansur, Fatma. *Bodrum: A Town in the Aegean.* Leiden: E.J. Brill, 1972.

Mihailovic, Kosta. *Socio-Economic Aspects of Interregional Migration in Yugoslavia.* Belgrade: Economic Institute, 1973.

Mills, C. Wright. *The Sociological Imagination.* New York: Oxford Univ. Press, 1959.

Murdock, George P. *Social Structure.* New York: Macmillan, 1949.

Nimkoff, M.F. *Comparative Family Systems.* Boston: Houghton-Mifflin, 1966, pp. 3-73.

Özbay, Ferhunde and Frederic C. Shorter. "Turkey: Changes in Birth Control Practice, 1963 to 1968," *Studies in Family Planning.* 1970, 51, 1-7.

Özbay, Ferhunde. "Türkiye'de 1963, 1968 ve 1973 yıllarında aile planlaması uygulamalarında ve doğurganlıktaki değişmeler" (Changes in Fertility and Family Planning Practice in Turkey: 1963, 1968 and 1973). Paper for the Second Turkish Demography Conference. Ankara: Hacettepe University, 1975.

Rainwater, Lee, Richard Coleman and Gerald Handel. *Workingman's Wife.* New York: Oceana Publishing, 1959.

Reich, Wilhelm. *The Mass Psychology of Fascism* (3rd edition, 1946). Harmondsworth, Middlesex: Penguin Books edition, 1975.

Robinson, R.D. "Turkey's Agrarian Revolution and the Problems of Urbanization," *Public Opinion Quarterly.* 1958, 22, 397-405.

Rosow, Irving and Daniel K. Rose. "Divorce Among Doctors," *Journal of Marriage and the Family.* 1972, 34, 587-98.

Schroeder, Clarence W. *Divorce in a City of 100,000 Population.* Peoria: Bradley Polytechnic Institute Library, 1939.

Shorter, Frederic C. and Belgin Tekçe. "Demographic Determinants of Urbanization in Turkey, 1935-1970." In Peter Benedict, Erol Tümertekin and Fatma Mansur (eds.), *Turkey: Geographic and Social Perspectives.* Leiden: E.J. Brill, 1973, 282-93.

Suzuki, Peter. "Encounters with Istanbul: Urban Peasants and Village Peasants," *International Journal of Comparative Sociology.* 1964, 5, 208-16.

Tekeli, İlhan. *Changes in the Rural Structure of Turkey Due to Agricultural Mechanization Within Market Conditions.* Ankara: Middle East Technical University Department of Regional Planning, 1976.

Terman, Lewis M. *Psychological Factors in Marital Happiness.* New York: McGraw-Hill, 1938.

Timur, H. "Civil Marriage in Turkey: Difficulties, Causes and Remedies," *International Social Science Bulletin.* 1957, 9, 34-36.

Timur, Serim. *Türkiye'de Aile Yapısı* (Family Structure in Turkey). Ankara: Hacettepe University Institute of Population Studies, 1972.

Turkish State Institute of Statistics (TSIS). *Divorce Statistics.* Ankara: State Institute of Statistics, 1968-1973, inclusive, and 1976.

————. *1935 Census of Population by Provinces, Districts, Cities and Villages—Provisional Figures.* Ankara: Central Office of Statistics, 1935.

————. *1950 Census of Population.* Ankara: General Statistical Office, 1961.

————. *1960 Census of Population: Population by Provinces, Districts, Sub-Districts, and Villages.* Ankara: State Institute of Statistics, 1963.

————. *1970 Census of Population of Provinces: Social and Economic Characteristics.* Ankara: State Institute of Statistics, 1970-73.

————. *1975 Census—Preliminary Results.* Ankara: State Institute of Statistics, 1975.

Udry, J. Richard. "Marital Instability by Race, Sex, Education, and Occupation Using 1960 Census Data," *American Journal of Sociology.* 1966, 72, 203-09.

United Nations. *1976 United Nations Demographic Yearbook.* New York: United Nations Publishing Service, 1977.

Weed, James A. "Age at Marriage As a Factor in State Divorce Rate Differentials," *Demography,* 1974, 11, 361-75.

Wolf, Eric R. *Peasants.* Englewood Cliffs: Prentice Hall, 1966.

Zaretsky, Eli. *Capitalism, the Family and Personal Life.* New York: Harper & Row, 1976.

SOCIAL PSYCHOLOGICAL PATTERNS OF HOMICIDE IN TURKEY: A COMPARISON OF MALE AND FEMALE CONVICTED MURDERERS

Serap Özgür and Diane Sunar

Like many other developing countries, Turkey has a high rate of criminal homicide; among 61 countries reporting to the United Nations, Turkey ranked eighth with a murder rate of 6.1 per 100,000 population.[1] This rate is considerably higher than the rates of some neighboring countries, such as Bulgaria (2.7) or Greece (1.5), and very much higher than the lower-ranking countries such as Portugal (.9) or the Netherlands (.3). Level of development cannot be regarded as the sole determinant of rates of criminal homicide, however, since countries with similar levels of development may have widely differing homicide rates: compare, for instance, Turkey (6.1) with Mexico (31.1), or the United States (4.5) with Canada (1.4). Nevertheless, most of the countries with higher homicide rates are relatively less developed countries of Latin America, Africa, and Asia, while most of the countries with lower homicide rates are relatively more developed European countries. (All figures are taken from the *U.N. Demographic Yearbook,* 1961.[2] It should be noted that these figures date from before the wave of terrorist killings in the 1970s, and therefore do not reflect levels of politically motivated violence.)

As the figures above indicate, murder is a serious social problem in Turkey. It will be our purpose in this paper, first, to examine this problem from a social psychological perspective; and second, to look at the characteristics of convicted homicide offenders, with particular attention to differences between male and female murderers.

Factors Contributing to High Homicide Rates

Why does Turkey have a high rate of criminal homicide? Since level of development does not provide an adequate answer, one must ask whether there are elements of Turkish culture which encourage individual violence. Wolfgang and Ferracuti (1967) have hypothesized that differences in homicide rates are to be explained in terms of cultural differences—more specifically, they hypothesize that high homicide rates are associated with a "subculture of violence," in which at least part of the population adheres to a system of norms and values which tolerates or even requires the use of violence in certain situations. The more an individual is integrated into this subculture, then, the more likely will his behavior be governed by its norms and expectations rather than by the norms and legal proscriptions of the larger society. As we shall try to show, some segments of Turkish culture do hold values which encourage violence, or in the extreme case, killing, under specifiable circumstances.

In traditional Turkish culture, as in most Mediterranean cultures, a central value which requires defense by violent means is honor (Peristiany, 1965). Honor may refer to a man's reputation as a participant in the community (*şeref*), or it may refer to his reputation as determined by the chastity of the women in his family (*namus*). An insult or other threat to a man's *şeref* must be punished in some way in order to maintain it as "clean"; in the extreme case, only the slaying of the offender will suffice to counteract the insult or threat. Threats to *namus* are somewhat more complicated, as they may originate in the behavior of a man's wife or unmarried daughter or sister, or in instigations by a man to unchaste behavior, or in insults or gossip concerning the man's ability to control his women. Again, however, any threat to *namus* calls for punishment, and *namus* which has been lost through actual unchaste behavior can be completely restored only by killing the (male) offender, and perhaps the guilty woman as well. Normally speaking, the defense of honor is a man's duty, but under unusual circumstances a woman may feel required to defend her *namus* herself.

Thus, as Safilios-Rothschild writes concerning Greek culture, "In the light of traditional values, killing in defense of family honor was not considered to be a crime; it was . . . a socially expected and approved behavior" (1969, p. 206). Moreover, in cases of loss of honor, there can be no such thing as legal redress; the person being directly responsible for the defense of his own honor, disputes concerning it can be settled only by personal, not legal, forms of justice (Pitt-Rivers, 1966). However, "honor crimes" are far from being purely personal events; on the contrary, they are and must be publicly known and communally validated to serve their function of cleansing a stained *şeref* or *namus*. As Meeker (1976, p. 251) puts it, "If vengeance were taken and no one heard of the matter, vengeance would not be worth taking."

The blood feud, a practice which is common in some parts of Turkey, may be considered a special case of the honor crime. The incident which initiates a blood feud may be a response to the loss of or threat to someone's *şeref* or *namus,* or it may spring from a more ordinary quarrel, land dispute, or the like. But whatever the origin, once the initial killing has occurred, members of the victim's clan feel honor-bound to avenge his death. This leads to a self-perpetuating cycle of vengeance in which members of both groups commit murder in the pursuit of their duty to protect their family's or clan's *şeref*.

These norms concerning *şeref, namus,* and vengeance survive most strongly in the more traditional segments of Turkish society— specifically, among those who reside in villages and small towns, or among the *gecekondu* residents in the large cities, who are generally recent migrants from rural areas. Despite the laws against murder and other forms of violence, and the near-certain imprisonment which awaits the murderer, these norms continue to be promoted by community acceptance of violence and to be enforced through fear of social ostracism and loss of honor and manhood.[3]

On the basis of these general remarks, we might predict that a high proportion of murders in Turkey would fit into the category of honor crimes (including blood feud), and that murders so classified would occur mainly in rural areas or in the *gecekondu* areas of the big cities. A number of studies (Stirling, 1965; Tezcan, 1972; Ünsal, 1973; Yavuzer, 1977; Ergil, 1978) tend to confirm both these predictions, as do some of the data to be presented later in this paper (Özgür, 1980).

The subculture of violence theory is most clearly supported in the Turkish case by the existence of traditions which encourage honor crimes. However, it is doubtful that honor crimes alone account for the high rate of homicidal violence in Turkey. Although fully reliable figures are not available, it seems unlikely that more than 25% of the (nonpolitical) murders are committed in defense of honor. Nevertheless, some elements of the "subculture of violence," other than the central value of honor, may serve to increase the homicide rate.

For one thing, the masculine ideal in an honor-centered culture is a man who is physically fearless, quick to take offense, and always ready to fight. While these characteristics are no doubt highly functional in the defense of honor, they may also imply a relatively low level of inhibition against aggressive or violent behavior in general. Megargee's (1966) study of convicted killers suggests that many of them could be typified as under-controlled personalities, who had weak internal restraints against an aggressive response to frustration. It seems likely that members of a "subculture of violence" may tend towards this under-controlled personality formation. Partial support for this surmise may be found in Çifter's (1970) study, in which the MMPI was administered to samples from Ankara, from the gecekondus of Ankara, and from villages. Scores indicative of a tendency to outward-directed aggression were higher in the village and gecekondu groups than in the urban group.

Second, in an honor-centered culture in which everyone must be constantly alert and ready to defend himself, acts of violence are in some sense normal and expectable. Not only internal, but external, social restraints against violence may be low.

Concomitant with this is the availability of weapons, or even the felt necessity to be constantly armed. Several studies indicate that, in fact, Turkish villagers tend to carry guns (Dönmezer, 1970; Tezcan, 1972; Ünsal, 1973). The fact that a gun is ready at hand in a moment of anger or frustration surely raises the probability of a fatal outcome. As Berkowitz (1960) argues, guns not only permit violence, they stimulate it as well. This hypothesis is supported by a study by Newton and Zimning (1969), who showed that countries with strict gun control had significantly lower homicide rates than countries with weak gun control.

The subculture of violence theory argues that high rates of homicide may stem directly from the normative expectations and constraints operative in some segments of society. Another theory, proposed by Henry and Short (1954) in a modern interpretation of Durkheim, provides quite a different perspective on homicide. According to this theory, the greater the external restraints to which an individual is subjected, the greater the likelihood of homicidal violence. External restraints may be "vertical," i.e., arise from the stratification system; or they may be "horizontal," i.e. arise from the relational system within which the individual is embedded. Thus, lower status persons are subjected to the restraints imposed by the social strata above them, and members of families and other social groups are subjected to the restraints of the relational system. In both cases, the individual has readily identifiable sources of stress or frustration to which he can attribute the ultimate blame for any act of violence. (Lack of external restraints, according to Henry and Short, is associated with anomie and suicide rather than murder.) While this theory was designed to explain intrasocietal distributions of suicide and homicide, it can be readily transposed to the cross-cultural question which is raised by the relatively higher homicide rates in less developed countries.

The external restraint theory would predict high homicide rates in developing countries if the following two conditions can be assumed to hold: 1) in the traditional cultures of these countries, individuals are tightly knit into the relational systems of family, clan, village, and the like; and 2) in developing countries, a large proportion of the population (as compared to the case in more developed countries) occupies low status positions. Both of these assumptions, if correct, imply strong external restraints on the individual, which in turn would imply relatively high murder rates.

Both of these conditions can be seen to obtain in Turkey. The traditional rural community in Turkey is often described as being characterized by a patriarchal family system and close family relations (Kolars, 1962; Stirling, 1965). Kâğıtçıbaşı (1977) argues that, in the face-to-face interpersonal relations of such traditional communities, everyone is a "significant other"—a situation which surely approaches the theoretical limit of horizontal external restraint.

Although Turkey is undergoing a very rapid urbanization process, according to the results of the 1980 census, approximately half of the population remains in rural areas; and in the largest cities, half or even more of the "urban" population consists of *gecekondu* dwellers, most of whom are migrants from rural areas and who maintain close ties with their former villages while perpetuating their traditional values and life styles to the extent possible in the urban context (Karpat, 1976; Şenyapılı, 1978). As villagers and *gecekondu* dwellers occupy low status positions in the stratification system of modern Turkey, it can be seen that the same groups which are subjected to the greatest horizontal external restraints are also subjected to the greatest vertical external restraints; and that these groups constitute well over half the population of the nation.

This position receives very strong support: across a large number of cultures, including Turkey, an overwhelming majority of murders are committed by persons from the lowest strata of their societies (Harlan, 1950; Toro-Calder, 1950; Henry and Short, 1954; Morris and Blom-Cooper, 1957; Wolfgang, 1958; Safilios-Rothschild, 1969; Mushanga, 1970; Ahuja, 1970; Emovon and Lambo, 1972; Connor, 1973; Ünsal, 1973; Ergil, 1978; Green and Wakefield, 1979).

It should be noted that the external restraint theory is not a rival of the subculture of violence theory. In the Turkish case, at least, the two theories complement one another, the latter predicting a high incidence of honor crimes and related homicides in the traditional segments of society, and the former predicting a high incidence of what we might call common murder in rural and lower-class urban (i.e. gecekondu) areas. Taken together, the two theories explain both the high incidence of murder in Turkey and its concentration in rural and gecekondu areas.

Cross Cultural Perspectives on Male and Female Murderers

Turning our attention now to a consideration of sex differences among murderers, we may see that, as with the class differences discussed above, there are trends so widespread as to be nearly universal.

Worldwide, crime (including murder) is more the province of men than of women. The ratio of female crime to total crime may vary from country to country, but even the highest figure indicates that women account for no more than 20% of all criminal arrests, and in most countries this percentage is much lower (Palmer, 1960). In Turkey, the proportion of female crime varies between approximately 2.5% and 3.5% (Ministry of Justice statistics, 1967-76).

Interestingly, however, murder accounts for a higher percentage of female crime than of male crime (this regardless of the fact that murders by males are much more numerous than murders by females). In Turkey, criminal homicide accounts for 9-10% of all male arrests, while it accounts for 15-20% of all female arrests (DIE statistics, 1967-76). From a statistical analysis of crime in 30 nations, Bowker (1978) concludes that, with increasing modernization, the trend is toward an increase in the female contribution to the total crime rate, together with a decrease in the proportion of female murders. One might almost say that, with modernization, female crime is becoming masculinized. This trend might have been predicted more than 80 years ago by Durkheim, who attributed women's low crime rate at that time to their low participation (relative to that of men) in collective life. Even if this trend towards increase in female crime rates exists, however, it has not yet altered the overall male–female distributions of crime in general and murder in particular.

Again following Durkheim (1897), who remarked that "while family life has a moderating effect upon suicide, it rather stimulates murder," we see that both male and female murderers are likely to be married. Here again there are sex differences: the female homicide offender is more likely to be married than the male homicide offender, by a ratio of three to two (Rosenblatt and Greenland, 1974). An exception to the tendency for murderers to be married may be found among blood-feud killers in Turkey (virtually all of whom are male): Ünsal (1973) found that only 27.4% of convicted blood feud offenders were married. This can perhaps be explained by the involved families' assignment of the duty of vengeance to young unmarried males whose subsequent imprisonment would not have serious consequences for family dependents.

Age patterns are also quite consistent across cultures. Generally, male murderers tend to be younger than female murderers. The man convicted of murder is most likely to be in his twenties, while his female counterpart is more likely to be in her thirties (Wolfgang, 1958; Bohannon, 1960; Lambo, 1962; Wolfgang and Ferracuti, 1967; Cole and Fisher, 1968; Tosun, 1968; Moran, 1971; Orban, 1971; Ünsal, 1973; Deiker, 1974; Rosenblatt and Greenland, 1974; Lunde, 1975; Ergil, 1978). Safilios-Rothschild (1969) reports a greater mean age for men than for women, but her figures cover honor crimes only.

It may be asserted that the female criminal, including the murderer, typically comes from a more disturbed background and has endured a more stress-ridden life than her male counterpart. Since both socialization practices and social sanctions militate strongly against female deviance in almost all cultures, traditional or modern, such a pattern is perhaps only to be expected. The strength of social norms prohibiting violence being much greater for women than for men, the strength of instigation must be correspondingly greater to provoke a violent response from a woman.

Thus we see that separation, divorce, and disturbed family relations are more common in the families of female as compared to male delinquents (Bagot, 1941; Wattenberg and Saunders, 1954; Monahan, 1957). Also, Felthous and Yudowitz (1977) found that a history of physically injurious paternal punishments is significantly associated with conviction for crimes of violence, and that such a history is significantly more frequent among female than among male offenders.

In addition to having a different type of family background, female murderers are reported to differ from male murderers in personality type. Of the personality types among murderers described by Megargee (1966), men are more likely to fit the "under-controlled" type, while women are more likely to be "over-controlled"—that is, to possess such strong inhibitions against aggression that even normal, socially acceptable outlets for aggression appear "off limits" to them. In contrast to the under-controlled type, who is likely to strike out aggressively upon slight provocation, the over-controlled type is likely to inhibit reaction until a very high level of frustration is reached, at which point the response may be extremely violent.

If one looks at the murderous act itself, again sex differences are apparent: in the choice of victim, the location of the crime, and the degree of premeditation.

The victims of most murders were, in life, close enough to their slayers to be classified as "primary contacts" (Wolfgang, 1958): spouse, family member, paramour, close friend, etc. However, this tendency is more pronounced for female murderers. In a variety of studies covering countries from the U.S. to India, the percentage of primary contacts among victims of male murderers ranges from about 45–60%, while the percentage for females ranges from about 75–85%. The differences are somewhat greater if only spouses and family members are considered (Svalastoga, 1956; Wolfgang, 1958; Bohannon, 1960; Driver, 1961; Yücel, 1969; Ahuja, 1970; Mushanga, 1970; Emovon and Lambo, 1972; Connor, 1973; Rosenblatt and Greenland, 1974).

The location of the crime is congruent with the choice of victim. Approximately half the murders committed by men take place in the home, while three-fourths or more of the murders committed by women occur in the home (Harlan, 1950; Wolfgang, 1958; Ergil, 1978).

Although adequate data on premeditation are not available, some suggestive hints may be found in the literature. The subculture of violence theory, applicable mainly to male violence, would predict that a high proportion of murders in such a subculture would have the character of "crimes of passion"—i.e., would be a spontaneous response to insult, perceived loss of honor, or the like. Also, the violence of "under-controlled" personalities, again, mostly men, would be predicted to be a spontaneous response to an anger-arousing situation. It is difficult to make clear-cut predictions about women. However, since female murderers tend to parallel middle and upper class murderers in terms of personality type (over-controlled), choice of victim (spouse or other family member), and scene of the crime (in the home) (Green and Wakefield, 1979), it may be expected that the incidence of premeditation may also be similar. Green and Wakefield (1979) found that premeditation was a feature of more than three-fourths of upper-class homicides. Rosenblatt and Greenland (1974), comparing male and female murderers, found that the women's crimes were less spontaneous than the men's. Ahuja's study of female murderers in India revealed that of the women who admitted their guilt, about 60% had planned the killing beforehand. Thus, although the point cannot be made conclusively, there is a substantial basis for believing that murders committed by women are more likely to be premeditated than those committed by men.

Predictions in the Present Study

The study to be described below had as its main purpose the comparison of male and female convicted murderers in Turkey. A wide range of comparisons was planned, from demographic characteristics to degree of expressed regret following the crime. Among the planned comparisons, three seem especially significant in terms of their social-psychological implications.

1) Motive for murder. Motives may be roughly classified as normatively approved (e.g., self defense, some honor crimes, etc.) or not normatively approved. On the basis of the preceding discussion, it may be predicted that women would be less likely than men to commit murder from a normatively approved motive.

At least three lines of argument can be made here. First, the subculture of violence, if it exists, makes normative prescriptions for male violence, but virtually prohibits female violence. Thus the honor crime, even though it may be socially approved for men, is generally forbidden to women. If anything, a woman is more likely to be the victim rather than the perpetrator of an honor crime. In addition, the relatively high level of male supervision and protection of women in a community in which *namus* is a central value makes it unlikely that a woman will encounter a situation (outside the family) in which she might need to defend her own life.

Second, the external restraint theory, which as we have seen predicts non-normative (common) homicide in traditional and low status groups, may be seen to apply with special relevance to women: women both are more enmeshed in relational systems, especially the family, and socially occupy a lower status position than men. It may be argued that the external restraint theory fails in the case of women, as the female murder rate is universally lower than that of men; but, as Henry and Short (1954) argue, there are very powerful countervailing forces, such as socialization practices and social sanctions, which probably serve to depress the female homicide rate much below what would be expected on the basis of external restraint alone. In any case, this theory would predict essentially non-normative murders among women.

Thirdly, the typically more disturbed social and family background of the female murderer (if it is found to hold true in Turkey) would predict more personal motives rather than normatively approved ones.

Against these lines of reasoning it may be argued that the social pressure against female violence is so forcible that only a woman whose motive for murder is socially approvable could find the strength to commit the deed.[4] However, the preponderance of theoretical expectation and previous findings leads us to prefer the prediction that male murder motives will be more normative than those of females.

2) Premeditation. As noted previously, there are reasons for believing that women are more likely than men to kill on the basis of premeditation. In addition to the considerations discussed above, it may be pointed out that a woman's relative physical weakness may push her towards premeditation; except in the case of child murder, any physical struggle would probably put the woman at a disadvantage. Even if the idea of murder should come to her in the heat of anger, she may postpone consummation of the act until such a time as she can be more assured of "success." We may predict, then, that a greater proportion of female than male murders will have been premeditated.

3) Degree of violence. There are at least three reasons for supposing that women will kill in a more violent manner than men. First, if it is true in Turkey, as it seems to be in other countries, that women more frequently kill their primary contacts, then it is likely that more intense resentment, anger and hostility will be involved. Second, Megargee's (1966) analysis of over-controlled personality types indicates that they tend to kill more violently than under-

controlled types. Since women more frequently fit into the over-controlled category, their murders may be expected to be more violent. Third, if our prediction concerning premeditation is correct, on that basis also a higher level of violence may be expected. If a murder is planned ahead of time, the killer fully intends the death of the victim, and greater violence may be employed simply to ensure the desired outcome. We expect, then, that murders committed by women will be more violent than those committed by men.

Method

The study to be reported below was conducted by interviewing 50 male and 50 female prison inmates who had been convicted of criminal homicide.

The Sample

Respondents were selected from among the inmates of the Çankırı closed prison, the Sivas semi-open prison, and the Izmir semi-open prison.

Since female convicted homicide offenders can be found only in small numbers, no systematic sampling was possible; almost all the available respondents were interviewed. Quota sampling, based on age categories, education levels, and rural vs. urban location of the homicide, was used in the selection of male respondents. All categories were adequately represented, with the partial exception of the under-30 age category, which was somewhat underrepresented.

The Interview

Each respondent was interviewed separately in a private room. In all cases the interviewer was of the same sex as the respondent. A brief introductory explanation was given, to the effect that the interview would be held in complete confidence; that it could not affect the respondent's legal situation, as they had already been convicted and sentenced; and that by reporting their true feelings they might be of help to people in similar situations in the future. All respondents were cooperative.

The interviews typically lasted about 30–45 minutes. Information given by the respondents was checked for reliability against information in their files, which had been previously examined. The respondents were not informed that their files had been read. Most of the information given in the interviews corresponded with that in the files, with some exceptions in the report of motives. It appeared to the interviewers that, in these cases of discrepancy, the motives reported in the interview were more probably the true motives than those recorded in the files.

Information sought in the interviews fell into five basic categories:

1) Demographic characteristics of the respondent.

2) Primary group relations. Questions regarding the respondent's relationships with family members, relatives, spouse (if married) and spouse's family, degree of contentment with home life, etc., fell into this category.

3) Secondary group relations. Questions regarding interpersonal relations apart from marriage and family were asked in this section, along with questions about activities, hobbies, religious beliefs, possible criminal contacts, etc.

4) Ratings of the acceptability of various homicide motives.

5) Description of the crime. Here the respondents were asked to give a spontaneous account of their crimes, and were encouraged to relate the story with no interruptions. Afterwards, where necessary, questions were asked in order to gain full information on the relationship of the victim, motive for the crime, degree of premeditation, degree of violence, location of the crime, weapon(s) used, etc.

A combination of closed and open-ended questions was used in all categories.

Description of the Samples

In this section, the male and female samples will be compared with regard to socioeconomic status (SES), age, marital status, mobility, location of the homicide act, motive and method of commission of homicide.

Socioeconomic Status

The measurement of SES in general is fraught with methodological pitfalls, but the measurement of the SES of a prison sample presents even more formidable problems, such as the lack of indicators like current occupation or income level, and incomparability of incomes at different times of arrest and imprisonment. Nevertheless, a rough estimate of the relative SES of these respondents may be made, based on the individual's occupation (or husband's occupation), education level (plus husband's education, for married women), and the individual's perception of his/her relative economic status.

The results were consistent across all three indicators: the male offenders were relatively lower in SES than the females.

Over three-fourths of the male group (78%) were classified as farm workers, which was considered the lowest status occupation, while less than half the females (44%) and less than one-third of the husbands of the maried female convicts (30%) were so classified. Only 22% of the male prisoners were classifed as public employee, laborer, tradesman, or entrepreneur, while 22% of the women and 62% of the husbands were so classified. About a third of the women (34%) were housewives. In terms of occupation, then, the female group was higher in SES than the male group (p ≤ .005).

Four levels of education were considered: illiterate, literate, elementary school graduate, and education beyond elementary school. The female offenders were less educated than the male offenders (p ≤ .04), as would be expected in view of male–female education differentials in Turkey (see Özbay, 1979; see also Kandiyoti in this volume), but the husbands of female offenders were more educated than the male offenders: 92% of the male offenders had an elementary school education or less, while almost 38% of the husbands had education beyond the elementary school level (p ≤ .005). Since a wife's SES is more strongly determined by her husband's characteristics than her own, this finding may be interpreted as indicating higher SES for the female than the male offenders.

Perceived relative economic status was used as a third indicator, since a direct comparison of incomes was not visible. Each respondent was asked to rate his/her pre-arrest economic situation in comparison to his/her surroundings (çevre). Fifty-two percent of the women, as opposed to 16% of the men, reported that their situation was better than the average; and only 14% of the women, as opposed to 30% of the men, reported that their situation was worse than the average (p ≤ .005).

Thus, from all three indicators—occupation, education, and perceived relative economic status—the female offenders ranked higher on SES than the male offenders.

Age

The male and female samples were compared as to age at the time the homicide was committed. Both groups tended to be young at the time of the murder: 68% of the women and 44% of the men were under the age of 27. However, 32% of the men (but only 10% of the women) were 38 years of age or older. Thus the women committed homicide at younger ages than the men (p ≤ .01).

Marital Status

No significant sex difference was found with regard to marital status. A large majority of both the male (68%) and the female (74%) groups was married.

Mobility

The geographical mobility of the offenders was determined by comparing their place of birth and the location of the homicide they had committed. Whereas 82% of the men committed homicide in the same rural area in which they were born, this was true of only 52% of the women. Whereas 32% of the women had moved either from a rural area to a city or from a smaller city to a metropolitan area, only 4% of the men had made such moves. (These figures are somewhat misleading, however, as many of the male sample showed a pattern of "temporary mobility": that is, they had left their villages for work in the cities or even abroad, but had returned after a time; still, only 4% of rural-born men committed murder in a city.) Sixteen percent of the women and 14% of the men were born and committed their homicides in urban or metropolitan areas. The female offenders, then, were geographically more mobile than the males (p ≤ .005).

Location of the Homicide Act

Under this heading we may consider two types of location: the rural or urban geographical location, and the physical site of the crime (home, field, street, etc.).

Consistent with the mobility data given above, more of the men (82%) than the women (52%) committed murder in rural areas; while more of the women (48%) than the men (18%) committed murder in urban or metropolitan areas (p ≤ .007).

As to physical site of the crime, the preponderance of the women (70%) committed murder at home, whereas most of the men (74%) committed murder in the street or field. Only 18% of the men killed at home, and 28% of the women killed in the street or field. A small percentage of both sexes (2% of the women, 8% of the men) committed murder in their place of employment. We may say, then, that most of the female homicides took place in the home, while most of the male homicides occurred in public places (p ≤ .0001).

Motive

Motives reported by the offenders were classified into seven categories:

1) Self defense. The homicide was committed under circumstances in which the only choices were to kill or be killed.

2) Property defense. The homicide was committed in the defense of land, money, or other belongings.

3) Honor. The homicide was committed in defense of the honor of either the offender or one of his/her relatives. *Namus* or sexual honor, rather than *şeref*, was usually at stake, and had generally been violated by rape or other sexual molestation.

4) Blood feud. The homicide was committed in revenge for the killing of a member of the lineage of the offender.

5) Domestic quarrels. The homicide was committed in the course of or as a result of quarrels between husband and wife or other household members.

6) Jealousy. The homicide was committed because of jealousy between co-wives, or concerning an extramarital liaison.

7) Aggressiveness. This category includes several types of murder motive, including: a) removal of an unwanted person, most frequently an extramarital lover who had come to be perceived as a threat; b) commission of homicide in the course of an armed robbery or similar crime; and c) commission of homicide in the course of a fight which had an essentially trivial origin.

The distribution of these motives by sex is shown in Table 1.

Table 1
Distribution of Homicide Motives by Sex (Frequencies)

Motive for Homicide	Female	Male	Total
1. Self Defense	1 (02%)	18 (36%)	19 (19%)
2. Property Defense	2 (04%)	10 (20%)	12 (12%)
3. Honor	22 (44%)	11 (22%)	33 (33%)
4. Blood feud	1 (02%)	3 (06%)	4 (04%)
5. Domestic quarrels	7 (14%)	0 (00%)	7 (07%)
6. Jealousy	5 (10%)	0 (00%)	5 (05%)
7. Aggressiveness	12 (24%)	8 (16%)	20 (20%)
Total	50 (100%)	50 (100%)	100 (100%)

$x^2 = 38$, df = 6, $p \leq .0001$

As can be seen in Table 1, the defense categories are predominantly male (56%, vs. 6% for women), while domestic quarrels and jealousy are, in this sample, exclusively female motives for murder (24%, vs. 0% for men). Honor, surprisingly, accounts for twice as many female as male murders (44% vs. 22%). Blood feud is, overall, the least frequent motive for murder in this sample (4%). Aggressiveness accounts for almost one-fourth of female murders, but less than one-sixth of male murders (24% vs. 16%).

Method of Commission of Homicide.
The methods used in homicide by the offenders were classified into four categories: shooting, stabbing (including attacks with knives, axes, and other sharp instruments), beating, and other (including poison, strangling, electrocution, and combinations of two or more methods). There were no significant sex differences in choice of method; a large majority of both males (78%) and females (68%) killed their victims by shooting them. The second most frequently used method was stabbing or cutting, with 10% of the men and 16% of the women choosing this method. Beating was used by 10% of the men and 8% of the women, and "other" methods were employed by 2% of the men and 8% of the women.

Other Comparisons
Further description of the samples, in terms of slayer–victim relationships, family backgrounds, and attitudes towards the crime, will be taken up at a later point, following a consideration of the predictions concerning normativeness, premeditation, and violence.

Predictions and Findings

Normativeness
Our first prediction was that men will be more likely than women to kill from a normatively approved motive. In order to assess the data on motives against this prediction, it was necessary first to classify motives according to their normative acceptability. For this purpose, the respondents were asked whether or not each of six possible motives was an acceptable reason for killing (the "aggressiveness" category was not included). Their responses are presented in Table 2. As can be seen in the table, the motives of self-defense and honor were almost universally accepted by this sample—over 90% of both males and females found both of these motives acceptable. Property defense was found an acceptable motive by men more often than women (70% vs. 47%), as was jealousy (40% vs. 24.5%), while domestic quarrels were found

acceptable by more women than men (44% vs. 20%). Approximately a third of both groups found it acceptable to kill in a blood feud.

Table 2
Percentage of Male and Female Offenders Accepting
Various Motives as Justifiable Grounds for Homicide

Motive for Homicide	Female	Male	Total
1. Self Defense*	91.8%	94%	92.9%
2. Property Defense*	46.9%	70%	58.5%
3. Honor*	93.9%	92%	92.9%
4. Blood feud*	32.7%	32%	32.2%
5. Domestic quarrels**	43.7%	20%	31.6%
6. Jealousy*	24.5%	40%	32.2%

* One female offender did not respond.
** Two female offenders did not respond.

Despite the sex differences, these responses show a fairly high degree of consensus, as self-defense and honor rate very high on acceptability, while blood feud, domestic quarrels, and jealousy were approved by less than one-third of the sample. Property defense seems to be an intermediate category, with somewhat over half the sample finding it acceptable. For our purposes, we shall adopt the criterion of approval by half or more of the sample for determining normative acceptability. Using this criterion, we see that self-defense, honor, and property defense are normatively acceptable (normative), while blood feud, domestic quarrels, and jealousy (along with the investigator's category of aggressiveness) are normatively not acceptable (non-normative) motives for murder.

When the motives reported by the homicide offenders are classified according to their normativeness, it may be seen that our hypothesis regarding sex differences was supported. Exactly half the female sample killed for normative reasons, and half for non-normative motives, while 78% of the males killed for normative motives, and 22% for non-normative motives (p $\leq$ .005).

A significant interaction between marital status and sex may be pointed out here: for the male murderers, there was no significant difference in normativeness between those who were married and those who were unmarried; but unmarried women more frequently murdered for normative reasons than did married women (76.9% vs. 40.5%, p $\leq$ .03).

Premeditation

Our second prediction was that murders committed by women would be more often premeditated than those committed by men. This prediction also is borne out by the data, as 62% of the women, as opposed to only 8% of the men, reported that they had planned the murder ahead of time (p ≤ .0001).

Violence

The third prediction was that female homicide would be more violent than male homicide. Degree of violence was determined by these criteria: a) if the murder was committed with only one act of violence (one shot, one blow, etc), it was classified as "less violent"; b) if two to seven acts of violence were performed, it was classified as "more violent"; c) if eight or more acts were performed, it was classified as "extremely violent." The women's murders were distributed almost equally across the three categories (32%, 34%, and 34%, respectively), while the men's murders were concentrated in the "less violent" category (60%, 24%, and 16%, respectively). Thus there is a clear tendency to greater violence in female homicides (p ≤ .01).

In the first section it was argued that a possible factor in determining the level of violence would be the degree of intention to kill (intention here is independent of premeditation, as it can come into being more or less simultaneously with the attack). The prisoners were asked what had been their intention at the time of the killing—to kill, to wound, or to frighten. There were fairly large sex differences in the responses. Male intentions were almost equally distributed (34%, 32%, and 34%, respectively), while over three-fourths of the women intended to kill (78%, 18%, and 4%, respectively). This difference was highly significant (p ≤ .0001).

If degree of violence is analyzed according to intention, a clear and predictable pattern emerges. Of the 56 murders committed with the intention to kill, 78.6% were committed with "more" or "extreme" violence. On the other hand, when the intention was to wound, 72% of the murders were committed with "less" violence (one act), and when the intention was to frighten, 84.2% of the killings were "less" violent. The relation between intention and violence was highly significant (p ≤ .0001).

Taking only the cases in which the intention was to kill, there is no significant relation between sex and degree of violence. We may conclude, then, that the greater violence employed by female murderers is a result of the fact that when they kill they do so intentionally, while men are more likely to kill without fully intending that the victim should die.

Discussion

It is apparent from the foregoing presentation that male and female murderers differ greatly in a wide variety of dimensions, from their demographic characteristics to their motives for murder and manner of committing it. In this section we will introduce a number of new variables, most of which also show male–female differences, and which may be useful in suggesting explanations for the differences already reported. Among these variables are slayer-victim relationships; family relationships before and after marriage; and offender's attitude toward his/her homicide act.

Slayer-Victim

As pointed out in the introductory section, the victims of most murders are among the "primary contacts" of their killers. This pattern holds true for the group examined here, as well: only 8% of the homicide offenders interviewed had killed a stranger. However, among their close contacts, men and women tend to choose different categories of victims. Table 3 shows the distribution, by sex of murderer, of the victim categories. The most striking difference is in the category of "member of immediate family," in which 42% of the female murders are concentrated, as opposed to only 16% of the male murders. In contrast, 74% of the men had killed a relative, neighbor, or friend, while only 36% of the women had done so. In this group the murder of a fiancé or lover was unique to the females; however, this may be an artifact of the underrepresentation of younger males in the sample. In sum, it appears that murder by a woman is much more likely than murder by a man to involve a victim from the immediate family or household, that is, a victim very close to the killer. On the other hand, when a man kills, the victim, while still a close contact, is likely to be at least one step removed from his family circle.

Interestingly, when the data on slayer-victim relationships are compared with those on physical site of the crime, a further contrast between the sexes becomes apparent. The locations of men's murders correspond almost exactly to what would be expected on the basis of the distribution of victims: 16% of their victims were family members, and 18% of their victims were relatives, neighbors, friends, or strangers, and 82% of their murders were committed

Table 3
Relationship of Victim to Slayer, by Sex of Slayer (Frequencies)

Victim	Female	Male	Total
1. Family Member	21 (42%)	8 (16%)	29 (29%)
2. Relative	8 (16%)	16 (32%)	24 (24%)
3. Neighbor	9 (18%)	12 (24%)	21 (21%)
4. Friend	1 (02%)	9 (18%)	10 (10%)
5. Lover or Fiancée	8 (16%)	0 (00%)	8 (08%)
6. Stranger	3 (06%)	5 (10%)	8 (08%)
Total	50 (100%)	50 (100%)	100 (100%)

$x^2 = 23.6$, df $= 5$, p$\leq$.0001

outside the home. The situation for women is quite different: while 42% of their victims were family members, a full 70% of their murders were committed at home; and while 58% of their victims were relatives, neighbors, friends, lovers or fiancés, or strangers, only 30% of their murders were committed outside the home. One possible implication that can be drawn here is that many of these women were subjected to some *namus*-threatening sexual attack in their homes by relatives or neighbors, and responded by killing their attackers (it will be recalled that 44% of the female murders had defense of honor as their motive). A second implication may be that, regardless of the formal nature of the relationship (relative, neighbor, etc.), there was a more intense emotional involvement with the victim in the case of the female murders. These two suppositions are not, of course, mutually exclusive.

Family Relationships

Part of the interview was devoted to questions about primary group relations. The first such question asked whether the respondents felt that they had received enough love and attention from their parents while growing up. The sex differences in response to this question were striking: while 92% of the men felt they had received sufficient parental attention, 36% of the women felt they had not (p $\leq$ .001). This finding is not surprising, in view of the traditional preference for sons and low status of daughters in the family (see, for instance, the articles in this volume by Kâğıtçıbaşı, Okman-Fişek, Kuyaş and Abadan-Unat). However, only 4.5% of the women who had been dissatisfied reported that the cause was favoritism shown to their brothers. About half of this group believed they were neglected either because they were adopted (13.6%) or because they were raised by a stepmother (36.4%). Another large group attributed their neglect to parental problems: 27.3% said their parents were indifferent to their children, and 18.2% believed their parents' quarrels prevented them from getting enough attention.

Responses to a second question also suggest that the source of these women's dissatisfaction with their parents does not lie entirely in the traditional undervaluation of daughters. When asked whether their parents got along harmoniously or not, 97.8% of the men replied in the positive, while 44% of the women replied in the negative (p ≤ .0001). Of the women who perceived their parents as disharmonious, 77.7% blamed their parents' problems on their fathers' excessive dominance, and 22.3% blamed their mothers' tempers or nervousness. Several interpretations of this sex difference may be offered. Perhaps daughters, feeling that they are undervalued, are readier than more secure sons to perceive their mothers' subjugation to domineering fathers; or perhaps being more restricted to the home, they are more exposed to parental quarrelling. Perhaps women are simply more open in expressing their feelings; the men certainly report happy family backgrounds with greater frequency than one might realistically expect. Nevertheless, it is possible that the more obvious interpretation is correct: that the female murderers come from more disturbed families than the males.

The sex difference in dissatisfaction with family life becomes even more marked in the responses of the married offenders to questions about their contentment with their home life after marriage (prior to imprisonment). The women express a strikingly greater level of discontent: 97.1% of the married males claim to have been content with their home life, while 59.5% of the married females say that they were not content with their home life (p ≤ .0001).

When asked whether they had been happier before or after marriage, the male and female prisoners responded, again, quite differently. Of the men, 91.2% reported that they were happier after marriage than before, while 62.2% of the women said they had been happier before marriage (p ≤ .001).

The post-marriage increase in happiness for the men can probably be explained in a fairly straightforward manner. In traditional rural families, which are the origin of the bulk of this sample, marriage brings about few changes in the young man's relation to his parents (which as we have seen is generally perceived in a very positive light), and brings new benefits, such as increased prestige and legitimate sexual satisfaction. That marriage brings an increase in happiness, then, is only to be expected in the case of men.

The picture for women is more complicated. For one thing, in these traditional rural families, the young woman has little or no choice of her marriage partner. Most frequently the girl is given by her father in exchange for a bride price (Stirling, 1965; Türkdoğan, 1976). In the vernacular, this transaction is discussed in terms of "buying" and "selling." There can be little doubt that the women are aware of and resent their status as property that can be bought and sold. Two of the respondents remarked about their marriages:

> My father was always thinking about selling me to his partner's son in order to get the bride price.

> It was a kind of exchange. My brother could get married to the girl he liked only if I married the girl's brother. I was nine years old when my parents forced me to get engaged for my brother's sake.

When asked whether they would prefer to be male or female should they have a chance to come into the world again, almost all of the offenders, both male and female, stated they would prefer to be male (99% and 89%, respectively).[7] The most frequently given reason for this preference is that men have "power" and "independence" (80% of both groups). This nearly-universal aspiration among the female offenders suggests that they are aware of and rebellious against their subordinate role vis-a-vis their fathers and husbands.

Not only is the woman virtually sold into marriage, regardless of what her preferences might be, she is usually removed quite decisively from contact with her own family. The most common pattern is for the young couple to live with the husband's parents, at least for a time. There the young wife is subordinated not only to her husband, but also to her father-in-law's patriarchal authority and to her mother-in-law's direct authority over her (see Kâğıtçıbaşı, 1981). Of the married male respondents in our sample, 71% lived in the same household with their parents after marriage. In striking contrast, 49% of the married female respondents reported "never" seeing their parents after they were married, and another 13.5% reported seeing them only "seldom." Only 38% of the women reported seeing their parents "very often," and none lived in the same household with her parents after marriage (p ≤ .0001). Of those women who said they never saw their parents, 77% said that they were not permitted by their husbands to see them, and the other 23% said they lived too far away to visit. The parents may also contribute to this separation. Even if the marriage situation seems intolerable, the parents may avoid contact with their daughter and strictly forbid her to come back to them. One of the respondents describes this sort of situation:

> I tried to escape several times and went to my parents. But they sent me back saying, "Your place is with your husband. Don't ever come back again." They forced me into this mess for the bride price, and if I returned they would have to give the money back. Murder was inevitable in my case.

Another factor in the female offenders' relative dissatisfaction in marriage may be the very early ages at which they typically got married. Almost 68% of the married women in the sample were married between 11 and 15 years of age. That is to say, they were removed from their parents and placed in a potentially (or actually) stressful situation while still children. When this early-marriage group is compared with the group who married at age 16 or older on their contentment with home life, 68% of the early-marriage group, compared with 42% of the later marriage group, expresses unhappiness with home life and marriage.

That early marriage is a potent source of stress is testified to by the fact that 85% of the husband killings, 88% of the female murders originating in domestic quarrels, and 83% of the female murders for "aggressiveness" (removal of an unwanted person) were committed by offenders who were married before age 15.

The male and female homicide offenders, then, present very different patterns in their family relations. The men come from family backgrounds which they perceive as satisfactory, on the whole, and they also claim to have been happy with their married life. In 90% or more of the cases, there is nothing in their report of family relations which would indicate abnormality, disturbance, or stress in a degree which would drive them to murder. On the other hand, a substantial proportion of the women report feeling neglected as children; memories of parental discord; dissatisfaction with their married life; isolation from their parents; and dissatisfaction with being female. While the interview conducted in this study did not yield fine-grained information on family relations of the sort which would permit detailed diagnoses and analyses, there is plentiful evidence that women in this sample had been subjected to many different kinds of stress, in many cases severe, and in many cases beginning in early childhood. It would seem that this group would have been in any case at high risk for some form of deviancy or delinquency.

Attitude Toward the Murder

The homicide offenders were asked whether they regretted or felt remorseful over having committed murder. Of the men, 92% reported that they had felt regret or remorse, while only 8% denied having such feelings. In contrast, only 24% of the women reported regret or remorse, and 76% denied having such feelings (p ≤ .0001). These findings are consistent with those on premeditation and intention to kill.

The offenders were also asked what they would do if faced with the same situation again. Twenty percent of the men, but 48% of the women, indicated that they would resort to murder again under the same circumstances. Slightly over a third of both groups (38% of the men, 36% of the women) said they would not kill if faced with the same situation again. An equally large group of men (36%) reported that they would migrate rather than murder, given the same circumstances, but only 6% of the women saw migration as an alternative solution to their problems. These sex differences are again highly significant (p ≤ .0001) and indicate that while a very large majority of the men believe that some course of action other than killing might be open to them under the same circumstances, approximately half of the women believe that their act of murder was in some way inevitable.

Two Representative Cases

At this point we would like to present two cases from the sample, one male and one female, each of which exemplifies rather fully the characteristics found to be typical of their groups.

A Representative Male Homicide Offender

This young man, to whom we will give the pseudonym Halil, was born to peasant parents in a village in Elazığ. His father was a barely literate farmer, and his mother an illiterate housewife. He was the second of seven children. His elder brother helped their father with the farm work, but after graduation from primary school, Halil and his other two brothers worked in factories. His sisters married and left the village. For six years he worked in Istanbul, returing to the village from time to time to help his father.

In his spare time he frequented the coffeehouse but stayed away from drinking and gambling.

He was brought up in what he considered to be a harmonious home atmosphere which was seldom a scene to quarrels or disputes. In general he was on good terms with his parents and other relatives.

When Halil was 23, he abducted a girl from his village, with her consent. After two days, he was caught and arrested. However, his family gave money to the girl's family as a bride price and the two families reconciled, allowing him to be set free and to marry the girl. After their marriage, he and his wife went to Malatya, where he worked as a construction worker for eight months. Then, upon his father's request, he went back to his village to help out on the farm.

Fifteen days after his return to the village, while he was out grazing the cattle with a friend, he was ambushed by his brother-in-law, who appeared ready to attack with the ax he had in his hand. Knowing his brother-in-law's strength and capabilities, Halil panicked and fired his rifle when the attacker was about five meters away. He thought the victim was wounded and asked his friend to take him to the doctor. Halil immediately went to the police and surrendered.

Halil reported that he was shocked and felt remorseful over his action. Since the murder was committed in self-defense and without the intention to kill, he was sentenced to only eight years' imprisonment.

A Representative Female Homicide Offender

This young woman, whom we shall call Kezban, was born in a village in Ödemiş. Her father, who had an elementary school education, worked as an electrician and construction worker, as well as working intermittently on the family's farm. Her mother, who was illiterate, worked on the farm. Her grandmother, who lived with them, helped with the household chores. Kezban had one brother, who was a small shop owner living in Ödemiş, and four sisters. After graduating from elementary school, she helped her parents with the farm work.

Kezban described her father as being a very nice person, but said that her mother was nervous and indifferent toward her. The family did not have close relations with other relatives.

At age 16, Kezban married an unemployed high school graduate from Ödemiş, without her father's consent. For the first two years following the marriage, the young couple lived with the husband's parents, with whom Kezban was on good terms. Meanwhile, three children were born to the couple—two daughters and a son.

Upon Kezban's continuous insistence that he find a job, her husband became a police officer and was assigned to Izmir. After six months, a new assignment took them to Antalya. Kezban reported that, although her husband had been relatively nice to her in the first years, after they left Ödemiş and he became self-supporting, he started drinking, gambling, and neglecting her. He began to have mistresses and to bring them home with him. To cap all this, one day he brought a young girl home and raped her there. After this incident, Kezban warned her husband that if he brought women to their house again she would kill him. He replied that he would do anything he wished and that she had no right to interfere.

On the day of the murder there was a long quarrel between them about his cruelty and malevolence toward her and the children. During the quarrel he beat her and threatened her with his gun. That night she decided to kill him. While he was sleeping she took his gun and shot him. Then, in a frenzy and losing all self-control, she stabbed him a number of times with a knife from the kitchen.

Immediately after the killing she went to the police and gave herself up. She reported no feelings of guilt or remorse, and still thinks that he deserved to be killed.

Comparison of the Cases

These two cases exemplify virtually all of the differences which the data have shown to distinguish the male and female homicide offender groups. To begin with demographic characteristics, Kezban can be considered higher SES than Halil: her elementary school-educated father had a trade in addition to farming, and her brother was a shopkeeper in town, while Halil's father was a barely literate farmer. Halil attained an elementary school education but remained at the level of blue collar laborer. Kezban also attained an elementary school education—somewhat unusual for a village girl—and married a man with a high school education who became a policeman. Kezban is also more mobile than Halil (or at least more permanently mobile): although Halil worked for several years in Istanbul, the village remained his home base, and he eventually returned to it, while Kezban migrated with her husband on a permanent basis and indeed experienced a move between cities as well as from village to city.

As to family background, Halil's reports are of a basically harmonious and satisfying family life, both before and after marriage, whereas Kezban recalls maternal indifference and a general isolation of her family from the wider kinship circle, and reports a radical disintegration of her relationship with her husband.

With regard to the murders themselves, typical differences again show themselves. Halil killed a relative with a single shot out on the fields, in self defense (a normative motive), without premeditation and without intent to kill. Following the murder he was contrite and remorseful. In contrast, Kezban killed her husband in their home following a violent quarrel, after having decided definitely to kill him. She carried out the murder in an extremely violent manner and felt no remorse afterwards, but rather felt her act was justified.

Conclusion

Looking at the data presented in this paper, one can see two quite different patterns in the making of a murderer.

The first pattern is primarily a male pattern and fits relatively well the expectations derived from the subculture of violence theory. The men in this sample were not in any conventional sense a troubled, delinquent, or criminal group. On the contrary, most were quite ordinary peasants or farm workers, who reported no significant family problems either in their childhood or adult lives. In most cases they killed on the spur of the moment, when threatened with physical attack, loss of honor, or possible loss of property, and frequently without a clear intention to kill. Their victims were for the most part outside the immediate family household and were confronted and killed in public places.

It would seem that murders of this type stem primarily from the normative system (honor), and its concomitant ideals (the vigilant, aggressive male), expectations (violent response to threat), and possibilities (firearms ready at hand). To be sure, some murders by men do not fit this pattern; but the fact that such a large proportion of them do fit it suggests that the high homicide rate in Turkey (which after all reflects primarily male murders) might be lowered by actions and policies directed at suitable aspects of the normative system rather than by interventions at the individual or family level. Strict gun control and stiffer penalties for blood feud and honor crimes, for instance, might disrupt the operation of the normative system at the most concrete level. More basic changes in the system are probably not within the province of policy and official action, but it may be predicted that the social changes

Turkey is now undergoing will undermine the traditional honor-centered system (as has already happened to a large extent in the cities) and eventually replace it with another system of values, possibly one less conducive to individual violence.

The second pattern, which is primarily a female pattern, is very different from the first. This second pattern has little relation to the normative system. Indeed, even the murders in defense of honor to some degree contravene the traditional expectation that the men of a family will protect and defend their women's *namus*. Rather, the female murders seem to represent an extreme reaction to extreme stress of various kinds.

One type of stress is indicated by the relatively high incidence of complaints of parental neglect in childhood. An unusually large proportion of the women in the sample were either adopted or were raised by a stepmother, which in itself may indicate potential psychological problems. However, these comprised only about half of those who felt they were neglected; the other half recalled parents who were too indifferent or too busy quarrelling to pay enough attention to their children—also a potential source of psychological strain.

A second type of stress is what we might call uprooting, which takes a variety of forms. Very early marriage is a prime example, and we have seen some of its pernicious effects in the foregoing discussion.

Another type of uprooting, more common among female than male murderers, can result from geographical mobility (i.e., rural-urban migration). Migration to the city inevitably calls into question at least some parts of the traditional culture into which the migrant has been socialized. In the relative absence of community sanctions and control, the individual may become confused and fail to meet the normative expectations of his/her traditional culture. In this connection it is worth noting that over 60% of the women who murdered in rural areas did so from normative motives (mostly honor), while only 38% of urban female murderers had normative motives. Of all the female murders committed for normative motives, 64% took place in rural areas, but only 36% in urban areas.

A third type of uprooting, which may be related to both early marriage and migration, is the sudden and total separation from parents imposed on the bride at marriage. Even if previous family relations have been less than satisfactory, this total separation, particularly at an early age, seems highly likely to trigger feelings of abandonment, helplessness, and resentment in the young woman.

Another type of stress may be, paradoxically, the relatively higher SES level of the female offenders. (Note that this interpretation can only be applied within narrow limits; virtually no murders were committed by middle class and upper class women.) Since her relative advantage in SES generally depends on her husband's educational or occupational characteristics rather than her own, the female murderer with relatively high SES may be suffering from yet another type of uprooting. On the other hand, a relative rise in SES may make a woman more conscious of her subordinate position and may make her aware that resistance and combat may be alternatives to passive endurance of intolerable pressures. Yet another possibility is that, with increase in SES (within limits), the man loses his ability to function as a traditional protector since that role would conflict with economic role in a more "rationalized" sector of the economy. Some respondents, in fact, reported being encouraged by their husbands to murder their molesters, since the husbands were afraid to risk their jobs or public employee status by carrying out the deed themselves. Thus, for a variety of reasons, a rise in SES may push a woman toward a more active defense of her own interests, including honor, with a resultant increased likelihood that murder may be one means of this defense.

In sum, we can say that the female murderer in Turkey, in comparison to her male counterpart, is usually from a more troubled background, has more personal and psychological problems, and has endured very high levels of stress which eventuate in personally motivated, premeditated, violent, and non-normative murder. Short-run measures, such as gun control, would be unlikely to have much effect on the incidence of this type of murder. On the other hand, strict enforcement of the laws forbidding child marriage and the institution of the bride price might do much to ameliorate some of the most distressing psychological strains rural women are subject to, and thus indirectly reduce the chances of perceiving homicide as the sole means of changing an intolerable situation. As in the case of men, it may be anticipated that social changes currently underway will do much to undermine traditional interaction patterns, normative expectations, and power relations. But it is as yet too early to predict the effects of those changes on the incidence or pattern of female homicide.

NOTES

[1]   This paper is based for the most part on an unpublished master's thesis presented to the Department of Social Sciences, Boğaziçi University in 1980 by Serap Özgür (Özgür, 1980).

[2]   The most recent year in which figures for Turkey are reported is 1961.

[3]   The prison sentence for honor crimes is rather light, however, typically four to six years, and cannot be considered a very strong deterrent to the maintenance of traditional norms. This situation may change in the near future, as there is a current move towards stiffer penalties for honor crimes.

[4]   In the original study (Özgür, 1980), a slightly different form of this argument was used as the basis for the prediction that women's murders would be more normative than men's. The direction of the prediction was reversed in this presentation to be congruent with the theoretical argument advanced here.

[5]   In order to avoid a proliferation of tables, data will be presented in the text insofar as possible. Where appropriate, all comparisons were tested for significance by the chi square test. In the interest of brevity, the data in some of the cells are omitted in this presentation. Where significance levels are given, however, it may be assumed that they apply to the full set of categories. For a full presentation of all frequencies and chi square levels, please see Özgür (1980).

[6]   In rural Turkey, adoption is more likely to reflect the adopting parents' desire for additional labor power than a psychologically-based desire to have a (another) child.

[7]   This preference for the male role among Turkish women is not restricted to homicide offenders, but has been found even among urban high school and university students (Toğrol, 1968).

BIBLIOGRAPHY

Ahuja, R. "Female Murderers in India: A Sociological Study," *Indian Journal of Social Work*. 1970, 31, 271-84.

Bagot, J.H. *Juvenile Delinquency: A Comparative Study of the Position in Liverpool and England and Wales*. London: Jonathan Cape, 1941.

Berkowitz, L. "Impulse, Aggression and the Gun," *Psychology Today*, Sept. 1960, 18-22.

Bohannon, P. *African Homicide and Suicide*.Princeton, N.J.: Princeton Univ. Press, 1960.

Bowker, L.H. "Women and Crime: An International Perspective." Paper presented at the Ninth World Congress of Sociology, Uppsala, Sweden, August 1978.

Çifter, I. "Direction of Aggression in Turkish Society." Paper presented at the Fifth National Congress of Neuropsychiatry, 1970.

Cole, K.E., S.S. Cole, and G. Fisher. "Women Who Kill," *Archives of General Psychiatry*, 1968, 19, 1-18.

Connor, W.D. "Criminal Homicide, USSR/USA: Reflections on Soviet Data in a Comparative Framework," *Journal of Criminal Law and Criminology*, 1973, 64, 1, 111-17.

Deiker, T.E. "Characteristics of Males Indicted and Convicted of Homicide," *Journal of Social Psychology*, 1974, 93, 151-52.

D.İ.E. (Devlet İstatistik Enstitüsü). State Institute of Statistics Publications, 1968-1977. Ankara: D.İ.E. Press.

Dönmezer, S. "Türk Toplumu Silahlanıyor mu?" (Is Turkish Society Getting Armed?) *Milliyet*, April 19, 1970.

Driver, E.D. "Interaction and Criminal Homicide in India," *Social Forces*, 1961, 40, 153-58.

Durkheim, E. *Le Suicide*. Trans. by George Simpson. New York: Free Press, 1951. Originally pub. Paris: Alean, 1897.

Ergil, D.A. "Sociological Analysis of Honor Crimes in Turkey," *ODTU Gelişme Dergisi/METU Studies in Development*, 1978, 12, 26-65.

Emovon, A.C. and T.A. Lambo. *A Survey of Criminal Homicide in Nigeria*. Ibadan: University of Ibadan Behavioral Science Research Unit, 1972.

Felthous, A.R. and B.Yudowitz. "Approaching a Comparative Typology of Assaultive Female Offenders," *Psychiatry*, Aug. 1977, 40.

Green, E. and R.P. Wakefield. "Patterns of Upper and Middle Class Homicide," *Journal of Criminal Law and Criminology*, 1979, 70, 2, 172-81.

Harlan, H. "Five Hundred Homicides," *Journal of Criminal Law and Criminology*, 1950, 40, 737-52.

Henry, A.F. and J.F. Short. *Suicide and Homicide*. Glencoe, Ill.: Free Press, 1954.

Kâğıtçıbaşı, Ç. *Cultural Values and Population Action Programs: Turkey*. Report prepared for UNESCO, 1977.

_____ . *Çocuğun Değeri: Türkiye'de Değerler ve Doğurganlık* (Value of Children: Values and Fertility in Turkey). Istanbul: Boğaziçi Univ. Press, 1981.

Karpat, K. *The Gecekondu: Rural Migration and Urbanization*. London: Cambridge University Press, 1976.

Kolars, J.F. "Community Studies in Rural Turkey," *Annals*, Association of American Geographers, 1962, 52, 4, 426-89.

Lunde, D.T. "Our Murder Boom," *Psychology Today*, 1975, 9, 35-42.

Meeker, M.E. "Meaning and Society in the Near East: Examples from the Black Sea Turks and the Levantine Arabs (I)," *International Journal of Middle East Studies*, 1976, 7, 3, 383-423.

Megargee, E.I. "Undercontrolled and Overcontrolled Personality Types in Extreme Antisocial Aggression," *Psychological Monographs*, 1960, 80, no. 611.

Monahan, T.P. "Family Status and the Delinquent Child: A Reappraisal and Some New Findings," *Social Forces,* 1957, 35, 250-58.

Moran, R. "Criminal Homicide: External Restraint and Subculture of Violence," *Criminology* 1971, 8, 357-74.

Morris, T. and L. Blom-Cooper. *Homicide, the Statistical Picture: A Calendar of Murder—Criminal Homicide in England Since 1957.* London: Michael Joseph, 1964.

Mushanga, M.T. *Criminal Homicide in Western Uganda: A Sociological Study of Violent Deaths in the Ankole, Kigeti, and Toro Districts of Western Uganda.* Unpublished M.A. thesis, Makerere Univ., Kampala, Uganda, 1970.

Newton, G.D. and F.E. Zimning. *Firearms and Violence in American Life.* Washington, D.C.: U.S. Government Printing Office, 1969.

Orban, P.T. "Social and Psychiatric Aspects of Female Crime," *Medicine, Science and the Law,* 1971, 11, 104-16.

Özbay, F. "Türkiye'de Kırsal/Kentsel Kesimde Eğitimin Kadınlar Üzerinde Etkisi" (Effects of Education on Women in Rural/Urban Areas in Turkey). In N. Abadan-Unat (ed.), *Türk Toplumunda Kadın* (Women in Turkish Society). Ankara: Türk Sosyal Bilimler Derneği, 1979.

Özgür, S. "Social Psychological Patterns in Homicide: A Comparison of Male and Female Inmates." Unpublished M.A. thesis, Boğaziçi Univ., 1980.

Palmer, S. *A Study of Murder.* New York: Crowell, 1960.

Peristiany, J.G. (ed.). *Honour and Shame: The Values of Mediterranean Society.* London: Weidenfeld and Nicolson, 1965.

Pitt-Rivers, J. "Honor and Social Status." In J.G. Peristiany (ed.), *Honour and Shame: The Values of Mediterranean Society.* London, Weidenfeld and Nicolson, 1965.

Rosenblatt, E. and C. Greenland. "Female Crimes of Violence," *Canadian Journal of Criminology and Corrections.* 1974, 16, 173-80.

Safilios-Rothschild, C. "Honour Crimes in Contemporary Greece," *British Journal of Sociology,* 1969, 20, 205-18.

Stirling, P. *Turkish Village.* New York: Wiley Science Editions, 1965.

Svalastoga, K. "Homicide and Social Contact in Denmark," *American Journal of Sociology,* 1956, 62, 37-41.

Şenyapılı, T. *Bütünleşmemiş Kentli Nüfus Sorunu* (The Problem of Unintegrated Urban Population). Ankara: Middle East Technical Univ. Press, 1978.

Tezcan, M. *Kan Gütme Olayları Sosyolojisi* (The Sociology of Blood Feuds). Ankara Univ. Faculty of Education Publications no. 24, 1972.

Toğrol, B. "Goals Chosen by Turkish Students in Response to Hypothetical Situations," *Istanbul University Studies in Experimental Psychology,* 1968, 6, 1-14.

Toro-Calder, J. *Personal Crimes in Puerto Rico.* Unpublished M.A. thesis, Univ. of Wisconsin, 1950.

Ünsal, A. "Kan Gütme Davaları" (Blood Feuds), *Cumhuriyet,* June 13-19, 1973.
Wattenberg, W.W. and F. Saunders. "Sex Differences Among Juvenile Offenders," *Sociology and Social Research.* 1954, 39, 24-31.
Wolfgang, M.E. *Patterns in Criminal Homicide.* Philadelphia: Univ. of Pennsylvania Press, 1958.
_____ and F. Ferracuti. *The Subculture of Violence.* London: Tavistock, 1967.
Yavuzer, H. *Ankara, İzmir ve Elazığ Çocuk Ceza ve İslah Evlerindeki Suçlu Çocukların Zekâ, Yakınçevre ve Kişilik Özellikleri Yönünden İncelenmesi Konusunda Deneysel Bir Araştırma* (An Experimental Investigation of Characteristics of Juvenile Delinquents in Reformatories in Ankara, İzmir,and Elazığ). Unpublished Docent thesis, Boğaziçi Univ., 1977.
Yücel, M. "Female Criminality," *Journal of Justice,* 1969, 60, 11.

CIVIL VIOLENCE IN TURKEY: ITS INFRASTRUCTURAL, SOCIAL AND CULTURAL FOUNDATIONS

Paul J. Magnarella

Shortly after the 12 September 1980 military takeover, General Kenan Evren, Turkey's Chief of the General Staff and President of the National Security Council, addressed his country saying, "In the course of the last two years, terrorism has caused 5,241 deaths and 14,152 wounded or disabled." He maintained that a "covered war" was being waged in Turkey "in utter disregard for any human consideration." For these and related reasons, "The Turkish Armed Forces have been obliged to take over the rule of the country in order to protect the unity of the nation and the country, to safeguard the fundamental rights of people. . . ." (Evren, 1980, p. 4).

Evren's depiction of Turkey's chaotic situation was not exaggerated. Acts of political violence between the radical right and left that affected everyone in-between had been accelerating during the late 1970s, reaching a crescendo in 1980.

Political terrorism was widespread in terms of Turkey's geography and the socioeconomic backgrounds of participants. In the absence of accurate official statistics, the Turkish publication *Briefing* surveyed available news sources to gauge the extent of civil violence during the months of February, March, and June, 1980. According to *Briefing*, there were 159 political murders in February spread over 27 of Turkey's 67 provinces. This was regarded as a comparatively calm month because universities were on vacation. Still, however, "just under two-thirds of the victims were students or youths or young workers, and almost a third were official figures or professional people, lawyers and policemen, being the two groups apparently most at risk" (*Briefing*, 10 March 1980). In March, the figures rose to 182 murders in 36 provinces, and in June they reached 224 murders in 40 provinces. *Briefing* added that the death toll only represented the tip of the iceberg. "Bombings, shootings, explosions are far more frequent than outright murder. . . . many of the terrorist movements, although rejected by the population as a whole, appear to be able to retain a substantial following among the young" (*ibid.*).

With respect to the socioeconomic backgrounds of those involved in civil violence, little is definitely known. To my knowledge, the only data available to the public were collected by journalist Emin Çölaşan, who administered a brief questionnaire to 287 political militants (125 leftists and 162 rightists) being held in Ankara's Kapalı Prison in late 1978. The results of this admittedly un-scientific sample were presented in *Milliyet* (18-21 April 1979) and again in Ergil (1980). The data revealed only small differences between leftists and rightists with respect to age, income, place of birth, occupation, and education. The large majority of both groups was under 25 years of age. Over a third were born in villages; about 30% were born in provincial capitals. Over 60% had spent the greater part of their lives in either Ankara, Istanbul or Izmir, and about half were *lise* (high school) and university students before entering prison. Although the inmates' families come from a wide range of income levels, it appears that the sample contained a larger proportion of low income families than the population as a whole.

On the basis of these data, we cannot conclude that left-wing militants are uniquely different from right-wing militants with respect to age, residence, occupation, or income characteristics. Both are discontent, generally young people who are committed to violent action as an appropriate means of political change. The data showing that 72% of the rightists and 64% of the leftists were living with their families and an additional 3% of each were living with relatives at the time of their imprisonment offer little support for the claim that "family breakdown" is a major cause of youth violence.

Back in the early 1970s, when I was studying tradition and change in Turkey, I wrote that Turkey was experiencing the genesis of a mass culture of material aspirations nurtured by the mass media and greater exposure to the lifestyle of the industrially advanced West.

> A tide of aspirations, swelling beyond the consumption limits imposed by the local economy, has created, what I call, a 'Culture of Discontent,'

characterized by manifest dissatisfaction with locally available income and consumption opportunities and a pressing desire to abandon Susurluk and even Turkey in pursuit of a 'better life'." (Magnarella, 1974, p. 180).

Turkey's recent situation was derived in part from this Culture of Discontent, which had been intensified under worsening economic and political conditions. In this chapter, I will offer a theory of civil violence and briefly outline some of the major economic, demographic, socio-cultural, political, and psychological factors contributing to civil violence in Turkey.

Relative Deprivation

In a significant article entitled "Psychological Factors in Civil Violence," political scientist Ted Robert Gurr maintained that the most systematically developed and empirically supported psychological theory explaining human aggression was frustration-aggression theory. He also argued that "many of the variables and relationships identified in social psychological research on the frustration-aggression relationship appear to underlie the phenomenology of civil violence" (1972, p. 36). Building on that theory, he proposed the framework of a general theory of the conditions that determine the likelihood and magnitude of civil violence. His basic premise was that:

> the necessary precondition for violent civil conflict is relative deprivation, defined as actors' perception of discrepancy between their *value expectations* and their environment's apparent value *capabilities*. Value expectations are the goods and conditions of life to which people believe they are justifiably entitled. The referents of value capabilities are to be found largely in the social and physical environment: they are the conditions that determine people's perceived chances of getting or keeping the values they legitimately expect to attain. (Gurr, 1972, pp. 37-38).

Gurr also previously wrote:

> The primary causal sequence in political violence is first the development of discontent, second the politicization of that discontent, and finally its actualization in violent action against political objects and actors. Discontent arising from the perception of relative deprivation is the basic, instigating condition for participants in collective violence. (1970, pp. 12-13).

Many social scientists have accepted Gurr's basic assumption that relative deprivation makes civil violence probable. Samuel Huntington (1971) adds that the modernization process of transitional societies intensifies relative deprivation by widening the gap between increasing aspirations and relatively inadequate capabilities, owing to insufficient levels of employment, production, and government resources.

A Theory of Civil Violence of Terrorism

Below I offer the outline of a theory of civil violence and terrorism fashioned after Gurr's, but with additions and modifications (especially infrastructural and ideological), that I believe apply to Turkey and other countries. I begin by altering Gurr's causal sequence as follows: The primary causal sequence in civil violence and terrorism is first the existence of infrastructural and perceptual (interpretative informational) conditions leading to the development of discontent; second, the acceptance of ideologies condemning those conditions creating discontent and advocating violent action to alter the conditions; third, violtent action. The more widespread and intense the above conditions, the more probable will be widespread and intense civil violence.

The infrastructural conditions would include the existence of:

1) a population size exceeding available economic opportunities;

2) marked differences in the distribution of wealth and "quality of life" goods and services among the population;

3) an insecure economic situation for many or most citizens, consisting of such factors as marked growth in inflation, high unemployment and underemployment, and no concrete signs of improvement in the near or intermediate future;

4) great demand for, but limited access to educational opportunities;

5) an inefficient, incompetent, ineffectual, corrupt and/or despotic government either incapable of or unwilling to devote substantial talent and resources to the solution of the above problems.

The perceptual conditions would include the perception on the part of a significantly large part of the population that:

1) it enjoys proportionally less of the country's economic and "quality of life" opportunities than others do;

2) other countries, especially neighboring countries, are enjoying much more economic and "quality of life" success than their own;

3) their government is either incapable of or unwilling to devote the requisite talent and resources to the solution of these problems;

4) given the prevailing socioeconomic and political arrangement, there is little or no hope for improvement in the near or intermediate future;

5) existing ideologies that condemn marked socioeconomic inequities and legitimize violent means for addressing the situation are valid.

A test of this theory would require the examination of a large number of cases to determine whether the specified infrastructural-perceptual conditions are highly associated with civil violence. Rather than provide such a test here, I offer a brief case study of the Turkish situation, which documents the concomitance of the specified infrastructural-perceptual conditions and civil violence as well as their parallel intensification.

Infrastructural and Perceptual Conditions

Population. Turkey's population has grown rapidly since World War I. It was only 13.6 million in 1927, but reached 20.9 million in 1950, 27.8 million in 1960, 35.6 million in 1970, and 45.4 million in 1980. The yearly growth rate during the 1960s and 1970s averaged 2.5%; in recent years about 1 million new people have been added to the country's population annually. Since the 1950s, Turkey's major urban populations have been increasing at about twice the national average, as many rural people abandon their villages in search of a better life in the cities.

Unfortunately, Turkey has not been able to provide basic health, housing, fuel, and related needs to much of her existing citizenry, not to mention the million plus expected annually. Relative deprivation is markedly visible in the *gecekondus* (shanty-towns) of most major cities. Over half the people of greater Ankara, Istanbul, and Izmir are gecekondu residents. Mango writes:

> the all-pervading bureaucracy has not been able to enforce a minimum of town planning, and the majority of urban Turks live in Jerry-built concrete jungles, without parks or open spaces, with polluted air to breathe—often one large slum punctuated by oases of bearable living, which seems to those outside them, as havens of luxury. Rapid change . . . has produced a social as well as economic crisis. The sheer misery of living . . . has bred radicalism. . . . (1979, p. 30).

In an August, 1980 interview, Istanbul mayor Kotil claimed that between 250,000 and 350,000 new people are added annually to Istanbul's population, then estimated at 5.5 million. The increases aggravate the city's already serious housing, employment and transportation problems. According to the mayor, terrorist organizations easily recruit gunmen from among the jobless in the gecekondus. One such gecekondu, Gültepe, had an unemployment rate of 25% and had experienced about 100 murders by both right- and left-wing terrorists since 1977 (Howe, 26 August 1980). A *New York Times* (13 August 1980) interview with Ankara's mayor, Ali Dinçer, produced a similar story. The mayor estimated that 70% of Ankara's 2.5 million inhabitants resided in gecekondu districts. He claimed that 50 to 60 of these districts were organized into "liberated zones" under the control of either left- or right-wing militants. These are areas in which government authority is ineffectual and access is limited to partisans. In February, 1980, the Istanbul newspaper *Hürriyet* claimed that 31 of Turkey's 67 provinces contained such "liberated zones."

Income Distribution. Available statistics for 1973 demonstrate that Turkey's income is very unevenly distributed, with only 27.4% of its households receiving 65% of the national income, while the remaining 72.6% of households get only 35%. The 1973 situation, as illustrated in Table 1, most probably persisted to 1980.

Table 1
Turkey's 1973 Income Distribution

Income Groups (in T.L.)	Households %	Income %
0- 5,000	12.2	01.5
5,000- 10,000	17.8	05.4
10,000- 15,000	20.0	10.1
15,000- 25,000	22.5	17.9
25,000- 50,000	18.1	25.4
50,000-100,000	06.8	18.6
100,000+	02.5	21.0

Source: *Turkey Almanac 1978* (Ankara: The Daily News, 1978) p. 178.

Unemployment, Foreign Work, and Labor Strikes. Turkey's employment situation steadily worsened during the second half of the 1970s. By early 1980, unemployment reached 20%, with underemployment certainly higher. Turkey's demographic-economic structure contained dangerous internal disjunctions. Due to rapid population growth, each year the number of new persons entering the labor market is about twice the number of new employment opportunities. That is, the work force has been increasing at about twice the rate of job opportunities, resulting in the addition of several hundred thousand new unemployed each year (*Milliyet*, 23 November 1979).

During the sixties and early seventies, labor migration to Europe appeared to provide a partial safety valve, as over a million Turks acquired jobs and more consumptive life styles in industrially advanced and economically successful countries. However, the demonstration effect associated with these experiences abroad added even greater demand pressures to Turkey's economy and government. Returning workers and their families demanded more consumer goods and government services; they bid up the prices of what was available, and expressed dissatisfaction with local work and living conditions.

Since the 1973-74 oil crisis, many European countries have experienced declining economic growth rates, and consequently have ceased importing large numbers of foreign workers. West Germany, the largest and, in many respects, the most attractive European employer of Turks, had (officially) 514,000 Turkish workers there in 1978, as compared with 605,000 in 1973 (*Milliyet*, 23 November 1979). As a result, many Turks who were nurturing the hope of eventually migrating to Europe for work became discouraged, disappointed, and resentful of a lost opportunity.

During the two years prior to the military takeover, over 120,000 Turks reportedly had requested asylum in Europe, especially in West Germany (Munir, 1980). Ironically, most of these people were not political extremists at odds with the Turkish government, but moderates who feared the Turkish government's inability to ensure their physical and economic security. European officials claim that many were essentially seeking economic asylum.

While not having a job and income is certainly miserable, many Turkish workers with jobs have shown that they are far from content with wages and working conditions. In recent years, Turkey's manufacturing industry has been hit by frequent and often violent strikes. As Table 2 shows, strikes increased by 371% over the 1974-77 period, and the corresponding number of man-work days lost jumped by 1,229%.

The first half of 1980 was another period of intensified strike activity. The Istanbul-based newspaper *Cumhuriyet* (10 June 1980) reported that as of 6 June 1980, 47,662 workers in various industries were on strike affecting 203 places of business. Of these, 41,735

Table 2
Turkish Labor Strikes

Number	1974	1975	1976	1977	% Increase 1974–77
Strikes	45	90	105	167	371
Workers involved	21,046	25,389	32,899	59,889	284
Man-work days lost ('000)	470.1	1,102.7	1,768.2	5,778.2	1,229

Source: *Türkiye Istatistik Yıllığı 1979 (Turkish Statistics Yearbook, 1979)*, p. 168.

workers (affecting 175 work places) were engaged in strikes organized by DISK (Confederation of Revolutionary Worker Unions), a politicized left-wing confederation which advocated the nationalization of all foreign trade, private banking and insurance; a complete redistribution of land; and a planned economy to improve the workers' lot (Landau, 1974, p. 93).

Inflation. According to the July, 1980 report of *Foreign Economic Trends,*

> The decade of the seventies has been a period of rising inflation in Turkey. At about seven percent in 1970, the rate of increase in prices had accelerated to 15-20 percent by 1975-76. In 1978 inflation approached 60%, and last year the Ankara Consumer Price Index increased by 72%, that for Istanbul grew by 82%, [and] the [national] Wholesale Price Index went up by 81%. (p. 6).

Inflation estimates for 1979 and the first half of 1980 reached 100% and beyond.

Turkish citizens have responded angrily. Government imposed price increases on various goods and services in February, 1980 were met with especially bitter protests. Leftist militants seized a half-dozen food trucks in Istanbul and distributed the contents to gecekondu residents. Ferryboat users refused to pay the 100% increase in tickets. In Ankara, militants plundered several supermarkets and several hundred student sympathizers of the anarchist Revolutionary Way burned an effigy of Prime Minister Süleyman Demirel while chanting slogans against the price increases. In Izmir, workers from a state-owned thread factory protested the government's economic policy by forcing some shops to close, blocking traffic, and cutting electricity, water, and transports to some sections of the city (Howe, 11 February 1980).

Coupled with this astronomical inflation at home was a marked decline in the value of the Turkish Lira (TL) on international money markets. From 1971 to December 1980, the Turkish Lira had been devaluated a total of 650% against the U. S. dollar. Whereas the dollar purchased TL 14 in 1971, it purchased TL 89.7 in December, 1980.

These devaluations and the reasons for them had at least two consequences of importance to the present analysis. For one, they meant that the cost of attractive import goods and many locally manufactured items, such as appliances, cars, even chemical fertilizers (all of which contain imported components), skyrocketed out of the reach of many disappointed consumers. The shortage of foreign exchange, which helped bring on the devaluations, meant that many basic necessities normally imported for Turkey's industry, such as petroleum, machinery, spare parts, and raw materials fell in short supply. Such import shortages, coupled with a local shortage of electric power, meant that Turkey's industry had to operate at between 40-60% below its capacity. This condition impacted negatively on the continually worsening job market.

Education. According to Turkish scholar Sherif Mardin (1978) and others (e.g., Szyliowicz, 1972; Cohn, 1970), the public's demand for education over the past quarter century created such a burden on the state-supported school system that educational quality was downgraded. Overcrowded classrooms, poorly paid instructors (some of whom were unqualified), a stress on memorization rather than experimentation, extremely limited individual student attention, etc., became characteristic of education throughout much of the system. The consequences were especially acute at the potentially volatile *lise* and university levels. In Turkey the university diploma is the key (but not the guarantee) to the world of attractive jobs; for many it is the minimal requirement for advancement in life. Mardin (1978, p. 250) writes: "In 1977, 360,000 students competed in the entrance examination to universities for 60,000 places. This leaves 300,000 candidates suspended in mid-stream, with no means of reintegrating them into the employment structure except as disgruntled minor employees with salaries that constitute a pittance by any standards." These people become recruitment targets for extremist groups.

Even many of those who earn diplomas are suspended and discontent. Back in 1970, University of Istanbul sociologist Muzaffer Sencer described a situation which still persists:

> This problem, Turkey's education-economic crisis, may be summarized as a massive swelling of students in various branches of higher education, wholly disproportionate with the needs of the community, and consequently, as an incapacity on the part of the graduates to hold their own without falling into the situation of "unemployed people with a diploma." In other words, those who graduate from institutions of higher education are for a large part incapable of finding the status and the work they deserve and thus face a situation in which their diplomas prove to be worthless. (1970, p. 12).

Many observations of student unrest in other parts of the world apply equally well to Turkey. For example, in his conclusions about student political activism in developing countries, Emmerson writes:

> In the university where underpaid, part-time professors lecture to anonymous crowds, where "education" means passing examinations and "learning" means cramming for them; where the student is unsupervised, unstimulated, and finally, unrewarded—under these conditions, student unrest is almost inevitable. (Emmerson, 1968, p. 401).

And although he is speaking specifically of Latin America, the following by Clutterbuck (1975, p. 23) could well refer to Turkey:

> Latin America remained the most active theatre for the urban guerilla, largely because of the rapid expansion of the cities and of the educational system to cope with it. Many young people emerged from universities with an awareness of the inequalities in their societies, but saw no avenues open to them in the existing systems for rectifying them. In nations with a long tradition of violence and *machismo*, some of them joined urban guerilla groups whose aims extended to exerting pressure for internal political change. . . .

Exposure. There are many indices of exposure, awareness and aspirational development. Some of them, like foreign work and formal education, have already been touched on. Here, I refer to education again. Over the decades, the Turkish government has made strenuous efforts to democratize education by making it available to more and more citizens. The growth in student numbers has been impressive. Looking at only the two ends of the educational continuum, primary school student enrollments jumped from less than a million in 1940-41 to about 5.5 million in 1977-78, while higher education enrollments rose from only 13,000 to a staggering 346,000.

The increases in radios and televisions have been equally meteoric. The number of registered radios grew from less than 100,000 prior to World War II to 4.3 million in 1977, while registered televisions skyrocketed from under 4,000 in 1971 to over 2.5 million in 1977.

Finally, the number of Turks who travelled outside the country for purposes either of tourism, education, pilgrimage or work increased steadily from one-half million in 1970 to 1.24 million in 1976. The vast majority travelled to countries whose standard of living exceeded that of Turkey. Turkey's 1977 Gross National Product per capita of $1,110 compared unfavorably with the $4,810 average for Europe and the $2,950 average for the Middle East (*1979 World Bank Atlas*). Hence, in whatever direction Turks looked, whether to the industrially-advanced West or to the oil-rich Arab South, they witnessed greater economic success. Being a proud people, many Turks were quick to develop and accept conspiracy theories to explain these observed differences. Why else would they be in such a comparatively dismal condition?

The foregoing briefly documents the intensification in recent years of Turkey's deep infrastructural (economic and demographic) problems. The situation is worsened by the Turks' growing demand for goods and services and by their government's inability either to solve the infrastructural problems or to meet increasing citizen demands. These conditions, along with the "demonstration effect" (witnessing greater economic success in other countries), have contributed to a severe state of relative deprivation on the part of many Turks. Even though they are discontent, the majority still hope for peaceful remedies. A significantly large and diffuse minority, however, have chosen the road of civil violence.

The next section briefly discusses some of those ideological organizations that condemn Turkey's socioeconomic condition and advocate change by violent means. It also comments on those aspects of traditional Turkish culture which predispose many Turks to violence.

Ideologies

There has been no shortage of persons and groups advocating political ideologies and methods (ranging from legal to violent) to rectify Turkey's social and economic problems. The most popular, legitimate political parties have been the left-of-center Republican People's Party and the right-of-center Justice Party. In recent years neither has been able to win a parliamentary majority, and the resulting coalitions have been largely ineffectual. Neither party advocates violence.

Over the past dozen years, a growing number of Turkish workers have been opting for more activist and socialist solutions to their own conditions. In terms of membership, one of the two largest labor confederations is DISK, which split from the moderate, "above politics," *Türk-İş* confederation in 1967 in order to politicize workers and advocate socialism. As of June 6, 1980, 88% of Turkey's total 47,662 striking workers were DISK members.

Prior to the 1980 military takeover there were reportedly over 50 extremist organizations operating in Turkey. The leftists were largely divided into pro-Moscow and pro-Maoist factions that fought among themselves as well as against the right and whomever else got in the way. Some of them made appeals to minorities in Turkey such as the Alevis and Kurds. The Turkish newspaper *Günaydın* (3 May 1977) described a number of these organizations "who are initiating incidents and writing their slogans everywhere from Fatih's cannon to Barbarossa's tomb to the walls of mosques." The following examples are taken from *Günaydın*.

Dev-Genç (Turkish Revolutionary Youth Federation) was originally organized in 1969 by Marxist students at Ankara University. Its goal is to educate the people in revolutionary action by conducting mass demonstrations. It maintains the following: the Soviet Union is not imperialist, just revisionist; local capitalists have joined hands with the imperialists to form an oligarchic dictatorship; the Kurdish people in the East are being oppressed; there is no need for Turkey to go through the process of national democratic revolution; the only way is revolution.

The organization's wall slogans include: "War of liberation against imperialism and oligarchy," "The only way is revolution," "Stop national oppression in the East."

One of the groups to grow out of *Dev-Genç* is the THKP-C (Turkish People's Liberation Party Front), originally led from Istanbul by Mahir Çayan, who died in 1972. It claims that socialist revolution in Turkey may be realized only through armed rebellion; that guerilla-type combat in the cities is necessary to create revolutionary terror and destroy the bourgeoisie, just as it did in parts of Latin America.

At least eight 'non-aligned' Marxist terrorist groups lay claim to the Çayan heritage, including the THKP-C Marxist Leninist Armed

Propaganda Unit whose members are accused of 35 murders, including several American servicemen. Much of this group was captured by Turkish authorities in Istanbul in February, 1980. Other groups include *Dev Sol* (Revolutionary Left) and *Kurtuluş* (Liberation), both with strong followings in Ankara's gecekondu areas.

One of the most important groups on the right is the young militant, anti-communist "grey wolves" supported by Alpaslan Türkeş's National Action Party (*Milliyetçi Hareket Partisi*). They advocate armed combat to stop the spread of communism in Turkey, and have combated leftists on university campuses and elsewhere. They call for the liberation of Turks living outside of Turkey under communist rule and for the consolidation of all Turkish people into one nation-state. They oppose birth control and envision a Turkey of 100 million population.

Other rightist groups supporting the same causes are TIT (Turkish Revenge Brigade) and ETKO (Captive Turks Liberation Army). Rightist organizations with a more religious bent include IKO (Islam Liberation Army) and TIB (Turkish Islamic Unit). According to *Briefing* (10 March 1980), the left outstrips the right by at least four to one both in terms of adherents and activities.

Hence, persons disillusioned with the regular political parties may choose from among a variety of extremist organizations offering either Marxist-Leninist, religious, or racial solutions to Turkey's problems.

Cultural Contributions

In addition to the infrastructural and ideological contributions to civil violence, there may be cultural ones. In the case of Turkey, many observers have commented on the positive value for violence under certain conditions inherent in traditional Turkish culture. Recently, Ankara University political scientist Doğu Ergil (1980) has offered an argument and analysis along these lines. He maintains there are two fundamental sources of violence in Turkish culture and society: (1) crimes of honor (*namus cinayeti*) and (2) blood feud. Both have their roots in rural society where limited economic possibilities often place individuals and groups in a position of intense competition and where official authorities are remote and alien. Consequently people have developed self-sufficient mechanisms to protect their families from enemies.

Namus refers to the honor associated with female sexual purity. The *namus* of a family is dependent on the sexual purity of its women. A family cannot possess degrees of it; they are either *namuslu* (honorable) or not. *Şeref* is social honor which one can earn and add to by behaving in accordance with societal norms. A *şerefli* (honorable) person protects the *namus* of his family and reacts aggressively against those who either threaten or stain it. A person's and a family's prestige in society is largely dependent on his/their *şeref* and *namus*.

Attacks on a family's sexual purity may be either physical or verbal. In such cases, it is primarily the responsibility of family males to retaliate. The ideal male is brave, unbending, aggressive, and determined to win. In matters of honor, he is quick to take offense. In cases of intense competition, he regards defeat as worse than death. Mardin (1978) maintains that Turkish families socialize their children to be warriors, with aggressive tendencies to be directed against any available outgroup. He endorses anthropologist Paul Stirling's depiction of the Turkish village as a "chip-on-the-shoulder" society. On the basis of research, the social psychologist Çiğdem Kâğıtçıbaşı (1970) concludes that a general dogmatic or intolerant behavior tendency, termed "core authoritarianism," is closely associated with early socialization in rural Turkish families.

In Turkey's rural areas, gun ownership and use are common. Ergil (1980) argues that the gun has become symbolic of the male sexual organ: using it is equivalent to asserting one's masculinity.

A crime of honor is a violence act one commits usually in retaliation against another who has threatened or stained one's women. The attack will be against the persons believed responsible for the threat or stain and against the women involved, if it is believed they were compliant.

Two examples of such honor crimes in Turkey were recently taken from Turkish newspapers and reported in the American press. One occurred in the southeastern Anatolian village of Gundikani. A 33 year old male and a 16 year old girl attempted to run off together, but were caught by the girl's family. Reportedly,

> family assemblies were held and the girl and man were tried and condemned to death without the intervention of state authorities. The man's head, arms, and legs were cut off and his body was thrown into the Tigris River. The girl was shot in the outskirts of the village (Howe, 26 February 1980).

In another case, "a young worker from the southern city of Adana was said to have killed his three sisters when he learned they had committed what he believed to be indecent acts" (*ibid.*). In cases of stained *namus*, the resulting aggression can be directed both inside and outside the family.

Ergil argues that crimes of honor are essentially a rural tradition transported to the cities by rural migrants. He supports his argument with data on 273 crimes of honor which occurred between 1970 and 1975 in Istanbul, Ankara, and Izmir—Turkey's three major cities. Of these crimes, 89% were committed by lower class persons, who had migrated to gecekondu areas from villages.

With respect to crimes in general, national statistics appear to support an even broader thesis than that proposed by Ergil. For example, in 1971 the percentage of men with rural occupations such as farmer, logger, etc. who were convicted of and imprisoned for crimes was almost five times larger than the percentage of men with such occupations in the national population (*Türkiye İstatistik Yıllığı*, 1979, pp. 123, 152).

The tradition most frequently commented on in connection with Turkey's civil violence is the blood feud. Mardin (1978, p. 231) writes:

> Student violence, by and large, is directed against other students. The pattern of attack, retaliation, revenge, and counter-offensive in which groups are involved is reminiscent of the blood feud in its regularity, symmetry and inevitability. . . .

In a similar vein, *Briefing* (10 March 1980, pp. 8-9) writes:

> The spate of political murders in Turkey has to be seen partly in the context of a fairly long history of blood feuding and local violence between rival families, factions, and communities.

A particular danger of the political blood feud is its self-perpetuating quality. Once initiated, it can continue for decades, as the revenge obligation is passed from brother to brother, father to son. Mario Modiano (1980) has commented on the blood feud in connection with the instigation of inter-ethnic and inter-sectarian antagonism for political purposes:

> Political extremists sought to exploit these revolutionary frustrations [of conflicting ideologies and rising expectations] by triggering the mechanisms of social, religious, and ethnic rivalry latent in the clan system that is still part of the main fabric of Turkish society. The politicians may now be losing control of the warring minorities, as the chain of violence becomes self-sustaining through the deep-rooted

tradition of the blood feud. And it is there that lie the potential seeds of a full civil war.

A third element of importance to the recruitment and activities of militant organizations is the peer group. In small towns and villages, especially, unisexual peer groups (resembling age-sets) are common. They are tightly knit and provide members with a great deal of social and emotional support. Such peer group relations can last almost a lifetime if the group is not divided by geographical separation. Young people with rural backgrounds who find themselves in the city feel a need to belong to a supportive peer group, and many join groups which carry an extremist political ideology. Often times the personal attachments are more important than the particular political ideology involved.

The case of V. C. Oduncu, a 17 year-old rural migrant to Ankara who was on trial for seven counts of murder in March of 1979, illustrates this point well. The report of his testimony and the prosecutor's remarks go as follows:

> In his testimony to the military prosecutor, released to the press, Oduncu said, "One day I was sitting in a coffee house in Salihli, a small southwestern town with two friends. A group came in. They beat us up with clubs and chains. Later I discovered that my friends were Idealists [members of one of the right-wing organizations] and that's why we were beaten. I became an Idealist too." The prosecutor's office said Oduncu was then charged with two assassinations of leftists and spent two years in jail. Released from prison, the prosecutor added, he joined his rightist friends again and acquired a gun. He was caught after allegedly robbing a jewelry shop and firing at a rival youth hostel. Last December, Oduncu escaped from prison with 12 others, the prosecutor said, adding that he allegedly was involved in five more assassinations until his recapture several weeks ago. Questioned about his political ideology, Oduncu was quoted as telling the prosecutor, "I am a rightist and I am opposed to leftists and communists. But I really don't know what rightist or leftist means" (*Gainesville Sun*, 14 March 1979).

Conclusion

As grave as Turkey's situation appears, it is not beyond remedy. Some of the major areas needing attention are obvious. Turkey must vigorously address its infrastructural problems. It must reduce the rate of population increase immediately and reach zero growth as soon as possible. Hopefully, Turkey has not already surpassed its optimum population size. Given its limited resource base, a Turkey of 100 million people as envisioned by the Grey Wolves, is an ill-advised goal.

Means should be developed to redistribute the nation's wealth more equitably. An effective land reform program coupled with greater government attention to the rural sectors would reduce urban migration and possibly even reduce the size of overcrowded cities. Rural life must be made more attractive. Elsewhere I have argued that Turkey's rejuvenation would be greatly facilitated by the development of a variety of postpeasantry socioeconomic styles in which labor-intensive agriculture is combined with light mechanization. Peasants have traditionally been associated with low levels of consumption and resource utilization. They can preserve and promote value systems and life-styles consonant with the coming age of increasing scarcity and conservation (Magnarella, 1979).

Needed also is a progressive tax reform which does not discourage or unduly penalize those private entrepreneurs who produce goods efficiently and provide satisfying work for many.

Consumer aspirations must be curbed. People should be discouraged from expecting goods and services that the country is incapable of providing to a large part of the population. Turkey must cease consuming more than it produces. In this connection, State Economic Enterprises must be operated more efficiently so as to produce more by reducing waste.

Turkey's politicians must begin giving the country a higher priority than they give their parties. More non-partisan cooperation in matters central to the nation's welfare must be exercised.

The main topics of this chapter—civil violence and its causes— have a discouraging and moribund quality. Fortunately, other qualities also comprise the Turkish scene. A number of years ago, I wrote:

> the idealized Turk is courageous, brave, and strong; moderate in all activities; respectful of the learned and elderly; loyal to kin and friends; guided by a keen sense of honor and shame; concerned with his and others' dignity; patient and enduring in the face of hardship; and generous, hospitable, and friendly (Magnarella, 1974, p. 165).

Contained in this description are many fine qualities upon which a secure, satisfying future can be built. Turkey, like many other developing countries, is facing a colossal challenge—one that is unprecedented in human history. The components and dynamics of today's problems are so unique that the paths to success traveled by the world's "arrived countries" no longer lead the way. New guides are needed. Those developing countries that discover new roads to economic achievement and political stability will become beacons to the world.

BIBLIOGRAPHY

Briefing. Ankara: 1980.

Clutterbuck, Richard. *Living with Terrorism.* New Rochelle: Arlington, 1975.

Cohn, E. J. *Turkish Economic, Social, and Political Change.* New York: Praeger, 1970.

Emmerson, Donald K., (ed.). "Conclusion." In *Students and Politics in Developing Nations.* New York: Praeger, 1968.

Ergil, Doğu. *Türkiye'de Terör ve Şiddet.* Ankara: Turhan Kitabevi, 1980.

Evren, Kenan. "The Statement of General Kenan Evren." Mimeograph distributed by the Turkish Embassy, Washington, D.C., Sept. 1980.

Gurr, Ted Robert. *Why Men Rebel.* Princeton: Princeton Univ. Press, 1970.

———. "Psychological Factors in Civil Violence." In I. K. Feierabend, R. L. Feierabend, and T. R. Gurr (eds.), *Anger, Violence, and Politics.* Englewood Cliffs: Prentice-Hall, 1972 [1968], pp. 31–57.

Howe, Marvine. "Angry Turks Resist New Policies and Higher Prices," *The New York Times* (11 Feb. 1980).

———. "Violence in Turkey Reflects Tradition," *The New York Times* (26 Feb. 1980).

———. "Turks Learning to Take Terror in Their Stride," *The New York Times* (26 Aug. 1980).

Huntington, Samuel P. *Civil Violence and the Process of Development.* London: Adelphi Papers, No. 83, 1971.

Kâğıtçıbaşı, Çiğdem. "Social Norms and Authoritarianism: A Turkish-American Comparison," *Journal of Personality and Social Psychology.* 1970, 16, 444–51.

Landau, Jacob M. *Radical Politics in Modern Turkey.* Leiden: E. J. Brill, 1974.

Magnarella, Paul J. *Tradition and Change in a Turkish Town.* New York: Halsted/Schenkman, 1974.

———. *The Peasant Venture.* Cambridge: Schenkman, 1974.

Mango, Andrew. "The Multiple Crisis in Turkey," *Asian Affairs.* 1979, 10, 125–31.

Mardin, Şerif. "Youth and Violence in Turkey," *Archives Européennes de Sociologie.* 1978, 19, 229–54.

Modiano, Mario. "Politicians Losing Control of Turkey's Warring Minorities," *The Times.* London (10 July 1980).

Münir, Metin. "Terror Forces Turks to Flee Their Homes," *The Sunday Times*. London (27 July 1980).

Sencer, Muzaffer. "Student Riots and the Graduate Unemployed," *Outlook*. 1970, 4, 184, 12–13.

Szyliowicz, Joseph S. *A Political Analysis of Student Activism: The Turkish Case*. Beverly Hills: Sage, 1972.

Turkey Almanac 1978. Ankara: The Daily News.

Türkiye İstatistik Yıllığı 1979. Ankara: Devlet Istatistik Enstitüsü Matbaası.

1979 World Bank Atlas. Washington, D.C.: World Bank.

CONTRIBUTORS

Nermin Abadan-Unat graduated from Istanbul Law Faculty in 1944, pursued graduate studies at the University of Minnesota in 1952-53 and obtained her Ph.D. from Ankara Law Faculty in 1955. She joined the Faculty of Political Science, Ankara University, in 1953 and is still teaching there. Her fields of interest are political sociology, political behavior, public opinion, mass communication, international migration and women's studies. In 1966 Professor Abadan-Unat established the Chair of Political Behavior and until 1978 remained its chairholder; she also directed the School of Journalism and Mass Communication attached to the Faculty of Political Science. She was a guest professor at the Geschwister-Scholl Institute, University of Munich, in 1969-70 and the City University of New York in 1973-74. Her main publications in Turkish include *Bureaucracy* (SBF, 1959), *Major Problems of Turkish Workers in Federal Germany* (DPT, 1964), *Elections of 1965* (SBF, 1966). In English she edited *Turkish Workers in Europe* (Brill, Leiden, 1976); and with Ruşen Keleş and others *Migration and Development* (Ankara, 1976). She also authored a number of articles in German, English and French. She served as vice-president of the Turkish Political Science Association and is the president of the Turkish Social Science Association. She was appointed in 1978 as contingent member of the Senate by the President of the Republic and served in this capacity for two years.

Alan Duben, a faculty member in the Department of Social Sciences, Boğaziçi University, Istanbul, has served as a consultant for the O.E.C.D. at Boğaziçi University in the area of urban studies. He previously taught at New York University. He received his Ph.D. in social anthropology from the University of Chicago in 1973. While at Chicago he was a fellow of the National Institute of Mental Health and the Ford Foundation. His publications include "Kinship, Primordial Ties, and Factory Organization in Turkey: An Anthropological View," *International Journal of Middle East Studies*, 1976; and "Class and Community in Urban Turkey," in C. A. van Nieuwenhuijze, ed., *Commoners, Climbers and Notables: A Sampler of Studies in Social Ranking in the Middle East*, Brill, 1977.

Sumru Erkut holds a Ph.D. in Social Psychology from Harvard University. She obtained her B.S. in Social Sciences in 1967 from the Middle East Technical University in Ankara. She has held full-time teaching appointments at the Middle East Technical University and Boston University and has taught part time at the University of Washington, Boston College and Wellesley College. She was also a research fellow at the Harvard University Center for Middle Eastern Studies. She is currently a research associate at the Wellesley College Center for Research on Women, where she is the associate director of the national review process of educational materials developed by grantees of the Women's Educational Equity Act Program. Her research has focused on factors affecting women's educational and occupational attainment, sex differences in the expectancy and attribution of academic achievement, models and mentors for college students, attitudinal modernity and cognitive development among rural Turkish children and Turkish students' attitudes toward careers.

Metin Heper, Ph.D. of Syracuse University, is Professor of Political Science at Boğaziçi University. He is interested in Turkish and Middle Eastern politics in comparative state and bureaucracy. He has been a research associate at Harvard University and the Hebrew University of Jerusalem and a visiting professor at the Southwest Texas State University and the University of Connecticut. He is the author of eight books: *Development Administration in Turkey: Conceptual Theory and Methodology* (with A. O. Berkman) (1980); *Gecekondu Policy in Turkey* (1978); *Decision Making in the Middle East Technical University* (1973); in Turkish: *Urban Migrants and Bureaucratic Organization* (forthcoming); *Traditionalism and Modernization in the Turkish Bureaucracy* (1977); *Bureaucratic Ruling Tradition in the Ottoman Empire and Turkish Republic* (1974); *Modernization and Bureaucracy: An Introduction to Comparative Public Administration* (1973); *Short Bibliography on Public Administration, 1958-1966* (1966). His articles have appeared in such journals as *International Journal of Middle East Studies, International Social Science Journal, Administration and Society, International Political Science Review, Res Publica,* and *International Review of Modern Sociology.* Currently, Professor Heper is working on *State and Bureaucracy in Turkey,* to be published by Eothen Press in England.

Çiğdem Kâğıtçıbaşı is head and professor of the Social Sciences Department of Boğaziçi University, Istanbul. She obtained her B.A. in psychology from Wellesley College in 1961 and her Ph.D. in social psychology from the University of California, Berkeley in 1967. Her research interests focus on family dynamics, sex roles, child socialization and early compensatory education, fertility and social change. She has authored six books in Turkish (*Psychological Dimensions of Social Change*, 1972; *Youth's Attitudes: A Cross Cultural Comparison*, 1973; *General Psychology*, 1975; *Impact of Sojourn: An Analysis of the Effects of an International Educational Exchange Program*, 1975; *Human and Humans: Introduction to Social Psychology*, 1976; *Value of the Child: Values and Fertility in Turkey*, 1981); and one in English (*The Changing Value of Children in Turkey*, 1982, East West Population Institute, Honolulu). Her other publications have appeared in a number of Turkish and international journals and edited volumes. She was a visiting professor at the University of California, Berkeley, in 1973 and at Columbia University in 1979.

Deniz Kandiyoti is associate professor of social psychology at the Department of Social Sciences, Boğaziçi University, Istanbul. She received her B.A. in psychology from the University of Paris (Sorbonne) in 1966 and her Ph.D. in social psychology from the London School of Economics in 1971. Her research interests have focused on social stratification, social psychological aspects of social change in urban and rural contexts, and more recently, sex roles. She has published numerous articles in Turkish and international journals and edited books on social change, sex roles and changing social structure in rural Turkey. Dr. Kandiyoti is active in the area of women's studies within the context of the International Sociological Association; she has been working in this field at the London School of Economics as a visiting research associate since 1980.

Mübeccel B. Kıray received a Ph.D. degree in sociology from Ankara University in 1946 and Ph.D. degree in anthropology from Northwestern University in 1950. Between 1960 and 1973 she chaired and taught at the Department of Social Sciences of Middle East Technical University in Ankara. Since 1973 she has been teaching at Istanbul Technical University and at Istanbul Academy of Economics and Business Administration, where she is the head of the sociology department. Her main publications include: *Ereğli: A Small Town Before Industrialization* (Ankara: DPT, 1964); with Hinderink *Social Stratification as an Obstacle to Modernization* (Praeger, 1970); *Izmir: A City Which Remained Unorganized: The Structure of Ismir's Business Life and Settlement Patterns* (Ankara, 1972); and an edited volume, *Social Stratification in the Mediterranean Basin and Development* (Mouton, 1972). Her other publications have appeared in numerous books and international journals. Dr. Kıray was guest professor at the London School of Economics in 1970-71.

Nilüfer Kuyaş, born in Istanbul, received her B.A. in philosophy from Wellesley College, Massachusetts, in 1977. In 1980 she completed her Master's degree in social psychology at Boğaziçi University with a thesis on women's status and power relations in the family. Her contribution to this volume is based on that thesis. Her plans for the near future include doctoral studies in the philosophy of social science.

Ned Levine is lecturer in Urban Planning at the University of California, Los Angeles, and member of the technical staff at the Jet Propulsion Laboratory, California Institute of Technology. He received his B.A. in psychology from the University of California, Berkeley in 1967; and his Ph.D. in social psychology from the London School of Economics in 1967. His research interests focus on comparative urbanization, individual adaptation to social change, noise abatement and control, and solar energy development. His recent publications, of relevance to Turkey, include "Antiurbanization: An Implicit Development Policy in Turkey" (*Journal of Developing Areas,* July 1980), and *Population Policy Formation and Implementation in Turkey,* with Sunday Üner, (Ankara: Hacettepe University, 1978). His other publications have appeared in a number of books and in various journals, among which are *Social Forces, Journal of Asian and African Studies, Sociology and Social Research,* and *Human Relations.*

Paul J. Magnarella is Professor of Anthropology at the University of Florida. He was awarded the Ph.D. in Social Anthropology and Middle East Studies by Harvard University in 1971. Dr. Magnarella's research interests include the impact of change forces on traditional society and culture both in developing countries and in the West. He has authored numerous articles on these topics as well as two books dealing specifically with Turkey: *Tradition and Change in a Turkish Town* (1971) and *The Peasant Venture* (1979).

Güler Okman Fişek received her B. A. from Connecticut College in 1967 and her M.A. and Ph.D. in Clinical Psychology from the University of Connecticut in 1970 and 1973 respectively. She did her internship in clinical psychology at Illinois State Psychiatric Institute and worked for a number of years in the United States as a licensed clinical psychologist. Since 1977 she has been teaching at Boğaziçi University. Her current areas of interest are group and family psychotherapy, the development of cognitive styles in various family contexts and the use of cognitive paradigms in clinical psychology. She is the co-author of a child development book, and a parent education book in Turkish prepared on early childhood development and education.

Emelie A. Olson has taught anthropology at Whittier College in Whittier, California, since 1973. She holds her M.A. (1968) and Ph.D. (1976) in Anthropology from the University of California at Los Angeles. She lived in Turkey for two extended periods, first in 1964-66 in a village in southwestern Turkey and later, in 1970-71, in Ankara. Her Ph.D. thesis was entitled *Family Planning and Husband-Wife Relationships in Contemporary Turkey.* She has also published a study examining the question of child abuse in Turkey in Jill Korbin, ed., *Cross-Cultural Perspectives in Child Abuse* (Berkeley: University of California Press, 1981). At present, she is engaged in research on images of women in the poetry of early Turkish mystics and on the role of religion in the lives of Turkish women.

Ferhunde Özbay graduated in 1966 from the Social Work Academy in Ankara. She completed her Masters degree at the Center for Population Studies of Hacettepe University. In 1970 she got a diploma in demography from Princeton University and then studied sampling at the University of Michigan. In 1975 she obtained her Ph.D. degree from Cornell University with a thesis on "Individual and Environmental Factors Affecting Fertility in Rural Turkey." Dr. Özbay taught at the Center for Population Studies of Hacettepe University until 1979 and at the Behavioral and Social Sciences Department, Ankara Academy of Economics and Business Administration until 1982. She is now at the Social Sciences Department of Boğaziçi University, Istanbul.

Serap Özgür, a native of Istanbul, completed her secondary education in Turkey and received her B.A. in 1977 from Portland State University in Oregon. In 1980, she received her master's degree in social psychology from Boğaziçi University. The study she did for her master's degree in social psychology was the basis of the article written with Diane Sunar which appears in this volume. In the near future she intends to pursue doctoral studies in criminology.

Diane G. Sunar received her B.A. in 1965 from Whittier College and her Ph.D. in 1972 from the University of California, Berkeley. After teaching for a year at California State College, Fullerton, she joined the Department of Social Sciences at Middle East Technical University in Ankara, where she taught from 1972 to 1979. Since 1979 she has been in the Department of Social Sciences at Boğaziçi University in Istanbul. Most of her published work has dealt with stereotyping in power relationships and with equity and justice norms and has appeared in journals both in Turkey and abroad.

Tansı Şenyapılı, born in Istanbul, received her B.A. in business administration in 1961 and her M.A. in city and regional planning in 1964 from Middle East Technical University. In 1963 she started working in the Department of Regional Planning of the Ministry of Resettlement and Reconstruction. In 1966 she received her M.A. in regional science from the University of Pennsylvania. Since 1971 she has been teaching in the Department of City and Regional Planning of the Middle East Technical University. She received her Ph.D. from Ankara University in 1977. With a grant from Centre for Environmental Studies of London she conducted a survey on the gecekondus of Istanbul, on which her book *The Problem of Unintegrated Urban Population* (1978) is based. She has also authored several articles.

INDEX